JUL 2 3 1997

S

DALY CITY PUBLIC LIBRARY

Y0-CZM-095

JOSEPH CONRAD:
THIRD WORLD PERSPECTIVES

Daly City Public Library
Daly City, California

JOSEPH CONRAD:
THIRD WORLD PERSPECTIVES

Compiled and Edited by Robert D. Hamner

An Original by Three Continents Press

A THREE CONTINENTS BOOK
LYNNE RIENNER PUBLISHERS
BOULDER & LONDON

S

©Robert D. Hamner 1990

A Three Continents Book

Published in the United States of America by
Lynne Rienner Publishers, Inc.
1800 30th Street, Boulder, Colorado 80301

Joseph Conrad: third world perspectives / compiled and edited by
Robert D. Hamner.—1st ed.
    p.   cm.
Includes bibliographical references.
ISBN 0-89410-216-8 (cloth)
ISBN 0-89410-217-6 (pbk.)
    1. Conrad, Joseph, 1857-1924—Criticism and interpretation.
2. Developing countries in literature. 3. Imperialism in
literature. 4. Colonies in literature. I. Hamner, Robert D.
PR6005.04Z753   1990
823'. 912—dc20   85-50524
                                   CIP

All rights reserved. No part of this book may be
used or reproduced in any manner whatsoever
without written permission of the publisher
except for brief quotations in reviews or articles.

Cover art by Max K. Winkler
©Three Continents Press 1990

ACKNOWLEDGMENTS

I am grateful to the following firms and individuals who have kindly granted permission to reprint copyrighted material.

Messrs. Withers, the Joseph Conrad Estate, for permission to reprint the numerous passages quoted from the essays, letters, stories and novels of Joseph Conrad that appear within the articles in this collection.

Chinua Achebe and Bolt and Watson, Ltd. "An Image of Africa." © University of Illinois Press.

Susan L. Blake. "Racism and the Classics: Teaching Heart of Darkness." *CLA Journal,* 25:4 (June 1982), 396-404. Reprinted by permission of the College Language Association.

Florence Clemens. "Conrad's Malaysia." *College English,* 2 (Jan. 1941), 338-46. Copyright © 1941 by the National Council of Teachers of English. Reprinted with the permission of the National Council of Teachers of English.

Sir Hugh Clifford. *North American Review.* "The Genius of Mr. Joseph Conrad." *North American Review,* 178 (June 1904), 843-52. Reprinted by permission of the University of Northern Iowa.

Michael Echeruo. Macmillan, Ltd. "Conrad's Nigger." In his *The Conditioned Imagination: From Shakespeare to Conrad.* Reprinted by permission, for world rights exclusive of USA, from Macmillan, London & Basingstoke.

Michael Echeruo. Holmes & Meier Inc. "Conrad's Nigger." In his *The Conditioned Imagination: From Shakespeare to Conrad.* Reprinted by permission, for rights in the USA.

Lloyd Fernando. The Modern Language Association. "Conrad's Eastern Expatriates: A New Version of His Outcasts." *PMLA,* 91:1 (Jan. 1976), 78-90. Reprinted by permission of the Modern Language Association of America, © 1976.

Jean Franco and *Punto de Contacto.* "The Limits of the Liberal Imagination: *One Hundred Years of Solitude* and *Nostromo.*" *Punto de Contacto,* 1:1 (1975), 4-16.

D. C. R. A. Goonetilleke and Barnes & Noble Books. "Conrad's Malayan Novels: Problems of Authenticity." In his *Developing Countries in British Fiction.* Rowman and Littlefield, © 1977, pp. 77-98, 258-60.

Wilson Harris and the University of Texas Press. "The Frontier on Which *Heart of Darkness* Stands." *Research in African Literatures,* 12:1 (Spring 1981), 86-93. Copyright © 1981 by the University of Texas Press.

Juliet McLauchlan. *Conradiana.* "Almayer and Willems—'How not to be.' " *Conradiana,* 11 (1979), 113-41. © 1979 by the Textual Studies Institute, Department of English, Texas Tech University.

Hans van Marle. *Conradiana.* "Jumble of Facts and Fiction: First Singapore Reaction to *Almayer's Folly." Conradiana,* 10:2 (1978), 161-66. © 1978 by the Textual Studies Institute, Department of English, Texas Tech University.

V. S. Naipaul, Gillon Aitken, and Alfred A. Knopf, Inc. "Conrad's Darkness." © 1974 by V. S. Naipaul. Reprinted from *The Return of Eva Peron with the Killings in Trinidad* by V. S. Naipaul, by permission of Alfred A. Knopf, Inc., for world rights exclusive of the British Commonwealth.

V. S. Naipaul and André Deutsch. "Conrad's Darkness." In his *The Return of Eva Peron with the Killings in Trinidad.* Permission for British Commonwealth and world rights exclusive of the USA and its dependencies.

Peter Nazareth and *Conradiana.* "Out of Darkness: Conrad and Other Third World Writers." *Conradiana,* 14:3 (1982), 173-87. © 1982 by the Textual Studies Institute, Department of English, Texas Tech University.

Edward Said and *Novel.* "Conrad: The Presentation of Narrative." *Novel,* 7:2 (Winter 1974), 116-32. Copyright Novel Corp., 1974.

C. Ponnuthurai Sarvan. *Conradiana.* "Under African Eyes." *Conradiana,* 8:3 (1976), 233-40. © 1976 by the Textual Studies Institute, Department of English, Texas Tech University.

D[avid] Timms and *Cahiers Victoriens et Edouardiens.* J. C. Hilson and D. Timms. "Conrad's 'An Outpost of Progress' or, the Evil Spirit of Civilization." *Cahiers Victoriens et Edouardiens,* 2 (1975), 113-28.

Permission to print the facsimile reproduction of Joseph Conrad was provided by The Beinecke Rare Book and Manuscript Library, Yale University.

For
Jared and Ryan
my sons

PREFACE

Joseph Conrad hardly needs an introduction to readers of Western literature. The purpose of this volume of essays is rather to highlight one increasingly vital facet of his contribution to the world of letters. Writing nearly half a century before the modern connotations of the term "Third World" came into existence, Conrad paved the way for a whole generation of new writers. At the same time his fictional trail through the Far East, Africa and the Americas has generated a growing flood of what might be called "colonial" criticism.

The following essays are representative of what many writers and critics from around the world have had to say regarding Conrad's treatment of peoples and places out on the frontiers where European civilization extended its imperial arms. In the process of selection, a distinction has been made between metropolitan critics of the industrialized West and critics from the former colonies. Out of the sixteen essays included, nine are by writers indigenous to newly independent nations of the Commonwealth, and a majority of these are established authors on an international scale. The remaining seven contributors, some of whom have lived in former colonies, have offered significant insights into Conrad's colonial fiction.

That there are many other essays which might have been chosen, the length of the bibliography at the end of this book is witness enough. It is not because they were lacking in quality, but rather in scope or in emphasis, or simply because various elements of duplication would have led to unfruitful repetition, that a number of fine articles had to be omitted. Hopefully, reders interested in pursuing specific leads contained in the text will examine pertinent references from the bibliography. The initial aim of this anthology is to provide exploration of developing trends in one specialized area of Conrad criticism.

Following the general introduction, brief explanations of the four major divisions of the book are provided. Since each essay speaks sufficiently for itself, within its own parameters, these explanatory notes are intended merely to suggest underlying relationships within the entire collection. Arrangement of the major divisions themselves corresponds approzimately with Conrad's writing career. He began with the Far East—and he drew from it later—adding Africa, the high seas, Europe and the Americas, in that order. This chronology of geographic expansion is reflected in the primary sources list. The tabulations accompanying the bibliography indicate in graphic form the rapidly growing interest in this aspect of Conrad's work. Because of Conrad's unique cross-cultural position, he provides a natural meeting ground for Conradian, Third World, comparative literature and socio-linguistic scholars. It is hoped that this book will act as a springboard for further dialogue.

Printing of the articles has followed the style of the originals wherever possible. Spelling and punctuation vary according to British, European and American practices of the journals and books quoted. The few exceptions are minor, to compensate for typographical inconsistency and to correct errors that might lead to misreading.

A collection of essays such as this would be impossible were it not for the cooperation of many people. Formal acknowledgments are provided in the appropriate place, yet there are several individuals who have been of great personal assistance. David Leon Higdon, editor of *Conradiana,* has provided advice and encouragement since I first broached the project to him four years ago. Adam Gillon, former editor of *Joseph Conrad Today* and current President of the Joseph Conrad Society of America has also been supportive in many ways. African scholar and editor of *Research in African Literatures,* Bernth Lindfors, and Don Herdeck, publisher and promoter of Third World studies, have been generous in their backing since the inception of the idea for this book. Peter Nazareth, who rediscovered his interest in Conrad along with my research, has provided continual encouragement. Anita Bryant Powers and Carol Hamner have stood by me through all the correspondence and word processing.

Funding to cover considerable permissions fees was provided by the Cullen Foundation, through the Faculty Enrichment Committee of Hardin-Simmons University.

TABLE OF CONTENTS

IV. Post-Colonial Legacy: In Conrad's Wake

INTRODUCTION

When Joseph Conrad (1857-1924) turned from life as a seaman in 1895 to assume writing as a profession, he virtually opened a new literary world. It would be an oversimplification to call him a colonial novelist in the line of his contemporaries Rudyard Kipling (1865-1936), and H. Rider Haggard (1856-1925), because his stories reach beyond their settings in time and place to themes still current in the post-colonial present. It would be equally misplaced to label him a Third World writer. Although his work proved the viability of colonial outposts as arenas of serious fiction, he did not live to see these "outposts of progress" acquire independence and nationhood.

As a European writing about Borneo, Malaysia, the Congo, Jamaica, and South America, Conrad seized upon the complexities of cultural confrontation. With his own blend of realism and impressionism, he brought to life for European readers alien environments that few could ever know personally. For better or worse, his depiction of "darker" races entered into the collective consciousness of his metropolitan contemporaries; and even when indications of his prejudices lead more recent critics to react negatively, his contribution to post-colonial Western literature remains formidable. At the same time, with his sense of the fragility of social institutions and the decline of empire, he laid the groundwork for newly emerging authors within the former colonies. Their exotic lands could be the setting for realistic drama, credible chararacters and relevant insights into human nature.

Evidence of Conrad's continuing influence as a writer about imperialism and as a predecessor of young Commonwealth authors may be measured in two significant ways. First, the number of essays and books that focus on his treatment of colonial subject matter has rapidly increased. In the early years, from 1896 until the colonies began to acquire independence in the late 1940's, beginning with India in 1947, there are a scant forty-two articles and one book—an average of less than one per year in this fifty-one year span. Between 1950 and 1969, the frequency is somewhat higher: twelve essays in the first decade and a sudden jump to sixty-five articles and six books from fifty-six different critics in the 1960's. There is an even greater surge in the 1970's: from ninety-nine individual writers there are 111 articles and eight new books dealing with some colonial/imperial aspect of Conrad's fiction. The pace continues in the 1980's.[1]

1

A second measure of Conrad's impact on Commonwealth literature is in the number of Third World critics and creative writers who contend with his presence—not the numbers alone, but the degree to which some of them are indebted to his example and his works. The numbers are there: since 1960, twenty-two critics from Africa, seven from the Caribbean and Latin America, and forty-one from Asia and the East have published reactions ranging from Nigerian novelist Chinua Achebe's condemnation of Conrad as a "bloody racist" to Kenyan novelist Ngugi wa Thiong'o's use of *Under Western Eyes* and *Lord Jim* as models for his own *A Grain of Wheat* (1968).

Achebe's charge has been answered by such fellow writers as Wilson Harris (Guyana) and Peter Nazareth (Uganda), among others.[2] Ngugi's debt to Conrad has spawned widespread recognition and at least three analytical essays.[3] From this it becomes apparent not only that Conrad is a figure with which to contend, but also that there is an expanding debate within the Third World regarding his legacy.

Rather than explore points of argumentation that will be raised within articles making up this volume, the purposes of an introductory overview might best be served in simply mentioning some of the major issues. Questions of racial discrimination have already been mentioned. When East meets West in Conrad, value systems are juxtaposed, pitting "civilization" against "barbarism." Not only are there strange customs and languages, but Christianity is tested against Islam, Buddhism, and "savage rites." Economic considerations are inevitable, whether imperialistic exploitation of material and human resources or capitalistic manipulation of a dependent country's internal policies is addressed. The political volatility of these sensitive areas is obvious.

Conrad is attuned enough to the complexity of appearances that he typically leaves situations open-ended, allows room for interpretation, preserves the frustrating ambiguity of reality. He is vulnerable, therefore, when the layered texture of his narrative style is taken literally to reveal his personal position. Since he builds his fictional world on observed, but imaginatively enhanced facts, biographical and psychological critics have found abundant resources for extrapolation. With the appearance of *Almayer's Folly* in 1895, the first reviewers weighed the accuracy of physical detail and the immediacy of truth. From that, others have gone on to question intentions and meaning, asking whether the stories merely exploit natives as pawns against exotic backdrops for the dramatization of European concerns.

Language alone becomes a crucial point. Not only did Conrad come as a foreigner to English as a third language (after Polish and French), but he took up the written word late, as a mature adult, approaching his forties. These successful adaptations in themselves would offer hope for colonial writers aspiring to reach larger audiences outside their native region. Beyond that, as Palestinian-born critic Edward Said has observed, Conrad's "practical and even theoretical" expression was "far in advance of *what* he was saying" (Said, *Novel,* 116). Linguistic analysis, with its own cultural and political implications, can be just as relevant to Conrad's treatment of exotic settings as his depiction of races and classes of men.

These are but a few of the larger concerns that have drawn critics from metropolitan countries and new nations to Conrad's fiction. While many of the arguments remain unsettled, terms are being defined and positions are being taken. It would have been too cumbersome and repetitious to present examples of all the various approaches to Conrad that are available. Instead, the essays included in this volume represent some of the most prominently cited issues and collectively they shed light on the overall status of Conrad criticism, vis-à-vis Commonwealth literature. It is appropriate that the colonies he introduced into the mainstream of Western literature should continue to utilize the riches he disclosed.

NOTES:

1 See annotated bibliography and accompanying table at the conclusion of this volume.

2 See annotated bibliography: Sarvan (1980), Harris (1981), Nazareth (1982).

3 See annotated bibliography: Kitonga (Nigeria 1970), Obumselu (Zambia 1974), Sarvan (Zambia 1976).

PART ONE

COLONISTS, COLONIAL: EARLY RECOGNITION

As might be expected, most of the first notices of Conrad's Eastern novels come from colonizers, in England and the United States. An explicit indication of the kind of prejudice Conrad faced in at least one segment of the home countries is voiced by a bigoted *Nation* reviewer who finds, "Borneo is a fine field for the study of monkeys, not men" (Rev. of *Almayer's Folly*, 17 Oct. 1895, 278). It is also likely that the review and letter published in the Singapore *Straits Times* in 1896, reproduced here in Hans van Marle's article, were written by Western expatriates in the Far East.

Sir Hugh Clifford's "The Genius of Mr. Conrad," which stands at the beginning of this anthology, seems an appropriate opening commentary not only because Clifford was Conrad's friend and correspondent, but because he knew on a more intimate basis all of the territories that were to find their way into Conrad's fiction. Foreign service had posted Clifford for years in Borneo, Africa, and the West Indies. When he says that Conrad's scenes and atmosphere are faithful to reality, but that his Orientals are reliable only in so far as they "represent the impression scored by Asiatics on a sensitive, imaginative, European mind," he speaks from greater authority of experience than Conrad ever claims (p. 16). A cautionary note has been sounded in this regard by social anthropologist Brian Street. Commentators on Conrad's verisimilitude tend to doubt or admire according to their own perceptions and the "criteria for 'truth' relate to the principles by which knowledge is selected and ordered rather than, as Clifford implies, simply to empirical knowledge" ("Joseph Conrad and the Imaginative Literature of Empire," p. 147).

Florence Clemens, also having lived for a more extended time in Malaysia than Conrad, is in a good position to be among the first to attest to the authenticity of Conrad's material. Referring to places, people, events and books about the region, she documents Conrad's observations and possible sources of information. Concluding these examples of contemporary reactions are the complaints of two Singapore *Straits Times* readers who object to Conrad's "jumble of facts and fiction" (p. 33). From the outset, basic questions center on the accuracy of reporting the Eastern scene. These concerns never disappear, but their various implications are explored in later criticism.

PART TWO

COLONIAL LEGACY: PINE AND PALM

In the following four essays, questions of Conrad's accuracy lead into considerations of his bringing together representatives of temperate climates (Pine) and darker races of the tropics (Palm). First, D. C. R. A. Goonetilleke draws attention to Conrad's European perspective in depicting two contrasting social systems. Goonetilleke concludes what is a fairly broad overview of the Eastern works with the observation that Conrad's most important themes are personal, rather than political (p. 56).

Lloyd Fernando's following essay is a warning against oversimplification of the confrontation of two alien value systems. "No set of values, Conrad found, is supported by any stronger sanction than habit or custom" (p. 67). The essential value of the Eastern scene is that it provides a dynamic catalyst for his greatest themes. Using *The Rescue* and other citations as points of reference, Fernando illustrates the disorientation of all Conrad's leading characters, "the true colonial condition which deflects from familiar goals the occupied and the occupiers alike" (p. 64).

Leading out of that idea, successive essays offer close analyses of two Eastern novels and one African story. McLauchlan illuminates the life-and-death antithesis in the values of Nina and Aissa on the one hand, and Almayer and Willems on the other. In both *Almayer's Folly* and *An Outcast of the Islands,* lives are spent in futile efforts to realize illusive dreams. As may be seen in the fourth essay, Conrad's moving the setting to the Congo works only a slight difference into the continuing themes. As Hilson and Timms point out, the exploitative Company treats Africans and its menial white employees alike as slaves. From the beginning, Hilson and Timms seize upon the social message of corruption "masquerading as philanthropy" (p. 108). Hypocrisy and self-deception, illusion and delusion play across the surface of Conrad's "objective" reality.

PART THREE

COLONIAL LEC\CY: BLACK AND WHITE

Were Conrad's philosophy and expression simple as black and white, reading him would be less complicated, but it would no longer be rich in various levels of meaning. Given his personal ambivalence and the inherent ambiguity of his rhetorically involved language, no categorical interpretation is likely to go unchallenged. Chinua Achebe in the opening essay of this section argues that the insidious corruption of racist imperialism is so pervasive that it even infects the author who attacks it in *Heart of Darkness.*

Achebe's sentiments are echoed in Michael Echeruo's complaint that Conrad relies upon a racially conditioned response in the portrayal of James Wait in *The Nigger of the "Narcissus."* Such charges as are raised by Achebe and Echeruo here, are reiterated or rejected by a number of critics. Among those who condemn Conrad's racism is Susan Blake, who provides an essay unique in this collection: unique in that it is unequivocally pedagogical. Blake offers a paradigm of how a novel as "great" as *The Heart of Darkness* can also provide classroom lessons in literary dehumanization. Then C. P. Sarvan's "Under African Eyes," in response to Achebe, summarizes the standard arguments in Conrad's defense. Not only does Sarvan offer explanations for problematic utterances by Conrad and his characters, he argues for Conrad's positive influence on the African novel. That influence is exemplified in Ngugi wa Thiong'o's imaginative use of *Under Western Eyes* and *Lord Jim* as models for his own first novel, *A Grain of Wheat*.

If undue prominence seems to be given to Achebe's comments, the reaction among his fellow Third World writers and Commonwealth scholars is ample evidence of Conrad's impact as a catalyst for new critical thought. He generates a division among Eurocentric and anti-imperialist partisans, but more significantly, discussion of his work provides a test case for the aesthetic principles of modern criticism. At the heart of the matter is the question whether, or in what capacity, established modes of Western thought are applicable to the new literatures of the Third World.

In the concluding essay for this third section, Guyanese novelist Wilson Harris argues, contrary to Achebe, that Conrad expands the potentialities of the novel, intimating a wholeness of vision which Conrad himself was never quite able to achieve. Drawing upon his South American perspective, Harris admires Conrad's undermining of "homogeneous cultural" imperatives which he had inherited along with the novel form. No small part of his contribution to literature is the dialogue he creates within closed systems and between alien cultures. His medium, as Harris observes, is the word, "qualitative and infinite variations of substance clothed in nouns" (p. 165).

PART FOUR

POST-COLONIAL LEGACY: IN CONRAD'S WAKE

Two of the major ways in which Conrad has influenced Third World literature have been anticipated in the preceding section. C. P. Sarvan has found Ngugi wa Thiong'o to be inspired directly by Conrad; Wilson Harris has advanced the proposition that Conrad opens the door for writers to explore beyond traditional consciousness, biases, and institutional forms. In this concluding set of essays, both Edward Said and V. S. Naipaul closely scrutinize aspects of Conrad's style: his narrative technique, his manner of using words so that language and images become "orchestration."

In his "Conrad's Darkness," novelist Naipaul confesses that when he came to writing he discovered that Conrad "had been everywhere before me. Not as a man with a cause, but a man offering, as in *Nostromo,* a vision of the world's half-made societies as places which continuously made and unmade themselves, where there was no goal" (p. 194). Naipaul, although he is a native Trinidadian, has been criticized for his own imperial biases: witness his phrase "half-made societies." One may wonder whether these underdeveloped nations are "half-made" because they fall short of Western models or because they have yet to reach a completeness of their own design. For some, Naipaul is the epitome of the artistic excellence that can emerge from a colonial experience. For others, he embodies the psychological casualty of imperialism. It is helpful for the reader to keep this controversy in view when Naipaul uses his personal reflections on "The Lagoon" to illustrate his difficulties in comprehending Conrad's major works, the essay yielding as much insight into Naipaul as into his predecessor.

Jean Franco turns to *Nostromo* and Gabriel García Márquez' *One Hundred Years of Solitude* for instructive comparison. The earlier novel exposes the ravages of economic imperialism in South America primarily from the conqueror's perspective. Columbian novelist Márquez dramatizes the other side of the same coin: a dependent population, "whose very imagination is no longer inviolate" (p. 201). Franco's provocative conclusion is that while "Conrad's verisimilitude could not prevent an ideological reading of *Nostromo* which confined Latin America to the realm of the absurd," there is a limit to the liberal imagination (p. 213). Feeling that Conrad offers biased stereotypes and that Márquez seems to accept the ideology, Franco fears for the efficacy of imagination when it becomes so isolated from reality as to deteriorate into harmless fantasy.

Even when no argument is being offered for direct influence, Conrad's having brought to life capitalist political manipulation in South America makes him a figure of contention. Had Franco delayed her study until the release of Francis Ford Coppola's filming of *Heart of Darkness* as *Apocalypse Now,* she could well have joined the chorus of critics interested in comparing Belgian imperialism with the United States' recent involvement in modern Vietnam.

Concluding the entire collection of essays, Peter Nazareth discusses Conrad as a mental liberator both for his own Victorian culture and for citizens of the Third World. Fittingly, Nazareth takes into account the ideas expressed by Achebe, Ngugi, Harris and Naipaul. "Out of Darkness: Conrad and Other Third World Writers" is both a summary and a tribute to Conrad who, "Nearly a hundred years later . . . is still helping refocus the Third World under Western Eyes" (p. 228). So long as the powerful continue to exert domination over weaker societies in any guise and under any pretense, Conrad remains relevant.

I. Colonists, Colonial: Early Recognition

THE GENIUS OF MR. JOSEPH CONRAD

Hugh Clifford, C.M.G.

"I do not like work—no man does," says Mr. Joseph Conrad in one of his books, speaking through the mouth of Marlow, a nomad of the seas, whom we must regard as the author's *alter ego*. "But I like what is in work,—the chance to find yourself. Your own reality,—for yourself, not for others,—what no other man can know. They can only see the mere show, and never can tell what it really means." The last clause of this paragraph contains, at the best, but a half-truth; for though work that has permanent value must always, almost of necessity, mean far more to the man who has put into it his whole soul than it conceivably can to others, the latter may, none the less, find in it the supreme attraction which Marlow, or Mr. Conrad, here claims for work in the abstract—the chance of seeing in it a revelation of the essence of the man who wrought it. This is the case to a more than usual degree with the books to which Mr. Conrad has put his name; and, therefore, a complete understanding of them and of their true significance is hardly to be won without the aid of some general information concerning their author. The books themselves reveal to us a personality distinct, individual, strange, and even a little enigmatical: a knowledge of the circumstances which formed and moulded it is necessary as supplying a commentary to the text, an explanation of much that otherwise is baffling. I have scant sympathy with the modern practice of lifting the curtain of privacy, of recording the incidents of a man's life for the satisfaction of an idle and unwholesome curiosity; but the work which Mr. Conrad has produced and is producing comes to us as the result, not only of an accretion of individual experience, but of a peculiar temperament which demands study for the proper comprehension of that to which it has given birth.

Mr. Conrad's books, I say it without fear of contradiction, have no counterparts in the entire range of English literature. They are peculiarly, arrestingly original. That is their key-note, their greatest distinction, alike in their thought and in their manner. The matter is, in a sense, the common property of all the world, or of that section of the world which he has roamed widely; but, from the outset, the reader is made conscious of an intensely individual point of view, a special outlook upon life, of a constructive imagination working upon lines different to those common to Englishmen, of a profound comprehension of the psychology of a certain class of character, and withal of a sombre force and a forthright sincerity that compel recognition of the essential truth revealed. The manner, as opposed to the matter, is even more striking, even more original. It is

11

wholly unlike that of any writer who has hitherto used the English language as his vehicle of expression, and may indeed be regarded, in some sort, as embodying a discovery of yet another use to which our tongue can be put. Curiously free from the trammels of recognized convention, at times rugged and even harsh, packed with phrases which, while they create the precise impression aimed at as they alone could do, yet have about them a certain exotic flavor, Mr. Conrad's style is one obviously born in its author, not fashioned painfully by his ingenuity, and so is felt to be free from all taint of affectation. Just as the Apostles after Pentecost "began to speak with other tongues, as the Spirit gave them utterance," so Mr. Conrad writes with the utterance that is *given* to him, the utterance which is his through the circumstances of birth, race, experience, training and even tradition, all of which, in his case, are widely different from those of any other great figure in English literature, ancient or modern. Behind and beyond and above this lies the power, the instinct, the genius, call it what you will, which alone enables a man to give articulate and artistic expression to his deeper thoughts, feelings and impressions, which makes these things take a form that can appeal forcibly to the intelligence of others; for, lacking this indefinable quality, the most original mind would be doomed, so far as literature is concerned, to silence and to obscurity.

It appears to me, therefore, that, before proceeding to an examination of Mr. Conrad's works, the main features of the author's history must be glanced at, since the latter are intimately connected with the former, are interwoven with them, and are, even, to some extent, the causes of which the books are the necessary, the inevitable, result. Joseph Conrad Korzeniowski, to give him for once the surname which, irritated doubtless by persistent mispronunciation, he has now for many years been content to drop, was born in Poland in 1856. The French language he acquired in infancy, together with his native tongue; but of English, which he uses today with such supreme success, he learned not a single word until he had attained his nineteenth year. The spirit of the nomad awoke in him early; and, in this age, the sea—the great highway which leads men up and down the world—speedily claims for its own those who have in them the itch of travel. None the less, his first adventure, undertaken when he was a mere lad, was a journey to Constantinople, his ambition being to fight for the Turks, then at war with Russia, the hereditary enemy of his country. Failing to obtain employment of the kind he sought, he next made a couple of voyages to the West Indies in a French ship, obtaining work as what, in the Australian Colonies, is called a "rouseabout." The life was probably hard enough, but by this time the sea had gripped the imaginative youngster, had asserted over him a sway not easily relaxed. To Europe, therefore, he returned in due course, his heart set upon making seamanship his profession.

Looking about him—this was in the days long before the age of the great shipping combines—he saw that the mistress of the sea was England, that her mercantile marine was the one which could offer to the adventurous spirit the amplest opportunity of wandering. To England accordingly, he came, settling down in Lowestoft; making the acquaintance of as many seafaring folk as possible, and presently shipping as an able seaman on board a coasting-vessel owned and commanded by one of his new friends. Studying the technicalities of his chosen profession with eager curiosity, Mr. Conrad was soon able to satisfy the requirements of the Board of Trade, and to obtain his mate's certificate, armed with which he made his first voyage to the East. The story of that voyage, and of the calamities which befell the ill-fated "Judea," has since been wonderfully told by Mr. Conrad in the sketch called "Youth," in which also is set forth the first impression wrought upon a virgin mind by the marvel, the glitter and the glory, of the East. Here is one passage. Marlow and his companions, escaping from the wreck, arrive at night at an Eastern port, and fall into the sleep of utter exhaustion.

"When I opened my eyes again, the silence was as complete as though it had never been broken. I was lying in a flood of light, and the sky had never looked so far, so high, before. I opened my eyes and lay without moving. And then I saw the men of the East—they were looking at me. The whole length of the jetty was full of people. I saw brown, bronze, yellow faces, and black eyes, the glitter, the color of an Eastern crowd. And all these beings stared without a murmur, without a sigh, without a movement. They stared down at the boats, at the sleeping men who at night had come to them from the sea. Nothing moved. The fronds of palms stood still against the sky. Not a branch stirred along the shore, and the brown roofs of hidden houses peeped through the green foliage, through the big leaves that hung shining and still, like leaves forged of heavy metal. This was the East of the ancient navigators, so old, so mysterious, resplendent and sombre, living and unchanged, full of danger and promise. And these were the men. I sat up suddenly. A wave of movement passed through the crowd from end to end, passed along the heads, swayed the bodies, ran along the jetty like a ripple on the water, like a breath of wind on a field—and all was still again. I see it now—the wide sweep of the bay, the glittering sands, the wealth of green, infinite and varied, the sea blue like the sea of a dream, the crowd of attentive faces, the blaze of vivid color—the water reflecting it all, the curve of the shore, the jetty, the high-sterned, outlandish craft floating still, and the three boats with the tired men from the West sleeping, unconscious of the land and the people and the violence of sunshine. . . The East looked at them without a sound. I have known its fascination since: I have seen the mysterious shores, the still water, the lands of brown nations, where a stealthy Nemesis lies in wait, pursues, overtakes so many of the conquering race, who are proud of their wisdom, of their knowledge, of their strength. But, for me, all the East is contained in that vision of my youth. It is all in that moment when I opened my young eyes on it. I came upon it from a tussle with the sea—and I was young—and I saw it looking at me. And this is all that is left of it! Only a moment; a moment of strength, of romance, of glamour—of youth!"

That is a description typical of Mr. Conrad's quality—the tiny picture, clean-cut as a cameo, that imprints itself upon the imagination, and yet has clinging about it the half-mystical haze of fancy and of sentiment which is one of the secrets of this writer's magic; but to me it possesses an added interest, because it is so obviously transcribed from a vivid and undimmed memory, because it shows that the man who saw it in his boyhood, and looked on it with the seeing eye, was even then noting, observing, pondering, above all *thinking,* was accumulating, atom by atom, stores of knowledge, of experience, impressions of men and of things, all of which were destined later to be put to so splendid a use, though he was at the time altogether unconscious of the power latent within him.

For nearly a score of years this process was continued, Mr. Conrad roaming abroad through the world of sea and land, in sailing-vessels and steam-tramps, on clippers or crawlers, hugging treacherous coast-lines, wriggling through the narrow waters of the archipelagoes, creeping up and down the channels of distant rivers, struggling with angry waves, or passing, day after day and night after night, across the unruffled ocean beneath domed skies empty of life. For nearly twenty years he visited half the ports of all the earth, rubbed shoulders with most of the races of mankind, and everywhere looked upon all things with the seeing eye which delved beneath the surface. What an education it was! He was distracted by no mere penman's zeal for the collection of "copy," had no thought of any artistic use to which in after years his slowly accumulated wisdom might be put: for the time, his whole being was concentrated upon the work of observing, simply because it was his nature to observe, and because the task brought to him an intense delight. His profession of seaman, which gave to him his fill of wandering, revealed to him uncounted things of which he had not dreamed, satisfied him utterly. He loved the' sea and his mastery of the sea—the long, lazy, uneventful intervals, and now and again a fight for the life; and all this while he never put pen to paper save to write up his log-book, or at rare seasons to compose a reluctant letter to his relatives in Poland when decency demanded such filial labor. But though he did not write, he read widely in two languages, English and French, the literary instinct in him driving him to select only the best ancient and modern works in those great literatures. Here again, still quite unconsciously, Mr. Conrad was arming, educating himself for the work which the future held for him; and what he learned became an integral portion of the man, because it was not acquired hurriedly and laboriously as a means to an end, but instinctively, gradually, slowly, lovingly, from sheer delight in the pleasure that it brought to him. And so, in the fulness of time, came the season of harvest following upon this long and mighty sowing.

It was in 1894 that Mr. Conrad was seized, suddenly and inexplicably, by a desire to rest. Almost from boyhood he had been a wanderer upon the face of the earth, had "labored in mid-ocean, wind and wave and oar,": now for a little space he would be idle, and would live ashore. Accordingly, he took lodgings somewhere in the Vauxhall Bridge Road—the "long, unlovely street" from which poor James Thomson, looking forth, beheld the woeful vision of "The City of Dreadful Night"—and made up his mind that for six whole months he would live indolently out of sight of the sea. He speedily discovered that idleness was very hard work. A toiler from his youth upward, inaction such as this irked him sorely; yet his pride would not suffer him to return to the sea which called to him so loudly.

He had promised himself six months ashore, and six whole months he would spend on the dry land. But how to fill this aching void of empty, useless hours? Then the spirit which had led him from the beginning, though he had been unconscious of its guiding hand, whispered in his ear. "Write!" it commanded, "Write!" He had just finished an engagement which had taken him, month in and month out, from Singapore to the ports of the east coast of Borneo. The impression of that island and of many of the men and women who lived there was fresh in his mind. Picture after picture, portrait after portrait rose up upon the retina of his memory, jostling one another, clamoring to be painted as he, he suddenly felt, alone could paint them. Material in abundance, unsought, but garnered unconsciously during many years, time, opportunity, all were his. An overpowering impulse to use these things was upon him, for genius, like murder, will out; so now, at the age of thirty-eight, the long period of probation and apprenticeship was ended, and Mr. Joseph Conrad had come to his own at last.

The fact that he debated within himself seriously as to the choice of the language in which he should elect to write, will be found to be full of significance to any thoughtful student of his work. French at first attracted him more than English. Flaubert and Guy de Maupassant fascinated him as did no modern English authors, and, so far as he can be said to have any literary parents, they are to be sought for in France, not in England or America. The love of the one and only word was a passion born quick and whole in him, and for a space he thought that the more delicate, subtle and dainty speech would best serve his purposes. But for many years he had sailed under the old Red Ensign; his friends were mostly English; his sympathies were with the men of English race whom he had found scattered through the crannies of the world. Men of British breed, it seemed to him, would perhaps understand the things of which he had to tell as no other men could do. In the end, therefore, he decided upon the use of English; but admiration of the French stylists, of French delicacy and workmanship, of French subtlety, of French illusiveness and allusiveness, remained strong in him, and to this influence he owes not a little of the force, the vividness, the distinction of his prose. Let any man possessed of the critical faculty read a page of Mr. Conrad's work with this knowledge in his mind, and he will find that a very real light is cast thereby upon the more effective peculiarities of his style. Add to this, that the author is a Sclav by birth and tradition, and that he possesses in an intensified form the sombre but strongly individual outlook of his people, and it will be recognized that he combines in his person a mental equipment of so unusual a character that, backed as it is by literary instinct and ability of a very high order, it could not fail to produce remarkable results.

The first book, begun in the circumstances which have been described, and finished after the author had returned to his ordinary avocations and was commanding a steam-launch on the *Congo*, was "Almayer's Folly," published in 1895. Like "An Outcast of the Islands," which appeared in the following year, it described certain phases of life on the east coast of Borneo, the central character in each case being a Dutchman. In the analysis of these white men Mr. Conrad achieved a considerable success, the lonely, broken, melancholy Almayer, with the altruism of strong affection forcing itself upward through his mean and trivial ambitions, being a peculiarly arresting figure. He was a creation—no mere puppet of mechanical contrivance—a man, intensely pathetic in his failure and his impotence, very weak, very human, very lovable, and the story of his tragedy moves us deeply. Similarly, Willems, the Outcast, is a character which exists, in which we cannot but believe. He is vital as truth itself, and the study of his degradation is as pitiless as it is strong. The Orientals in both these books, however, are much less successful. To me they are interesting, not because they are really Asiatics, but because they represent the impression scored by Asiatics upon a sensitive, imaginative, European mind. Mr. Conrad had seen them and known them, but he had seen as white men see—from the outside. He had never lived into the life of brown people. The whole *motif* of "Almayer's Folly"—the attraction which a Bugis chief has for the Dutchman's half-caste daughter—is based upon a misunderstanding. It is in the Eurasian that color-prejudice and contemptuous hatred of the native have their culmination. Almayer's life might well have held a tragedy for him and for his children, but it would have come to them by no such channel as that here imagined by Mr. Conrad.

This, however, is a matter of only secondary importance. True or false, the figures in these books live for us, and above and beyond them are the power of presentment, the marvellous faculty for the absolute creation of atmosphere, the genius for description, and the individual, finished style which these, Mr. Conrad's earliest works, display. Take, for instance, this picture of a Malayan daybreak:

> The smooth darkness filling the shutter-hole grew paler and became blotchy with ill-defined shapes, as if a new universe were being evolved out of sombre chaos. Then outlines came out, defining forms without any details, indicating here a tree, there a bush; a black belt of forest far off; the straight lines of a house, the ridge of a high roof near by. Inside the hut, Babalatchi, who had lately been only a persuasive voice, became a human shape leaning its chin imprudently on the muzzle of a gun and rolling an uneasy eye over the reappearing world. The day came rapidly, dismal and oppressed by the fog of the river and by the heavy vapors of the sky—a day without color and without sunshine: incomplete, disappointing, sad.

That, to one who knows by heart the melancholy dawns of southern Asia, is well-nigh perfect, yet it loses by divorcement from its context, for it is used with consummate art to give just the touch of sombre mystery which the narrative there needs.

In 1898 two new books appeared, "Tales of Unrest," a collection of five short stories, and "The Nigger of the 'Narcissus.' " The former displayed all the qualities of Mr. Conrad's earlier books, the tales called "Karain" and "The Lagoon," respectively, containing some marvellous descriptive passages. Both these stories, however, dealt with the psychology of Asiatics, and to the expert were interesting rather than satisfying. "The Nigger," on the other hand, gave us, for the first time, Mr. Conrad at his very best. Of "plot" it had barely a vestige, but Mr. Conrad proved himself to be independent of the mere constructive faculty. It told of a voyage from Bombay to an English port round the Cape of Good Hope in a sailing-ship; the characters were all seamen of the British merchant service; there was not a woman's name from cover to cover; the hero was a malingering negro. No machinery could conceivably have been more simple, and nothing short of genius could have served to put it to such splendid use. In an interesting note, published in the "New Review" for December, 1897, Mr. Conrad set forth his theories of art, and from this interesting human document one passage may be quoted here.

> It is only through complete, unswerving devotion to the perfect blending of form and substance; it is only through an unremitting, never-discouraged care for the shape and the ring of sentences that an approach can be made to plasticity, to color; and the light of magic suggestiveness may be brought to play for an evanescent instant over the commonplace surface of words: of the old, old words, worn thin, defaced by ages of careless usage. The sincere endeavor to accomplish that creative task, to go as far on that road as his strength will carry him, to go undeterred by faltering, weariness or reproach, is the only valid justification for the worker in prose. And if his conscience is clear, his answer to those who, in the fulness of a wisdom which looks for immediate profit, demand specifically to be edified, consoled, amused; who demand to be promptly improved, or encouraged, or frightened, or shocked, or charmed, must run thus: My task which I am trying to achieve is, by the power of the written word to make you hear, to make you feel—it is, before all, to make you see. That—and no more, and it is everything. If I succeed, you shall find there according to your deserts; encouragement, consolation, fear, charm—all you demand; and, perhaps, also that glimpse of truth for which you have forgotten to ask.

That, in a few words, is a statement of Mr. Conrad's literary creed, and with what triumphant success has he attained to his ideal! "The Nigger" is a book which must be read from cover to cover: it cannot be dealt with fairly by extract or quotation. But he who reads it, or "Youth," or "Typhoon," or any of Mr. Conrad's works, will be made to hear, to feel—before all, to *see;* he will find himself deafened by the roar of the storm, aching in sympathy with the weary men who cling to the canting deck, and realizing the individuality of each of them so vividly that he would recognize any one among them were he to meet him in the street. Whether we ask for it or no, we have in Mr. Conrad's books more than a glimpse of the truth, truth vital and eternal,—the thing that is wonderfully depicted, yet veiled by the mystery and magic of imaginative art.

"The Nigger" marks an epoch in Mr. Conrad's literary career, because it proved him to possess, in addition to his other qualities, extraordinary psychological insight of a peculiar kind, and showed that his mind—the mind of the Sclav, more delicate and more subtle than the mind of the Englishman,—was able to analyze human nature in a fashion distinctively its own. Since 1898, three more books have come from Mr. Conrad's pen—"Lord Jim," "Youth," and "Typhoon,"—the first an elaborate psychological study, the others collections of short stories. Space forbids a detailed examination of these volumes, any one of which would suffice to make the reputation of an author. Of the three, "Lord Jim" is the most important, and, indeed, is in some respects the greatest of Mr. Conrad's books. On the other hand, it suffers because we are asked to believe that the story as written was told by the seaman Marlow to his friends after dinner, an illusion which it is impossible to sustain. "Lord Jim" resembles nothing more nearly than some delicate piece of mosaic, of which each of the myriad tiny fragments that compose it is essential to the whole. It is built up, sentence by sentence, paragraph by paragraph, almost word by word, and lacking any phrase it would be marred and incomplete. In a word it is *written,* as in this age of speed and hurry few books are written; but, putting aside all question of its length, the very subtlety of this study of a man's soul makes its delivery by word of mouth in the circumstances described a sheer impossibility.

"Youth" and "Typhoon," though conceived upon a smaller scale, contain work no whit less remarkable than "Lord Jim" with its host of living characters. In the former volume, "The Heart of Darkness" grips me as does no other short story in our literature. From its opening, with the description of the sea-reach of the Thames and thoughts of the days when Britain too was a land of Darkness to the Roman invaders, the mystery and the gloom of savage places obsesses the imagination. The description of the great African river crawling seaward through the sombre forest, of the incomprehensible savage life upon its banks, of the mean and paltry schemers who exploit that vast wilderness, fascinates, possesses and oppresses you with its insistent horror. And so, step by step, you are led up to Mr. Kurtz, the man to whom the wilderness had whispered "things about himself which he did not know, things of which he had no conception till he took counsel with that great solitude," and the culmination of horror is reached in this high priest of the innermost shrine of the Heart of Darkness.

In a wholly different strain are told the stories of the old sea-captain, toiling for the daughter whom he loves, and concealing for her sake the blindness which is creeping over him; of Falk, the man who survived because he was the fittest, but at the price of devouring human flesh; of the girl whom Falk loved, the girl of opulent charms, who exists as a being so completely realized, yet who never speaks a word in our hearing; of the great typhoon, its fury and its might thrown up wonderfully upon the background of a dense, slow, heavy mind—the mind of the captain, who brings his ship to port through sheer inability to appreciate the tremendous character of his antagonist. All these and their fellows, whom I cannot even name, live for us. They are vital, full of meaning, true. In every instance, to use Mr. Conrad's own phrase, he has "snatched, in a moment of courage, from the remorseless rush of time, a passing phase of life," and, approaching the task "in tenderness and faith," he has held up "unquestioningly, without choice and without fear, the rescued fragment before all eyes and in the light of a sincere mood." He has shown "its vibration, its color, its form; and through its movement, its form and its color, has revealed the substance of its truth—has disclosed its inspiring secret: the stress and passion within the core of each convincing moment."

His is a notable achievement, a tremendous success, and we have cause for thankfulness because circumstances have chanced to give to this man of keen observation, delicate perception and subtle intelligence a unique training and experience, and withal so complete mastery over our magnificent language—the language which he only began to learn in his nineteenth year.

CONRAD'S MALAYSIA

Florence Clemens[1]

The familiar opening line of *The Rescue*[2] induces a transmigration to "the shallow sea that foams and murmurs on the shores of the thousand islands, big and little, which make up the Malay Archipelago." Although white men and women, exiled far from their homes, are at the heart of Joseph Conrad's Malaysian fiction, the native life forms the necessary isolating background and is of great importance. As yet there has been no finer writing about Malaysia itself and, for the most part, no truer.

Conrad has long been respected for the photographic accuracy of his observation and memory. His training as a seaman developed what was a natural trait in him. As a navigator he had to know the nature of "the shallow sea" and the position and character of "the thousand islands." As an artist he saw them with rare clarity and then was able to mirror them exactly. To travelers bound for the East Indies Conrad's novels are invaluable preparation for the scene. Those who have already been there instantly recognize his faithful reflection of the islands. Should anyone, lacking the opportunity to visit Malaysia, patiently compare Conrad's background to its smallest detail with descriptions by trustworthy travelers, geographers, ethnologists, and government investigators, he would find but little in the fiction to which the observations of experts do not attest.

Geographically, Conrad's Malaysia is very nearly perfect. There are, for example, no more accurate descriptions of the sand bar at the mouth of the Meinam River than those in "The Secret Sharer," "Falk," and *The Shadow Line*. In "The End of the Tether" the Singapore of Conrad's day appears with maplike precision. The "avenue of big trees" did "run straight over the Esplanade."[3] "A queer white monument" did "peep over bushy points of land" beyond "the work shops of the Consolidated Docks Company."[4] It was exactly a "three-mile journey"[5] from the public library to New Harbour docks. No clearer idea of Borneo's huge, forested bulk, with its muddy rivers fed by heavy tropical rains, can be gained from books than from *Almayer's Folly, An Outcast of the Islands,* or *The Rescue.* Only rarely did Conrad part from his own geographical experience.

Correct in the physical background, Conrad's fiction is further strengthened by his accurate knowledge of the complicated pattern of Malaysian life. He recognized the influences which have made the Indies a meeting place of various oriental tenets and of East and West in general.

21

He understood the early Spanish and Portuguese jealousy over the rich spice trade. The Pepper Coast of *Lord Jim* had been the scene of struggles between the two. The Eurasians of *An Outcast of the Islands* and *Lord Jim* are very acute studies of the present population which has resulted from the infusion of blood from those bitter rivals. In his own day the Dutch-British contest for control of the islands naturally produced a spirit of rivalry and mutual antagonism in the colonists from those two nations. The native potentates of Sambir of *Almayer's Folly* and *An Outcast of the Islands* were afraid of the foreign greed for power and attempted to balance Holland against England in order not to fall prey to either while gaining as much as possible from both. "Freya of the Seven Isles" has as its main theme the Dutch-British distrust, fanned into fear and hatred.

The Acheen War of the 1870's was the result of a broken agreement made by Holland and Great Britain to respect the integrity of the Kingdom of Atjeh in Sumatra. The agreement was primarily concerned with an attempt at adjustment between the Dutch and English. An exchange of lands was made, and the English left Sumatra to the Dutch, but the Dutch promised to keep Sumatran waters free from pirates. The Dutch found it difficult to keep their part of the treaty, and both countries, fearing American, French, or Russian influences in Atjeh, agreed to deprive that state of its promised independence. Resistance was stubborn and took years to subdue. This Acheen War enters the plots of "Karain," "The End of the Tether," and *Almayer's Folly*.

Piracy forms in the island history a romantic and sinister chapter of which Conrad did not neglect to avail himself. Foreign intervention produced the Malay pirate system, the most formidable the world has witnessed. It was a cruel and desperate attempt to evict the intruders. Among the strongest pirate nations were the Sulu and the Illanun. The story in *An Outcast of the Islands* of the destruction of the Sulu robber gang to which Babalatchi and Omar belonged is an authentic account of European methods used in attacking a pirate nest. Daman's Illanun pirates of *The Rescue* were struggling for existence even after piracy had obviously fallen. *The Rescue* refers directly to Sir Thomas Cochrane's victory in the "Diana" over the pirates.[6]

Conrad's books prove his understanding of the leading part Mohammedanism has played in Malay life. His treatment of Dain Maroola of *Almayer's Folly* as a Brahman prince from Bali and his description in "Karain" of ancient Buddhist ruins in Java give the proper slight emphasis to the waning Buddhist and Brahman influences that in the eighth century had produced the highest civilization the islands have known. Mohammedanism came to the archipelago from India by way of traders, gradually overthrowing the Brahman and Buddhist ways of life until it became firmly established in the fourteenth century. Before that the Malays were divided into innumerable tribes scattered over the many islands. They spoke different dialects and were distinct and apart. The Mohammedan traders realized the value of a common language and took for this purpose the Malay spoken in the Menangkabo district of Sumatra. This dialect is now the trade speech of the islands. Those who learned it became Mohammedan with it. As the proselytizing language of the Moslems, it became impregnated with the expressions peculiar to that faith.

Mohammedanism came peacefully to Malaysia for the most part, but one fanatical war of conversion was carried on in Sumatra by the Padris, who moved against the heathen Bataks in the Sumatran highlands. The Dutch eventually became involved; and the long war, which had started as a Moslem reform against the use of opium, betel nut, and tobacco, ended with the annihilation of the Padris in 1837. The plot of *The Rescue* is affected by this war, for Jörgenson fought in it and Belarab had been outlawed because of his part in it.

Mohammedan Malays are Conrad's chief native characters, but among them move an important foreign minority—the Arabs, the great trading class of the archipelago. They are the leaders in commerce and in religion who have identified themselves with the Malays through intermarriage and yet kept aloof as a superior power. Omar had been the Arab leader of the Sulu pirates of *An Outcast of the Islands.* Abdulla, Conrad's great Arab character of *Almayer's Folly, An Outcast of the Islands,* and "Because of the Dollars," is the epitome of Arab and Mohammedan influence in Malaysia. Conrad's outstanding Malay leaders—Pata Hassim and Belarab of *The Rescue,* Lakamba and Babalatchi of *Almayer's Folly* and the *Outcast,* Karain of "Karain," and Doramin of *Lord Jim*—use devout Islamic expressions but are less painstaking than the Arabs in observing the ordinary practices of the Mohammedan—ablutions and prayer, alms-giving, fasting, and pilgrimages. The Mohammedan way of thinking has cut a deep channel in their minds, but there are whole areas of their thought untouched by it. These Malays of Conrad's lived at the time when the power of the petty feudalistic kingdom was vanishing under foreign dominion. They were concerned with preserving the ancient forms of government. They attempted to get along amicably with the intruders through open friendship and secret deceit or by hiding their kingdoms in remote parts, or they had already lost control and were trying to regain it.

In his presentation of the complicated Malaysian life, Conrad did not fail to introduce the ubiquitous, hard-working Chinese, laboring in every capacity open to him. The clerks of Hudig's trading-house in Macassar, the miners at Samburan, the boatmen and shopkeepers at Singapore, the house servants of Almayer and Heyst, and the ship-owner in "Because of the Dollars" represent the Chinese in Malaysia, and Conrad embodied in them the racial characteristics which sharply differentiate the Chinese from the Arabs and the Malays.

To Conrad's remarkable powers of observation we owe his valuable record of the appearance of native life. In this he is as accurate and concrete as in his geographical description. In countless passages he has constructed the scene as it passed before his own eyes. There are the harbors or river fronts filled with native craft, "outlandish and high sterned."[7] There are the villages, Karain's, Belarab's, or Lakamba's, composed of kampongs of palm trees with labyrinths of paths twisting across the bare earth beneath them and houses of bamboo and palm leaves, set on stilts, in their midst. The curved roofs of mosques gleam above the foliage. The outlying orchards and fields separate the towns from the jungle. There are excellent interiors in the fiction, homes belonging to Babalatchi, Lakamba, and Doramin. That his interiors of mat-furnished homes with primitive kitchens, weaving-rooms, and men's and women's quarters are all true to the actual Malay household in every aspect can be proved by comparing them with such careful, detailed records as may be found in the contributions of students, for example, those of R. O. Winstedt to the *Papers on Malay Subjects.*

Malay costume comes in for the same close and brilliant attention. When Conrad has presented Mas Immada or Dain Maroola or Pata Hassim or Taminah, we know how they appeared in their sarongs and bajus, their turbans and headkerchiefs, their flawed jewels and krises. We even learn that because Mas Immada was from Wajo in Celebes her sarong was in the "national check of grey and red."[8] The etiquette of the kris as presented throughout Conrad is in perfect accord with the accounts of numerous authorities. Hassim wore his kris correctly on the left side."[9] Karain was acting as any properly taught Malay would when he "covered the handle of his kris in a sign of respect,"[10] as he examined the coin bearing Queen Victoria's likeness. Daman, on the other hand, allowed the handle of his kris to appear when he meant to insult. "The Koran, in a silk cover, hung on his breast and, just below, the plain buffalo horn handle of a kris stuck into the twist of his sarong, protruded to his hand . . . . 'There is blood between me and the whites,' he pronounced violently."[11]

So it is that Conrad's eastern fiction is in itself an authority on the general political situation in the archipelago and on the material Malay scene. For these elements it may be read with perfect trust. Only when it is studied for information on the difficult matter of native psychology can doubts arise as to Conrad's preparedness for handling his subject with complete mastery. This angle should attract the attention of some Malay student whose analysis would be acceptable. The only Conrad critics with the proper preparation whose opinions have reached the public are Frank Swettenham and Hugh Clifford. On reading *Almayer's Folly,* they felt that Conrad's "pictures of Malays were the result, as it were, of a series of flashlight impressions absorbed by a mind of strangely sensitive and imaginative quality, rather than any deep understanding of the people we both knew so well."[12] Hugh Clifford, after enthusiastically praising Conrad's westerners in the East, declared that "the Orientals . . . . are much less successful. To me they are interesting, not because they are really Asiatics, but because they represent the impression scored by Asiatics upon a sensitive imaginative European mind. Mr. Conrad had seen them and known them, but he had seen as white men see— from the outside. He had never lived into the life of the brown people."[13] Again, he mentioned "Karain" and "The Lagoon" as "containing some marvellous descriptive passages. Both these stories, however, dealt with the psychology of Asiatics, and to the expert were interesting rather than satisfying."[14] That is all from one whose long, intimate experience with Malays would have made his careful appraisal of Conrad's native psychology of great value. He became

Conrad's warm personal friend and apparently had no strong desire to point to any fault in his work.

Conrad himself was fully aware of his own lack of training along this line. In the Author's Note to *A Personal Record* he tells of his first meeting with Clifford, who accused him of knowing nothing of the Malay mind. "I was perfectly aware of this. I have never pretended to any such knowledge, and I was moved— I wonder to this day at my impertinence—to retort: 'Of course I don't know anything about Malays. If I knew only one hundredth part of what you and Frank Swettenham know of Malays I would make everybody sit up.' "[15]

Careful comparative study of Conrad's fiction and the writings of Alfred Wallace and Sir James Brooke proves that Conrad turned to them for help where his own experience ended, although he never in his prefaces and letters acknowledged his need of them. Of Brooke's diaries there is no public mention, but, according to Richard Curle, Wallace's *The Malay Archipelago* was Conrad's "favorite bedside companion."[16] From Brooke, Conrad secured characters, incidents, and scenes. Thus Rajah Allang of *Lord Jim* is traceable to Brooke's diaries, and Brooke himself was very influential in the formation of the Lingard of *The Rescue*. The entire plot of *The Rescue* is based on happenings which Brooke recorded. All Conrad's native intrigues are influenced by the actual intrigues which involved Rajah Brooke. Alfred Wallace supplied a multitude of phrases and words, incidents, backgrounds, and one entire character—Stein of *Lord Jim;* and Conrad, accepting Wallace as the greatest authority of his time on the Malay, founded the Malay nature he portrayed on Wallace's estimate of the race. The prefaces prove that a number of native characters have the physical appearance of people Conrad actually saw. Lakamba and Babalatchi are two. On the other hand, such typical physiques as those of Pata Hassim and Dain Maroola agree throughout with the detailed description of the physical Malay as recorded by Wallace. Wallace was likewise full and detailed in his estimate of Malay nature. In brief, he attributed to the Malay these chief qualities; impassivity, reserve, deceiving diffidence, undemonstrativeness, circuitous speech, courtesy, lack of humor, and a short range of mental activity. Good or bad, Conrad's Malays hold to this pattern. They were compressed into the Wallace mold.

This secondhand estimate of Malays has two results. For one, Conrad's Malay nature is not very far wrong, for Wallace and Brooke were good judges. For the other, it is at least once removed from reality, and, so being, is probably never quite right.

It appears that Conrad knew only the trade Malay language, which he would need in his commercial travels. There are sixty-five Malay words scattered throughout the fiction, and all of them are of the trade Malay type soon learned by foreigners. In *A Personal Record*[17] Conrad mentions listening to a conversation between the Rajah of Dongala and Captain C. in which the only word he understood was the name "Almayer." Malay is a florid, highly ornamented language, full of figures of speech, bits of poetry—quoted often to refer to an unquoted line in the same poem—coined words, proverbs, and special vocabularies for particular moments of the day, occupations, places, or occasions. In itself the language tells a world about the Malay mind. By not knowing it, Conrad was distinctly handicapped as a recorder of Malay thought. Perhaps the language alone of "Karain" and "The Lagoon" was enough to occasion Hugh Clifford's remark that those stories are "interesting rather than satisfying to the expert."

A little more may be hazarded in attempting to guess Clifford's lack of satisfaction. "Karain" and "The Lagoon," as he pointed out, are the two tales in which white characters are not at the center of the stage. These stories rest on Malay nature itself. Both involve runaway couples, and no literature abounds more in just such situations than the Malay. Lovers who to prevent separation escape their own environment and the disasters that attend such actions are favorite Malay subjects. In that, then, the stories are not untrue to the region. It happens, however, that both these stories are strongly concerned with the supernatural, another theme dear to the Malay mind. Here is where Conrad's lack of knowledge betrays him.

"Karain," for example, is a perfectly understandable character. The abduction of Matara's sister and the long search he and Matara made for her darkened his mind. He was bound to Matara as to a blood brother, and he had to help Matara do the killing which the Malay considers just. On the other hand, he could not bear to see Matara's sister die. These two loyalties wore on him through the years until he became unbalanced on this one subject. He actually saw the sister, a mournful figure who sat by their fires and tried to dissuade him from his intention, but at first he knew this was an illusion, and he kept it a secret from Matara. When he killed Matara to save the sister, he became truly insane. He saw Matara following him always, until the Englishman's charm allayed his fears and dissipated the ghost. Any mad westerner, his mind clouded by indecision and remorse, might have the same illusions. Conrad's own Almayer became subject to them.

To Malays, however, ghosts, or *hantu,* are amazing creatures. No kindly human form returns after death to the living. To minds more swayed by ancient animistic than by present Moslem teachings the *hantus* seem actual and not the figment of an overwrought imagination. From earliest childhood, the Malay is taught about the multitude of invisible or occasionally visible good and evil presences by whom he is always surrounded. He learns elaborate means of fooling or placating or winning them. To a real Karain, Matara might have returned, but not as himself. The spirits of the murdered are among the most dreaded and horrible of *hantu.* Matara's ghost would probably have been an enormous, oppressive, indefinitely shaped being, almost too fantastic for a westerner to imagine, and his spirit revenge would have been something unthinkable.

In spite of their weaknesses as Malays, Conrad's native people are very interesting; and, if they might mislead us, should we take them too literally as Malay folk, they, on the other hand, are much like Malays in their ways and exactly like them in their appearance and dress. As to their homes and their country, Conrad has given us in these only the real Malaysia.

NOTES:

1   For three years resident in the Straits Settlement. This article and kindred papers in the *South Atlantic Quarterly* for July and the *Scientific Monthly* for November are based upon her Ohio State University thesis.

2   (New York: Doubleday, Page & Co., 1925), p. 3.

3   *Selected Stories of Joseph Conrad* (New York: Doubleday, Doran, 1930), p. 190.

4   *Ibid.*, p. 194.

5   *Ibid.*, p. 209.

6   *Ibid.,* p. 23.

7   "Youth," in *Selected Stories of Joseph Conrad,* p. 37.

8   *The Rescue,* p. 65.

9   *Ibid.*

10 *Tales of Unrest* (New York: Doubleday, Page & Co., 1923), p. 49.

11 *The Rescue,* p. 222.

12 Hugh Clifford, "Joseph Conrad: Some Scattered Memories," *Bookman's Journal and Print Collector,* II (October, 1924), 3.

13 "The Genius of Mr. Conrad," *North American Review,* CLXXVIII (June, 1904), 843.

14 *Ibid.,* p. 849.

15 (New York: Doubleday, Page & Co., 1925), p. vi.

16 *The Last Twelve Years of Joseph Conrad* (London: Sampson, Low, Marston & Co., 1928), p. 120.

17 *Ibid.,* p. 75.

JUMBLE OF FACTS AND FICTION: THE FIRST SINGAPORE REACTION TO *ALMAYER'S FOLLY*

Hans van Marle

"We are all reading your books out there," so Joseph Conrad was told in the early autumn of 1909 by a visitor "out of the Malay Seas." This visit from an admiring reader had such a psychological impact on Conrad ("It was like the raising of a lot of dead," as he put it) that Captain Carlos M. Marris crops up in letters to J. B. Pinker, Hugh Clifford, and Edward Garnett.[1] Three years later Conrad dedicated *'Twixt Land and Sea* to Marris, no doubt because this English sailor, who had settled in Kedah in northern Malaya, had supplied most of the facts behind "Freya of the Seven Isles" (as I hope to demonstrate at a later date).

In his article on four unpublished letters of Conrad's to Mr. and Mrs. T. Fisher Unwin from the holdings of the West Sussex County Record Office, Mario Curreli has shown that reviews of *An Outcast of the Islands* reached its honeymooning author from his publisher's office in the summer of 1896.[2] Dr. Curreli's annotation indicates that one of these notices, printed in the London *Indian Magazine and Review* for June 1896, concerned not only Conrad's second novel but also *Almayer's Folly*. In his text the semi-anonymous reviewer A. K. referred to "a writer in a Singapore newspaper," who had identified the fictional Captain Lingard of Conrad's *début* "as a successful trader... well known for many years in the Eastern Isles"–clear evidence, thus, that Conrad's first novel had been read out East shortly after it was published.

It turned out not to be all too difficult to trace A. K.'s reference and the review to which it took exception. The *Straits Times* for 16 January 1896 proved to contain an unsigned review of *Almayer's Folly* by one of Conrad's first readers "out there." The text of the review, which has thus far escaped all bibliographers, is given below under No. I.

The next day's issue of the *Straits Times* contained the immediate reaction of an indignant subscriber who apparently not only had read the novel but had also known the actual Captain Lingard–who, he felt, had not been done justice. Evidently the novel had given him reason to equate the fictional Lingard with the man he had known. In doing so, he must have been the very first to break Conrad's hardly a secret code, preceding by some four months another Singaporean whose review Professor Norman Sherry was able to trace.[3]

Two things are obvious from this spirited letter to the editor of the *Straits Times,* the text of which is given below under No. II. In the first place, Conrad's

29

Tom Lingard was an easily recognizable figure for old hands in Singapore, and in the second the real Captain William Lingard was a highly interesting historical figure in his own, non-fictional right. Elsewhere I have tried to sketch summarily Lingard's importance to historians.[4] A projected fuller treatment of his life will, I hope, do justice both to his memory and to Conrad's keen awareness of his exemplary relevance for nineteenth-century Southeast Asian history.

Amsterdam

I
ALMAYER'S FOLLY.
A ROMANCE OF THE INDIAN ARCHIPELAGO

This story is the tragedy of a European–"the only European on the East Coast"–degraded to the level of his surroundings by long years of residence among the sordid intrigues and petty interests of a native village in Borneo. It tells us also the fate of a girl–the daughter of that European–living under the same miserable conditions, too well educated to be unconscious of their degrading influence; but too high-spirited to return to the creature-comforts of a civilisation which is socially merciless to people of mixed blood.

Kaspar Almayer had been a clerk in a mercantile firm at Macassar at a time when that port was a rendezvous for all those bold spirits who, fitting out schooners on the Australian coast, invaded the Malay Archipelago in search of money and adventure. The boldest of these men was one Tom Lingard—he whom all the natives recognized as the Raja Laut or King of the Sea because of his trading successes and desperate fights with the pirates who then infested those waters. On the occasion of one of these conflicts he had captured a young native girl whom, in well-meant but mistaken kindness, he adopted as a daughter and sent to the convent for an education. Some time afterwards having taken a fancy to young Almayer he offered to make him the husband of the girl and the heir of a fortune. Almayer hesitated. The golden prospects held out to him were seriously discounted by the thought of the life-companionship of an ignorant and half savage Sulu girl to whom four years of convent life had imparted only a very thin veneer of civilisation. On the other hand, there was the possibility of accidents–the girl might die or might run away–and he would be left to enjoy alone a fortune which his abilities were certain to increase. The marriage accordingly took place but the hopes of Almayer were doomed to disappointment. The fortune was dissipated in hopeless attempts to reach an imaginary Eldorado in Central Borneo. The Raja Laut returned a penniless adventurer, to disappear in the labyrinth of London life and after twenty years of failure and disappointment, Almayer found himself a broken-down trader in a petty Borneo village, ruined by the competition of Arab and Chinese rivals. The unhappiness of his position was in no way diminished by the continued existence of Mrs. Almayer with her shrill voice, her scanty sarong, and her passion for disfiguring the house with the broad red marks of indiscriminate betel-chewing. She, too, had been disappointed in her marriage, having found

Almayer very different from the ideal pirate of her girlish dreams, and she never failed to taunt him with the fact that she was "his own Christian wife married according to his own Blanda Law"[5] knowing that this was the bitterest thing of all—the greatest regret of that man's life.

Nina Almayer, the only child of this ill-assorted marriage, had been sent at an early age to Singapore to receive whatever education that great civilising centre could bestow. There, under the maternal wing of one Mrs. Vinck, she received Christian teaching, social training and a good glimpse of civilised life, until she reached an age when her Eastern charms began to divert attention from the more orthodox beauty of the Misses Vinck. The education accordingly ended in a scene of humiliation, in an outburst of contempt from her white teachers for her mixed blood. "She would not stay," said Capt. Ford who brought her back to her father. "Sit still; what can you do? It is better so. She was never happy over there. Those two Vinck girls are no better than dressed up monkeys. They slighted her. You can't make her white. It is no use your swearing at me; you can't."[6] She was thus brought back with her father and mother to exercise a melancholy choice between the civilisation that despised her and the barbarism that she had learnt to despise. The story of "Almayer's Folly" is the story of this choice.

It is a sad story. The author has drawn with great power and fidelity the miserable results of a mixed marriage under existing social conditions. He does not allow us to feel that the end might have been different in the case of an abler man than the weak and foolish Almayer: No man, however able, can force his will upon Society. The social prejudice against mixed blood, unjust in itself, has been aroused by the narrowing influence of local education and limited interests, and serves to save many foolish lives from mental shipwrecks. Its general utility does not, however, prevent its operating with very cruel harshness against individuals. "She was very beautiful disposing," said the Dutch officers of Nina Almayer, "but after all, a half-caste girl!"[7] To Almayer she was much more than a mere half-caste girl. When the hard social ideas of his countrymen had created an insurmountable barrier between him and his daughter, his mind went back to the happy years of her childhood when his joy in her was undimmed by the thought of her inevitable future. "In the dim light of the rooms with their closed shutters, in the bright sunshine of the verandah, wherever he went, whichever way he turned, he saw the small figure of a little maiden with a pretty olive face, with long black hair, her little pink robe slipping off her shoulders, her big eyes looking up at him in the tender trustfulness of a petted child. He had done all he could. Every vestige of Nina's existence had been destroyed; and now with every sunrise he asked himself whether the longed-for oblivion would come before sunset, whether it would come before he died?"[8]

"Ah, Tuan!" said the one eyed diplomatist of that Borneo Village, "the old times were best. Ever I have sailed with Lanun men and boarded in the night silent ships with white sails. That was before an English Rajah ruled in Kuching. Then we fought amongst ourselves and were happy. Now when we fight with you, we can only die!"[9] Are these really the views of the natives? Incidentally it may be stated that our author is weak in his Malay, that he is in error in representing Bali as one kingdom and in describing a prince of Bali as a Brahmin. These blemishes do not detract from the general truthfulness of the book. The power of the European has substituted a sullen peace for the open war of the past. It has done so in the interest of trade, not of civilisation, however much we may disguise the fact. Civilisation makes no proselytes; it indeed rejects them with its barrier of racial prejudice. Left to themselves the natives are forced to judge civilisation and Christianity by the Europeans with whom they are brought most in contact, by the ethics of the trader and the manners of the beachcomber. The result is deplorable but it has none the less to be faced.

"Almayer's Folly," by Joseph Conrad. T. Fisher Unwin, Paternoster Sq. (Straits Times, 16 January 1896)

II
"ALMAYER'S FOLLY":
TO THE EDITOR OF THE "STRAITS TIMES"

SIR.–Perhaps you will allow me, as one who knew well the late Captain Lingard, the "Rajah Laut" of Bornean waters, to refute a few of the pernicious libels on his memory which are perpetrated by the author of "Almayer's Folly," and reproduced, to some extent, by its reviewer in your columns yesterday. Captain Lingard was a man who was well known in Singapore up till the time of his death,[10] holding the respect and esteem of all who knew him, and was not the man to engage in such a questionable line of conduct as the author describes. For many years he sailed his own ships and cargos, between Singapore and Borneo, and had amassed a very considerable fortune. It is quite true that he had serious losses in the latter end of the "seventies," but they were incurred in the perfectly legitimate trading ventures in which he had, all through his career in the East, been engaged in, and not in the wild and vain effort of discovering an eldorado in the interior of Borneo.[11] Never, up till his death, was he in such a state as to be described as a penniless adventurer. Even now, after the lapse of so many years, Captain Lingard's estate has large interests in Borneo, and it was only a year or two ago that a representative of his family, a nephew, I think, passed through here on his way to realise them.[12]

It was in one of his numerous voyages to Borneo that he attacked and destroyed a large and powerful fleet of Lanun pirates, and succeeded in rescuing a Dutch man-of-war brig, which they had surrounded and almost captured. For his conspicuous bravery on this and other occasions, and the signal aid he rendered to the Netherlands India Government, he received the thanks of the king of Holland, and was decorated with the order of the "Lion of the Netherlands," which he was proud to wear on dress occasions.[13] It was on account of this action, and of the wholesome terror with which his behaviour inspired the pirates, that he acquired the name of "Rajah Laut" among the Malays.[14]

Quite possibly, the story of the Sulu girl, who was married to Almayer,[15] and their subsequent adventures, may be founded on fact, but it is a pure fiction on the author's part to connect them in this way with the career of Capt. Lingard, the "Rajah Laut." Novelists, of course, are allowed a considerable amount of license, but the line ought to be drawn somewhere, and, when it comes to such a questionable jumble of facts and fiction such as the opening chapters of "Almayer's Folly," it is only fair in the interests of truth, and in justice to the memory of those who are maligned, that a protest should be made.

I have no interest in referring to any minor errors, in what is, undoubtedly, a powerful and interesting work, but surely the author and his reviewer must know very little of Dutch Indian Society when they dwell so deeply on the social disabilities of the results of mixed marriages, "the half-caste girl" as it is put. Had the scene been laid in British India, no doubt the social bar is as strong and deep as the author makes it. It has been shown admirably in some of Kipling's sketches. But to imply that it exists to anything like the same extent in Dutch Indian Society, is ludicrous. Society in these colonies is so thoroughly permeated with the tinge of colour that it would be considered a most extraordinary thing to hint at any such disability being recognised.[16] More especially is it so in the class of society in which Almayer, a mercantile clerk in Macassar, would be likely to move in. The writer is evidently drawing on his British Indian experience, if he has had any, and foolishly applying it to a very different set of circumstances.

I am, & c,

G.[17]

(*Straits Times,* 17 January 1896)

NOTES:

1   G. Jean-Aubry, *Joseph Conrad: Life & Letters* (London: Heinemann, 1927), II pp. 103, 109, 133. The first quotation above occurs on p. 133, the other two are on p. 103. Captain Marris' unpublished introductory letter to Conrad, dated 18 July 1909, is in the Beinecke Library, Yale University.

2   Mario Curreli, "Four Unpublished Conrad Letters," *Conradiana,* 8:3 (1976), 209-17.

3   Norman Sherry, *Conrad's Eastern World* (Cambridge: Cambridge University Press, 1966), p. 118.

4   A. van Marle, "De rol van de buitenlandse avonturier" (The Role of the Foreign Adventurer [in Nineteenth-Century Indonesia]). *Bijdragen en Mededelingen*

betreffende de Geschiedenis der Nederlanden, 86:1 (1971), 32-39. See also A. B. Lapian, "The Sealords of Berau and Mindanao: Two Responses to the Colonial Challenge," *Masyarakat Indonesia,* 1:2 (1974), 143-54.

5   *Almayer's Folly* (London: Dent, 1946), p. 40.

6   *Ibid.,* pp. 30-31.

7   *Ibid.,* p.126 (for "disposing" the quotation should read "and imposing").

8   *Ibid.,* pp. 201-02.

9   *Ibid.,* p. 206 (for "Ever" read "Even").

10   For Captain Lingard's life, see Sherry, *passim.* He died in Macclesfield, Chesire, on 27 May 1888, and the *Straits Times* for 5 September 1888 contained an obituary.

11   The son of William Charles Olmeijer (the Almayer of Conrad's title) voiced similar misgivings about the lust for gold ascribed to his father when I interviewed him in the late 1950s. The son apparently did not know that his father had actually petitioned for permission to prospect for gold in the interior of Borneo: see G. J. Resink, "Tulisan dan tanda tangan Charles Olmeijer" (Handwriting and Signature of Charles Olmeijer), *Medan Ilmu Pengetahuan,* 1:4 (December 1960), 358-62 (with English summary and reproduction of the handwritten petition, dated 1 December 1890.)

12   Lingard's will (at Somerset House, London) shows that he left his assets in England (including the *Royal Oak,* a public house in the center of Macclesfield) to a nephew there, while those in Southeast Asia went to another nephew, the James Lingard who has given his name to *Lord Jim.* Before Captain Lingard returned to England in 1883 he had bought his daughter a house in Singapore: Sherry, pp. 113, 134.

13   The writer of the letter is telescoping two separate events into one. The attack by the pirates was averted in 1875, with Lingard's wife handling the ship's gun (Lingard's own letter in *Makassaarsch Handelsblad* for 1 January 1876 and Sherry, pp. 103-04). Lingard was made a Knight in the Order of the Netherlands Lion in 1869 for his aid in saving a Dutch man-of-war stranded on a reef close to "his" Bornean river.

14   The title of Rajah Laut (more or less equivalent to First Lord of the Admiralty) was officially bestowed upon Lingard by the Sultan of Berau (the "Brow" of *Almayer's Folly,* p. 42) in 1862 for his help in warfare against a neighboring ruler, the Sultan of Bulungan. According to official Dutch reports, Lingard occasionally donned the garb and insignia of his Berau dignity.

15   The actual Mrs. Olmeijer was not a Sulu girl adopted by Captain Lingard, as Conrad has it, but the Eurasian daughter of a Dutch colonial soldier. On the other hand, the real Lingard had married a relative of Olmeijer's (Sherry, p. 94).

16   I have written at length about this "tinge of colour" and its social implications in "De groep der Europeanen in Nederlands-Indië, iets over ontstaan en groei" (The European Group in the Netherlands Indies: Remarks on Origin and Growth), *Indonesië*, 5(1951-2), 97-121, 314-41, 481-507 (English summary, pp. 506-07).

17   Since G's letter was published the same day it was written, it can safely be assumed that he was a Singapore resident. The *Singapore and Straits Directory 1896* (Singapore: Singapore and Straits Printing Office) lists several dozen residents of the city whose family name begins with a G. Reflecting a characteristically colonial geographical mobility, all but three of them do not yet appear in the 1879 edition *(The Singapore Directory for the Straits Settlements 1879*, Singapore: Keaughran). Probably the most likely candidate among these three is Alexander Gettle, who was secretary of the Chamber of Commerce and United States Vice-Consul in 1879 and a Municipal Commissioner seventeen years later. The two others are G. Gaggino, a ship chandler, and Alexander Jasper Gunn. The latter, the more likely of the two to sign with one initial only, was exchange broker and public accountant in 1888 and Gettle's successor at the Chamber of Commerce in 1896. For all its details, Charles Burton Buckley, *An Anecdotal History of Old Times in Singapore* (Singapore: Fraser and Neave, 1902), could not help me in establishing the authorship of the letter under consideration beyond all doubt, though Gettle would seem best placed to state that he "knew well the late Captain Lingard" in the years before "Europe had swallowed up the Rajah Laut" *(Almayer's Folly,* p. 28, echoed in *An Outcast of the Islands,* p.364).

II. Colonial Legacy: Pine and Palm

CONRAD'S MALAYAN NOVELS: PROBLEMS OF AUTHENTICITY

D. C. R. A. Goonetilleke

And, behold, here was a writer, of whose very existence I had not previously heard, at work in the same field and displaying withal a degree of finish, a maturity and originality of style, a sureness of touch and a magical power of conveying to his readers the very atmosphere of the Malayan environments, which to me was so familiar, yet whose knowledge of the people, about whom he wrote with such extraordinary skill, was superficial and inaccurate in an infuriating degree.

Hugh Clifford, 'Concerning Conrad and his work

Conrad was in the Far East between 1883 and 1888, but the actual time he spent there was no more than a year. Moreover, his Eastern experiences were gained as second mate of the *Palestine,* first mate of the *Vidar,* and master of the *Otago.* As an active seaman, he spent little time ashore.[1] Thus, his first-hand experience of Eastern countries and peoples was slight. Indeed, Norman Sherry estimates that Conrad spent altogether only about twelve days (three days each during the four times the *Vidar* called) at Tandjong Redeb,[2] which he transmutes into Sambir and Patusan in his fiction. Given his extremely slight experience of the Malay Archipelago, it is in a way a logical consequence that the authenticity of his Eastern fictive world should be called in question. But is it as false as it has been often made out (by writers like Hugh Clifford and F. R. Leavis)?[3]

Let us first examine Conrad's presentation of the Malayan setting. Its quality in his first two novels is much the same as in *The Rescue.* One can put one's finger on it by comparing a typical passage from Conrad with a typical and similar passage from an average contemporary writer about Malaya such as Clifford. Here is Conrad (in *Almayer's Folly*):

As he skirted in his weary march the edge of the forest he glanced now and then into its dark shade, so enticing in its deceptive appearance of coolness, so repellent with its unrelieved gloom, where lay, entombed and rotting, countless generations of trees, and where their successors stood as if mourning, in dark green foliage, immense and helpless, awaiting their turn. Only the parasites seemed to live there in a sinuous rush upwards into the air and sunshine, feeding on the dead and the dying alike, and crowning their victims with pink and blue flowers that gleamed amongst the boughs,

39

incongruous and cruel, like a strident and mocking note in the solemn
harmony of the doomed trees.[4]

Here is Clifford (in 'The East Coast'):

These forests are among the wonderful things of the Earth. They are immense
in extent, and the trees which form them grow so close together that they tread
on one another's toes. All are lashed, and bound, and relashed, into one huge
magnificent tangled net, by the tickest underwood, and the most marvellous
parasitic growths that nature has ever devised. No human being can force
his way through this maze of trees, and shrubs, and thorns, and plants, and
creepers; and even the great beasts which dwell in the jungle find their strength
unequal to the task, and have to follow game paths, beaten out by the passage
of innumerable animals, through the thickest and deepest parts of the forest.[5]

The emphasis in the first passage is on nature dead or dying and, in the second, on
nature alive; but both are alike in their concern with nature in its raw plenitude.
They are not purely factitious descriptions of 'the Malayan exotic' (in Leavis's
phrase).[6] Both writers are trying to render genuinely Malayan settings, and their
observations are accurate. But the touches of striking, human metaphor for
inanimate nature in the Clifford, unlike in the Conrad, are lost in the obtrusively
literary rhetoric. Descriptive epithets such as 'countless', 'immense', 'most
marvellous' can be considered at best only vaguely impressive; the impressive-
ness is soon lost in the woolliness and exaggeration. This kind of description
occurs in both passages. Conrad's prose is less repetitive and less artificial than
Clifford's. But the laboured effects in both appear to arise from an identical source
– the struggle of European writers who are trying to come to terms with
environments alien to them and render them in terms suited to Western readers for
whom they would generally be even more unfamiliar. Still, when Conrad comes
to *Lord Jim*, he develops 'that special power of conjuring up for the reader an alien
environment'[7] and retains it to much the same degree in *Victory*:

Patusan is a remote district of a native-ruled state, and the chief settlement
bears the same name. At a point on the river about forty miles from the sea,
where the first houses come into view, there can be seen rising above the level
of the forests the summits of two steep hills very close together, and separated
by what looks like a deep fissure, the cleavage of some mighty stroke. . . .[8]

The spoken idiom is rather plain; but it is clear and has a living naturalness. The
locale here is presented as it strikes a sensitive observer (Marlow, when he first
sees it); it thereby gains immediacy and verisimilitude. Yet, Conrad's main
settings, whether in *Almayer's Folly* or *Lord Jim*, are rendered with sufficient
precision to make them identifiably Malayan, but without a high degree of
specification which would locate them in particular places in Malaya. London in
The Secret Agent is nothing but London, whereas Sambir or Patusan is not

Tandjong Redeb in Eastern Borneo and nothing else besides. Of course, some regions within the same country, whether they be tropical or temperate, usually resemble one another. But Conrad's descriptions themselves possess a general quality which works with this likeness, to make it possible for them to be taken as relating to a number of regions in the Malay Archipelago. This factor contributes to the general significance of the novels, which is that they reflect life in the Archipelago as a whole and life in a universal sense.

Let us consider the role of the Malayan environment in Conrad's novels. J. I. M. Stewart argues that 'external nature as a sinister and alarming mystery constitutes – it is perhaps not too much to say – the central emotional focus of the novel' [*Almayer's Folly*]. [9] But his reasoning appears unconvincing to me. It is true that Conrad at times refers to 'external nature as a sinister and alarming mystery'; but this manner of description, as in the extract analysed above, is usually part of Conrad's failure to present well the alien surroundings and is not 'central'. It is also true, for instance, that Almayer calls Sambir 'this infernal place' when he feels that his hopes are shattered after Dain Maroola's supposed death; it is true that Dain imagines that Nina and he 'would be together on the great blue sea that was like life – away from the forests that were like death'. But such references by the characters are infrequent and are evoked by particular occasions. They do not contribute to build the kind of central symbolism Stewart posits – the jungle which 'speaks mysteriously of deeply buried dreads' and is set over against the ocean, the way out to happy civilised living. [10]

There are characteristic ways by which the setting becomes more than surroundings. One way is evident in the scene in *Victory* when Heyst and Lena are contemplating the threat to their lives posed by the arrival of desperadoes, a threat particularly serious as Wang has stolen their revolver and left them:

> Beyond the headland of Diamond Bay, lying black on a purple sea, great masses of cloud stood piled up and bathed in a mist of blood. A crimson crack like an open wound zigzagged between them, with a piece of dark red sun showing at the bottom. Heyst cast an indifferent glance at the ill-omened chaos of the sky.

Conrad is using nature to charge the atmosphere in a simple theatrical 'pathetic-fallacy' manner. At other times he attempts to link the natural scene with the human situation more closely, as when Willems first sees Aissa in *An Outcast of the Islands*: 'She seemed to him at once enticing and brilliant – sombre and repelling: the very spirit of that land of mysterious forests, ...' Willems views the 'native' woman as a symbol of her tropical environment in a way typical of exotic romances.

In Conrad's Malayan fiction, then, the alien surroundings, whether their presentation is undistinguished as in *Almayer's Folly, An Outcast of the Islands* and *The Rescue* or competent as in *Lord Jim* and *Victory,* appear clearly authentic. They seem rather conventionally exotic only during his infrequent attempts to relate them actively to the human drama. He has the good sense to see all his characters, European and Malayan, in true relation to both the imperial system and the Malayan social system. We noticed that Europeans are usually at the centre of his Malayan novels and that, except in *Victory,* the Malayans are not unimportant. His kind of emphasis suggests that his perspective is European, but it is not distorted: the Europeans enjoyed an importance in the colonies enormously out of proportion to their numbers because they belonged to the 'ruling race' if not to the ruling nation; indeed, the Europeans in Conrad's Archipelago were in a more powerful position than those in Kipling's India, during the same period too, because the country was more 'undeveloped'.

The world of his Eastern novels was ruled by the Dutch and, to a very small extent, by the Portuguese and Spanish. In *Lord Jim,* Gentleman Brown had travelled among Spanish settlements and had been arrested by a Spanish patrol. In *Victory,* the crookedness of Portuguese officials in Timor is illustrated by the way they tried to cheat Morrison. The novels, however, are set almost wholly in Dutch territory. Among his milieux, only Macassar in *An Outcast of the Islands* and Sourabaya in *Victory* are important enough to have a number of Europeans who form exclusive societies. We noticed that his chief settings are all remote. The characters afford insights into Dutch rule in the course of their actions and conversations. Lingard is a powerful 'British Free Merchant'; it is he who appoints Almayer and Willems, the two Dutchmen, to Sambir. Stein, a Bavarian, traded in dangerous areas such as Patusan 'by special permit from the Dutch authorities'; Cornelius, a Portuguese, and Jim, an Englishman, are his nominees. Moreover, both the large-scale traders and their agents enjoy a considerable measure of independence. Thus, Conrad shows how the Dutch allowed other Europeans to trade rather freely on the outskirts of their empire and even set up pockets of influence. But the overall sway of the Dutch is felt even in these spots: Babalatchi intrigues with the Arabs to oust them; Hassim speaks of 'tributes' paid by the Malayans to them; Jewel and Hassim are openly defeatist. The Dutch as colonial masters enter the outposts directly only once – when certain officers come to Sambir to arrest Dain Maroola. We have seen how effectively Conrad dramatises their encounter with Almayer.

Conrad, then, conveys an accurate impression of Dutch rule in so far as it affects his milieux. It is interesting to find that he strives to depict life in these places as it actually moves in its complex way. But his presentation of the interaction of Dutch rule, other European colonialists, the Arabs and Malayan society is not wholly successful. Intrigue and villainy play a prominent part and they have a real social basis in his kind of developing milieux. Yet they set him delicate artistic problems: with the same material, Conrad could write *The Secret Agent* and Alfred Hitchcock make *Sabotage.* Let us first examine the European side: take Cornelius and Gentleman Brown in *Lord Jim,* Jones, Ricardo and Pedro in *Victory.* Cornelius is a trading agent who tries to oust and even kill another, Jim, to save his position by scheming with Brown and his men, as well as with Malayans (Kassim, Tunku Allang and their men). When he guides Brown and his men through a secret tributary to attack Dain Waris, the episode appears melodramatic. But his treachery often takes the form of convincingly human drama. Conrad skillfully presents his overwrought attempt to persuade Jim to accept his 'little plan wherein for one hundred dollars – or even for eighty – he, Cornelius, would procure a trustworthy man to smuggle Jim out of the river, all safe'; with equal skill, Conrad dramatises Cornelius' behaviour soon after:

> Then Cornelius appeared from somewhere, and, perceiving Jim, ducked sideways, as though he had been shot at, and afterwards stood very still in the dusk. At last he came forward prudently, like a suspicious cat. 'There were some fishermen there – with fish', he said in a shaky voice. 'To sell fish – you understand'. . . . It must have been then two o'clock in the morning – a likely time for anybody to hawk fish about!
> Jim, however, let the statement pass, and did not give it a single thought.

Cornelius's absurdly defensive actions and speech betray his guilt and cowardice. Jim's nonchalance reveals his courage and happy unawareness of Cornelius' viciousness. Gentlemen Brown is different from the Portuguese. He belongs to the category of European ruffians who prowl around developing countries, cruder versions of the 'Interlopers'. As Conrad puts it in the novel, 'What distinguished him from the ordinary buccaneers like Bully Hayes or Pease was the arrogant temper of his misdeeds and a vehement scorn for mankind at large and for his victims in particular'. Conrad's account of how Brown captured his schooner is cursorily melodramatic, but Brown is usually a credibly human villain as in his key scene with Jim which was discussed above.

Jones in *Victory* bears a certain similarity to Brown who 'was supposed to be the son of a baronet'; Jones claims to be a 'gentleman'. Both carry over into the criminal world something of the airs of their former 'social sphere'. But Jones is not violent as Brown is, and, when violence is necessary, he directs his men to use it. The essential differences between Jones, Ricardo and Pedro are suggested by Heyst's description to Lena when she sees them for the first time from her bungalow: '. . . Here they are before you – evil intelligence, instinctive savagery arm in arm. The brute force is at the back...'. But the three desperadoes do not become symbols of these qualities. There are other similarly explicit attempts to endow them with a symbolic importance: Lena sees Ricardo as 'the embodied evil of the world' (when she employs duplicity to save Heyst); Jones regards himself as 'a sort of fate' (as he talks to Heyst shortly before he learns of Lena's presence on Samburan). An acceptable symbolic extension of meaning is almost impossible in their presentation because, in the first place, they do not come alive sufficiently as real human beings. Leavis thinks that they are 'a kind of Morality representation, embodiments of counter-potentialities',[11] but it seems to me that Conrad does not follow allegorical modes as Leavis suggests. When Shakespeare depicts the witches in *Macbeth,* he starts from contemporary popular belief and life, and presents them as embodiments of evil; he does not attempt to make the witches human and they remain moral forces throughout the play. Conrad's villains, however, are not allegorical figures of this type. Nor do they resemble figures from a Morality play like *Everyman:* the writer of such a play commences with moral concepts and, then, tries to lend them human interest. Conrad's method of portraying the desperadoes is not allegorical but symbolic. He begins with human beings[12] and, then, tries to invest them with a symbolic moral significance. But his effort in this direction is a failure, as I indicated above. M. C. Bradbrook is wrong to consider Jones 'the Living Skeleton, the Heart of Darkness';[13] none of the criminals gains a serious symbolic significance. Still, because they are not exactly like the villains of popular melodramatic fiction, say, of Peter Cheyney, Leslie Charteris or 'Sapper', who begin from nothing but melodramatic convention and remain within this convention, they offer an human interest. It is marked in their early appearances in Schomberg's hotel:

> The secretary retracted his lips and looked up sharply at Schomberg, as if only too anxious to leap upon him with teeth and claws.
> Schomberg managed to produce a deep laugh.
> 'Ha! Ha! Ha!'
> Mr Jones closed his eyes wearily, as if the light hurt them, and looked remarkably like a corpse for a moment. This was bad enough; but when he opened them again, it was almost a worse trial for Schomberg's nerves. The spectral intensity of that glance, fixed on the hotel-keeper (and this was most frightful), without any definite expression, seemed to dissolve the last grain of resolution in his character.
> 'You don't think, by any chnce, that you have to do with ordinary people, do you? inquired Mr Jones, in his lifeless manner, which seemed to imply some sort of menace from beyond the grave.
> 'He's a gentleman', testified Martin Ricardo with a sudden snap of the lips, after which his moustaches stirred by themselves in an odd, feline manner.

The 'discomfiture' of the pusillanimous Schomberg and the breakdown of his 'resolution' appear completely human. Jones's quietly menacing speech and demeanour as well as Ricardo's crude actions and sense of social inferiority are realised as fully as if they were part of any domestic scene, lurid though they could easily have become. The key to Conrad's descriptions of all these desperadoes is found in Schomberg's reaction to them as 'a spectre, a cat, an ape' (shortly before he directed their attention to Heyst). All their actions are too often conceived within the framework of these three exaggerated analogies, and this is partly why they soon begin to appear cardboard melodramatic caricatures rather than human criminals. As they play a larger role in *Victory* than all the other characters and as they play an important role in its *dénouement,* the weakness in their presentation mars the novel more than any other.

The various kinds of intrigue and villainy on the Malayan side of the colonial context convey the same mixed impression of realism and melodrama, but they are usually linked with political considerations. These characteristics are exemplified by *Almayer's Folly.* The cunning way by which Dain escapes the Dutch officers – the use of the dead body of one of Dain's boatmen after dressing it as if it were his own and battering its face – is a glaring and gruesome instance of melodrama. But the intriguing of Babalatchi and Lakamba – to get rid of the Dutch influence with the help of the Arabs, to trade with the latter and find out the location of Lingard's goldfield – is often put realistically:

'If the Orang Blanda come here, Babalatchi, and take Almayer to Batavia to punish him for smuggling gunpowder, what will he do, you think?'

'I do not know, Tuan'.

'You are a fool', commented Lakamba, exultingly. 'He will tell them where the treasure is, so as to find mercy. He will'.

Babalatchi looked up at his master and nodded his head with by no means a joyful surprise. He had not thought of this; there was a new complication.

'Almayer must die', said Lakamba, decisively, 'to make our secret safe. He must die quietly, Babalatchi. You must do it'.

Babalatchi assented, and rose wearily to his feet. 'To-morrow?' he asked.

'Yes; before the Dutch come. He drinks much coffee', answered Lakamba, with seeming irrelevancy.

Babalatchi stretched himself yawning, but Lakamba, in the flattering consciousness of a knotty problem solved by his own unaided intellectual efforts, grew suddenly wakeful.

'Babalatchi', he said to the exhausted statesman, 'fetch the box of music the white captain gave me, I cannot sleep'.

A prominent feature of Babalatchi's appearance is his single eye, but this does not necessarily make him a melodramatic villain: 'a fine old one-eyed fellow called "Souboo"' was among Captain Sherard Osborn's Malayan seaman.[14] Both Babalatchi and Lakamba appear very human plotters. The unsuccessful 'statesman' is in low spirits and the usually inefficient chief is animated as he feels he has hit upon certain bright ideas. They speak of death and murder imperturbably; Lakamba casually suggests to Babalatchi a specific method of murder when he refers to Almayer's coffee-drinking habit. Murderous intrigue, as suggested above, was an ordinary occurrence in places such as Sambir. The primitive chief uses an opera of Verdi from a hand-organ as a lullaby, a kind of ironic situation to be had in developing societies coming into contact with the West.[15] Indeed, all Conrad's insights here come off as authentically Malayan drama. He is aware of a need to fashion an English equivalent for the Malayan vernacular of his characters. Terms like 'Tuan' and 'Orang Blanda' are obviously Malayan; they are part of a simple idiom which is differentiated from Standard English in its structures. It is an alien English which is alive and sounds natural. Hugh Clifford attempts to meet the same need when Panglima tries to dissuade Wan Beh from accompanying him through 'the rebel party' in *Wan Beh, Princess of the Blood:*

'Whither goest thou?'' he asked.

'With thee, sweetheart', she said simply.

'Thou can'st not', said he shortly. . . .

. . . Malay-like his energy was not equal to arguing the point further. 'Let her be', he said to his followers. 'She for ever made trouble for me; it is her custom. What can one do? *Kras hati ta' takut mati* – the hard heart feareth not to die! Let her be'.

The speech of both characters has been fashioned crudely and appears extremely artificial. The English is stilted and full of archaisms. It is awkward to transliterate a Malay proverb and follow this with an English translation; indeed, such a thing would hardly occur in private conversation between Malayans.

The politics in Conrad's Malayan world is mainly intrigue. What are its directions and how accurate is Conrad's portrayal of them? Arnold Kettle refers to Dain Waris and Hassim, and says: 'these young Malayan aristocrats are conceived as Polish rather than Malayan nationalists'.[16] V. S. Pritchett goes further along the same lines: he thinks that Conrad's Malayans 'are really transplantations from Polish history'.[17] Firstly, are the Malayans nationalists? Let us discuss this question mainly in relation to the Malayans in Patusan (*Lord Jim*). Dain Waris is content to accept unquestioningly Jim's foreign over-lordship as if it were in the natural order of things; the other members of his community hold Jim in even greater awe. Before Brown came to Patusan, it is Doramin alone who thinks in terms of a successor to Jim. To Doramin's mind, the issue of a successor arises only after Jim of his own accord decides to leave Patusan. Moreover, Doramin's 'secret ambition' is to see his son 'ruler of Patusan' – that is, as a tribal chief. He is disturbed by the possibility that Jim's stay, if permanent, may prevent his son's succession; but he never thinks of requesting or forcing the 'white lord' to step aside. When he shoots Jim in the last scene, he is executing tribal justice. Let us now look at the opponents of the Bugis. They accept Jim's sway and stop their usual active hostilities towards the Bugis. But the attitudes of their leaders, Tunku Allang and Kassim, change in response to the new situation created by the arrival of Brown and his men:

> Kassim disliked Doramin and his Bugis very much, but he hated the new order of things still more. It had occurred to him that these whites, together with the Rajah's followers, could attack and defeat the Bugis before Jim's return. Then, he reasoned, general defection of the townsfolk was sure to follow, and the reign of the white man who protected poor people would be over. Afterwards the new allies could be dealt with. They would have no friends.

Because the enemies of the Bugis share in the general awe of Jim, they wish to attack the Bugis in his absence and with the help of the newly-arrived Europeans. They are friendly with Cornelius because he, too, is against Jim. They are hostile to Jim and the other Europeans for purely tribal, not nationalist, reasons. The attitudes of the Malayans in Conrad's other settings are of a piece with those of the inhabitants of Patusan. Babalatchi and Lakamba in Sambir intrigue with the

Arabs against the Dutch for tribal financial gain. Hassim and Immada revere Lingard as Dain Waris does Lord Jim; they require Lingard's help to fight for the rightful tribal succession in Wajo. Certain Malayans seem to reveal one of the basic characteristics of nationalists, opposition to alien rule: but this hostility is motivated by tribal considerations and cannot be considered nationalistic. Moreover, the Malayans were more often submissive to the Europeans than hostile; nor did they feel themselves to be on an equal footing with the Europeans. None of them reveals even a semblance of the other basic characteristic of nationalists, a sense of corporate identity. Conrad's Malayans think only in terms of their particular small tribe; although they live on or near the East coast of Borneo, they do not have a conception of belonging to the larger entity, Indonesia. But they are not tribalists. The need to be very conscious of and to defend the tribal order does not arise because it is not seriously endangered in Conrad's remote settings – not by the Dutch, not by individuals such as Almayer or Lingard or Lord Jim, not by a firm such as Stein's.

Conrad's Malayans, then, are tribal. Could one consider characters such as Dain Waris and Hassim 'aristocrats', as Kettle does? They are members of a privileged class by virtue of their ancestry and wealth. But theirs is the ruling class of tribal society — not an aristocracy in the usual sense of the term a privileged class in 'democratic' or 'undemocratic' civilised society. Thus to use the term 'aristocrats' for members of a tribal ruling class is to misapprehend their socal role and level of development.

Are there reasons to justify Kettle's point that they 'are conceived as Polish rather than Malayan nationalists'? Zdzislaw Najder describes succinctly the 'three major groups' of Polish nationalists in the nineteenth century:

> First, the appeasers, who wanted to preserve Polish national identity but within the scope of the Russian Empire (their most prominent representative was Count Aleksander Wielopolski, 1803-77). Secondly, the 'Whites' who thought about rebuilding the Polish Kingdom of the pre-partition time without basically changing its internal structure and preserving its feudal outlook; they relied heavily on the hope of foreign, mostly French and British, support of the Polish cause. Thirdly, there were the 'Reds' of various shades, who linked the fight for national independence with programmes for social reforms (particularly land reform and the abolishment of serfdom) and counted rather on a successful armed uprising than on the results of international political manoeuvring. The appeasers were, of course, dead against the two other groups. However, even the two 'patriotic groups, the Whites and the Reds, opposed each other violently, especially just before and in the early stages of the January 1863 insurrection.[18]

All these kinds of Polish nationalists of upper-class background are very different from the tribal leaders in Conrad's kind of milieux. The Poles live in a feudal system; in fact, the 'appeasers' and the 'Whites' do not wish to change it. On the other hand, all the Malayans belong to a tribal system. The Polish 'Whites' and 'Reds' are nationalist; the 'appeasers' are aware of their 'national identity' and value it. The Malayans are not nationalist and not even conscious of a 'national identity'. The conflicts between, say, Doramin's group and Tunku Allang's group in Patusan or Belarab's group and Tengga's group in the Land of Refuge are tribal, not like the nationalist antagonism of the Polish groups. The Malayans believe in primitive religion; the organised religion with which they were coming into contact, was Islam. On the other hand, the Poles were Catholics, though Conrad himself rejected Catholicism. Thus, the Malayans and the Poles live and think in cultural contexts which are very dissimilar and at different stages in the evolution of different civilisations. Moreover, the Malayans in Conrad's kind of milieux could not be expected to be conscious of nationality or be nationalistic in any way, Polish or Malayan, because nationalism did not emerge in that part of the world until shortly after *Lord Jim* was first published (in *Blackwood's Edinburgh Magazine,* 1899); as J. D. Legge observes,

> The emergence of a nationalist movement in the first decades of the twentieth century was essentially a new phenomenon. There had been movements of resistance against the Dutch from time to time in the past—the Java War of 1825 or the struggle in West Sumatra in the 1820s and 1830s for example—and these, in retrospect, might seem to have been the forerunners of a later, more coherent, resistance to colonial rule. Indeed they have been so regarded by modern nationalists themselves, and the leaders of the early revolts have become heroes of the modern republic. More correctly, however, these were prenationalist movements, isolated, uncoordinated responses to particular discontents, sporadic in character and reflective of fissures within Indonesian society as well as hostility to the spread of Dutch power.[19]

Thus nationalism could have entered *Victory* and *The Rescue*. But they, like the early novels, are set in more or less remote environments, and there were no articulated national feelings in such places: as George McTurnan Kahin notes, 'long before and throughout the period of Dutch rule Java was the political and cultural centre of Indonesia and the supporter of most of its population'.[20]

Was Indonesian nationalism, when it did emerge, like Polish nationalism? The Indonesian nationalists were members of a tiny educated elite – as late as the 1930s the literacy rate in Indonesia was 6% – who were drawn from both the upper class and lower social strata. Three of the major factors which gave rise to nationalism and led to its development, were Dutch education, Islam and Marxism. Thus the Indonesian nationalists were markedly different from their Polish counterparts.

There is, then, no justification for thinking that Conrad's young Malayan leaders are 'aristocrats', that they 'are conceived as Polish rather than Malayan nationalists' and that his Malayans 'are really transplantations from Polish history'. His Malayans are conceived as Malayans in his particular selected environments at the specific chosen period. I agree with Kettle when he states that Conrad's 'feeling for the native peoples is sincere'. But Kettle proceeds to support the point in this way: 'Dain Waris in *Lord Jim,* Hassim in *The Rescue* are presented with the greatest sympathy and dignity, indeed they are among Conrad's few characters (apart from the women) who can be said to be idealised'.[21] Can we agree? Consider Dain Waris. Conrad introduces him through Marlow: "Of small stature, but admirably well proportioned, Dain Waris had a proud carriage, a polished easy bearing, a temperament like a clear flame. His dusky face, with big black eyes, was in action expressive, and in repose thoughtful'. This description is somewhat 'idealised'; but the idealisation is Marlow's, not Conrad's. The author's realism is more pronounced and ironic earlier in the introductory passage:

> Of Dain Waris, his own people said with pride that he knew how to fight like a white man. This was true; he had that sort of courage—the courage in the open, I may say—but he had also a European mind. You meet them sometimes like that, and are surprised to discover unexpectedly a familiar turn of thought, an unobscured vision, a tenacity of purpose, a touch of altruism.

Marlow records a true insight of Conrad into the primitive Malayan mind, its sense of racial inferiority to the 'white' men. At the same time, Conrad exposes limitations of Marlow's amiable conservatism. Marlow has a racialist bias. He speaks highly of Dain because he sees in him certain qualities which he associates only with the Europeans, virtually because Dain does not seem to him a Malayan. He views Dain as Mrs Aphra Behn did Oroonoko, though much less crudely. First he focuses attention on Dain in particular. Then he widens his vision to take in Dain's whole race and the full extent of his racialism stands revealed. The Malayans were primitive but even among people at this level of development one would expect to discover, say, more than 'a touch of altruism sometimes'. Thus Conrad presents Dain through Marlow with critical realism. But is he effectively portrayed? In his case, Conrad sets himself a particularly difficult task of character-creation – Dain is very different from an ordinary Malayan (more so than Jewel) and not European – and is not equal to its demands. He brings Dain into the action occasionally but not dramatically, only descriptively as in this instance. Dain never speaks. Indeed, he seems to me the least alive and striking of the characters in *Lord Jim*.

Conrad's portrayal of Dain, then, is realistic but, on the whole, a failure. But what of Hassim? and Immada? Conrad himself introduces them:

> He was clad in a jacket of coarse blue cotton, of the kind a poor fisherman might own, and he wore it wide open on a muscular chest the colour and smoothness of bronze. From the twist of threadbare *sarong* . . . His upright figure had a negligent elegance. But in the careless face, in the easy gestures of the whole man there was something attentive and restrained.
> . . . .
> . . . Her black hair hung like a mantle. Her *sarong*, the kilt-like garment which both sexes wear, had the national check of grey and red, . . . She walked, brown and alert, all of a piece, with short steps, the eyes lively in an impassive little face, the arched mouth closed firmly . . .

Conrad describes them carefully, precisely and fully. In the case of Immada, for instance, he does not 'launch out' into a conventional 'glowing description' of a Malayan 'damsel' which Alfred Wallace parodies: "The jacket or body of purple gauze would figure well in such a description, allowing the heaving bosom to be seen beneath it, while 'sparkling eyes', and 'jetty tresses', and 'tiny feet' might be thrown in profusely'.[22] This kind of commonplaceness mars Sherard Osborn's description of Baju-Mira[23] but not, as I said, Conrad's presentation of Immada. Moreover, Conrad dramatises the characters of Hassim and Immada as in the scenes with them examined above. They are secondary characters portrayed successfully.

Of course, Conrad regards Dain Waris, Hassim and Immada very favourably but one cannot say, with Kettle, that they are 'idealised'. Conrad is also aware that Malayans suffer from certain deficiencies of character. He portrays these with much the same critical realism and with much the same degree of success as their virtues, as in the case of Babalatchi and Lakamba. We have noticed that he does not succumb to the current prejudices of the Clifford and Kidd type or, worse, of the Charles Kingsley and Frank Marryat type.[24] On the other hand, there were the minority views of, say, Alfred Wallace and Sir Frank Swettenham. Here is Wallace (in *The Malay Archipelago*):

> The higher classes of Malays are exceedingly polite, and have all the quiet ease and dignity of the best-bred Europeans. Yet this is compatible with a reckless cruelty and contempt of human life, which is the dark side of their character. It is not to be wondered at, therefore, that different persons give totally opposite accounts of them—one praising them for their soberness, civility and good nature; another abusing them for their deceit, treachery, and cruelty.[25]

Here is Swettenham (in *Malay Sketches*):

> The real Malay is a short, thick-set, well built man, with straight black hair, a dark brown complexion, thick nose and lips, and bright intelligent eyes. His disposition is generally kindly, his manners are polite and easy. Never cringing, he is reserved with strangers and suspicious, though he does not show it. . . .
> They [Malay women] are generally amiable in disposition, mildly – sometimes fiercely – jealous, often extravangant and, up to about the age of forty, evince an increasing fondness for jewellery and smart clothes. . . .[26]

Conrad's balanced awareness of the Malayans is a development on views such as these. In fact, Wallace's *The Malay Archipelago* was Conrad's 'intimate friend for many years' (in the words of Richard Curle).[27] From first-hand experience and reading he knows more about Malayans than about negroes and Chinese, and he is more interested in them. That is why he puts them into his fiction far more than the others. He presents these people alien to him with their alien speech in their alien context with a mixture of success and failure as in the case of the Europeans there.

His Malayan world is predominantly authentic in all its varied spheres. His degree of success and failure is explicable. He is able to rise above conventional Western prejudices against Malayans for much the same reasons as he is able to transcend those against Chinese, whereas he yields slightly to those against negroes. The prejudices against Malayans were less strong than those against negroes; among the favourable views of South-East Asians expressed by Europeans are those of Sherard Osborn on Nicodar Devi and Baju-Mira,[28] Fred McNair on the Maharajah of Johore,[29] and Graham Greene on the women of Indo-China.[30] Westerners knew of great Asian civilisations in the past; Malayan civilisations had not regressed into as primitive a stage as African ones, and Conrad had experienced the difference. Westerners suffered less from guilt about ill-treatment of Malayans than of negroes and Chinese: there was no slave or coolie trade in Malayans; Dutch rule in 'Indonesia' and British rule in 'Malaysia' were less harsh than other colonial regimes in Asia and Africa. Presumably it is because of this problem of guilt that Sherard Osborn betrays conventional prejudice against the Chinese, but considers his whole book, *My Journal in Malayan Waters,* an attempt to give 'a fair impression of the much-abused Malay'.[31] Thus, the same European could yield to conventional prejudices against one 'coloured' race but not other 'coloured' races, and different Europeans could have prejudices against different 'coloured' races, for historical reasons.

M. C. Bradbrook says: 'it would be generally agreed that Conrad's first three books [she is referring to *Almayer's Folly, An Outcast of the Islands* and the first efforts of *The Rescue*] show promise but not achievement. They are uneven because he was too close to the experience he used and also too close to his models'.[32] She is right in her judgement that Conrad's early endeavours show promise but not achievement, but her reasons do not seem to me correct. Conrad was not 'too close to the experience he used': 'the experience' in the East was gathered between 1883 and 1888; *Almayer's Folly* was published about seven years later. It is doubtful whether he thought in terms of 'models' as such (Bradbrook mentions Flaubert), though he was influenced by writers such as Flaubert and Maupassant.[33] The closeness to his 'models' or, more probably, his sources of influence was not decisively debilitating: weaknesses in his first efforts such as poor psychological 'exploration', conventional romance and melodrama are also found in his last novels, as we noticed above. The unevenness of his early fiction and his last Malayan novels should be related partly to their period of composition; in the case of the former, to his artistic immaturity and, in the case of the latter, to the unsteadiness of an artist past his prime. The conventional romance is partly a consequence of that disinclination to render intimacies common in nineteenth-century fiction. However, the artistic challenges involved in presenting various male–female relationships between people of different races, of different degrees of development and different character (Almayer and his wife, Willems and Aissa, Jim and Jewel) in alien environments call into play a degree of realism unusual for Conrad in this field. There is still another important cause for the unevenness of his Malayan fiction: Conrad did not know enough; his rhetorical vein reflects, and appears partly an attempt to conceal, an ignorance. We noticed at the beginning of this chapter that his experience of the East was slight. He had to depend heavily on books about it and pure imagination. This did not suit his kind of talent, which fed mainly on personal experiences and contacts. Norman Sherry has worked out much of the factual background of Conrad's Eastern works in *Conrad's Eastern World,* and it suggests that there is an even closer connection between the workings of Conrad's imagination and his personal experiences and facts than we have hitherto been aware of. Conrad's artistic difficulties increased because he, a writer from a European context, was presenting life in the Malay Archipelago, a developing environment alien to him, to a European reading public for whom it was even more alien.

Conrad himself was aware that he knew too little about Malaya: in a letter to Hugh Clifford in 1898, he says,

> I suspect my assumption of Malay colouring for my fiction must be exasperating to those who *know.* It seems as though you had found in my prose some reason for forgiving me. Nothing could be more flattering to a scribbler's vanity or more soothing to the conscience of a man who, even in his fiction, tries to be tolerably true.[34]

On the other hand, he was not unconscious of the solid reading behind his fiction; he wrote to William Blackwood on 13 December 1898 about an article by Clifford:

> I am inexact and ignorant no doubt (most of us are) but I don't think I sinned so recklessly. Curiously enough all the details about the little characteristic acts and customs which they hold up as proof I have taken out (to be safe) from undoubted sources – dull, wise books.[35]

But his sense of his ignorance and of his want of first-hand experience were more deeply embedded in his consciousness as deficiencies affecting his art, particularly after he became more familiar with Clifford as a man and as a writer.

Before he met Clifford, he had reviewed his *Studies in Brown Humanity* in the *Academy* for 23 April 1898. Conrad seldom reviewed books but this review was meant (he told Clifford in a letter) as 'a tribute not only to the charm of the book but to the toil of the man; to the years of patient and devoted work at the back of the pages'.[36] In the review itself, he had praised Clifford as 'the embodiment of the intentions, of the conscience and might of his race'.[37] Clifford became one of his best friends and he later counted his friendship as 'amongst his precious possessions'.[38] In his 'memoir article' Clifford summarises aspects of their friendship relevant to my concerns:

> His lament was that, while I possessed unusual knowledge, I made of it an indifferent use; mine that though his style was a Miracle, his knowledge was defective; yet is was upon this unpromising foundation that a friendship was

built up which endured without a falter for a quarter of a century, and ended only on that sad day in August, 1924, when I stood mourning at my old friend's graveside in the quiet Kentish cemetery where he lies sleeping.[39]

In the review mentioned above, Conrad said:

> Each study in this volume presents some idea, illustrated by a fact told without artifice, but with an effective sureness of knowledge. . . .
> Nevertheless to apply artistic standards to this book would be a fundamental error in appreciation . . . . And this book is only truth, interesting and futile, truth unadorned, simple and straightforward. . . . One cannot expect to be, at the same time, a ruler of men and an irreproachable player on the flute.[40]

This view, both respectful and critical, was Conrad's habitual reaction to Clifford's work. Clifford said:

> . . . the author [of *Almayer's Folly*] had none but a superficial acquaintance with the Malayan customs, language and character. . . .
> . . . one who had not had the opportunity of entering into the life of the people of the country, as I and some of my friends had done, had been able in that first book to convey so much of the magic and singular charm possessed by Malaya and to limn the lives of the people with a force and imaginative touch which had never been equalled by any other writer.[41]

Although Clifford was scarcely treating Conrad's work as *literature,* his 'authoritative' criticism was bound to have effects on an author as hard on himself as Conrad was, still unestablished, and still rather isolated as a comparative newcomer to England. By the time he came to write *Lord Jim,* his confidence in his mastery of the Malayan experience seems to have been shaken. Consider Jim's comment on the ring given him by Stein: 'The ring was a sort of credential – ("It's like something you read of in books", he threw in appreciatively) and Doramin would do his best for him'. Introducing the Gentleman Brown episode, Marlow says: "This astounding adventure, of which the most astounding part is that it is true,. . . .'. Jim makes an observation to Marlow on the relationship of Dain Waris, Doramin and his wife: ' "It's well worth seeing", Jim had assured me while we were crossing the river, on our way back. "They are like people in a book, aren't they?" he said triumphantly'. These remarks are meant to establish the 'foreignness' of Jim's and Marlow's reactions to an alien way of life. I think they also betray a doubt in Conrad about the convincingness not only of these particular items but also of all his Malayan material. He seems to be anticipating readers' objections to its authenticity. Those remarks are put into the mouths of Jim and Marlow not only as appropriate to their characters but also to forestall possible objections. His doubt of his own powers lies behind other aspects of his art: the Malayans speak much less than in his first two novels and Dain Waris not at all; he makes Jewel speak an English closer to the Standard than, say, Babalatchi and justifies it, rather than attempting to give her a Malayan English.

In *Victory* the Malayans do not appear in terms of drama and hardly matter; in *The Rescue* they play a considerably less important part than in the early novels. These tendencies could be due either to a further flagging of his originally rather slight sense of Malay life, or to his awareness that he did not know enough to write well about the Malayans, or to both. In his prime, from 1901 to 1911, he never made the mistake of attempting to articulate themes with too little material to go on – although it has to be noted that *Nostromo* was composed from a minimum of what would usually be called first-hand experience.

The fact is that an artist's experience cannot be weighed solely by amounts of time spent or by his veritable presence in such-and-such a place. At times what Conrad calls 'most vivid impressions' and 'highly valued memories'[42] can trigger off perceptions of exceptional depth, apparently because they fit in with tendencies that his sensibility is already preoccupied with. This is the case with Conrad's interest in the ironies of hypocrisy and self-deception. In *Lord Jim* he writes: '. . . There were very few places in the Archipelago he had not seen in the original dusk of their being, before light (and even electric light) had been carried into them for the sake of better morality and – and – well – the greater profit, too'. Conrad is here describing Stein, not directly but through Marlow. The point is not the characterising of Stein but the Conradian irony – made clearer and more mordant by Marlow's relutance to utter the key words at the end – regarding the hypocrisy of conservative English thinking about imperialism which Marlow typifies. He speaks of an altruistic moral ideal as the prime goal of empire-building; this acts as a cover for the chief motive of 'greater profit', and it also helps him to maintain his dignity in his own eyes and in the eyes of the public (at home and abroad), to salve his conscience, and to fool the credulous. Conrad also shows that Marlow is unaware of his dishonesty: the hesitancy in his speech is not the author's but the character's. Thus Conrad has dramatised, during the heyday of Empire, a national trait of his adopted country. Twenty years later Forster wrote:

> Hypocrisy is the prime charge that is always brought against us. The Germans are called brutal, the Spanish cruel, the Americans superficial, and so on; but we are perfide Albion, the island of hypocrites, the people who have built up an Empire with a Bible in one hand, a pistol in the other, and financial concessions in both pockets. Is the charge true? I think it is; but while making it we must be quite clear as to what we mean by hypocrisy. Do we mean *conscious* deceit? Well the English are comparatively guiltless of this; they have little of the Renaissance villain about them. Do we mean *unconscious* deceit? muddle-headedness? Of this I believe them to be guilty. [43]

In *The Rescue* Carter is credited with 'the clear vision of a seaman able to master quickly the aspect of a strange land and of a strange sea'. It is likely that Conrad himself had this 'clear vision of a seaman' and that this is what enabled him so quickly to grasp essentials of life in the Archipelago and in Latin America. He was perhaps helped also by his Polishness. We have noticed his ability to rise above common imperial attitudes, and we know that as a Pole he had suffered, with his family, under the empire-building of the Tsars. In his autobiography he pays tribute to

> the Polish temperament with its tradition of self-government, its chivalrous view of moral restraints and an exaggerated respect for individual rights: not to mention the important fact that the whole Polish mentality, Western in complexion, had received its training from Italy and France and, historically, had always remained, even in religious matters, in sympathy with the most liberal currents of European thought.[44]

This cultural heritage must have helped him to achieve his extraordinary liberal-mindedness. So, he considered, did his kind of aristocratic origins:

> An impartial view of humanity in all its degrees of splendour and misery together with a special regard for the rights of the unprivileged of this earth, not on any mystic ground but on the ground of simple fellowship and honourable reciprocity of services, was the dominant characteristic of the mental and moral atmosphere of the houses which sheltered my hazardous childhood: – matters of calm and deep conviction both lasting and consistent, and removed as far as possible from that humanitarianism that seems to be merely a matter of crazy nerves or a morbid conscience.[45]

Because these Polish attitudes were 'matters of calm and deep conviction both lasting and consistent', we are justified in finding in his Polishness at least some of the roots of his extraordinarily humane and keen awareness of realities in other countries dominated from abroad. The political aspects of his Polish background appear explicitly in the opening of 'Prince Roman':

> '. . . Of course the year 1831 is for us an historical date, one of these fatal years when in the presence of the world's passive indignation and eloquent sympathies we had once more to murmur *'Vae Victis'* and count the cost in sorrow. Not that we were ever very good at calculating, either, in prosperity or in adversity. That's a lesson we could never learn, to the great exasperation of our enemies who have bestowed upon us the epithet of Incorrigible. . . .'
>
> The speaker was of Polish nationality, that nationality not so much alive as surviving, which persists in thinking, breathing, speaking, hoping, and suffering in its grave, railed in by a million of bayonets and triple-sealed with the seals of three great empires.[46]

Here Conrad reveals his anger at the indifference of the world to Poland's plight, his sympathetic sense of her inherent weakness, of her subjection, of her valiant but abortive striving. Nationalism was a prominent part of Conrad's family tradition; the Korzeniowskis were 'Reds', while the Bobrowskis were generally 'appeasers'. These Polish interests and feelings of Conrad could have found a psychological release and a congenial field for expression in the developing countries of the Far East because of the similarity of their predicament under imperialism. V. S. Pritchett suggests that 'Conrad seems to have turned the Polish exile's natural preoccupation with nationality, history, defeat and unavailing struggle, from his own country to these Eastern islands'.[47] What Pritchett does not note is that in Conrad's Malayan fiction, though the Malayans, the subject people, are more or less important in all the works except *Victory,* it is the Europeans, the members of the 'ruling race' and his fellow 'white' men, who matter most; that though the roles of 'Tuan Jim' and the 'Rajah Laut' have a social significance, the most important themes are always personal and not political; and that in his remote milieux at that particular time there was nothing like the national struggles against imperialism found in Poland. Thus Conrad's Polishness is relevant, in a rather indirect and unverifiable way, to a consideration of his Malayan fiction; but the East evokes new independent interests and emphases.

NOTES:

1   For instance, compare Old Singleton in Conrad's *The Nigger of the 'Narcissus'* 'who in the last forty-five years had lived no more than forty months ashore'.

2   Norman Sherry, *Conrad's Eastern World* (Cambridge, 1966), p. 139.

3   The epigraph to this chapter is characteristic of Hugh Clifford's criticism of Conrad. F.R. Leavis, *The Great Tradition*, p. 210.

4   Joseph Conrad, *Almayer's Folly,* in *Almayer's Folly and Tales of Unrest* (London, 1947 ed.), pp. 166-67. Cf. *An Outcast of the Islands* (London, 1951 ed.), p. 49; *The Rescue* (London, 1949 ed.), p. 5.

5   Hugh Clifford, 'The East Coast', from *In Court and Kampong* (1897), in *Stories by Sir Hugh Clifford,* p. 16.

6   Leavis, *The Great Tradition,* p. 210.

7   Clifford, 'The Art of Mr. Joseph Conrad', in *The Spectator,* 29 November 1902, pp. 827-28.

8   Conrad, *Lord Jim,* pp. 161-2. *Cf. Victory* (London, 1954 ed.) pp. 2-3.

9   J. I. M. Stewart, *Joseph Conrad* (London, 1968), p. 39.

10   *Ibid.,* p. 40.

11   Leavis, *The Great Tradition,* p. 229.

12 Conrad speaks of originals in life for his desperadoes in his 'Author's Note' (1920), *in Victory* (London, 1960 ed.), pp. xi-xv.

13 M.C. Bradbrook, *Joseph Conrad: Poland's English Genius* (New York, 1965 ed.), p. 65.

14 Sherard Osborn, *My Journal in Malayan Waters* (London, 1861 ed.), p. 69.

15 For instance, compare E. M. Forster's account of an Indian 'public wedding' in which Islamic prayer and Western music mix – Forster, 'Adrift in India', in *Abinger Harvest* (London, 1967 ed.), p. 330.

16 Arnold Kettle, *An Introduction to the English Novel* (London, 1962 ed.), Vol. 2, p. 71.

17 V.S. Pritchett, *The Living Novel* (London, 1960), p. 145.

18 Zdzislaw Najder, *Conrad's Polish Background* (London, 1964), pp. 3-4.

19 J. D. Legge, *Indonesia* (New Jersey, 1964), p. 112.

20 George McTurnan Kahin, *Nationalism and Revolution in Indonesia* (New York, 1963 ed.), p. 2.

21 Kettle, *Introduction to the English Novel* (London, 1962), p. 71.

22 Alfred Russel Wallace, *The Malay Archipelago* (London & New York, 1890), p. 168.

23 Osborn, *My Journal in Malayan Waters* (London, 1861), p. 175-76.

24 Frank S. Marryat writes: '. . . the Malays who inhabit the coast of Borneo are a cruel, treacherous, and disgusting race of men, with scarcely one good quality to recommend them. . . . In their physiognomy these Malays are inferior to the Dyaks: they have a strong resemblance to the monkey in face, with an air of low cunning and rascality most unprepossessing'. - Marryat, *Borneo and the Indian Archipelago* (London, 1848), pp. 99-100.

25 Wallace, *The Malay Archipelago,* p. 448.

26 Frank Swettenham, 'The Real Malay', in *Malay Sketches* (London, 1895), pp. 2,8.

27 Quoted from Sherry. *Conrad's Eastern World,* p. 142. Conrad refers to 'Alfred Wallace's famous book on the Malay Archipelago' in *The Secret Agent* (London, 1961 ed.), p. 118.

28 Osborn, *My Journal in Malayan Waters,* pp. 133-4, 175-6.

29 Fred McNair, *Perak and the Malays: 'Sarong and Kris'* (London, 1878), pp. 207-8.

30   'Indo-China was the first country I fell in love with after West Africa. It was partly
     the beauty of the women – it's extraordinary – . . .'–'Graham Greene takes the Orient
     Express', *The Listener,* 21 November 1968, p. 674.

31   Osborn, *My Journal in Malayan Waters,* pp. 225, 360.

32   Bradbrook, *Joseph Conrad,* p. 14.

33   I do not propose to discuss the nature of these influences or attempt to find out the
     years when they operated appreciably. I shall briefly suggest the difficulty of these
     tasks: in 1918 he told Hugh Walpole that he had not read Flaubert till *Almayer's
     Folly* was finished (Stewart, *Joseph Conrad,* p. 38), but 'the novel was begun on the
     margins of a copy of *Madame Bovary'* (Bradbrook, *Joseph Conrad,* p. 14); and
     Conrad's memory was extraordinarily retentive.

34   Letter of Clifford, 17 May 1898, in Jean-Aubry, *Life and Letters,* Vol. 1, p. 237.
     See also Conrad, 'Author's Note' to *A Personal Record,* pp. iv, v.

35   William Blackburn (ed.), *Joseph Conrad: Letters to William Blackwood and
     David S. Meldrum* (North Carolina, 1958), p. 34.

36   Letter to Clifford, 17 May 1898, in Jean-Aubry, *Life and Letters,* p. 237.

37   Joseph Conrad, 'An Observer in Malaya' (1898), in *Notes on Life and Letters*
     (London, 1949 ed.), p. 58.

38   Conrad, 'Author's Note' to *A Personal Record* (London, 1960), p. iv. He inscribed
     Chance 'to Sir Hugh Clifford whose steadfast friendship is responsible for the
     existence of these pages'. See also *Letters to Blackwood and Meldrum,* p. 64.

39   Quoted from Jessie Conrad, *Joseph Conrad and his Circle* (London, 1935), pp. 76-77.

40   Conrad, 'An Observer in Malaya', in *Notes on Life and Letters,* p. 60.

41   Clifford, *A Talk on Joseph Conrad and his Work* (Colombo, 1927), pp. 4-5.

42   Conrad, letter to the 'Ranee' Brooke, 15 July 1920, in *Letters to Cunninghame
     Graham,* p. 210.

43   E. M. Forster, 'Notes on the English Character' (1920), in *Abinger Harvest,* p. 22.

44   Conrad, 'Author's Note' to *A Personal Record,* pp. vi-vii.

45   Ibid., p. vii.

46   Joseph Conrad, 'Prince Roman', in *Tales of Hearsay and Last Essays* (London,
     1955 ed.), p. 29.

47   Pritchett, *The Living Novel,* p. 145.

CONRAD'S EASTERN EXPATRIATES:
A NEW VERSION OF HIS OUTCASTS

Lloyd Fernando

I

The Bay which was the setting for "Karain," a short story by Conrad, has now been identified as Palu Bay on the west coast of the Celebes. The claims of the Teunom River in Atjeh as a partial source for the Patusan setting in *Lord Jim* have been strengthened by a Polish journalist's actual year-long trip in the Indonesian Archipelago.[1] A book of photographs by this journalist, Andrzej Braun, is in preparation, picturing most of the locales, certain or probable, for Conrad's Eastern fiction. The building plans of ships that Conrad sailed in have been compiled, and scale models of some are being built. An eight-volume edition of the letters is nearing completion, and there is even talk of a revised Collected Edition of all of Conrad's works. A benign empire of Conrad scholarship now spreads across the globe with, at last count, national editors in twenty-seven countries. The fiftieth anniversary of Conrad's death was 1974, and conferences were held in Texas, where a wealth of Conrad memorabilia is to be found, and in Kent where he died.

The prototypes of the major characters and settings of Conrad's Eastern fiction have been more or less completely identified, with the completion of Norman Sherry's two valuable books and Jerry Allen's compendious one.[2] One place which Conrad literary sleuths have somehow missed is Samburan, the island on which Heyst and Lena act out their strange drama in *Victory;* similarly, the desolate coast on which Lingard lost the battle of his life in *The Rescue* has not been pinpointed. These and a few other remaining minor items will no doubt be dispatched very soon.

In important respects, however, critical interpretation has not kept pace with factual discoveries. Essentially, we still belabor the major insights of such critics as Douglas Hewitt, Albert Guerard, and Thomas Moser. The journey into the self, the test of character in isolated surroundings, the workings of fate or chance, the horror of primitivism in man, such themes had been elucidated to such a point of fineness that the burst of factual exploration into Conrad's sources, particularly in the mid-1960's, brought welcome relief. Still this fresh surge of activity which has led to genuine advances in Conrad scholarship may put us in danger of being content to beat futilely round the well-known facts (Marlow's phrase) much as Jim's Court of Inquiry did.

II

What is the grammar of Conrad's facts? How are we to find our way about and beyond them with any certainty? To put the problem bluntly, can the 900 Muslim pilgrims whose safety was in the balance in *Lord Jim* merely be an embellishment for the moral problem of a pleasant enough young Englishman? What significance do the Africans in chains whom Marlow encounters at the first trading post in *Heart of Darkness* have, beyond serving as a reminder of the excesses of a colonial age and lending the somber vividness of an impressionistic painting to a truly great short novel? Are Nina and Dain, Hassim and Immada, Belarab and Tengga and their compatriots no more than a company of shadows, providing a backdrop for Western dramas about man's isolation in the universe? We remember that Ricardo and Schomberg in *Victory* both "looked on native life as a mere play of shadows" (*Victory,* p. 167; Pt. II, Ch. viii). Heyst and Lena did too. The fates of the Malaysian characters, it is true, were not Conrad's primary quarries. "No one of any particular consequence will have to die [in *The Rescue],*" he told J.B. Pinker at the end of 1918. "Hassim and Immada will be sacrificed, as in any case they were bound to be, but their fate is not the subject of the tale."[3] Thus far we have the face value of his Malaysian sources, the most important of which Sherry has skillfully laid bare. We are now obliged to evaluate Conrad's knowledge of the Malaysian region and examine the degree to which his fictional art was affected by it. This essay will show that the relation between factual knowledge and art was, in Conrad's case, not less than profound; in the process the Malaysian Archipelago and its peoples will appear in a dynamic perspective never described before.

From the wealth of facts that recent scholarship has placed before us, we can begin by admitting that Conrad did not, after all, have an intimate knowledge of Malaysian life. His Eastern world has been established, rather, as the world of a truly sensitive expatriate. An expatriate is taken to mean, quite simply, one who lives in a foreign country for a greater or lesser period of time without coming to look on himself as one of its nationals. Conrad knew no Malay and therefore could not have obtained any deep insights into Malay life. He certainly had no intimate Malay friends, and his acquaintanceship with other Malaysians does not appear to have extended significantly beyond shipping clerks, waiters in colonial-style hotels, and other persons whom a visitor or seaman will encounter of necessity during his travels. The period Conrad spent in the Malaysian region was a few brief months, and he based some of the major characters of his Malaysian fiction on originals he scarcely met—with the exception of Almayer, who was also an expatriate despite the length of time he had spent in Berau. Mostly he learned about them from books and newspapers, and from gossip written or supplied by other expatriates. The Eastern world he portrays really falls within the expatriate round of hotels, other expatriate acquaintances, shore gossip, books by other expatriates, some of them distinguished in colonial history, and a skillful seaman's knowledge of certain harbors, bays, rivers, creeks, and shores. Even when Conrad locates his action in the interior as in Patusan (*Lord Jim*) and Berau (*Almayer's Folly* and *An Outcast of the Islands*), his impressionistic method serves also as a pragmatic authorial device for making do with what he has actually garnered. The river mists, the flashes of lightning and thunder, the driving rain, and the reliance upon narrators, while dramatically atmospheric, also serve the more humble duty of decently casting a veil over what Conrad does not know. His Malaysian characters remain either shadowy, like Dain Waris in *Lord Jim*, or exotic external portrayals like Babalatchi and even Aissa in *An Outcast of the Islands.*

In brief, we can no longer doubt the validity of Sir Hugh Clifford's view, expressed nearly seventy years ago, that the "Orientals" in Conrad's work are interesting "not because they are really Asiatics, but because they represent the impression scored by Asiatics upon a sensitive, imaginative, European mind. Mr. Conrad has seen...as white men see—from the outside. He had never lived into the life of brown people."[4] Clifford has particular qualifications for expressing this criticism. He was a scholar of the Malay language, a writer of minor fiction based in the Malay Peninsula, and a colonial administrator who had spent long years in villages and settlements far removed from the town centers of colonial power. Conrad retorted with some justice that while Clifford possessed unusual knowledge he put it to indifferent use in his fiction.[5] In a letter to William Blackwood he admitted wryly, "Well I never did set up as an authority on Malaysia," but his defense is curious since it actually concedes that his sources were expatriate and secondhand: "All the details about the little characteristic acts and customs which they hold up as proof [of ignorance] I have taken out (to be safe) from undoubted sources—dull wise books. In 'Karain' for instance, there's not a single action of my man (and a good many of his expressions) that cannot be backed by a traveller's tale—I mean a serious traveller's" (13 Dec. 1898).[6]

It is continually astonishing therefore to contemplate the extent of Conrad's success in evoking Malaysian locales on the basis of his limited personal knowledge. Equally, it is not unfair to assert that Conrad steered deftly round the realities of Malaysian life, remaining within shallows acutely defined by an unerring novelistic instinct. To appreciate the nature of his genius we must balance what he lacked in intimate knowledge with what he contributed by way of prodigiously sensitive understanding. A famous phrase of his about his Malaysian fiction gains a new significance when looked at in this light. He spoke of the Malaysian Archipelago as that area "from which I have carried away into my writing life the greatest number of suggestions."[7] The facts that he carried away have been uncovered with dramatic clarity; the "suggestions" have left us comparatively bemused. One cannot completely evaluate the worth of Conrad's Malaysian fiction unless these, too, come under equally close scrutiny, and their relationship to the facts has been explicated.

He did not feel his limited personal knowledge to be a handicap in writing his stories. "Facts can bear out my story," he asserted, in a letter to Blackwood about *The Rescue,* "but as I am writing fiction not secret history—facts don't matter" (Sept. 1897; Blackburn, p. 11). He was emphatic, even about the adverse effects of relying too much on facts. Rather testily he wrote to Richard Curle who had shown him an article Curle had written entitled "Conrad in the East":

> Didn't it ever occur to you, my dear Curle, that I knew what I was doing in leaving the facts of my life and even of my tales in the background? Explicitness, my dear fellow, is fatal to the glamour of all artistic work, robbing it of all suggestiveness, destroying all illusion. You seem to believe in literalness and explicitness, in facts and also in expression. Yet nothing is more clear than the utter insignificance of explicit statement and also its power to call attention away from things that matter in the region of art.[8]

Norman Sherry's sober exploration of Conrad's method of transmuting fact to fiction has been of considerable help.[9] Conrad took actual events, settings, personal names, and even details of physical appearance, grafted some onto certain other basic ones chosen previously, and illuminated his amalgams with the power of his own shaping genius. His acute psychological analyses show that emotions actually belie the facts in situations that test human nature in solitary surroundings. As a result, his work achieves truth "in the Aristotelian sense, in the likelihood and possibility of its action" (*Conrad's Eastern World,* p. 272). The value of this systematic progression from the particular to the general is admirably demonstrated by Sherry. Some difficulties remain. The Eastern setting, the Eastern characters have not been brought yet into an organic relation with the novelist's main concerns. Conrad is still left vulnerable to the charge that these elements merely lend color and glamor to his novels and stories.

Efforts to get round this difficulty have not been wholly satisfactory either. Jocelyn Baines has boldy assigned to the East the role of a nemesis which brings the proud Westerner low. "Almayer, Willems and above all Kurtz (because primitive life possessed similar powers in Africa as in the East) appear as trophies of that Nemesis," Baines asserts.[10] This view is bound to nurse the persistent assumption, the traditional cliché, of the East being the agent that corrupts the idealistic Westerner and leads him to decadence and squalor. The film of *An Outcast of the Islands* made many years ago with Trevor Howard in the role of Willems ended on just such a note, perverting Conrad's own conclusion. The so-called "primitivism" of the East appears as an inferior or malevolent way of life inimical to civilized values. Critics like Adam Gillon and Leo Gurko appear to be unaware of the racist assumption that undermines any usefulness this view might have. "The East is filled with white men who lost their spirit, grew soft, and declined into vague misfits," writes Gurko, adding in an extraordinary footnote, "or fell into the pit of miscegenation. The white men in Conrad like Almayer and Willems who marry Malay women usually come to a bad end, and their degradation is specifically symbolised by their crossing of racial barriers." Gurko does not believe that Conrad holds the civilized as "good" and the primitive as "bad," but that "as life frames they are different and in the end incompatible."[11] If this really were Conrad's conclusion, his novels would not fully deserve the regard in which we hold them. Unfortunately, we cannot obtain redress by taking the opposite and more sympathetic view, advanced by William Bysshe Stein, of traditional Eastern dignity assailed by Western colonial greed.[12] More homework remains to be done.

III

In his Preface to *The Nigger of the "Narcissus"* Conrad defined art as "a single-minded attempt to render the highest kind of justice to the visible universe" (p. vii). It will profit us, therefore, to take in the social and historical perspectives (these being aspects of the visible universe) that emerge from all his wonderful factual details considered together, before proceeding to a reformulation of his cosmic view. In doing so we will remember his cautionary observation in the Author's Note to *Almayer's Folly* about how the facts of the visible universe can mislead. The critic may think "that in those distant lands all joy is a yell and a war dance, all pathos is a howl and a ghastly grin of filed teeth." Conrad continues: "Under the merciless brilliance of the sun, the dazzled eye misses the delicate detail, sees only the strong outlines, while the colours, in the steady light, seem crude and without shadow. Nevertheless. . . there is a bond between us and that humanity so far way" (pp. vii-viii).

Taking first his people, the really central characters in the Malaysian novels and stories are Europeans—English and Dutch principally—which is not surprising since they represent the principal colonial powers in the area at the time. The basic conception of these characters accords with current clichés. Tom Lingard, the Englishman, is kindly in a paternal way; Schomberg, the German hotelkeeper, and Heemskirk, the Dutch gunboat commander, are the brutal Teutons; Jim is a weak but romantic hero; Heyst, the Scandinavian, is the neutral observer; and Willems and Tom Lingard together reflect a collusion between Dutch and English colonial interests. Of course, the novels and stories are also densely populated with secondary Malaysian characters—Malays, Arabs, Eurasians, and Chinese. Certain stock assumptions influence their portrayals too. The Chinese are inscrutable traders or waiters in hotels, the Eurasians are sycophantic toward Europeans, while the Arabs are crafty and wealthy. The Malay characters, who are the most prominent, are depicted as noble, given to intrigue, practical [sic.], or unreliable. They represent the principal challenge the Malaysian region offers to the alien invaders.

Proceeding next to events, those relating to the careers of the individual European protagonists have enjoyed the almost undivided attention of critics. The fates of Willems, Almayer, Jim, Tom Lingard and Heyst have been discussed voluminously enough in print. But another kind of event, growing out of accumulated detail, presents an extraordinarily complex and confusing picture of local politics in the Archipelago as a whole. Conrad gives us a picture of the states of the region thrown into rivalry or conflict with each other, or forming or disbanding alliances in the face of a new challenge to traditional social realities– colonial power creeping over the islands from centers established in Singapore, Batavia (now Jakarta), and Surabaya. Much action takes place in remote areas nominally under the egis of the British or Dutch but too far from the centers of power to be effectively governed. An occasional gunboat pays a visit, a Dutch or British flag is hoisted on ceremonial occasions, and token allegiance is affirmed. Rebellions are planned, arms are smuggled, uprisings are quelled or have limited success, private agonies are enacted.

The equally heterogeneous Europeans are similarly affected, drawing together in hotel lounges, trading firms, or on board ships from recognized affinities of an ethnic kind, and from common interests in trade of overlordship. In this confusing picture of "inter-island politics" ("Karain," p. 13) they pursue their harried careers as traders, seamen, buccaneers, down-and-outs, colonial administrators, and genuine idealists, creating pocket European settlements in major ports, the more daring going farther afield into little known bays, creeks, and villages in search of fortune. An air of freebooting hangs like a pall over Conrad's more precise narratives. The scramble for acquisition of new territories thriving on contempt for the local inhabitants contrasts with the increasing powerlessness of the Malaysians to resist an inexorable and forced affiliation with the intruding foreigners. Intrigues become complex, heroism mingles with deceit, and pathos with treachery, lack of pride, and self-seeking. There is a tragic absence of real purpose, and an appropriation of the best by the strongest, while life-styles, ideals, and methods become hopelessly confused. We have, in brief, an evocation of the true colonial condition which deflects from familiar goals the occupied and the occupiers alike. Conrad, the seaman, travelling from port to port, encounters personalities and learns of events in both centers as well as remote areas. His principal characters and incidents, by their authenticity as shown in recent scholarship, serve as buoys in an uncharted sea, helping us to recognize this historical reality, while Conrad leads us into the enigmatic nature of the third kind of event he is concerned to portray.

Here we begin to approach Conrad in his most powerful as well as his most vexatious vein. He declared, while he was completing his very first novel, *Almayer's Folly,* that he was concerned with "the clash of nebulous ideas."[13] The phrase is typical of Conrad's nearly impenetrable rhetoric. Part of the purpose of this essay is to suggest that the rhetoric has the quality of a deliberate code, as well as to propose some ways of cracking it. It is not to flog a worn-out colonial theme that we have drawn out the social realities that comprise the substance of Conrad's Malaysian novels (and indeed many of his other novels, too). His greatness is not enhanced or diminished a jot by such a simple-minded approach to the commingling of East and West in such brutalizing circumstances. Rather one must ask what larger purposes are served by his authentic evocation of societies, not just individuals, in simultaneous processes of expansion and decay. And our answers must be organically connected to what we already know of his undisputed achievement. .

Taking the arena of the Malaysian Archipelago as a whole, Conrad saw societies in the process of birth and decay as a result of their forced conjunction. His principal characters are unconsciously affected by this resonance in the conduct of their lives. On the mundane level, there are conflicts of law or authority, as in the three-cornered contest in *Almayer's Folly* between Dutch, British and Malaysian jurisdiction, or in the benevolent brigandage of Captain Tom Lingard's gunrunning expedition in *The Rescue*. In the novels, Conrad sometimes refers to the "lawlessness" of the area or of particular characters. He does not mean by this mere criminality but, quite literally, a condition where the true laws are hard to discover if they exist at all. Where sets of laws are in conflict, and resolution is to be found in the power of arms, the characters find themselves thrown on their own resources, and their political ties with their countries of origin begin to weaken as much as their concept of justice. Some grasp their opportunities with fevered brilliance like Jim in *Lord Jim*, others with blatant malevolence like Jones in *Victory*.

Of even greater moment is the dissolution of emotional and ethical bonds with one's own race group which takes place under these conditions. Conrad makes one of his rare and revealing disclosures about his personal sensibility when referring to the experience behind the creation of *Almayer's Folly*. He admits that "part of my moral being which is rooted in consistency was badly shaken." He continues, "The discovery of new values in life is a very chaotic experience; there is a tremendous amount of jostling and confusion and a momentary feeling of darkness. I let my spirit float supine over that chaos."[14] The temptation to interpret these new values as Eastern values should be firmly turned aside. It would be too easy to reduce the moral challenges Conrad's characters faced to that of making a choice between Eastern and Western values. That would introduce an unjustified triviality into Conrad's great subject and lead us to fall once again into the clichés, already referred to, about the East as emblematic of primitivism or savagery, or alternatively, of untarnished innocence. At this crucial point we must strike out in a new direction to escape both of these unsatisfactory and limiting choices.

IV

Conrad's expatriates are not only European exiles (English, Dutch, German, and Belgian), but Malay exiles (Wajo, Ilanun, Bugis, Javanese, Dyak, and Balinese), Chinese, and others of mixed descent. Dain Maroola in *Almayer's Folly* is a Balinese prince who has fled to Sambir to obtain arms for resuming his fight against the Dutch. Nina the Eurasian girl, for whom Almayer plans a glittering future in Europe, leaves her father and flees with Dain to a new life on Bali. Babalatchi the Sea Dyak in *An Outcast of the Islands* is even compared to Aeneas (p. 54; Ch. v). During his checkered career he has transferred his allegiance and his domicile several times. Aissa the Arab-Malay whom Willems loves is the daughter of a Brunei chief Omar el Badavi who has himself moved repeatedly as a result of local strife and incursions into the territory by white men. Rajah Hassim in *The Rescue* is a Wajo driven out of his land by a rival group, planning his ill-fated return from exile with Tom Lingard's assistance. While the principal actors in Conrad's Malaysian dramas are undoubtedly Europeans, this common condition of exile in the historical sense makes them kin to their Malaysian counterparts. The epigraph to Conrad's first novel, *Almayer's Folly,* aptly summarizes his inclusive concern for the predicament of all his characters, Western and Eastern: "Qui de nous/n'a eu sa terre promise,/son jour d'extase/et sa fin en exil" ("Who among us has not had his promised land, his day of ecstasy, and his end in exile"). Whether by inclination or under duress they have left their original societies and blunderingly seek to affiliate with or form new societies. To label such exiles outcasts in the sense of rejects of established societies misrepresents their condition; rather, they are thrown into a position in which they not only labour under the loss of old ties but are also tantalized by the possibility of forming new ones.

The social and political realities in which Conrad's protagonists move, therefore, cannot be regarded as a backdrop or as merely evidence of the historical disintegration of the Archipelago at the time, and certainly not as exotic detail for bored housewives, although they serve these functions very well. The visible social realities serve a uniquely symbolic function of portraying concretely some deeper aspects of the condition of the expatriate, no matter what his country of origin. Men break out of (or are driven out of) their own social groups and seek to form new ones for dubious or uncertain motives. They embrace thereby a hazardous process of psychological adjustment because the old conventions exert unpredictable stresses on conduct as much as the new ones may repel or entice. Conrad does not intend to suggest that the newly encountered Eastern values are capable of displacing Western ones in the scale of general human values, or again that in the confrontation the opposite will happen, namely that Western values will be confirmed in their superiority. No doubt part of the shock of discovery experienced by Almayer, Willems, Jim, Aissa, Tom Lingard and others is simply the sudden awareness, the blinding recognition, that there really is an alternative life-style. No doubt they also respond to this life-style with varying degrees of weakness or strength, fascination or repulsion, respect or contempt. But the encounter equally undermines the bedrock of conviction in the beliefs and values of one's own group, absorbed over a lifetime. An entire civilization begins to tremble at the foundations. The complex of moral values and conventions of race and customs is disconcertingly seen to possess a frightening arbitrariness. The expatriate mind, caught on the rebound from the revelation of an alien life-style, finds it cannot confidently reaffirm these original values, although it may yearn for the mysterious unsuspected composure they had always previously provided. As a result, it "floats supine over. . . chaos." The conventional idea of Conrad the exile and of his protagonists as outcasts has failed to develop this crucial meaning of the author.

Conrad was rather more explicit about this confusion in his earlier than in his later work. In one of his short stories written in 1896, "An Outpost of Progress," he declared that courage, composure, confidence are individual virtues but belong to the crowd which blindly upholds them through its institutions, its morals, it police, and its opinion. This becomes clear when the confrontation with alien surroundings "brings sudden and profound trouble to the heart":

> To the clear perception of the loneliness of one's thoughts, of one's sensations—to the negation of the habitual, which is safe, there is added the affirmation of the unusual, which is dangerous; a suggestion of things vague, uncontrollable, and repulsive, whose discomposing intrusion excites the imagination and tries the civilised nerves of the foolish and the wise alike. (p. 89)

No set of values, Conrad found, is supported by any stronger sanction than habit or custom. An ethical system nurtured over centuries and taken for granted comes crashing down, and the concept of growth and maturity of the human personality itself dissolves in the vapid air. Before laying aside *The Rescue* in 1898 Conrad wrote, in a letter to Cunninghame Graham, "There is no morality, no knowledge, no hope; there is only the consciousness of ourselves which drives us about a world that whether seen in a convex or a concave mirror is always but a vain and fleeting appearance" (31 Jan. 1898).[15] There are good grounds for believing that here was the locus of the "suggestions" Conrad took away from the Archipelago. There is not appearance and reality; there is only appearance and the sense of the defeated consciousness. Conrad told Graham in the same letter, "Egoism is good, and altruism is good, and fidelity to nature would be best of all, and systems could be built, and rules could be made—if only we could get rid of consciousness. What makes mankind tragic is not that they are the victims of nature, it is that they are conscious of it" (Watts, p. 70). In his best work his fictional method came to rely upon a characteristic ponderousness as the only means of bearing this enigmatic discovery. Conrad the expatriate saw the expatriate as uniquely placed to experience the exciting possibilities of fresh extensions of the human mind, human culture, and human society. That these potential extensions were of infinite depth and direction and still ultimately of no lasting validity was what made the prospect frightening beyond any power of words to convey. Conrad frequently used the word "chaos" to convey this unfathomable sector of life itself, even as he employed words like "masquerade" and "fleeting appearance" when referring to conventional notions of the human personality. While completing *Almayer's Folly* he wrote to Marguerite Poradowska, "All is yet chaos, but, slowly, the apparitions change into living flesh, the shimmering mists take shape, and—who knows?—something may be born of the clash of nebulous ideas" (29 March or 5 April [?]; Gee and Sturm, p. 64). Robert Secor's analysis of Conrad's technique of shifting perspectives in *Victory* is one of the few notable attempts to approach this issue from a concentrated study of his rhetoric.[16]

It was the East that brought Conrad this perception, the fact of intercultural contact which revealed undiscovered and infinite dimensions of moral growth. While writing *An Outcast of the Islands* he asked Garnett, "Where is the thing, institution, or principle which I do not doubt?!" (8 March 1895).[17] Traditional concepts of character, too, vanished under the burden of the realization that human nature had hardly been plumbed, and would never be wholly plumbed. An unnoticed passage in one of Conrad's letters written about this time offers a clue to the kind of problem of character Conrad saw revealed by this experience of what may be called detribalization. "Personality," he declared, "is only a ridiculous and aimless masquerade of something hopelessly unknown." One can never truly become the wholly completed, finished personality that life in a closed society deludes one into thinking is possible. One will never "be," one is "ever becoming." Here is the extract in full:

> If one looks at life in its true aspect then everything loses much of its unpleasant importance and the atmosphere becomes cleared of what are only unimportant mists that drift past in imposing shapes. When once the truth is grasped that one's own personality is only a ridiculous and aimless masquerade of something hopelessly unknown the attainment of serenity is not very far off. Then there remains nothing but the surrender to one's impulses, the fidelity to passing emotions which is perhaps a nearer approach to truth than any other philosophy of life. And why not? If we are "ever becoming—never being" then I would be a fool if I tried to become this thing rather than that; for I know well that I never will be anything. I would rather grasp the solid satisfaction of my wrong-headedness and shake my fist at the idiotic mystery of Heaven. (23 March 1896, Garnett, p. 46)

V

In the Malaysian novels, Conrad's "fools" are his expatriates who have not "the solid satisfaction" of belonging decisively to a given group, and through whom he studies the farthest approaches to this mystery. They adopt a number of postures on approaching or entering this realm which challenges them to change at the same time as it mocks their attempts to do so as being of absolutely no importance. The less sensitive ones like Almayer assimilate to a bare minimum in the new group, remaining disturbed by bad dreams. Or they may, like Willems in *An Outcast of the Islands,* switch loyalties back and forth between the old and the new and suffer agonies appropriate to their sensibility. The real perils of this condition are reserved for the more sensitive expatriates who are lured by the prospect of new, unlimited growth of the human personality in the moral and emotional realm they (and Conrad) have discovered, and who seek to burst their conventional bonds of race and culture. They are emphatically not different versions of the same character in the way that much Conrad critism has upheld. In this view Conrad very nearly wrote the same book over and over again. Thomas Moser in his influential study echoes the suggestion attributed to Virginia Woolf that *The Rescue* might be seen as "an attempt to rewrite *Lord Jim* twenty years later."[18] Conrad did not deal with the same character over and over again but with the same problem whose infinite complexity demanded a multiplicity of approaches in different works. Through his protagonists he explored some of the important alternative responses that men could fall into or adopt in the mysterious territory uncovered by the experience of contact with other cultures. Whatever the nature of each response, and whichever the style, all were doomed to failure.

The idealistic Jim of *Lord Jim* despairs on realizing that the unsuspected strength of the bond with his original group has led him to a second betrayal of the foreigners in his care. At sea as well as on land, the Muslims who "surrendered to the wisdom of white men and to their courage, trusting the power of their unbelief" (*Lord Jim,* p. 17; Ch. iii) find their implicit faith spurned. The intellectual Axel Heyst in *Victory* who believed in total aloofness from human society and lived on a solitary island in the Archipelago dies affirming the unavoidable supremacy of the cohesive principle, the ineradicable need in every man to be part of a group.[19] (His silent Chinese waiter, Wang, who parallels him, likewise accepts membership in the Alfuro tribe, into which he had married but from which he had kept aloof.) The romantic brigand Tom Lingard in *The Rescue* accepts the ultimate truth of the message of Jaffir's ring that he must "forget everything" including the delusion that in matters of culture contact one can meddle dispassionately. For the highly intelligent imperialist Kurtz in *Heart of Darkness* (which was written under the same creative impetus as the Malaysian novels) was reserved the harshest lesson: inflexible belief in the superiority of Western civilization (or the values of one's own group) is indistinguishable from quintessential barbarity. Such a belief leads one to think that all other groups must assimilate to one's own group for their own good. The godlike virtues are one's own, the barbaric ones those of others. By the cruelest irony, to be god to a new group is to belong utterly to it and not to one's own. Intense pleasure at being deified by the group one wishes to draw into one's own mingles eventually with intenser pain at the realization that godhood more effectively annihilates one's ties with the original group. The more intensely one wants to assimilate others into one's own group, even from compassionate motives, the more one becomes a fit subject for pathology. Kurtz is drawn nearer than any other character of Conrad's into the heart of the mystery and is finally destroyed by it. Marlow, watching Kurtz, is Conrad's sole expatriate who momentarily surrenders his group membership but has a revelation of inevitable spiritual chaos and comes back to reaffirm with stoic mien his membership in his original group. It certainly looks as if Conrad sought to show that the principal keys available to humankind are powerless to unlock this "idiotic mystery of Heaven." The epigraph from Milton's *Comus,* used for *Victory's* first edition, to which Robert Secor has drawn attention, could stand at the head of all Conrad's work: "a thousand fantasies/ Begin to throng into my memory/of calling shapes and beckoning shadows dire." The abiding paradox which the expatriate grasps with bitter understanding is that it is as important to belong as it is to adventure into the unknown. If one remains

securely within one's own group without a personally experienced awareness of
what it means to leave it, one sacrifices the capacity for creative thought about
human relations and remains a prisoner to imposing delusions. One must, like
Marlow, cross the shadow line and return in order to understand both the
arbitrariness and therefore the unimportance of one's own values and the
necessity, for sanity, of pragmatic assent to them.

The unique revelations about human nature disclosed to the expatriate
mind represent the greatest "suggestions" (quite apart from the facts) that Conrad
took away from the Malaysian Archipelago and that profoundly influenced his
fiction. In the most important sense the historical disarray of the geographical
region after the intrusion of white men serves as an inclusive metaphor for the
chaotic regions of the mind on whose threshold the expatriate particularly finds
himself. It is not to say, of course, that the Archipelago possessed uniquely some
intrinsic virtue or value over other areas in imparting to Conrad an understanding
of the nature of the bond, as he put it, "between us and that humanity so far away."
That would be the reverse kind of chauvinism to the European kind which has
been refused here. It is rather to say that the region was a catalyst for the
development of Conrad's greatest themes which occupied him for a life-time. He
encountered the region at a crucial point in the history of relations between East
and West. He went on to see the same phenomena in all their frighteningly
mingled variety in other parts of the world as well.

VI

One needs to look at Conrad's novelistic art afresh to understand the further
intricacies of the expatriate mind into which he penetrated with unexampled
sagacity. Much that has seemed unnecessarily perverse or obscurantist is bound
to become clearer in the light of the approach adopted here. Conrad's Polish
background itself might be brought into a more even relation with the concerns
that jelled in the novelist during his voyages in the Eastern Seas. One is glad to
note evidence that the early unkindness with which he was treated for having, as it
is said, "betrayed" Poland, and the subsequent desire to define a narrowly Polish
Conrad, have given way in recent years to the more rewarding approach of looking
on his genius as Poland's gift to the world.[20]

A detailed scrutiny of individual works from the standpoint outlined here
must be left to another occasion, but we could use one novel at least as a
touchstone for the usefulness of what has been said. Conrad conceived and
completed a third of *The Rescue* within three years of the start of his literary
career. His difficulties in writing it, his fits of despair, his driving uncertainty about
the worth of what he was attempting, these are too well documented in the letters
to need detailed substantiation here. During three years of increasing desperation
he turned frequently to other writing projects which he completed, returning again
and again to *The Rescue* "like a man certain of defeat." He confessed to Edward
Garnett his fears that it would destroy his reputation.[21] His fears have been partly

justified. No major novel of his has received in recent years more adverse criticism than this one.[22] Conrad has been accused of treating immaturely the portrayal of Lingard and Mrs. Travers, the two principal characters in the novel, and of evading the sexual consequences of their encounter. Perhaps in relation to what Conrad called "the human interest of the tale" in his letter to Blackwood (Sept. 1897; Blackburn, p. 9), such strictures may be warranted. However, the illumination the novel offers in another area of the expatriate condition has been missed.

Among the copious references to *The Rescue* in Conrad's letters are two that clearly set out his creative intentions for it—his letter of September 1897 to William Blackwood (Blackburn, p. 9) and one written to J. B. Pinker at the end of 1918 (Jean-Aubry, II, 212). Both are remarkably good expositions which should correct some serious current misconceptions. There are many kinds of romance, Conrad said, and this one is not fit for juvenile readers "on account of the depth and complexity of the feelings involved" (Jean-Aubry, II, 212). He was never in any doubt that in referring to this novel as a romance, he was more concerned with Lingard and "the wreck of the greatest adventure of his life" than with Lingard's love affair with Mrs. Travers. He wanted to convey in the action of the story "the stress and exaltation of the man under the influence of a sentiment which he hardly understands and yet which is real enough to make him as he goes on reckless of the consequences" (Sept. 1897; Blackburn, p. 10). He aimed, he said, "at stimulating vision in the reader." This is not the phraseology of an author who wishes to deal with a passionate love affair. "Lingard—not the woman—is the principal personage," he said. If we concentrate narrowly on the relationship of Lingard and Mrs. Travers we have a story in the realistic mode à la G. A. Henty about white people trapped among the Malays.[23] Conrad was a master at developing his themes in unexpected directions from this kind of imperialistically inspired cliché. Willems in *An Outcast of the Islands* enacts the cliché of the white man who becomes physically enslaved by "a savage woman." Jim emulates the real-life Rajah Brooke settling "native squabbles" and eventually becoming ruler or lord over Patusan. Kurtz is the heroic white missionary figure dedicating his whole life to bringing civilization to "primitive" people. Conrad takes over the admired (or feared) stereotypes of the colonial age and subtly exposes their shallowness. In *The Rescue,* to treat the love affair of Lingard and Mrs. Travers as the dominant element is to be content, wrongly, with the stereotype of the masterful white man in hostile "native" territory who at some point or other says, "Take me to your chief."

Onto this stereotype Conrad grafted materials in his usual way. Some events and people he had seen, for others he depended on hearsay, and yet others he had read about. Lingard grows out of the real-life William Lingard, who in the 1870's "had a great if occult influence with the Rajah of Bali," and out of the real-life Rajah Brooke whose journals Conrad had read in Rodney Mundy's *Narrative of Borneo and Celebes* (1848).[24] A man named Wyndham who far many years kept the Sultan of Sulu supplied with arms and gun-powder also contributed to the portrait. Conrad tells us that in 1850 or 1851 Wyndham "financed a very lively row in Celebes" and subsequently came to a "lamentable" end (Sept. 1897; Blackburn, p. 10). It is noteworthy that in the original manuscript entitled "The Rescuer" (British Museum Ashley MS 4787, fols. 141-42) Wyndham appears as a character in his own name. There really was a French brig named "Amitié" which was stranded on the coast and attacked by Malays. The captain of the brig himself told Conrad the story. Finally, the important incident of Jaffir, the messenger who carries a ring from his chief to tell of an ambush, was also drawn from the Brooke journals (See letter dated 15 July 1920; Watts, p. 210). Once again the basic facts of the story are true, but it is "the stress and exaltation" of a sentiment Lingard labors under, though hardly understanding it, that Conrad is after.

He concentrates his imaginative resources upon the moment of contact, as between true equals, of East and West. This is not a realistic notion but a romantic one. The two who nurse it are Lingard and Rajah Hassim, both expatriates. Lingard "had wandered beyond that circle which race, memories, all the essential conditions of one's origin, trace round every man's life" (*The Rescue,* pp. 121-22; Pt. III, Ch. i), while Rajah Hassim is "the [Wajo] chief of ten fugitives without a country" (p. 136; Pt. III, Ch. iii). Only such people can entertain the idea of a romance of East and West (or of any other differing social groups). They are sufficiently liberated by circumstances and experience from the customary orientations of their respective cultures to believe in a great vision of equal and successful commingling. *The Rescue* is a celebration of that vision, as *Heart of Darkness* is its dirge. The latter is characterized by overweening arrogance, the former by "colossal" stupidity (*The Rescue*, p. 314; Pt. v, Ch. iii).

Appropriately for a romance there is a ring, an emerald one, symbol of betrothal. At their first meeting Rajah Hassim saves Lingard from some hostile Malays. At their next encounter, Lingard repays the debt, saving Hassim who is in flight after having been deposed from his kingdom. On this occasion Lingard ignores the message of Hassim's ring that he should "Depart and forget" (*The Rescue*, p. 81; Pt. II, Ch. iii) and instead becomes directly involved in the rescue of his friend. He then finds himself committed to helping Hassim recover his kingdom, and thereby embarks upon "the greatest adventure of his life"—the challenge of discovering how to help without endangering or interfering with his friend's way of life. Lingard returns the ring on this occasion in the belief that he can keep his involvement free of self-interest; Rajah Hassim is to send it to him again if he needs help. At the end of the novel Hassim is trapped in ambush and does send the enigmatic gift once more. Jaffir the messenger hands it to Lingard's lieutenant, saying, "Rajah Hassim asks for nothing. . . . Nothing is changed, only the friendship is a little older and love has grown....Just hand it to him" (p. 379; Pt. VI, Ch. iii). The ring might mean once again, "Depart and forget," or it may be a request for help at a critical juncture and so a solemnization through fire of a momentous equal alliance. But by this time Lingard is involved in a more conventional romance with Mrs. Travers who, on being asked to hand the ring to Lingard, decides instead to suppress what she does not understand (p. 407; Pt. VI, Ch. iv). The cryptic message failing to get through, Rajah Hassim is killed and the enterprise to reinstate him collapses. The ring, in effect, through quirks of human nature, had been made to repeat its original message, "Depart and forget." What had once been pregnant with meaning, opening into ideal realms of human communication, becomes in the end devoid of significance, "a dead talisman" (p. 467; Pt. VI, Ch. ix), and is flung into the sea by the confused Mrs. Travers.

The structure of the action rests on an admirable figure pointing to Conrad's lifelong concerns. Both the stranded yacht and Belarab's camp represent the respective societies from which Lingard and Rajah Hassim seek to be independent in pursuit of their dream. The two locations represent the obstinate presence of established social groups which exert pressure on the expatriate in each case to conform in terms of mutual hostility toward the other. Rajah Hassim, escaping his group, is killed in ambush. Lingard is prevented from receiving Hassim's final appeal for interlocking dependence by the one he thought understood his ideals best. The fire, "the stress and exaltation" go out of Lingard. He will roam the seas for a few years more, a successful trader with his ship, but cured once and for all of "the greatness of his day-dreams, his engaged honour, his chivalrous feelings" (p. 405; Pt. VI, Ch. iv). Finally, he is to vanish into Europe without trace (*Almayer's Folly,* p. 28; Ch. ii).

Conrad's exploration of the obscure pathways of the expatriate psyche would not have been complete without *The Rescue.* He had studied how either frailty, or pettiness, or outright villainy overtakes the unwary traveler in the loneliest regions of the human mind. If he had really been convinced that contact with the so-called primitive cultures of Asia and Africa could bring only disaster to the individuals concerned, he would not have carried his exploration into this obverse aspect of the heart of darkness or sought strenuously to give a place to the genuine idealism with which the mingling of cultures could be entertained. Without *The Rescue* we should have thought the less of him. But, in fact, the novel was conceived and partly written, with great agonies of effort, during the intensely creative early period of Conrad's career as a novelist. He put it aside repeatedly to write the works for which he is better known: "An Outpost of Progress," "Falk" (a story, by the way, dealing with a white man in the East Indies who once ate human flesh), and two of his greatest successes, *Lord Jim* and *Heart of Darkness.* He may have needed to come to terms first with a clear appraisal of the perversions (or subversions) of human ideals which intercultural contact appears to entail almost inevitably. (The last 200 years of human history are sufficient evidence of that.) He saw that this contact encouraged all too often the victimization of one group by another, summing up this trend in the expression "Ote toi de la que je m'y mette" (colloquially: "Get out of there so I can get in"). He commented wryly that this doctrine was much easier to practice than the reverse (see letter dated 31 Jan. 1898; Watts, p. 71). But his own fertile expatriate mind saw beyond the historical realities to a dream of human inter-communication based on the subtlest kind of mutual respect. It was colossally stupid to expect it to be realized, but novelistically sound to seek to depict it as a romance.

Conrad's conviction about the nature and value of fiction endorses this view:

> And what is a novel if not a conviction of our fellowmen's existence
> strong enough to take upon itself a form of imagined life clearer than reality
> and whose accumulated verisimilitude of selected episodes puts to shame the
> pride of documentary history?[25]

His prolonged difficulties in writing *The Rescue* need not be taken solely as they
have tended to be hitherto, as mere exemplification of Conrad's creative process.
Conceived at the beginning of his career as being of a piece with the rest of his
work, and completed only toward the end of his writing life some twenty years
later, its theme may be said to cast an aura, a romantic aura if you will, over almost
his entire creative output. In this sense it offers an ideal frame of reference within
which his other incisive studies could well be placed. Conrad's preoccupation
with this novel over a lifetime indicates the point of fineness (in both senses of the
word) to which he finally brought the "suggestions" he took away from the
Malaysian Archipelago. While Tom Lingard's life may be seen in reverse
chronology in the novels taken as they were published, an essential rightness
informs Conrad's intricate progress from historical fact to the most elusive
"suggestion" of all.

The *Rescue* is undeniably faulty in execution especially when taken
rigorously as a work of art. The text underwent several revisions before arriving
at its present state from the partly complete manuscript written between 1896 and
1900. These changes, which have already been studied by Walter F. Wright and
Thomas Moser, deserve further examination in the light of the present reinter-
pretation of Conrad's expatriates (See Moser, pp. 145-57, 219-20). Even in its
finished state, roughly the first half of *The Rescue* has a firmer, more controlled
quality than the latter half. Lingard, the captain of a brig which he calls a bit of
country all his own (*The Rescue*, p. 75; Pt. II, Ch. ii), is well drawn as the
resourceful expatriate poised on the brink of a great event whose significance he
understands without being able to articulate it. His initial encounters with Rajah
Hassim have movement, life and color. In the Author's Note to this novel Conrad
says that he saw the action plainly enough, but that what he had lost for the
moment "was the sense of the proper formula of expression" (p. vii). He doubted
the power of his prose "to master both the colours and the shades" (p. ix). In other
words, he found his nebulous, romantic theme eluding his grasp. "My story is
there is a fluid–in an evading shape. I can't get hold of it," he told Garnett. "I can't
see *images.*" Finally, since he was unable to capture the essence of his theme, he
decided to "try for the visual effect."[26]

He succeeded in his latter aim only too well. Particularly in the second half,
the novel is not so much grand as grandiose. Conrad lavishes color, stressing the
visual elements of his narrative the more he loses confidence in his ability to depict
what he had set out to to. Loss of control makes the writing itself stagy. Nearly
every gesture, action, or event is imbued with a grossly overworked air of fateful

significance. Matters come to a head when with startlingly misplaced irony the author nicknames his hero "the Man of Fate" (*The Rescue,* p. 310; Pt. v, Ch. iii). That, unfortunately, is what Lingard has been made to become, with all the derisiveness such a title must inevitably attract. The heavy-handed image undermines the conception of the character himself and subverts the author's chief purpose of offering a convincing perspective on "the cost of romantic necessity" (*The Rescue,* p. 115; Pt. II, Ch. vii). This section (Pt. v) was written after Conrad took up the novel once again in 1916, apparently partly out of a wish not "to leave this evidence of having bitten off more than I could chew" (7 July 1919; Garnett, p. 263). The "Man of Fate" is not the only image to mar the concluding episodes. The damage is compounded when Mrs. Travers likens all the characters (including herself) to actors "walking on a splendid stage in a scene from an opera, in a gorgeous show fit to make an audience hold its breath" (*The Rescue,* p. 300; Pt. v, Ch. iii). This analogy, too, reveals authorial indulgence rather than precise image-making. No doubt in drawing it Mrs. Travers betrays a streak of insensitivity useful to Conrad's narrative purposes, and there is even a distant kinship between the operatic imagery (*The Rescue,* pp. 300-11; Pt. v, Ch. iii) and his key preoccupation with a world of vain and fleeting appearance, whether seen in a convex or a concave mirror. But Mrs. Travers' remembrance of "the fatal inanity of most opera librettos" (p. 301) poisons the comparison, converting the theme of the romance of contact between cultures into an idea for a mere extravaganza with a principal named Lingard who does not recover from being pelted by pseudoromantic sobriquets like "Rajah Laut," "King Tom," and "Man of Fate."

VII

One must reserve for a subsequent occasion a more detailed reexamination of Conrad's novelistic technique in relation to the central thematic interest of his Eastern expatriates, both white and brown. The crux of his art is the ultimate obscurity in which he shrouds them all. H. G. Wells, in what was really a sympathetic review, referred to Conrad's trampling army corps of dependent clauses produced by the author's toiling after effect.[27] But E. M. Forster's wonderfully pithy observation that "the secret casket of [Conrad's] genius contains a vapour rather than a jewel" succinctly catches both the admiration and the impatience we feel in reading Conrad. Who does not echo Forster's ironic anguish as he asks, "Is there not . . . something noble, heroic, beautiful, inspiring half a dozen great books; but obscure, obscure?"[28] This essay has sought to show that Conrad's lifelong search for "the proper formula of expression" stemmed from his efforts to make us see beyond the facts, not to the jewel but indeed to the vapor into which every effort to understand lives beyond our own eventually disperses. In the Malaysian novels Conrad's expatriates are tantalized by the ideal of a true bond of humanity among all, but haunted by the specter of failure because a pristine chaos mocks every effort of the human personality to master it. "Tell them. . . No. Nothing," Jim says. "What's written [that shall come to pass]?" asks Lingard of Rajah Hassim, who answers, "No one knows" (*The Rescue,* p. 77; Pt. II, Ch. ii). The message of the ring is "Depart and forget," the whole endeavor is "absolutely unimportant" (*The Rescue,* p. 467; Pt. VI, Ch. ix). "Is there no guidance?" Heyst asks, and his father replies, "Look on–make no sound" (*Victory,* p. 175; Pt. III, Ch. i). Even Willems' final realization is "Nothing mattered. He cared for nothing" (*An Outcast of the Islands,* p. 356; Pt. v, Ch. iv). Intelligence is of no account in this confrontation, Conrad held; "Questions of right and wrong . . . are things of the air . . . . Feelings *are,* and in submitting to them we can avoid neither death nor suffering . . . but can bear them in peace" (16 May 1918; Garnett, p. 258).

Only Marlow achieves this still point of Buddhistic nonattachment at the end of his travail in *Heart of Darkness.* We are far away from Aristotelian or any other kind of rational truth now. Truth in Conrad has no face and that is the final horror. Conrad structures his rhetoric on narrators who function like baton-passing relay runners, bringing back to the reader garbled reports, and report of reports of aspects of the truth. Even Kurtz in his dying moments crying out, "The horror! The horror!" is only a narrator. Thus it is not Conrad's obscurity, but rather the obscurity of the outer reaches of life itself of which both his expatriate characters and his readers get an inkling. We may concede, with H. G. Wells, that the style is like river mist, that "great banks of printed matter creep upon the reader, swallowing him up," but we cannot deny the sense of deep and permanent unease in which Conrad's fiction leaves us. Conrad himself said, in reference to *The Rescue* but in a way that resonates to the rest of his works, "You see, what I wanted to say is by no means easy and I wrote it out in a perverse mood. But I still think something of the kind ought to be said—more concisely—in other words" (2 June 1896; Garnett, p. 55). The point is that no other writer of the English language has yet produced those words.[29]

NOTES:

1   I.P. Pulc, "Andrzej Braun's visit to Atjeh," *Conradiana,* 5, No. 2 (1973), 86-94. See also Andrzej Braun, "In Conrad's Footsteps," *Conradiana,* 4, No. 2 (1972), 33-46. All references to Conrad's works are to the Dent Collected Ed., 21 vols. (London: Dent. 1946-55).

2   Sherry, Conrad's *Eastern World* (Cambridge, Eng.: Cambridge Univ. Press, 1966) and *Conrad's Western World* (Cambridge, Eng.: Cambridge Univ. Press, 1971); Allen, *The Sea Years of Joseph Conrad* (London: Methuen, 1967).

3   G. Jean-Aubry, *Joseph Conrad: Life and Letters* (New York: Doubleday, 1927), II, p. 212.

4   "The Genius of Mr. Joseph Conrad," *North American Review,* 178, June 1904, 842-52.

5   See Jessie Conrad, *Joseph Conrad and His Circle* (London: Jarrolds, 1935), pp. 76-77.

6   William Blackburn, ed., *Joseph Conrad: Letters to William Blackwood and David S. Meldrum* (Durham: Duke Univ. Press, 1958), p. 34. Hereafter cited as Blackburn.

7   Author's Note to *The Shadow Line,* p. xii.

8   Richard Curle, ed., *Conrad to a Friend* (New York: Doubleday, 1928), p. 113.' Curle's article, "Conrad in the East," eventually appeared in *Yale Review,* 12 (April 1923), 497-508.

9   See Sherry, *Conrad's Eastern World,* Chs. xiv and xv.

10   *Joseph Conrad:* A Critical Biography (London: Weidenfield, 1959), p. 88.

11   *Joseph Conrad: Giant in Exile* (New York: Macmillan, 1962), pp. 97, 117-18. See also Adam Gillon, *The Eternal Solitary: A Study of Joseph Conrad,* (New York: Bookman, 1960), pp. 104-05.

12   "The Eastern Matrix of Conrad's Art," *Conradiana,* I, No. 2 (1968), 1-13.

13   John A. Gee and Paul J. Sturm, eds., *Letters of Joseph Conrad to Marguerite Poradowska* 1890-1920 (New Haven: Yale Univ. Press, 1940), p. 64. Letter dated "29 March or 5 April (?) 1894." Hereafter cited as Gee and Sturm.

14   Author's note to *An Outcast of the Islands,* p. vii.

15   C. T. Watts, ed., *Joseph Conrad's Letters to R. B. Cunninghame Graham* (Cambridge, Eng.: Cambridge Univ. Press, 1969), p. 71. Hereafter cited as Watts.

16   *The Rhetoric of Shifting Perspectives: Conrad's Victory,* Pennsylvania Univ. Studies, No. 32 (University Park: Pennsylvania State Univ., 1971).

17   Edward Garnett, ed., *Letters from Joseph Conrad* 1895-1924 (1928; rpt. New York: Charter Books, 1962), p. 33. Hereafter cited as Garnett.

18   Moser, *Joseph Conrad: Achievement and Decline* (Hamden, Conn.: Archon, 1966), p. 145. Cf. "A Disillusioned Romantic," *Times Literary Supplement,* 1 July 1920, p. 419; rpt. in Norman Sherry, ed., *Conrad: The Critical Heritage* (London: Routledge, 1973), pp. 332-35. Albert Guerard, *Conrad the Novelist* (Cambridge, Mass.: Harvard Univ. Press, 1958), p. 84, endorses this view too.

19 See Osborn Andreas, *Joseph Conrad: A Study in Non-Conformity* (New York: Philosophical Library, 1959), p. 163.

20 See Gillon, Ch. i.

21 Letters dated 2 June 1896, 5 Dec. 1897, and May 1898; Garnett, pp. 54, 120, 139.

22 See, e.g., F. R. Leavis, *The Great Tradition* (London; Chatto, 1948), p. 183 et passim; Moser, pp. 146-50, 219; Guerard, pp. 84-85; and Gurko, pp. 255-62.

23 One of G.A. Henty's works of popular fiction is entitled *In the Hands of the Malays.*

24 See letters dated Sept. 1897, 15 July 1920; Blackburn, p. 10; and Watts, p. 210.

25 *A Personal Record* (London: Dent, 1948), p. 15.

26 Letters dated 29 March 1898, May 1898, and Aug. 1898; Garnett, pp. 135, 139, 141. Conrad's italics.

27 *Saturday Review,* 16 May 1896, pp. 509-10; excerpted in Sherry, *Conrad: The Critical Heritage,* pp. 73-76.

28 Sherry, *Conrad: The Critical Heritage,* p. 346.

29 This essay was completed during sabbatical leave granted by the Univ. of Malaya at the end of 1971. Thanks are also due to the Director, Institute for the Arts and Humanities Studies, Pennsylvania State Univ., for a Fellowship awarded at the same time and to the Curator of the Rare Books Room, Pennsylvania State Univ., Charles Mann, for making his personal library freely available for my use.

ALMAYER AND WILLEMS – "HOW NOT TO BE"

Juliet McLauchlan

Critical assessment of Conrad's first two novels has been limited, even falsified, because most critics have seen them as little more than two very similar tales about white men who go to complete ruin in a tropical setting. More disastrously, the most influential critics, notably Thomas Moser and Albert Guerard, have not only found the love stories unconvincing but have cited them as perfect examples of Conrad's supposed loss of conscious control of his material, when he tries to deal with a basically "uncongenial subject," love.[1] It is, thus, widely accepted that *Almayer's Folly* and *An Outcast of the Islands* are unimportant 'prentice-work, and that Conrad had not yet found the truly Conradian themes of his greatest fiction. Recent close study has convinced me that neither, in fact, is a love story as such; that Conrad no more wrote "love stories" than he wrote "sea stories;" and that mainstream Conradian themes dominate both novels. These include the futility of seeking happiness through material wealth or through adherence to the non-values of supposed "civilization," moral isolation and corruption, through the debasement of truly civilized and human standards of honor and rectitude, and the tragic tendency of human beings to try to live by and within illusions.

I. ALMAYER'S FOLLY: Almayer's Dream—and Nina's

Almayer's Folly is sustained metaphor, built upon a life-death antithesis which is worked out in close conjunction with some of the major themes just mentioned. The conflicting dreams of Almayer and Nina lie at the heart of the novel.

So far as Almayer is concerned, some critics have accepted to a limited extent that the novel is concerned with dreams, with illusion-versus-reality, but they do not appear to have noticed that Almayer's vague "dreams of wealth and power," his longing for "the lost glories of Amsterdam," are paralleled exactly by Nina's dreams of "savage glories," both dreams having sprung from a mother's tales.

On the very first page Almayer is unpleasantly jarred from his "dream of a splendid future" to the "unpleasant realities of the present hour." His response is characteristic: "He absorbed himself in his dream." He is still "gifted with a strong and ardent imagination" just as he was when he "saw. . . great piles of

79

shining guilders and realized all the possibilities of an opulent existence. . . the indolent ease of life" which he once counted on enjoying as Lingard's son-in-law. Now, once more he is living a dream, which depends this time upon Dain's return. He blames "circumstances" for the fact that "fortune was gone," but so strong a hope remains that he has only a vague remembrance of being called by his wife "some time during the evening," "probably" for dinner. Having immediately established the strength and over-riding reality of Almayer's illusion and its vagueness, Conrad proceeds to show in detail why and how he is indeed "thoroughly recalled to the realities of life:" "by the care necessary to prevent a fall on the uneven ground where the stones, decaying planks, and half-sawn beams were piled up in inextricable confusion." (12) Almayer creates and recreates in imagination a totally illusory world of "civilized" splendor, to be attained by the acquisition of vast wealth, epitomized in the gold and diamonds to which first Lingard and now Dain are supposed to lead the way. In this dream-world, his one joy will be to watch the (unspecified) triumphs of his beloved daughter in a remote Dutch society. So much does he live in this dream that the realities of life come to seem less and less real to him, and he becomes ever more incapacitated for action, depending ever more on outside help and luck to bring the fortune which is to make his daughter's happiness and thus his own. Conrad consistently (as at the novel's opening) shows this in terms of concrete detail: the "splendid banquet" of his vision is set against the "plateful of rice" which is actually in front of him, the "rich prize" which he imagines to be "within his grasp" against the "tin spoon" in his hand. Always the dream is vague, the real situation particularized.

Paralleling this, Nina's dream becomes similarly absorbing. Understandably her "traditionless father's" vague dreams for her future have no meaning, reality, or attaction. Instead she becomes irresistibly fascinated by her mother's stories of bravery, savagery, and the totally different "splendour" of a primitive society. Even in Almayer's own imagination, his dream for Nina takes on no concrete form, far less for the girl herself; and her experience of "civilization" has not been such as to give any basis for romantic dreaming. Indeed she has developed only contempt and hatred for all white people except her father. The basic conflict of the novel lies in the different ways in which the two dreams develop. Amidst surroundings of "squalid neglect"[2] Almayer is living in an "enchanting vision," while *simultaneously* Nina is building in imagination an "entrancing picture." (The phrases occur within two pages of each other–16, 18.) Since both father and daughter appear here to be equally spellbound, both "vision" and "picture" may at first seem to be equally illusory. Even in the word "vision," however, there is the strong suggestion of something illusory, while a "picture" is very often a representation of something real. In this case Almayer's vision of treasure, and a resulting life of civilized opulence, becomes more and more totally unrealizable as Lingard disappears permanently, as Almayer himself comes to lose the co-operation of the other scheming traders, and as he suffers the betrayal of his hopes by Dain. Worst, he suffers the final and insupportable loss of his daughter, who alone has given meaning and purpose to his dream. Nina's dream, her "picture," on the other hand, becomes reality as she meets in Dain "the embodiment of her fate," the very "creature of her dreams." (It is critically fashionable to scorn Conrad's early novels but his balance and control here are masterly.)

When Almayer's totally illusory dream is shattered, he is himself shattered; and, as elsewhere in Conrad's fiction, we see that although it may well be impossible to live by an illusion, it is even more impossible to live without it. For Almayer the shattering of his illusion is closely associated with death: "His face was like the face of a man that has died struck from behind–a face from which all feelings and all expression are suddenly wiped off by the hand of unexpected death" (196). The blankness of both face and voice are perfect images for the emptiness and deathlike quality of an existence which becomes no more than an anguished attempt to forget what cannot be forgotten. Our sense of the illusory nature of the vision by which he has tried to live is heightened by the fact that it seems to be the *child* Nina who haunts him so painfully, to whom he continually speaks and pleads. Broken, enfeebled, he hears the "childish prattle" of many years before. This seems to me to make nonsense of any contention that there is an incestuous element in Almayer's paternal love. The only textual evidence for this (and it is very slim) comes in the reference to Nina's light touch on her father's head and his later feeling of betrayal when he realizes that at that very moment of filial affection she was planning to meet Dain. It seems basic to Almayer's tragedy that he should so continue to see Nina as a child when the child has become a woman and has made it clear that his "way" cannot be hers. In this novel, the "folly" of the title is sometimes associated with foolishness, sometimes with madness (echoing the French), sometimes with the building itself. Almayer's true folly has been the madness of rearing a dream-structure in which he has dwelt for so long. The actual building is the perfect image for the metaphorical "folly" he has reared for himself and Nina, which they will never inhabit. The multiple nuances of the word clearly meant much to Conrad, as he was impressed by the difficulty, even impossibility, of finding an equivalent for the Polish translation. He considered *Almayer's Daughter* before deciding upon the Polish word meaning madness.[3] Either choice involved losing the richness of the English word.

Central to Almayer's tragedy, also, is his inability at a crucial stage to accept a quite different dream from that in which he has been so long absorbed. He actually comes to consider another, and the repetition of the word "heart" emphasizes the pull of his love against his folly:

> What if he should suddenly take her to his heart, forget his shame, and pain, and anger, and–follow her! What if he changed his heart if not his skin and made her life easier between the two loves that would guard her from any mischance? His heart yearned for her. What if he should say that his love to her was greater than. . .[but]

"I will never forgive you, Nina!" he shouted, leaping up madly in
sudden fear of his dream. (192)

In effect he is fearful of a dream of life and love which alone might have saved him.
He refuses life itself, for it is after the departure of the lovers that he virtually
ceases to exist.

What of Nina's dream? To a large extent it appears to "come true." What
value can be given to it? Is any of its "splendour" real–if by "real" we mean
providing some adequate basis for living? It is real in this way insofar as it is an
integral part of the life-death antithesis which forms the metaphorical basis of
the novel. For Nina, life and Dain are synonymous. To both men Nina is essential
to life, but only Dain can offer life in return. To her father Nina cries:

"Could you give me happiness without life? Life!" she repeated with sudden
energy that sent the word ringing over the sea. "Life that means power and
love," she added. . . . (190)

The last news of Nina comes as a kind of affirmation, for in Dain's kingdom
they are celebrating the birth of an heir. Nina appears to have chosen life, life's
very essence being its continuation from one generation to the next. Significantly,
it is this news which constitutes the final blow for Almayer, driving him to the last
desperate refuge of dreams induced by opium, deepening despair, madness, and
finally death.

There is something to be added about the value, if any, of Nina's dream-
come-true. Is her life, then to be a mere idyll? An escape to an island paradise?
To any such sentimental ending, we have had, as has Nina herself, the corrective
from her mother, whose "mature wisdom" (Babalatchi's words) is simply
knowledge of the demands of life in a kingdom like Dain's. She can warn of the
inevitable realities. There will be splendors: Nina will be a great ranee; "and if you
be wise you shall have much power that will endure"; she will live "far away in
splendour and might"; but the mother warns of some aspects of the realities of
such a position. Nina can readily enough accept her mother's dictum that "power
will lie in not letting him look too long into your eyes," even that "if he lingers,
[Nina must] give him the kriss yourself and bid him go." But there is a less
acceptable warning, and its importance is obvious since the older woman
hesitates in "irresolute thoughtfulness" before continuing "abruptly," after a
pause: "Listen Nina, in after years there will be other women." To Nina's "stifled
cry" the mother repeats her words "firmly":

"I tell you that, because you are half white, and may forget that he is a great
war chief, and that such things must be. Hide your anger and do not let him
see on your face the pain that will eat your heart. Meet him with joy in your
eyes and wisdom on your lips, for to you he will turn in sadness or in doubt. As
long as he looks upon many women your power will last, but should there be
one, one only with whom he seems to forget you, then–" (153)

Although Nina feels that she "could not live," that "it could not be," the mother rebukes her for crying and counsels her to "show no mercy" and even to "strike with a steady hand." Her mother's influence has long been strong, so it seems that this ruthless advice may well enable Nina to face and come to terms with her emergence from idyllic dream into a complex and difficult reality.

The fate of the girl Taminah shows exactly how vital it is for Nina to act as she does in order to be able to live and love. The slave-girl, by virtue of being a slave-girl, has no choice of escape. Before the coming of Dain:

> In that supple figure. . . behind those soft eyes . . . slept all feelings and all passions. . . . And she knew nothing of it all. She lived like the tall palms. . . seeking the light, desiring the sunshine, fearing the storm, unconscious of either.(112)

Her life has been simply existence. Once she has met Dain his approach sends her

> into a wild tumult of newly-aroused feelings of joy and hope and fear. . . [she] drank in the dreamy joy of her new existence. . . till the full consciousness of life came to her through pain and anger. (114-15)

So intense are these passions and her savage jealousy that she is driven to try to betray her lover, since anything seems preferable to imagining his happiness with Nina. Babalatchi buys her, wishing for "the sight of a young face and the sound of a young voice" but Taminah's nature and needs are precisely Nina's; deprived of the metaphorical sunshine of her life, of which she has had no more than a tantalizing glimpse, bought for an old man's pleasure, she can only pine and die.

Nina's dream does, then, become reality. It would not have done so without a struggle to achieve freedom. Some ruthlessness is involved since it is truly a struggle for life; and she does not always find it easy. Her hardest fight seems to be the first and crucial one when:

> Her breast [is] torn by conflicting impulses . . . her heart deeply moved by the sight of Almayer's misery. . . longing to bring peace to that troubled heart, she heard with terror the voice of her overpowering love commanding her to be silent. As she submitted after a short and fierce struggle of her old self against the new principle of her life. (103).

The struggle is decisive. Her mother easily leads her to overcome her "passing desire to look again at her father's face" and, leaving to meet Dain: "She understood now the reason and the aim of life. . . and threw away disdainfully her past" (152). Later when Almayer pursues the lovers, she can tell him that when he spoke of gold: "our ears were filled with the song of our love. . . Then I began to live. . . And I mean to live. I mean to follow him. . . . I love you no less than I did before, but I shall never leave him, for without him I cannot live" (179-80). The assurance of the continuance of his daughter's love comes as no comfort, since it is

coupled with such determination to depart with Dain, even with willingness to die
rather than fail to do so.

Imagery and the Life–Death Antithesis

As is characteristic throughout Conrad's fiction, imagery consistently rein-
forces the major theme of the novel, the life-death conflict between the two
dreams. On the one hand, the tangled, prison-like growth of the tropical forest is
heavily suggestive of corruption and death, as are the darkness, dimness, and cold
moonlight of some of the crucial scenes. On the other hand, the sky, sea, air and
sunlight are all linked with the absolute necessity for Nina and Dain to escape to
the freedom of a life together. This is evident in a passage which has often been
quoted and too often used as the basis of a gross misinterpretation of Conrad's
treatment of love not only in *Almayer's Folly,* but more generally. The received
critical idea (especially as expounded by Moser in the chapter already cited) is
that the passage links ideas of fertility and feminine sexuality with death. Instead
it abounds in imagery linking sexuality (both masculine and feminine) with life,
and with the need for these young lovers to escape from Sambir and Almayer's
dream for Nina. Whatever the passage may be, it is certainly not the writing of
someone who could not come to terms with the sexual and could thus describe it
only in terms of corruption and death.

The passage, upon which I shall comment without quoting *in toto,* begins
(71) with some positive feeling in that the "little nutshells" are sheltered in the
enclosed bay, yet the "black water," "dim light," the "high canopy of dense
foliage" through which the light can penetrate only by struggling, all suggest
imprisonment and menace. Far overhead, there is, however, the "broad day," day
being associated always with freedom and life for the lovers. Many words and
phrases in the latter half of the passage are extremely evocative of unrestrained
sexual pleasure, of the ecstasy and striving for oneness which is characteristic of
all lovers: the plants are "entwined, interlaced in inextricable confusion,"
"climbing madly and brutally over each other," involved in a "desperate
struggle." The "strong and harsh perfumes" are similarly evocative in the
context. The suggestion of harshness is appropriate to the "savage" natures of
both lovers, but savagery in this novel is associated with the natural and beautiful
and with life rather than with any baseness–mainly by the beauty of the associated
imagery. The "shower of dew-sparkling petals" which falls in a "continuous and
perfumed stream" on to the lovers, the "sleeping water" and the "ring of luxuriant
vegetation bathed in the warm air," achieve a fine mingling of the sensual, the
savage, and the beautiful. Of particular significance within the metaphorical
context of the novel as a whole, is the determined "shooting upward," the
"climbing madly in. . . a desperate struggle towards the life-giving sunshine
above" (71). The lovers are associated with the bright blossoms which must
struggle upwards into the sunshine, and the whole passage stresses yet again the
life-death antithesis.

In a related passage which has also attracted similar critical attention and led to similar misinterpretation of Conrad's treatment of women and love, Dain is waiting for Nina so that they may escape. In sunlight he is aimlessly wandering around the "clearing":

> As he skirted in his weary march the edge of the forest he glanced now and then into its dark shade, so enticing in its deceptive appearance of coolness, so repellent with its unrelieved gloom, where lay, entombed and rotting, countless generations of trees. . . . Only the parasites seemed to live there in a sinuous rush upwards into the air and sunshine, feeding on the dead and the dying alike, and crowning their victims with pink and blue flowers that gleamed amongst the boughs, incongruous and cruel, like a strident and mocking note in the solemn harmony of the doomed trees.
>
> A man could hide there, thought Dain, as he approached a place where the creepers had been torn....As he bent down...an acrid smell of damp earth and of decaying leaves took him by the throat, and he drew back with a scared face, as if he had been touched by the breath of Death itself. The very air seemed dead in there–heavy and stagnating, poisoned with the corruption of countless ages. . . . Was he a wild man to hide in the woods and perhaps be killed there–in the darkness–where there was no room to breathe? He would wait for his enemies in the sunlight, where he could see the sky and feel the breeze. (166-67)

It seems perverse to take this as anything but a specific *rejection* by Dain of the death and corruption which the forest represents. The essential link between the forests of Sambir and death is made yet more explicit as Dain begins to reassure himself that evening. It is now dark but: "she would come. . . . Yes, when the next day broke, they would be together on the great blue sea that was like life–away from the forests that were like death" (169). Nothing could be clearer than that. It is only by ignoring the sustained life-death antithesis of *Almayer's Folly,* so apparent here, and by overemphasizing isolated aspects of imagery, that it becomes possible to conclude either that there is "an intense pessimism, obscurely implicated with some sexual morbidity"[4] here, or that Nina's love constitutes some sort of threat to her lover's masculinity.[5]

After Nina has joined Dain beside the dying fire, the contrast between Sambir and Dain's country heightens our awareness of the antithesis. In this great final scene in the jungle where all is danger, and the darkness is pierced only by the fire and moonbeams, Dain speaks:

> of his own island, where the gloomy forests and the muddy rivers were unknown. He spoke of its terraced fields, of the murmuring clear rills of sparkling water that flowed down the sides of great mountains, bringing life to the land and joy to its tillers. . . . He spoke of vast horizons swept by fierce winds. . . . (173-74)

Here is the fertile, the majestic, the spacious, all far removed from the joyless gloom of the rivers and forests of Sambir. And Dain speaks movingly of the fascination of the sea, of its beauty and capriciousness, its treachery, its mystery, in terms very similar to Conrad's own in the later *The Mirror of the Sea*. In *Almayer's Folly* the sea constitutes the very road, the only road of escape. In bright sunlight the lovers set off:

> in that crude blaze of vertical sun, in that light violent and vibrating, like a triumphant flourish of brazen trumpets. [Their boat heads southward, aided by the sea-breeze which] shivered with its breath the glassy surface of the water. (194)

We last see the prau as a small

> patch of yellow light on the red background of the cliffs . . . .[It] had caught the sunlight and stood out, distinct with its gay tint. . . . till it cleared the last point of land and shone brilliantly for a fleeting minute on the blue of the open sea . . . [As it continues southward] the light went out of the sail [and it] disappeared. . . in the shadow of the steep headland. (195)

The bright dream has become reality, but reality will be shadowed, difficult and complex. This is no sentimental escape to a paradisal island.

Around the motionless Almayer, who has been watching the lover's prau:

> the air was full of the talk of the rippling water. The crested wavelets ran up the beach audaciously, joyously, with the lightness of young life, and died quickly, unresistingly, and graciously, in the wide curves of transparent foam on the yellow sand. (195)

Predominant here are images of joy, courage, life, and sensual love, shadowed by hints of transience and death. Almayer himself has already rejected his possible dream of life and love. Now his deliberate "burial" of Nina's footsteps in a line of "miniature graves" constitutes his first pathetic attempt to forget his daughter. His "effort to shout out loud again, his firm resolve to never forgive" issues in a soundless movement of his lips; his intended firmness becomes a "dejected and feeble progress across the sand, dragging his feet." Already he feels the presence of that "invisible companion" the child Nina. It is later Ali's conviction that Almayer has "turned sorcerer," talking to "a spirit in the shape of a child. . . a bad and stubborn spirit," Ali thinks, for "Master spoke to the child at times tenderly, and then he would weep over it, laugh at it, scold it, beg of it to go away, curse it. . . ." Almayer's haunted, death-in-life existence brings him to near-madness; from living in an impossible vision of the future, he comes to exist only in ghostly visions of the past, and from this "anguish and pain" only death can ultimately free him.

Universal Significance?

So distinguished a critic as Jocelyn Baines can dismiss *Almayer's Folly* with adverse stylistic criticism of a few isolated passages and content himself with only one major criticism:

> Although Almayer is a type and the situation which confronts him is typical, there is no question of his transcending his particularity as do, for instance, Charles and Emma Bovary, who, without losing their individuality, come to symbolise aspects of human nature and the human predicament. The misfortunes of Almayer have little reference beyond himself.[6]

But this damning critical verdict springs from inadequate attention to the novel as a whole and to its pattern of imagery. The "folly" of this particular father is only an extreme presentation of the foolishness, even madness, the total futility, of erecting a structure for someone else's life, particularly for a beloved child's life, with no understanding of its personality and real needs. Besides the universal relevance of this situation, there is the folly of living in a dream, an illusion, as does Almayer. This is shown in all its destructiveness. Nina Almayer, a half-caste, torn between parents with totally opposite longings for her future, becomes a powerful metaphor for any young person forced to assert the right to lead an independent life. The sharp racial antagonism of the Almayer parents becomes a metaphor for an extreme incompatability of parental background and viewpoint. The fact that Almayer's dreams for Nina are so clearly grounded in illusion, and the close association of his dreams for her with death, show how vital it is for her to escape, and the escape thus takes on value from its association with life. This is coupled with Nina's positive rejection of what her father considers to be "civilized" life. In line with this, the commercial success which lies at the heart of Almayer's dream, the "treasure" and vast "fortune" which will make dream reality, are shown in this novel to be valueless by contrast to life, love, freedom of choice. Thus we see here the announcement of a major and recurring Conradian theme: it is folly and death to trust to "material interests."

II. AN OUTCAST OF THE ISLANDS

There is undoubted pathos, perhaps even a hint of tragedy, in the story of of Almayer. Here is a father capable of genuine feeling for his daughter–blind and possessive though his love may be. Almayer and Willems are by no means the twin instances of white degradation which they have sometimes been taken to be, and Jocelyn Baines comes close to recognizing a crucial difference when he notes (though disapprovingly) that "it is difficult to feel affection or compassion for Willems, who is contemptible without even being pitiable."[7] As Baines notes further, Conrad stated in his Author's Note that "the story itself was never very near my heart" (ix). One can understand this, and even agree with Baines, and yet admire greatly what Conrad has achieved. It is right to feel contempt for this character, for in Willems Conrad has carefully embodied many of the negative qualities which he most detested. He has, deliberately, created a thoroughly contemptible man.

Through Willems' downfall Conrad is primarily concerned to show an attempt to live totally without principles. As he lacks any sense of honor, Willems' motivation and behavior are shown to afford no possible way to live. They lead him into the fatal path of betrayal and thus constitute instead an inevitable way to death. Equally important, Conrad is concerned to show a human being incapable of love, or indeed of any real human feeling. Willems experiences only overpowering lust, unsoftened by affection or compassion, and stands as lust's ugly embodiment. Particularly brilliant is the portrayal of that satiety and revulsion in which such an empty passion must end. Finally, the major Conradian theme announced in *Almayer's Folly,* in a different form, becomes central: greed for riches, linked in Willems to a lust for power, is futile and contemptible. In the three sections which follow I shall consider in some detail these themes in turn—although they are so inter-related that it is not possible to maintain arbitrary divisions.

Willems as Wanderer

In the autumn of 1894, when Conrad was just beginning to write *An Outcast of the Islands*, he wrote to Marguerite Poradowska: "Mrs. M. Wood has stolen my title. She has just published a book called *The Vagabonds,* and here I am in a pretty stew."[8] Both Babalatchi and Lingard are shown as being in some sense vagabonds, vagabonds of the sea. What of Willems? The novel contains numerous references to the roads, tracks, or paths which Willems imagines himself to be following often with accompanying descriptions of his mode of proceeding: walking, stumbling, wading, marching, rushing, among others. All are basic to the novel's account of Willems' totally unsuccessful way of life. Sometimes Conrad records Willems' own view of his progress or his predicament; often (perhaps even more effectively) he *shows* different forms of Willems' physical movements; occasionally (and with great effect), the accompanying imagery heightens the total impression.

The dominant metaphor in *An Outcast of the Islands* is subtly presented in the novel's opening sentence, and it is worth looking closely at the effects which Conrad has achieved—since this also is widely held to be poor 'prentice-work. These effects depend upon interaction of words unexpectedly qualified by juxtaposition. That Willems has "stepped off the straight and narrow path" seems to record some deliberate departure from a course governed by strict, perhaps orthodox, principles, but the phrase "of his peculiar honesty" undercuts the connotations of the cliché to import the sense of a moral standard personal to Willems, perhaps odd, not generally acceptable. The commendable firmness of his "unflinching resolve" is similarly undercut: there is something suspect about the effortlessness with which he imagines that he can regain the path. He will simply "fall back into"–what?–not the path, it seems,–"the monotonous but safe stride of virtue." Willems counts on swinging back into and maintaining a purposeful pace, which he himself links firmly to the great word virtue, with all the moral weight carried by that word since classical times. Although unexciting, this course must be accepted for safety's sake. Willems regards his straying (into embezzlement, we soon learn) as a sort of short pleasure-trip, which will not take him beyond the "wayside"; but the word "quagmires" sounds a note both comical and ominous. Who could sensibly plan a "little excursion" into a morass and count on extricating himself at will(3)?

Very economically, Conrad has revealed a great deal about Willems; he is emerging as a figure of total moral confusion and self-delusion. It comes as no surprise when we find that the "path of his peculiar honesty" has proved to be: "such a faint and ill-defined track that it took him some time to find out how far he had strayed amongst the brambles of the dangerous wilderness he had been skirting for so many years" (21). The significance here is that long before Willems finds himself surrounded by the gloomy forests and tangled undergrowth of Sambir, he has been operating dangerously near to a trackless, menacing wilderness–the moral wilderness in which he will ultimately discover himself to have become a "lost man".

The irony of his position, just before his dismissal by Hudig, lies in his conviction that he has only temporarily "stepped off the path of honesty" (the phrase with only slight variations, occurs three times); that he is still "following the road to greatness"; that it is indeed "plainly before his eyes" (11). At first, but only momentarily, he has felt "dismayed" to find how far he has strayed, but he has since displayed "that courage that will not scale heights yet will wade through the mud–if there be no other road" (21). Ironically, he has now come almost to the point where he can make restitution, after having for some time "devoted himself to the duty of not being found out."

His actual dismissal puts an end to this particular form of self-delusion; and here we begin to "see" Willems embark upon a course which will reach its climax (after Lingard's final departure) in his daily "aimless wanderings," and which will lead him ultimately to his death. Smarting under Hudig's insults and physically reeling, he "stumbled heavily," over what is merely a "thin rope's end," "as if it had been a bar of iron." It is not any real obstruction which causes him to stumble, but his senseless headlong rush. As usual his response to what happens to him is a "passion of anger," directed here against what is really his "guilt," but which he defines to himself as "an idiotic indiscretion." Equally characteristic of Willems is his conviction that he has been "driven" to it by "the stupid concourse of circumstances." It seems to him "a fatal aberration of an acute man," and he can only conclude that "he must have been mad." It will be in almost exactly these terms that he will later try to explain to Lingard his betrayal and to excuse it by putting upon Aissa the blame for his fatal infatuation. Yet the fact is that, in Conradian terms, the whole course of Willems' life is aberrational– from the path of honor.

Shortly, we again "see" Willems' blind mode of proceeding. Overcome by "an impulse of mad anger" towards the cringing Leonard da Souza, he knocks him down "before he knew what had happened," then "tore blindly down the street," coming to himself only when he finds that he is outside the town "stumbling on the hard and uneven earth," wondering "How did he get there?" (29). Overmastered by bursts of destructive passion, Willems thus stumbles through life guided only by his impules, having never espoused moral principles. He can never see a better way, for to Conrad there is no way for the morally blind.

Just prior to the arrival of Lingard, there does seem, momentarily, to be some hope for Willems. Stung by the sense of all that he has lost: "he came out of himself, out of his selfishness. . . out of the temple of self"[9], but almost immediately his thoughts "wandered" back towards the home of his unhappy youth, forcing him to realize that he cannot return to that. He is "drifting into suicide" when Lingard appears and takes him in hand.

Thus Conrad presents Willems at the beginning of the novel—Willems before he meets Aissa. What sort of path leads him towards her? Ironically, it is a way into which he drifts himself; even more ironically, it is what Babalatchi later calls "a way for their destruction and our own greatness." Indeed the great irony of Willems' ever more aberrational course is that it comes to be consistently governed by Babalatchi's determination to "make use of Willems for the destruction of Lingard's influence." He rightly predicts he can do this because "white men . . . [are] always the slaves of their desires"(60).

After Lingard has left Willems with Almayer, those "two specimens of the superior race" soon come to hate each other and the situation becomes "intolerable." So it is that Willems:

> took to wandering about the settlement . . . There was only one path. . . . On the other side the virgin forest bordered the path, coming close to it, as if to provoke impudently any passer-by to the solution of the gloomy problem of its depths. . . . There were only a few feeble attempts at a clearing here and there. . (65-66)

Gradually he goes farther afield:

> He skirted in his little craft the wall of tangled verdure. . . where the spreading nipa palms nodded their broad leaves over his head as if in contemptuous pity of the wandering outcast. . . he could see the beginnings of chopped-out path-ways, and . . . would land and follow the narrow and winding path, only to find that it led nowhere, ending abruptly in the discouragement of thorny thickets. . and the big trees would appear on the bank, tall, strong, indifferent in the immense solidity of their life, which endures for ages, to that short and fleeting life in the heart of the man who crept painfully amongst their shadows in search of a refuge from the unceasing reproach of his thoughts. (66-67)

I have quoted these passages at considerable length because of their metaphorical significance. There are obvious echoes from the passage previously quoted (21).

The "dangerous wilderness" has now become an actual one, but it is still a moral wilderness which Willems is skirting and into which he will definitively stray from the path of honor.

It is when he finally follows a path which seems "frequented" that he finds Aissa's path. During the months of his infatuation, there is to Willems no path, road, or way of life save that which she indicates to him, that which she, indeed, permits him to follow. Willems makes one attempt to return to trading, but even if Almayer were to accept him, all the evidence indicates that Aissa would never accept any way of life but her own. Always we are aware that Babalatchi is the guiding force. It is Babalatchi who at a crucial point convinces Willems that he must "submit" to Aissa's will (that he help Abdulla). If he does not, he may "have to live without her." At this Willems: "gasped and started back like a confident wayfarer who, pursing a path he thinks safe, should see just in time a bottomless chasm under his feet" (125-26). Willems' fixed idea at the height of his infatuation is to take Aissa right away, but she consistently urges him towards the path of greatness as her people envisage it – very much along the lines laid down by Mrs. Almayer for Nina in her role as Dain's wife. Very ironically, the only time we see Willems acting competently and commandingly is when he is in desperate pursuit of Aissa, thus furthering Babalatchi's aims. (He has now clearly committed himself to the fatal path of betrayal.) Solely because he cannot otherwise have Aissa with him, he successfully undertakes an exacting navigational operation (with all that this implies about his potential as "one of us"). He comes very close here to becoming a hero in Aissa's terms, but then fails to follow her way by failing to kill their enemies, especially Lingard. His later total rejection of Aissa herself and of the way of life and love to which she ardently wishes him to dedicate himself disappoints her cruelly. As for Willems himself, he has brought himself to an impasse. Now that he wants nothing more to do with Aissa and must again face Lingard, he seems to intend some sort of return to Lingard's way. His physical progress here is revealing of the impossibility of such a return. Appearing at the end of Lingard's encounter with Aissa:

> He stood. . . his hands grasping the lintel. . . writhed about . . . Then he made a sudden rush head foremost down the plankway. . . .
>
> When he felt the solid ground. . . under his feet, Willems pulled himself up in his headlong rush and moved forward with a moderate gait. He paced stiffly . . . [keeping his eyes on Lingard's face as if trying to read the man's feelings or intentions] the silence which had been lifted up by the jerky rattle of his footsteps fell down again . . . . Through this silence Willems pushed his way, and stopped about six feet from Lingard. He stopped simply because he could go no further [although] he had started from the door with the reckless purpose of clapping the old fellow on the shoulder. (256-57)

An impasse indeed, for Willems has already rejected Lingard's way. To Lingard, whose own honesty is "unswerving," there is only "the right way and the wrong way." He walks "the road of life . . . proud of never losing his way," with always that "firmness, steadfastness of purpose," which are alien to Willems. Although Lingard is acting "in obedience to his benevolent instincts" as he goes about "shaping stray lives he found here and there," it is in keeping with Conrad's ironical presentation of this "way" of treating others, that Lingard's way of "retribution" (in a very exact sense) is shown to be immeasurably cruel. During the highly dramatic scene when Lingard dooms Willems to an unending imprisonment in Sambir, all ways are effectively closed to him. This is a "scene" in which the accompanying imagery plays a most effective part. The "silence" through which Willems has "pushed his way" was "the silence of the cloudy sky and of the windless air, the sullen silence of the earth oppressed by the aspect of coming turmoil, the silence of the world collecting its faculties to withstand the storm" (257). Throughout the coming encounter the storm presents metaphorically the Jove-like (or Jehovah-like) wrath of Lingard, who is the personification of retributive power and action. Willems shouts his appeal "towards the sombre heaven, proclaiming desperately under the frown of thickening clouds the fact of his pure and superior descent" (271). While the encounter continues, the clouds have ominously "thickened into a low vault of uniform blackness." Continuing the storm imagery, this also corresponds to the blackness of Lingard's thoughts as he tries to come to terms with the problem of Willems as his own "mistake," his own "shame"; and it suggests too the darkness which will now, metaphorically, surround Willems, right up to the ultimate darkness of his death. In the "stifling gloom" around the three figures, Lingard pronounces sentence, and the violence of the elements is appropriately suggestive of his relentless power over Willems. Flashes of lightning split the clouds, followed instantly by deafening thunder. Willems is as one struck indeed by the fire and thunderbolts of a vengeful heaven. The crushing weight of his punishment comes in Lingard's words: "You say you did this for her. Well, you have her" (276). This prompts Willems suddenly to catch his hair in his hands "and remain standing so." After Lingard has told Aissa: "I have told him that he must live here all his life . . . and with you" (276). Aissa looks at Willems "who remained still, as though he had been changed into stone in the very act of tearing his hair" (277).

The total confusion of the elements which accompanies Lingard's disappearance from view mirrors the collapse of Willem's whole world with the departure of this man whom for "all his life he had felt. . . behind his back." As Lingard's canoe moves upstream so the "thunderstorm. . . was working its way up the river with low and angry growls"(282). During a short period of "formidable immobility," "the voice of the thunder was heard, speaking . . . like a wrathful and threatening discourse of an angry god." The rising wind envelopes Willems "with a cloud of water-dust" that hides from his sight Lingard and everything else, waking him from his "numbness in a forlorn shiver." The surrounding element is no longer air but water, "cutting his respiration." He stands "gasping" while assaulted, as by some malevolent power, "from everywhere," "in a vertical downpour," until finally "from under his feet a great vapour of broken water floated up." Even worse, he feels "the ground become soft—melt under him." As he experiences the full force of Lingard's anger and "justice," the definitive withdrawal of his support, the ground under Willems' feet loses its firmness. The imagery heightens the effect as we see Willems slip and slide in the mud which the earth has now become. This whole passage is a magnificent metaphor for the dissolution into near chaos of Willems' world. Filled with an "insane dread" of the water surrounding him, and of the "fire and water" which seem to be "falling together, monstrously mixed, upon the stunned earth," now he can indeed see no way.

> He wanted to run away, but when he moved it was to slide about painfully and slowly upon that earth which had become mud so suddenly under his feet. . . . [Aissa follows him] in his toilsome way up the slippery declivity of the courtyard, from which everything seemed to have been swept away. . . . They could see nothing. (284)

So they proceed "under the roll of unceasing thunder, like two wandering ghosts." Although they finally gain the shelter of the house, Willems' choice now lies as Lingard has said, between the "forests" and the "river." We feel here the full harshness of Lingard's retribution. Yet there is no real alternative for Willems. He has no way of his own; he wants only to escape from Aissa's way; he has rejected the way of Lingard, who regards him as being "not fit to go amongst people," and is unwilling to let him "escape from him by going out of life." He regards Willems' life as "finished": Willems is "buried here." So it seems to Willems too as Lingard departs. Apart from his futile dreams of escape, there occurs to him only one possible way: back into his former passion for Aissa. But passion is dead: it cannot provide a way. From now on images of death surround Willems; hardly anything else seems tangible to him. Significantly, his last "long stride," his "step nearer," his taking off "with a long bound for a tearing dash," carry him straight to his death, for the "dash" prompts Aissa to fire (360). To Mahmat, Willems has resembled "the tiger when he rushes out of the jungle at the spears held by men." Totally selfish to the end, Willems is carried to his death by one of his characteristic bursts of passion. As Lingard's way of justice is so ambivalently presented (we are surely not intended to endow his sense of justice with moral value), it is right that Willems gets what he deserves *because this way of life can come to no other end*. Death alone can bring escape of a sort to one who has never been able to see or find a satisfactory way to live.

Willems' aberrational way of life is closely linked with his worship in the "temple of self" and with the accompanying fear of losing that precious self. He comes to equate loss of the self with sexual abandon. There is a suggestion of this in his first encounter with Aissa. Passing close to her, he has felt "the touch of a look darted at him from half-open eyes" which "touched his brain and his heart together." He has been "spun" around by a combination of "surprise and curiosity and desire" after passing her. Now "charmed," Willems experiences "the brusque stirring of sleeping sensations awakening suddenly to the rush of new hopes, new fears, new desires–and to *the flight of one's old self*" (69, my italics).

Willems' fear of losing the self comes close to the obsessional in the course of the novel. He does not realize that, as a lifelong worshipper in the "temple of self," he is living a form of imprisonment. Nor can he realize that there is nothing of value to lose in this self-imprisoned personality. Before he commits himself to Aissa he experiences a horror of losing the self through abandonment to sexual desire. Ironically, in the sense that for a considerable period he becomes enslaved by sexual desire, he does experience loss of self. When lust has turned to revulsion, it is for this that he comes to loathe himself, unaware that the true self has in fact been lost through loss of honor.

Fairly early in his involvement with Aissa, Willems experiences misgivings which are expressed in terms of the novel's dominant metaphor, and which foreshadow his end. He has come to be guided only by the newfound "ecstasy of the senses," yet feels uneasily that the passing moments are marking "his footsteps on the way to perdition. Not that he had any conviction about it, any notion of the possible ending on that painful road." Morally blind, he cannot see the right course; self-deluding, he will persuade himself to follow the wrong one. At this crucial juncture he pushes away scruples about betraying Lingard, telling himself: "His clear duty was to make himself happy. . . . Happiness? Was he not, perchance, on a false track? Happiness meant money. Much money. At least he had always thought so till he had experienced those new sensations. . . ."(142). Willems is right but, with a multiple irony characteristic of *Outcast,* right for the wrong reasons. He *is* on a false track. This applies in the deepest moral sense because he will now follow the fatal path of betrayal. In a more ironical sense, it is the wrong track because it will lead him away from his real goal, money: if he followed here the honorable path by remaining loyal to Lingard, there would be some future chance of his gaining "happiness" through possession of money. When his lust has turned to revulsion, happiness once again seems attainable only in this way, but by that time Lingard's influence is less strong and Willems has lost Lingard's benevolent support.

A few pages later, in a sort of dream, Willems actually "sees" himself going off into a sort of wilderness scene, but misses the ominous significance of what he sees. He has closed his eyes in an "ecstasy of delight," and is "dreamily, perfectly happy": "but for the annoyance of an indistinct vision of a well-known figure; a man going away from him and diminishing in a long perspective of fantastic trees" (145). Wanting to see him disappear, Willems watches, but is startled to recognize the figure as himself. It takes him some time to get over the shock of seeing himself "go away so deliberately, so definitely, so unguardedly; and going away–where?" This is splendidly in keeping with Conrad's whole conception of Willems' behavior as aberrational, and with the fact that Willems himself always sees his aberration confusedly, while Conrad and the reader see it plainly for what it is. Willems' anger and bewilderment are indicative of his moral confusion: "He felt indignant. It was like an evasion [Conrad means this in the French sense of escape], like a prisoner breaking his parole–that thing slinking off stealthily while he slept" (145). As with the earlier image he has formed of himself as a "slippery prisoner," he sees himself going off "inevitably," but everything is vague: for he can never really see what he is doing.

The "escape" motif pervades the novel. Willems escapes from his own attempted tight control, to become enslaved by his desires. When satiated, he escapes from Aissa's spell only to return to the temple of self. Aissa reports to Lingard his metaphorical escape, which frightens Lingard because he imagines Willems will physically escape his "justice." Willems cannot do so; he cannot because of his own nature escape his death. Yet death is in some way his escape, as already noted. As Lingard puts it, Willems is finally "delivered by the mercy of God from his Enemy," by death. Who is the Enemy? Lingard has been his enemy to the extent that he has meted out a terrible punishment by keeping him in a life which is not life at all. But the real enemy would seem to be the self in which Willems has lived imprisoned, the moral blindness which has led him to his death. His moral confusion reaches its peak when he says to Lingard: "As far as you are concerned, the change here had to happen sooner or later; you couldn't be master here for ever. *It isn't what I have done that torments me. It is the why.* It's the madness that drove me to it" (269-70). In the italicized words this Conradian "hero" damns himself. The act of betrayal, which constitutes his real corruption, means nothing to him. He can never see that his one aberration has been from the path of honor and rectitude. Willems has neither: thus any moral obligation which he ought to feel is always overmastered by his desires.

The Presentation of Love in An Outcast of the Islands

Shakespeare's Sonnet 129 epitomizes the nature of Willems as a figure of lust:

> The expense of spirit in a waste of shame
> Is lust in action; and till action, lust
> Is perjured, murd'rous, bloody, full of flame,
> Savage, extreme, rude, cruel, not to trust;
> Enjoy'd no sooner but despised straight;
> Past reason hunted, and no sooner had,
> Past reason hated, as a swallow'd bait,
> On purpose laid to make the taker mad
> Mad in pursuit, and in possession so;
> Had, having, and in quest to have, extreme;
> A bliss in proof, and prov'd, a very woe;
> Before, a joy propos'd: behind a dream.
> All this the world well knows; yet none knows well
> To shun the heaven that leads men to this hell.

Shakespeare's Iago provides a similar parallel for Willems' experience of a "love" which is closely akin to what Iago calls "our raging motions, our carnal stings, our unbitted lusts." Love to Iago is only "a sect or scion" of these. He of course believes that lust can be controlled by reason; for Willems this is impossible. Iago thinks, too, in terms of the satiety which overtakes Willems, and this sort of sexual nature is best expressed when Emilia tells Desdemona that men:

> . . . are all but stomachs, and we all but food;
> They eat us hungerly, and when they are full
> They belch us. (*Othello,* III, 4)

The ugliness here is exactly expressive of the revulsion which Willems comes to feel towards Aissa.

His first words to the girl are simply "You are beautiful." Afterwards he continues his "monotonous song of praise and desire":

> She was beautiful and desirable, and he repeated it again and again; for when he told her that, he had said all that there was within him–he had expressed his only thought, his only feeling. (76)

That is the key to Willems' "love." Further discussion must be linked with consideration of very widely-held views on Conrad's presentation of love in this novel.

As with *Almayer's Folly,* Thomas Moser and Albert Guerard have most influenced the general critical view. Pursuing his theory that love was for Conrad "the uncongenial subject," Moser writes:

> Conrad seems aware of Willems' lack of masculinity as he was not of Dain's; Lingard comments explicitly that Willems "is not a man at all." Certainly Willems *presently* loses interest in Aissa's sexuality. When she clasps him round the neck in a burst of passion, he stiffens "in repulsion, in horror." Toward the end of the novel, Willems decides that he must resign himself to perpetual exile in Sambir and let the woman help him to forget. He takes Aissa suddenly in his arms and waits "for the transport, for the madness," but all he feels is "cold, sick, tired, exasperated with his failure." The next morning he gets up with a "disgusted horror of himself."[10]

Somewhat similarly, Albert Guerard claims that:

> The girl is specifically equated with the tropical life that "works in gloom," that is "only the blossoming of the dead," that "contains nothing but poison and decay." The novel's only area of unconscious or half-conscious creation tells us that Willems is horrified by sex from the first and from the first, threatened by impotence.[11]

Guerard also claims that although Willems' passion is: "immediate and . . . strong enough to conquer racial pride and any lingering loyalty to Lingard. . . [it] is *presently* mingled with disgust, and in the end leads to sexual failure" (my italics).

Having long felt uneasy about these views, I have become convinced that they are demonstrably misinterpretations. Moser's chronology is confused. He writes as if the "repulsion" and "horror" affect Willems at some unspecified early stage in the relationship. Yet they, too, come "towards the end of the novel"– immediately after Lingard's final departure. It is not, then, "presently" that Willems' desire fades. It comes as part of that later satiety which leads to revulsion and disgust. Guerard also uses the word "presently," but his error is not one of chronology. The "disgust" which Willems admittedly feels from the very first, has nothing to do with sexual impotence, or the threat of it. Far from it. It is rather similar to Kurtz's mingled feelings of desire and loathing (except that Kurtz never seems to pass to a state of satiety or total revulsion). To Willems, the desire for Aissa is from the first quite irresistible, yet simultaneously he loathes *himself* for "surrendering to a wild creature the unstained purity of his life, of his race, of his civilization" (80).

Both Moser and Guerard ignore the fact that Willems passes through the stage of mingled self-disgust and over-powering desire to become totally besotted. After five solid weeks in the company of Aissa (to whom he is "indeed a man"–so much for his impotence, it would seem), Willems tells Almayer that he now knows what "perdition" is, and his ravings to Almayer during the few days when he is deprived of her company show him to be totally overmastered by his passion. His exaggerated, even melodramatic, speech and behavior do not reflect Conrad's inability to express "love" but simply underline the extent of Willems' enslavement. "Without her" he cannot imagine living and can think only of taking her away from everyone else: "to fashion–to mould–to adore–to soften. . . Oh! Delight!....I would be all the world to her!" (92) With the truest sort of irony, Willems gets exactly what he wants–when he no longer wants it: he becomes "All the world to her," when he has come to wish only to escape from her.

Willems' infatuation becomes most evident in scenes where it is rendered through other people's responses, or through "definite images." When he is finally being allowed to return to Aissa he attacks Lakamba "in the senseless fury of white men," shouts curses which sound to Lakamba like the raving of a mad dog; as he shouts Aissa's name, Lakamba expresses contempt "for the inhuman sound"; and we finally "see" Willems as he frantically kicks open the gate, rushes "like a tornado," and disappears into the house, Aissa in his arms (107-08).

A finer scene, truly Conradian in its oblique presentation, comes later as Almayer reports disgustedly to Lingard the treatment he has received. We see Willems tyrannizing in the way he loves; we see too an indulgent and besotted Willems at the height of his infatuation:

> By his orders they laid me out on the floor, wrapped me in my hammock, and he started to stitch me in, as if I had been a corpse, beginning at the feet. While he worked he laughed wickedly . . . . Whenever I moved they punched me in the ribs. He went on taking fresh needlefuls as he wanted them, and working steadily. Sewed me up to my throat. . . That woman. . . clapped her hands. I lay on the floor like a bale of goods while he stared at me, and the woman

shrieked with delight. Like a bale of goods!. . . . Finally, by his directions, they flung me into the big rocking-chair. I was sewed in so tight that I was stiff like a piece of wood. He was giving orders . . . . They obeyed him implicitly. Meantime I lay there in the chair like a log, and that woman capered before me and made faces; snapped her fingers before my nose. . . . Now and then she would leave me alone to hang round his neck for awhile, and then she would return before my chair and begin her exercises again. He looked on indulgent. . . She drags him before my chair. "I am like white woman," she says, her arms round his neck. (183-84)

It is the revulsion which inevitably follows such infatuation, and not any "threat of impotence" or sexual inadequacy in Willems, which accounts for his feelings when, near the novel's close, he fails to find consolation with Aissa. Seeing little hope of realizing his dreams of a return to "civilization," Willems feels overpowering despair and loneliness. When Aissa appeals to him to let her come into the house with him, his responses are made very interesting by a qualifying phrase which quite undercuts normal expectations. His heart is "moved, softened with pity," *not* with any ordinary human feeling for another, but "for his own abandonment"! Even his anger against "her who was the cause of all his misfortune vanished before his extreme need for some consolation." Characteristically, he first blames her and then sees a return to her arms in terms of degradation: "he planned the deliberate descent from his pedestal, the throwing away of his superiority, of all his hopes, of old ambitions, of the ungrateful civilization" (337). (At this point, consider again Willems' plea to Lingard to spare him on the grounds of his "pure and *superior descent*" [27, my italics]). Echoed here, from a different standpoint altogether, that phrase can be seen as an oxymoron. Willems always thinks in terms of his superiority, and by "descent" *he* means lineage. To the reader however, "descent" suggest instead the baseness of this man, the abysmal level upon which he operates.) "For a moment" he imagines he can forget in her arms, and feels "the *semblance* of renewed desire" (my italics). She offers him her submissive and patient devotion, responding to his embrace with joy, and it is in this context that he "waited for the transport, for the madness, for the sensations *remembered and lost*" (the italicized phrase, omitted by Moser, suggests very concrete past experience). Despite his failure to recapture any of the old sensations, he does spend the night with her; naturally he is exhausted and despairing the next day. There is nothing so dead as a dead lust.

If *Outcast* is a love story at all it is because of the portrayal of Aissa. Willems, it must be stressed, is incapable of love. Aissa is "the girl with the steadfast heart," "strong," "fearless," "Woman in body, but in heart a man." With her "violent impulses," her "merciless heart" where enemies are concerned, she is by no means sentimentalized but, savage though she is, she possesses qualities which make her actually superior to her white lover. Her way of life is not presented as the way Willems, or a truly civilized man, should follow, but Conrad directs his contempt towards the debased standards of the supposedly civilized Willems. Lingard sees her, rather as Babalatchi does, as "a woman whose heart, I believe, is great enough to fill a man's breast: but still you are a woman, and to you, I, Rajah Laut, have nothing to say" (246). Rather against his will Lingard respects her, and feels "some emotion arising within him, from her words, from her tone, her contact . . . at the close sight of that strange woman, of that being savage and tender, strong and delicate, fearful and resolute . . ."(249). In her Lingard reluctantly recognizes qualities of strength, courage, and loyalty, which make her much more admirable to him than such a moral weakling as Willems. For Willems Lingard has lost all respect, and it is in this context that he declares to Babalatchi: "That man is not like other white men. You know he is not. He is not a man at all. He is . . . I don't know" (230). The implications here are simply not sexual. To Lingard, whatever else Willems may be (and the old seaman is genuinely puzzled), he clearly cannot be a man, lacking as he does the essential qualities of courage, steadfastness, and rectitude.

All this places Aissa morally. In terms of certain basic moral qualities she is more of a human being than is Willems. What of the sexual aspects of her presentation? Predominantly, her appearance and movements are linked with the light and brightness of the sun, the play of air and water, femininity, warmth, freshness, the colors of hair and clothing. I shall quote several passages at some length to show that the dominant images in *Outcast* do *not* in fact equate feminine sexuality with death. They achieve something far more subtle.

The "scene" which preludes Aissa's first appearance embodies great natural beauty, with clear suggestions of sexuality, none of death:

> a flash of white and colour, a gleam of gold like a sunray lost in shadow, and a vision of blackness darker than the deepest shade of the forest. He. . . fancied he had heard light footsteps—growing lighter—ceasing . . . The grass on the bank of the stream trembled and a tremulous path of its shivering, silver-grey tops ran from the water to the beginning of the thicket. And yet there was not a breath of wind. Somebody had passed there. He looked pensive while the tremor died out in a quick tremble under his eyes; and the grass stood high, unstirring, with drooping heads in the warm and motionless air. (68)

Great natural beauty also surrounds her as we "see" her first:

> she stood straight, slim, expectant, with a readiness to dart away suggested in the light immobility of her pose. High above, the branches of the trees met in a transparent shimmer of waving green mist, through which the rain of yellow rays descended upon her head, streamed in glints down her black tresses, shone with the changing glow of liquid metal on her face, and lost itself in vanishing sparks in the sombre depths of her eyes. (69)

Just as the first passage above, with its stillness and light tremors, is evocative of a sort of sexual expectancy, so in the passage below fragrance and beauty are evocative of sexual languor and expectancy as Willems waits for Aissa a little later:

The brilliant light of day fell through the irregular opening in the high branches of the trees and streamed down, softened, amongst the shadows of the big trunks. Here and there a narrow sunbeam touched the rugged bark of a tree with a golden splash, sparkled on the leaping water of the brook, or rested on a leaf that stood out, shimmering and distinct, on the monotonous background of sombre green tints. The clear gap of blue above his head was crossed by the quick flight of white rice-birds whose wings flashed in the sunlight, while through it the heat poured down from the sky, clung about the steaming earth, rolled among the trees, and wrapped up Willems in the soft and odorous folds of air heavy with the faint scent of blossoms and with the acrid smells of decaying life. And in that atmosphere of Nature's workshop Willems felt soothed and lulled into forgetfulness of his past, into indifference as to his future. The recollections of his triumphs, of his wrongs and of his ambition vanished in that warmth, which seemed to melt all regrets, all hope, all anger, all strength out of his heart. And he lay there, dreamily contented, in the tepid and perfumed shelter. . . . (74-75)

Despite the predominance of beauty in the imagery, there are clear suggestions of something more ominous. Before considering why this should be so, it will be helpful to quote the passage from which Guerard has abstracted a few phrases (above):

She moved a step forward and again halted. A breath of wind that came through the trees, but in Willems's fancy seemed to be driven by her moving figure, rippled in a hot wave round his body and scorched his face in a burning touch. He drew it in with a long breath, the last long breath of a soldier before the rush of battle, of a lover before he takes in his arms the adored woman; the breath that gives courage to confront the menace of death or the storm of passion.

Who was she? Where did she come from? Wonderingly he took his eyes off her face to look round at the serried trees of the forest that stood big and still and straight, as if watching him and her breathlessly. He had been baffled, repelled, almost frightened by the intensity of that tropical life which wants the sunshine but works in gloom; which seems to be all grace of colour and form, all brilliance, all smiles, but is only the blossoming of the dead; whose mystery holds the promise of joy and beauty, yet contains nothing but poison and decay. He had been frightened by the vague perception of danger before, but now, as he looked at that life again, his eyes seemed able to pierce the fantastic veil of creepers and leaves, to look past the solid trunks, to see through the forbidding gloom–and the mystery was disclosed–enchanting, subduing, beautiful. He looked at the woman. Through the checkered light between them she appeared to him with the impalpable distinctness of a dream. The *very spirit of that land of mysterious forests,* standing before him like an apparition behind a transparent veil–a veil woven of sunbeams and shadows. (69-70)

In a related passage, Willems is lying looking up at Aissa afraid to move for fear of frightening her:

her head [is] lost in the shadow of broad and graceful leaves that touched her cheek; while the slender spikes of pale green orchids streamed down from amongst the boughs and mingled with the black hair that framed her face, as if all those plants claimed her for their own–the animated and *brilliant flower of all that exuberant life* which born in gloom, struggles for ever towards the sunshine.(76).

Throughout the novel, the wilderness, trackless, "dangerous," stands as the ultimate threat to Willems in his aberrational course through life. Although he is frightened by the darkness and threatening aspects of the *actual* wilderness, Aissa's beauty will blind him completely to the real danger of the *moral* wilderness of whose existence he is not even aware. Ironically, he looks into the gloomy depths of the forest, which are linked here with death, decay, and poison, and imagines, as he looks back at the girl, that he sees in *her* the actual personification of their "mystery," which is "enchanting, subduing, beautiful"; thus there is nothing to be feared. So it comes about that, "dazzled" by this "flower," Willems will see none of the perils of the moral wilderness into which he will plunge in pursuit of her. Every time Conrad links the wilderness and death, it should evoke for the reader this fatal threat to Willems.

Guerard and other critics have maintained that the novel should have ended with Willems' abandonment by Lingard, but the ending as devised by Conrad is essential to the full presentation of the nature of Willems and of Aissa.

The devotion of which this primitive woman is capable is finely visualized in the beauty of Aissa's appearance and movements as she comes to Willems at the beginning of the novel's last "scene." The renewal of their love-making has prompted in Aissa rapturous feelings quite opposite to the revulsion we have seen in Willems. This is reflected in her beauty and her exaltation. The first hint of this comes from the old woman, w! ¬ has seen her pass the sleeping Willems: "I saw her look at you and pass on with a great light in her eyes. A great light" (348). This is the "picture" as she appears, "her hands full of flowers":

She [has] turned the corner of the house, coming out into the full sunshine, and the light seemed to leap upon her in a stream brilliant, tender, and caressing, as if attracted by the radiant happiness of her face. She had dressed herself for a festive day for the memorable day of his return to her, of his return to an affection that would last for ever. The rays of the morning sun were caught by the oval clasp of the embroidered belt that held the silk sarong round her waist. The dazzling white stuff of her body jacket was crossed by a bar of yellow and silver of her scarf, and in the black hair twisted high on her small head shone the round balls of gold pins amongst crimson blossoms and white star-shaped flowers, with which she had crowned herself to charm his eyes; those eyes that were henceforth to see nothing in the world but her own resplendent image. And she moved slowly, bending her face over the mass of pure white champakas and jasmine pressed to her breast, in a dreamy intoxication of sweet scents and of sweeter hopes. (351-52)

Not only is Aissa radiantly happy, she is centering her hopes firmly on their having a child to constitute "a bond which nothing on earth could break." At that precise moment, with the unexpected appearance of Joanna, Willems is centering his hopes with equal firmness upon a return to "civilization." By setting Willems' baseness and insensitivity against Aissa's hopeful joy and capacity for devotion Conrad achieves here a contrast central to his presentation of a thoroughly contemptible character. "[Willems] had a flashing vision of delivering a stunning blow, of tying up that flower-bedecked woman in the dark house..." (352). A little later: "He thought with [characteristic] fury: I will kill them both" (353). As always, Willems cares only for himself; doubtless he would kill both women if that would make possible his own escape. He is quite unaware that he has finally penetrated to the very depths of the moral wilderness. Aissa's dream is shattered by the terrible revelation that Willems has both a wife and a child. It is dramatically necessary that Willems should meet his death as he does: his final betrayal of Aissa prompts her to behavior appropriate to her "savage" nature and background. She is not only the "brilliant flower" of the wilderness but (more inclusively) "the very spirit of that land of mysterious forests." Though steadfast, her heart can become "merciless"; though capable of devotion and loyalty, her nature is subject to "violent impulses." Swept now by jealousy, hatred, and the acute pain of betrayal, she acts in accordance with her father's imagined whisper "Kill! Kill!" It is not with a melodramatic *crime passionnel* that this novel ends but with a retributive act surpassing even Lingard's: betraying Aissa. Willems finds a death which is meted out according to the code of that dangerous wilderness into which he has definitively strayed through his betrayal of Lingard. Conrad's touch is very sure as the metaphorical and the actual merge here.

Wealth and Power

Most characteristic of Willems is his conviction that happiness is attainable through wealth—and really in no other way. Once again, there is a superficial resemblance to Almayer, but their dreams are fundamentally different. Almayer's centers upon the future of his child; his joy will arise from his being able to see her happiness, as he imagines. Willems' dream centers solely on self. It precedes and survives his passion for Aissa and is associated with an ugly desire to exercise power over others. A particularly ugly aspect of his lust for power is that it goes with an utter contempt for people of a darker, less "civilized" race, although Willems prides himself on being free of such prejudice.

The early pages of the novel show this aspect of Willems' character as vividly as they show his moral confusion. To "tyrannize," to "patronize," these are "the delights of his life." Willems enjoys a quite idiotically inflated sense of his white superiority:

> He loved to breathe the coarse incense they offered before the shrine of the
> successful white man ... he was their providence; he kept them singing his

> praises in the midst of their laziness, of their dirt, of their immense and
> hopeless squalor: and he was greatly delighted. . . . he could give them all they
> wanted without ruining himself. In exchange he had their silent fear, their
> loquacious love, their noisy veneration. It is a fine thing to be a providence,
> and to be told so on every day of one's life. . . . Willems revelled in it. . . . his
> greatest delight lay in the unexpressed but intimate conviction that, should he
> close his hand, all those admiring human beings would starve. . . . They lived
> now by the grace of his will. This was power. Willems loved it. (4-5)

Willems, the consistent worshipper in the "temple of self," expects others to
worship there too. There is a distinct irony in his fatuous arrogance when it is set
against his complete helplessness as he later finds himself at the mercy of
Lingard's godlike power. There is nothing so ugly as this in the pathetic Almayer.
In all of Conrad's fiction only the manager in *Heart of Darkness* and Massy in
"The End of the Tether" are more coldly selfish in their devotion to wealth and
power than is Willems. To swerve from this one way to hapiness would seem to
Willems aberrational. Yet in Conradian terms Willems' way is aberrational from
the start, especially since he has from the start strayed from the path of rectitude.
Willems actually prides himself on the dishonourable methods by which he has
been, as he imagines, so successful: he has bribed, smuggled, and indulged in all
manner of illicit dealings:

> he disapproved of the elementary dishonesty that dips the hand in the cash box,
> but one could evade the laws and push the principles of trade to their furthest
> consequences. Some call that cheating. Those are the fools, the weak, the
> contemptible [he assures himself]. (8)

Conrad also shows the whole unreliable basis of Willems' fatuous
self-confidence. He is a man of "gross ignorance":

> There is always some one thing which the ignorant man knows, and that thing
> is the only thing worth knowing; it fills the ignorant man's universe. Willems
> knew all about himself. . . . He. . . conscientiously. . . expounded his theory of
> success. . . [his] text [being] Where there are scruples there can be no power.

In the context of this novel, it is hardly necessary to underline the irony in
"Willems knew all about himself." In fact he knows nothing about selfhood in
Conradian terms.
        As elsewhere in Conrad, a basic inadequacy in Willems is indicated by
his decisive rejection of life at sea as too "hard and exacting." Although Lingard,
in his vanity and gullibility, is treated very ironically, the "simple-hearted old
seaman" is doubtless right in his view that: "the boy was hopelessly at variance
with the spirit of the sea [feeling] instinctive contempt for the honest simplicity
of that work which led to nothing he cared for" (17). Instead Willems' "trading
instincts developed themselves astonishingly." Lingard remains convinced that

the sea is the only place for an honest man, but is equally convinced that Willems will "never make a seaman"; he "didn't think there was enough money in it" (42).

Near the novel's close Conrad gives a final brilliant reminder of the nature of Willems and his illusory dreams of "civilization" and success. Abandoned by Lingard, Willems longs only for escape and for a return to his old way of life:

> For hours together we would stand in sunlight while the sea breeze sweeping over the lonely reach fluttered his ragged garments; the keen salt breeze that made him shiver now and then under the flood of intense heat. He looked at the brown and sparkling solitude of the flowing water, of the water flowing ceaseless and free in a soft cool murmur of ripples at his feet. (329)

Despite the positive imagery here, which resembles that in *Almayer's Folly,* Willems' dreams have nothing to do with real freedom, escape, or life. As he imagines that he might escape by building a raft, his dreams are revealing. Characteristically he imagines:

> drifting down with the current, down to the sea . . . . There were ships there—ships, help, white men. Men like himself. Good men who would rescue him, take him away, take him far away where there was trade, and houses, and other men that could. . . appreciate his capabilities; where there was proper food, and money; where there were beds, knives, forks, carriages, brass bands, cool drinks, churches with well-dressed people praying in them. He would pray also. The superior land of refined delights where he could sit on a chair, eat his tiffin off a white tablecloth, nod to fellows–good fellows; he would be popular; always was–where he could be virtuous, correct, do business, draw a salary, smoke cigars, buy things in shops–have boots. . . be happy, free, become rich. O God! (329-30)

In his second novel we see here Conrad's full artistry at work. A sound satirical sense combines with his sense of fun (often underestimated) to produce a rich passage, remarkable for its careful juxtaposition of customs, forms, and actual objects to reveal exactly the triviality of Willems' idea of civilized existence, correct (even "virtuous") behavior, and the bases of social relationships. Care for words here extends to the smallest details: "could [not would] be virtuous" implies that circumstances will enable Willems to be virtuous, and this is quite in line with his conviction that his lapses are caused by external forces, not by any fault within himself. This contrasts delightfully with the word "would" in the marvellous "He would pray also"; he has no doubt he can pray if he decides in an appropriate context to do so. This is a Conradian *tour de force,* prefiguring the brilliance of some of the later expository presentation of character, as with Sotillo, Bento, Massy, and others.

Through Almayer (in contrast to Dain and Nina) and, supremely, through Willems, Conrad has shown in *Almayer's Folly* and *An Outcast of the Islands* "how not to be."

Aylesbury, England

NOTES:

1 Thomas Moser, *Joseph Conrad: Achievement and Decline* (Hamden, Conn.: Archon Books, 1966), Chapter Two. Page references to Conrad's novels within the text are to the Dent Collected Edition (London, 1947, 1949).

2 David Leon Higdon and Floyd Eugene Eddleman, "Collected Edition Variants in Conrad's *Almayer's Folly*," *Conradiana,* 9 (1977), 85, show that Conrad cut out a line and a half after the phrase "squalid neglect": "Great red stains on the floor and walls testified to frequent and indiscriminate betel-nut chewing." They rightly conclude that Conrad could not have done this "to avoid offending an over-sensitive reader," because he refers several times elsewhere to this habit of Mrs. Almayer's. They further conclude that there seems to be "no good reason" for omitting it, and suggest that "its loss results in a far less specific, vivid image and that the sentence had served excellently as an extension and substantiation of the picture of squalid neglect." I should like to suggest a good reason for the change Conrad made. The emphasis in this first chapter is entirely on Almayer's own fecklessness. It would weaken the reader's sense of this if Mrs. Almayer, too, carried responsibility for the squalor. She has, after all, long lived apart, amongst her women in a riverside hut which she seldom leaves.

3 Zdzislaw Najder, *Conrad's Polish Background* (London: Oxford University Press, 1964), pp. 262, 271. Here Conrad discusses the matter with his counsin Aniela Zagorska, who translated *Almayer's Folly* into Polish.

4 J.I.M. Stewart, *Joseph Conrad* (London: Longmans, 1968), p. 48.

5 Here I must refer to a passage which is not quite central to my argument, except insofar as it *is* central to the controversial question of Conrad's presentation of love in this novel. Thomas Moser holds that Conrad habitually equates feminine sexuality with death, that he shows it to threaten masculinity to the point of rendering Dain, Willems, and other Conradian lovers impotent. In support of this theory, he writes that when Nina starts to kiss Dain he "tries to prevent the kiss by saying 'we must part now.' " Instead of going, Nina kisses him; his response must disappoint her: "He closed his eyes, surprised and frightened."

   Two points vitiate this as a critical assessment. First, in his quotation, Moser breaks off in the middle of a sentence. Dain is not simply "surprised and frightened"; he is "surprised and frightened at the storm raised in his breast. . . [and, after Nina's departure] he remained motionless [with eyes closed] afraid to lose the sense of intoxicating delight he had tasted for the first time." Second, his "We must part now" has nothing to do with the kiss. It follows the passage already quoted and breaks a long (and presumably intimate) silence. Nina asks if he will "be long away" and Dain replies "Long!. . . would a man willingly remain long in a dark place? When I am not near you Nina, I am like a man that is blind. What is life to me without light?" Nina is so moved by his words and by the "confirmation" she reads in his eyes, that in "an immense wave of gratitude and love" she longs to make some "outward and visible sign of all she felt." Remembering from her "civilized" past the white man's custom of kissing on the lips, Nina kisses her lover in this way. "Now he wanted but immortality, he thought, to be the equal of gods, and the creature who could open so the gates of paradise must be his–soon would be his forever!. . . He must go on board . . . yet he was loth to leave the place where he had learned to know what happiness was."

6   Jocelyn Baines, *Joseph Conrad: A Critical Biography* (London: Weidenfeld and Nicolson, 1960), p. 164.

7   Baines, p. 162.

8   John A. Gee and Paul J. Sturm, *Letters of Joseph Conrad to Marguerite Poradowska* (Port Washington, New York: Kennikat Press, 1973), p. 84.

9   R. G. Hampson, "The Mystic Worshipper and the Temple of Self," *Journal of the Joseph Conrad Society (U.K.),* 2:4 (1977), pp. 9-11, discusses interestingly the contrast Conrad makes between Willems' temple which "is openly dedicated to himself," and Almayer's. Almayer appears to worship at the shrine of his little daughter, but "the real idol in the shrine that Almayer's idealization makes out of his daughter's cot is Almayer himself."

10   Moser, p. 56.

11   *Conrad the Novelist* (Cambridge: Harvard University Press, 1958), pp. 81, 180.

CONRAD'S "AN OUTPOST OF PROGRESS" OR, THE EVIL SPIRIT OF CIVILIZATION

J.C. Hilson and D. Timms

I

"An Outpost of Progress" is the lightest part of the loot I carried off from Central Africa, the main portion being of course "The Heart of Darkness".[1]

It may be that Conrad's well-known statement about his two African tales has misled his critics, for many have alleged that "An Outpost of Progress" is merely a preliminary sketch for the later and more considerable work, and that it may be valued only as such. J. I. M. Stewart's remarks may be quoted as a typical response to the story:

> Technically, "An Outpost of Progress" is an immature story. The initial situation is stated rather than dramatized, and the conclusion is huddled and melodramatic. Yet the generalized account of Kayerts, Carlier and their plight is full of point. . . "Heart of Darkness", in fact, is a reworking of the theme of "An Outpost of Progress", with incomparably enhanced power . . . In "An Outpost of Progress" too much of the wider significance of the fable is established for us merely in an authorial commentary: what the story "says" is not adequately conveyed as a direct reverberation of the presented facts.[2]

Even A. T. Tolley, its most sympathetic critic, ultimately considers that, compared with *Heart of Darkness*, the tale is "undeniably inferior" and "shows the sort of thing that could be achieved by treating 'head-on' the theme of going to pieces in the jungle."[3]

In both African tales, Conrad is far more interested in what happened to the whites in the Congo than in what happened to the blacks. In *Heart of Darkness,* he deals with the effects of Africa on a talented white man, but, in the earlier story, what interests him is the effect of the Company, and the "Progress" and "Civilization" it represents, on the white men who work for it. In fact, Conrad's original title for "An Outpost of Progress" was "A Victim of Progress". Kurtz believes he can immerse himself in Africa for his own purposes, but to his "horror" finds that he has become part of the society he exploits. Initially, though, he is in his ideals and talents the personification of the bogus ethic that the

107

Company presents to the world. Kayerts and Carlier are quite the reverse of Kurtz in character and accomplishments, and suffer in a different way. "Progress" victimizes Kayerts and Carlier, not the heart of darkness. The psychological effects and symbolic value of Africa are largely outside Conrad's terms of reference in "An Outpost of Progress": to make a preliminary simplification, his main purpose in this story is social comment.

"An Outpost of Progress" is about two ineffectual and rather stupid white men who are left in charge of a rundown, useless trading post by the Managing Director of a large trading company. The only other inhabitants are a negro clerk, Makola (who likes to call himself Henry Price), his family, and ten negro workers. The white men run the post in a haphazard way, trading for food and a little ivory with the local natives. But their routine is upset when by the machinations of Makola the ten negro workers are sold to some itinerant slave-dealers for ivory. Though Kayerts and Carlier are at first appalled, they gradually ease their consciences by blaming Makola entirely, and by telling themselves that the thing is done and they must make the best of it. The local natives, having lost a few men themselves to the slave-traders, fear lest more of their number may be taken, and stay away from the trading post, so that trade dries up completely. The white men's supply of food consequently fails. Their companionship is strained, until, in a quarrel that starts from a very petty beginning, one of the men is accidently shot in the confusion of a ludicrous chase round their hut. The following morning, the Managing Director, who has been delayed two months beyond his promised return, arrives at the station. He finds that Kayerts has hanged himself from the cross on the grave of the previous station chief.

That the themes of "An Outpost of Progress" differ from those of *Heart of Darkness* should be clear from our analysis of the earlier tale below. Moreover, its techniques are more complex and consistent than, say, J. I. M. Stewart would have us believe. The themes of "An Outpost of Progress", we shall suggest, are established by certain aspects of its internal organization — by what we are shown as much as by what we are told — and by the ironic ambiguity surrounding certain phrases and concepts.

II

While he was stationed at Kinshasa in the Congo, Conrad wrote to his aunt: "Truly, while reading your dear letters, I forget Africa, the Congo, the black savages and white slaves (of whom I am one) who inhabit it".[4] That paradoxical phrase "white slaves" condenses the point of "An Outpost of Progress". The story is explicitly about slavery, black *and* white: Kayerts and Carlier are slaves as well as slave-dealers, victims as well as pioneers. Ultimately, "An Outpost of Progress" is an attack, written with "bitterness" and "indignation", on what Conrad himself called "masquerading philanthropy."[5]

The full measure of the attack on "masquerading philanthropy" and the depth of Conrad's feelings are established in the tale partly through the ironically

pitying tone of the narrator's commentary. More importantly, though, Conrad
carefully weaves into the fabric of the story a pattern of parallels and correspon-
dences which make his point dramatically. There are similarities, for instance,
between Kayerts and Carlier and the negro station-hands who are later sold into
slavery by Makola. The structure of the tale emphasises this. Part I begins with a
description of Kayerts and Carlier and their arrival at the station: Part II with an
account of the negro workers and *their* advent.[6] This structural link is strengthened
by verbal parallels. Kayerts and Carlier and the ten natives are unhappy exiles
from home: Kayerts "regretted the streets, the pavements, the cafes, his friends
of many years; all the things he used to see, day after day" (91), and Carlier
"regretted the clink of sabre and spurs on a fine afternoon, the barrack-room
witticisms, the girls of garrison towns" (92). The negroes also have their regrets:
"They were not happy, regretting the festive incantations, the sorceries, the
human sacrifices of their own land: where they also had parents, brothers, sisters,
admired chiefs, respected magicians, loved friends, and other ties supposed
generally to be human" (100). Carlier, we are told, was a non-commissioned
officer of cavalry "in an army guaranteed from harm by several European
Powers" (88) — an army, in other words, that no longer functioned as a fighting
force. Similarly, the negro workers are enfeebled warriors. They "had lost their
splendid physiques", partly because the rice-rations on which they are fed by the
Company do not agree with them (100-101). Later, Kayerts and Carlier are
reduced to a diet of "rice boiled without salt" (109), and this is an important factor
in their mental and physical decline.

In their treatment by the Company, too, white men and black are alike.
Kayerts and Carlier have been told that their stay at the station will be six months,
but they are left much longer, because the Director has more important things
to do. Again, the case of the natives provides an ironic counterpoint. They too had
been hired for six months, but had now "been serving the cause of progress for
upwards of two years" (100). The tasks they are set are much the same, and both
white and black perform them incompetently. The Director tells Kayerts "to plant
a vegetable garden, build new storehouses and fences, and construct a landing-
stage" (88); the negro workers "were mustered every morning and told off to
different tasks—grass-cutting, fence-building, tree-felling, etc., etc." (101). And
just as the Director contemptuously and rightly assumes that none of the work he
has given Kayerts and Carlier will be done, so "no power on earth could induce
the negro workers to excute efficiently" their job (101).

More important than all these considerations, the white men and the
negroes are manipulated by two men who, though ostensibly unlike, serve the
same ends and employ the same means: Makola and the Managing Director of the
Great Trading Company. Makola, more than Kayerts and Carlier, is the real
representative of the Company at the station — a Director-surrogate. And as the
duality of his nature and actions suggests, he is the living symbol of the
ruthlessness and duplicity of the Company. That he survives and breeds while
white men die indicates that the continuity of the Company is invested in Makola

and his methods rather in the white men. He has two names: he insists that his name is Henry Price",[7] but the natives (for reasons which are, perhaps sinisterly, indeterminate) call him "Makola". He speaks English and French, and understands bookkeeping: he is apparently a "civilized nigger" (102). This, however, is a veneer, for Makola "cherished in his innermost heart the worship of evil spirits" (86). But the irony is that these aspects of Makola are not contradictory: they come together in his function as keeper of the station's storehouse. In this storehouse, where he "pretended to keep a correct account of beads, cotton cloth, brass wire and other trade goods it contained" (86), Makola "spent all his days"(97). The storehouse is a kind of temple, and is even called "the fetish" (93). Moreover, the narrator explains that it may have come by its name because it contains the "spirit of civilization" (93). The implication is clear. If the worshipper of evil spirits, Makola, haunts the storehouse, which contains the "spirit of civilization", then these spirits must be one and the same. And later, of course, the ivory received in exchange for the ten negro workers is laid before the storehouse. It is an offering to this ambivalent spirit. The identity between the evil spirits and the spirit of civilization is perhaps further reinforced by the fact that Gobila, whose seemingly naive thoughts about the white men are often accurate foreshadowings of their fate, thinks that "Evil Spirits. . . had taken possession of his white friends "(107).

Makola's actions point to the conclusion that the methods of civilization and the methods of savagery are also the same. When he first suggests to Kayerts and Carlier that they need more ivory, Makola invokes the name of the Director: "These workmen of ours are no good at all . . . Station in very bad order, sir. Director will growl. Better get a fine lot of ivory, then he say nothing" (101). Makola's attitude towards the negroes mirrors the Director's scornful unconcern for the fate of Kayerts and Carlier, and indicates a common aim — the acquisition of ivory by whatever means. Carlier shows his awareness of this when he says that the Director "has seen worse things done on the quiet" than the bartering of workers for ivory (109).

Doing things on the quiet is the feature of the "civilizing" system on which Conrad's indictment of "progress" focuses. The stability of this station, and by implication of the whole trading process in the Congo has presumably been maintained by hypocrisy, by covering up dubious methods and presenting to the world a philanthropic mask. And in the central incident of "An Outpost of Progress", Conrad supplies a kind of parable of the Company's Congo activities which demonstrates that their continuance depends upon such hypocrisy. Critics usually suggest that the absurd scramble round the hut is triggered by a dispute over a few lumps of sugar. However, although the sugar is one of the factors in the escalation of tension between the two men, it is not the *immediate* cause of the battle. We shall quote at length to show the full development of the quarrel:

"Let's have a decent cup of coffee for once. Bring out that sugar, Kayerts!"
"For the sick," muttered Kayerts, without looking up.
"For the sick," mocked Carlier. "Bosh!. . . Well! I am sick."

"You are no more sick than I am, and I go without," said Kayerts in a peaceful tone.

"Come! out with that sugar, you stingy old slave-dealer."

Kayerts looked up quickly. Carlier was smiling with marked insolence. And suddenly it seemed to Kayerts that he had never seen that man before. Who was he? He knew nothing about him. What was he capable of? There was a surprising flash of violent emotion within him, as if in the presence of something undreamt-of, dangerous, and final.

But he managed to pronounce with composure. "That joke is in very bad taste. Don't repeat it."

"Joke!" said Carlier, hitching himself forward on his seat. "I am hungry—I am sick — I don't joke! I hate hypocrites. You are a hypocrite. You are a slave-dealer. There's nothing but slave-dealers in this cursed country. I mean to have sugar in my coffee today, anyhow!"

"I forbid you to speak to me in that way," said Kayerts with a fair show of resolution.

"You! — What?" shouted Carlier, jumping up. Kayerts stood up also. "I am your chief," he began, trying to master the shakiness of his voice.

"What?" yelled the other. "Who's chief? There's no chief here. There's nothing here: there's nothing but you and I. Fetch the sugar — you pot-bellied ass."

"Hold your tongue. Go out of this room," screamed Kayerts. "I dismiss you — you scoundrel!" (110-111)

Kayerts can begin by denying Carlier's request for sugar "in a peaceful tone", and his composure cracks only when Carlier calls him a "slave-dealer". Carlier has here stated what, we would argue, is the kernel of the story. He attacks all those who come to Africa in search of profit, and the hypocrisy by which they conceal from themselves and the outside world the uncivilized methods of their "civilizing". But the stability of their relationship depends upon a tacit agreement to ignore the truth. Similarly, the fiction of the Company's civilizing mission can be maintained only if the truth about its trading methods is suppressed: as we note above, Carlier has also recognized that the Director has "seen worse things done on the quiet." In a sense, Carlier has to die because of his perceptiveness. All along, he has been sharper than his partner, penetrating the rhetoric of the Director's pep-talk, for instance, which had so impressed the naive Kayerts. His mistake is to give voice to his knowledge: in mentioning the unmentionable, Carlier has broken the circle of hypocrisy.

When Carlier is shot, Makola steps forward to fulfil his role as true representative of the hypocritical system by offering Kayerts help in concealing the circumstances of Carlier's death:

After meditating for a while, Makola said softly, pointing at the dead man who lay there with his right eye blown out —

"He died of fever". Kayerts looked at him with a stony stare.

"Yes", repeated Makola, thoughtfully, stepping over the corpse, "I think he died of fever." (114)

Since Makola suggests that "he died of fever" will be sufficient public explanation of Carlier's death, we might infer that there is something suspicious about the death of the station's first chief, who, it is reported, also died of fever. This suspicion is heightened by Makola's threatening comment when Kayerts rebukes him angrily over the sale of the negroes: "You very red, Mr. Kayerts. If you are so irritable in the sun, you will get fever and die — like the first chief!" (104). Makola advises Kayerts to "bury Carlier tomorrow" (114). But before that tomorrow arrives, Kayerts undergoes a series of psychic tremors in which he seems to decide alternately to acquiesce in the hyprocrisy and to recoil from it in horror. By morning he is utterly perplexed, and is still sitting with the corpse when he hears the whistle of the steamer carrying the Managing Director. He stumbles out into an early morning white fog, dense enough to conceal anything further away than a few feet. This symbolizes the moral atmosphere, the enveloping hypocrisy in which the victim of progress is lost, unable to see or move surely. Makola, of course, has no such disability: where Kayerts "groped his way", Makola "flitted by in the mist" (116), running to answer the steamer's whistle by ringing the bell which is effectively Kayerts's death knell. The Managing Director, when he lands, finds Kayerts hanging from a cross "irreverently. . . putting out a swollen tongue" at him (117). It was, of course, at the Director's instigation that the cross was erected over the grave of the previous station chief. Since Makola must have been left in charge before the new white men came, we may take it that the Director's orders were carried out through or by Makola. The "civilized nigger" and the savage civilizer have cooperated in making a gallows of the most potent symbol of civilization.

Why does Kayerts kill himself? This, surely, is at the heart of Conrad's condemnation of "progress". When he hears the whistle of the steamer, Kayerts follows its meaning:

> Progress was calling to Kayerts from the river. Progress and civilization and all the virtues. Society was calling to its accomplished child to come, to be taken care of, to be instructed, to be judged, to be condemned; it called to him to return to that rubbish heap from which he had wandered away, so that justice could be done.
> Kayerts heard and understood.(116)

This passage states the alternative to the course of action suggested by Makola. Kayerts can participate in the hypocrisy, or he can confess that he killed Carlier and return to civilization to face the consequences. But by so bringing things into the open, Kayerts will become liable to the "justice" of "civilization". He knows that even though Carlier was killed as the result of a grotesque accident, a hypocritical code will condemn him for having murdered an unarmed man.[8] And Conrad suggests the iniquity by means of another verbal parallel. For the phrase "taken care of" here recalls an earlier passage:

> Society, not from any tenderness, but because of its strange needs, had taken care of these two men, forbidding them all independent thought, all initiative, all departure from routine; and forbidding it under pain of death. (91)

Society does "take care of" Carlier and threatens to "take care of" Kayerts: what he hears and understands in the ship's whistle is that, whether he chooses to keep quiet about Carlier or to return to Europe and face civilization's justice, he will be perpetuating the hypocrisy. His suicide is an attempt to resolve a "choice of nightmares" similar to that which faces first Kurtz, then Marlow, in *Heart of Darkness,* an attempt to release himself from the victimization of "progress". But perhaps the final irony of all lies in the fact that the suicide itself will presumably enable the Director and Makola to treat Kayerts and Carlier in the same way as they treated the previous chief. They will be buried as having died of fever, and the circle of hypocrisy will remain intact. Perhaps this is the confirmation of Gobila's belief that Kayerts and Carlier are simply reincarnations of the previous station chief.

There *is* an existential irony in Kayerts's death, but this does not contradict the point made at the end of the first section of this paper. Professor C. B. Cox distinguishes between *two* motives for suicide in Conrad: suicide as a solution of a personal and social dilemma, and suicide as a response to a conviction that existence in a meaningless universe is absurd.[9] In "An Outpost of Progress", Conrad brings these together. Though Kayerts seems to understand, as we argue above, that his suicide is of the "social" type, by making him die as he does, Conrad dramatizes its existential implications, since the circumstances show that there is in fact nothing beyond the emptiness of society and civilization. Kayerts calls "Help! . . . My God!" (115), and is answered by the whistle of the steamer. Nonetheless, he stumbles through the fog, and calls again "in his ignorance" to an "invisible heaven" for help. Finally, he sees the shape of the cross and finds his way to it. It offers not salvation, but a piece of wood from which to hang himself. This takes us back to *Heart of Darkness*, of course, but we would suggest that where, in the later work, Conrad considers the existential void and sees the social one as an analogue of it, in "An Outpost of Progress" he sees the emptiness of civilization and implies a void beyond.

III

Conrad's own feelings about "An Outpost of Progress" were oddly confused. When he first wrote the story, he told Edward Garnett that he turned to it as a relief from writing *The Rescue* which was proving difficult.[10] But when Garnett sent his opinion of the story, Conrad recanted:

> You are right in your criticism of *Outpost.* The construction is bad. It was bad because it was a matter of conscious decision, and I have no discrimination — in artistic sense . . . Let me assure you that your remarks were a complete disclosure to me. I had not the slightest glimmer of my stupidity. I am now profoundly thankful to find I have enough sense to see the truth of what you say. It's very evident that the first 3 pages kill all the interest. And I wrote them of set purpose! I thought I was achieving artistic simplicity!!!!!![11]

In 1906, however, Conrad submitted the story to *The Grand Magazine,* for a series entitled "My Best Story and Why I think So". Not the least interesting feature of why Conrad thought so was that the reason offered was, more or less, the reason he had earlier given to Garnett for *disliking* it:

> This story, for which I confess a preference, was difficult to write, not because of what I had to write, but of what I had firmly made up my mind not to write into it. What I have done is done with. No words, no regrets can atone now for the imperfections. . . I remember perfectly well the inflexible and solemn resolve not to be led astray by my subject. I aimed at a scrupulous unity of tone, and it seems to me that I have attained it here.[12]

And only four years later came another *volte-face* when Conrad claimed that *Tales of Unrest*, in which "An Outpost of Progress" had been incorporated, was his least favourite work.[13]

At first sight, all of this might seem the perfect illustration of Lawrence's maxim "trust the tale, not the teller": but a closer scrutiny of Conrad's comments above reveals that teller and tale are essentially in harmony. For despite Conrad's inability to make up his mind over whether he *liked* "An Outpost of Progress" or not, about one thing he does seem to have been clear. He consistently saw in the tale a consciousness and directness of intent, and above all an effort to narrow its scope and keep its subject uncluttered. This is further corroborated by a statement he made in connection with *Heart of Darkness*: "It is a story as much as my *Outpost of Progress* was, but, so to speak, 'takes in' more — is a little wider — is less concentrated on individuals."[14] The insistence by Conrad's critics that the story is immature depends to a great extent on a point that we have tried to deny: that "An Outpost of Progress" is a lesser *Heart of Darkness,* inferior in lacking the symbolic suggestiveness of the later work. This implication itself rests on an *a priori* assumption that symbolic suggestiveness is superior to a more direct technique. This may be so, but it is nevertheless misleading to see the explicitness of "An Outpost of Progress" as the "essay-like explicitness" of A. J. Guerard's complaint.[15] Rather, it is that of a carefully shaped work of art, with a single purpose.

NOTES:

1   "Author's Note", *Tales of Unrest* (London, 1947), p. vii (This, and all subsequent page references, which will be given in parentheses within the text, are to the "Collected Edition" of Conrad's works, published by J.M. Dent & Sons, Ltd).

2 *Joseph Conrad* (London, 1968), pp. 75-77. See also Albert J. Guerard, *Conrad the Novelist* (Cambridge, Mass. and London, 1958), pp. 64-65; Norman Sherry, *Conrad's Western World* (Cambridge, 1971), pp. 125-132.

3 "Conrad's 'Favorite' Story", *Studies in Short Fiction*, III (1965), 319.

4 Letter to Marguerite Poradowska, 26 September, 1890. Quoted in *Heart of Darkness,* ed. Robert Kimbrough (Norton Critical Edition: New York, 1963), p. 120.

5 Letter to T. Fisher Unwin, 22 July, 1896. Quoted in Jocelyn Baines, *Joseph Conrad* (Harmondsworth, 1971), p. 218.

6 "An Outpost of Progress" was first published in two parts, in the issues of the magazine *Cosmopolis* for June and July, 1897, and the story retains this division in subsequent editions.

7 Other commentators have noted that Makola's alias is significant: cf. Edward W. Said, *Joseph Conrad and the Fiction of Autobiography* (Cambridge, Mass., 1966), p. 142.

8 Conrad clearly attached great significance to the fact that Carlier was unarmed: "I am sure you will understand the reason and meaning of every detail. . . the meaning of Carlier not being armed." (Letter to Edward Garnett, 22 July, 1896. *Letters from Joseph Conrad, 1895-1924* ed. Edward Garnett, Indianapolis, 1928), p. 62. Conrad's insistence on the importance of this detail is explained if, as we argue, the false justice of society should be seen as a central factor in Kayerts's dilemma.

9 "Joseph Conrad and the Question of Suicides," *Bulletin of the John Rylands Library;* LV (1973), pp. 285-299. It is certainly tempting to see in "An Outpost of Progress" a classically "absurd" situation. The word "absurd" itself occurs several times, and the tragicomic relationship between two inept characters — a Laurel and a Hardy — is much like that between Vladimir and Estragon in *Waiting for Godot.*

10 Letter to Edward Garnett, 5 August 1896, *Letters from Joseph Conrad*, p. 64.

11 Letter to Edward Garnett, 14 August, 1896, ibid., p. 66.

12 Quoted by A. T. Tolley, op. cit., p. 314.

13   See A. T. Tolley, op. cit., p. 315.

14   Letter to William Blackwood, 31 December, 1898. Quoted in Kimbrough, op. cit., pp. 129-130.

15   Op. cit., p. 64.

III. Colonial Legacy: Black and White

AN IMAGE OF AFRICA

Chinua Achebe

It was a fine autumn morning at the beginning of this academic year such as encouraged friendliness to passing strangers. Brisk youngsters were hurrying in all directions, many of them obviously freshmen in their first flush of enthusiasm. An older man, going the same way as I, turned and remarked to me how very young they came these days. I agreed. Then he asked me if I was a student too. I said no, I was a teacher. What did I teach? African literature. Now that was funny, he said, because he never had thought of Africa as having that kind of stuff, you know. By this time I was walking much faster. "Oh well," I heard him say finally, behind me, "I guess I have to take your course to find out."

A few weeks later I received two very touching letters from high school children in Yonkers, New York, who—bless their teacher—had just read *Things Fall Apart*. One of them was particularly happy to learn about the customs and superstitions of an African tribe.

I propose to draw from these rather trivial encounters rather heavy conclusions which at first sight might seem somewhat out of proportion to them: but only at first sight.

The young fellow from Yonkers, perhaps partly on account of his age but I believe also for much deeper and more serious reasons, is obviously unaware that the life of his own tribesmen in Yonkers, New York, is full of odd customs and superstitions and, like everybody else in his culture, imagines that he needs a trip to Africa to encounter those things.

The other person being fully my own age could not be excused on the grounds of his years. Ignorance might be a more likely reason, but here again I believe that something more willful than a mere lack of information was at work. For did not that erudite British historian and Regius Professor at Oxford, Hugh Trevor Roper, pronounce a few years ago that African history did not exist?

If there is something in these utterances more than youthful inexperience, more than a lack of factual knowledge, what is it? Quite simply it is the desire—one might indeed say the need—in Western psychology to set Africa up as a foil in Europe, a place of negations at once remote and vaguely familiar in comparison with which Europe's own state of spiritual grace will be manifest.

This need is not new: which should relieve us of considerable responsibility and perhaps make us even willing to look at this phenomenon dispassionately. I have neither the desire nor, indeed, the competence to do so with the tools of the

119

social and biological sciences. But, I can respond, as a novelist, to one famous book of European fiction, Joseph Conrad's *Heart of Darkness*, which better than any other work I know displays that Western desire and need which I have just spoken about. Of course, there are whole libraries of books devoted to the same purpose, but most of them are so obvious and so crude that few people worry about them today. Conrad, on the other hand, is undoubtedly one of the great stylists of modern fiction and a good storyteller into the bargain. His contribution therefore falls automatically into a different class—permanent literature—read and taught and constantly evaluated by serious academics. *Heart of Darkness* is indeed so secure today that a leading Conrad scholar has numbered it "among the half-dozen greatest short novels in the English language."[1] I will return to this critical option in due course because it may seriously modify my earlier suppositions about who may or may not be guilty in the things of which I will now speak.

Heart of Darkness projects the image of Africa as "the other world," the antithesis of Europe and therefore of civilization, a place where a man's vaunted intelligence and refinement are finally mocked by triumphant bestiality. The book opens on the River Thames, tranquil, resting peacefully "at the decline of day after ages of good service done to the race that peopled its banks." But the actual story takes place on the River Congo, the very antithesis of the Thames. The River Congo is quite decidedly not a River Emeritus. It has rendered no service and enjoys no old-age pension. We are told that "going up that river was like travelling back to the earliest beginning of the world."

Is Conrad saying then that these two rivers are very different, one good, the other bad? Yes, but that is not the real point. What actually worries Conrad is the lurking hint of kinship, of common ancestry. For the Thames, too, "has been one of the dark places of the earth." It conquered its darkness, of course, and is now at peace. But if it were to visit its primordial relative, the Congo, it would run the terrible risk of hearing grotesque, suggestive echoes of its own forgotten darkness, and of falling victim to an avenging recrudescence of the mindless frenzy of the first beginnings.

I am not going to waste your time with examples of Conrad's famed evocation of the African atmosphere. In the final consideration it amounts to no more than a steady, ponderous, fake-ritualistic repetition of two sentences, one about silence and the other about frenzy. An example of the former is "It was the stillness of an implacable force brooding over an inscrutable intention" and of the latter, "The steamer toiled along slowly on the edge of a black and incomprehensible frenzy." Of course, there is a judicious change of adjective from time to time so that instead of "inscrutable," for example, you might have "unspeakable," etc., etc.

The eagle-eyed English critic, F. R. Leavis, drew attention nearly thirty years ago to Conrad's "adjectival insistence upon inexpressible and incomprehensible mystery." That insistence must not be dismissed lightly, as many Conrad critics have tended to do, as a mere stylistic flaw. For it raises serious questions of artistic good faith. When a writer, while pretending to record scenes, incidents and their impact, is in reality engaged in inducing hypnotic stupor in his readers through a bombardment of emotive words and other forms of trickery, much more has to be at stake than stylistic felicity. Generally, normal readers are well armed to detect and resist such underhand activity. But Conrad chose his subject well—one which was guaranteed not to put him in conflict with the psychological predisposition of his readers or raise the need for him to contend with their resistance. He chose the role of purveyor of comforting myths.

The most interesting and revealing passages in *Heart of Darkness* are, however, about people. I must quote a long passage from the middle of the story in which representatives of Europe in a steamer going down the Congo encounter the denizens of Africa:

> We were wanderers on a prehistoric earth, on an earth that wore the aspect of an unknown planet. We could have fancied ourselves the first of men taking possession of an accursed inheritance, to be subdued at the cost of profound anguish and of excessive toil. But suddenly, as we struggled round a bend, there would be a glimpse of rush walls, of peaked grass-roofs, a burst of yells, a whirl of black limbs, a mass of hands clapping, of feet stamping, of bodies swaying, of eyes rolling, under the droop of heavy and motionless foliage. The steamer toiled along slowly on the edge of a black and incomprehensible frenzy. The prehistoric man was cursing us, praying to us, welcoming us—who could tell? We were cut off from the comprehension of our surroundings; we glided past like phantoms, wondering and secretly appalled, as sane men would be before an enthusiastic outbreak in a madhouse. We could not remember because we were travelling in the night of first ages, of those ages that are gone, leaving hardly a sign—and no memories.
>
> The earth seemed unearthly. We are accustomed to look upon the shackled form of a conquered monster, but there—there you could look at a thing monstrous and free. It was unearthly, and the men were—No, they were not inhuman. Well, you know, that was the worst of it—this suspicion of their not being inhuman. It would come slowly to one. They howled and leaped, and spun, and made horrid faces; but what thrilled you was just the thought of your remote kinship with this wild and passionate uproar. Ugly. Yes, it was ugly enough; but if you were man enough you would admit to yourself that there was in you just the faintest trace of a response to the terrible frankness of that noise, a dim suspicion of there being a meaning in it which you—you so remote from the night of first ages—could comprehend.

Herein lies the meaning of *Heart of Darkness* and the fascination it holds over the Western mind: "What thrilled you was just the thought of their humanity—like yours. . . .Ugly."

Having shown us Africa in the mass, Conrad then zeros in on a specific example, giving us one of his rare descriptions of an African who is not just limbs or rolling eyes:

> And between whiles I had to look after the savage who was fireman. He was an improved specimen; he could fire up a vertical boiler. He was there below

me, and, upon my word, to look at him was as edifying as seeing a dog in a parody of breeches and a feather hat, walking on his hind legs. A few months of training had done for that really fine chap. He squinted at the steam gauge and at the water gauge with an evident effort of intrepidity—and he had filed his teeth, too, the poor devil, and the wool of his pate shaved into queer patterns, and three ornamental scars on each of his cheeks. He ought to have been clapping his hands and stamping his feet on the bank, instead of which he was hard at work, a thrall to strange witchcraft, full of improving knowledge.

As everybody knows, Conrad is a romantic on the side. He might not exactly admire savages clapping their hands and stamping their feet but they have at least the merit of being in their place, unlike this dog in a parody of breeches. For Conrad, things (and persons) being in their place is of the utmost importance.

Towards the end of the story, Conrad lavishes great attention quite unexpectedly on an African woman who has obviously been some kind of mistress to Mr. Kurtz and now presides (if I may be permitted a little imitation of Conrad) like a formidable mystery over the inexorable imminence of his departure:

> She was savage and superb, wild-eyed and magnificent. . . She stood looking at us without a stir and like the wilderness itself, with an air of brooding over an inscrutable purpose.

This Amazon is drawn in considerable detail, albeit of a predictable nature, for two reasons. First, she is in her place and so can win Conrad's special brand of approval; and second, she fulfills a structural requirement of the story; she is a savage counterpart to the refined, European woman with whom the story will end:

> She came forward, all in black with a pale head, floating towards me in the dusk. She was in mourning . . . . She took both my hands in hers and murmured, "I had heard you were coming" . . . She had a mature capacity for fidelity, for belief, for suffering.

The difference in the attitude of the novelist to these two women is conveyed in too many direct and subtle ways to need elaboration. But perhaps the most significant difference is the one implied in the author's bestowal of human expression to the one and the withholding of it from the other. It is clearly not part of Conrad's purpose to confer language on the "rudimentary souls" of Africa. They only "exchanged short grunting phrases" even among themselves but mostly they were too busy with their frenzy. There are two occasions in the book, however, when Conrad departs somewhat from his practice and confers speech, even English speech, on the savages. The first occurs when cannibalism gets the better of them:

> "Catch 'im," he snapped, with a bloodshot widening of his eyes and a flash of sharp white teeth—"catch 'im. Give 'im to us." "To you, eh?" I asked; "what would you do with them?" "Eat 'im!" he said curtly. . .

The other occasion in the famous announcement:

> Mistah Kurtz—he dead.

At first sight, these instances might be mistaken for unexpected acts of generosity from Conrad. In reality, they constitute some of his best assaults. In the case of the cannibals, the incomprehensible grunts that had thus far served them for speech suddenly proved inadequate for Conrad's purpose of letting the European glimpse the unspeakable craving in their hearts. Weighing the necessity for consistency in the portrayal of the dumb brutes against the sensational advantages of securing their conviction by clear, unambiguous evidence issuing out of their own mouth, Conrad chose the latter. As for the announcement of Mr. Kurtz's death by the "insolent black head of the doorway," what better or more appropriate *finis* could be written to the horror story of that wayward child of civilization who willfully had given his soul to the powers of darkness and "taken a high seat amongst the devils of the land" than the proclamation of his physical death by the forces he had joined?

It might be contended, of course, that the attitude to the African in *Heart of Darkness* is not Conrad's but that of his fictional narrator, Marlow, and that far from endorsing it Conrad might indeed be holding it up to irony and criticism. Certainly, Conrad appears to go to considerable pains to set up layers of insulation between himself and the moral universe of his story. He has, for example, a narrator behind a narrator. The primary narrator is Marlow but his account is given to us through the filter of a second, shadowy person. But if Conrad's intention is to draw a *cordon sanitaire* between himself and the moral and psychological malaise of his narrator, his care seems to me totally wasted because he neglects to hint however subtly or tentatively at an alternative frame of reference by which we may judge the actions and opinions of his characters. It would not have been beyond Conrad's power to make that provision if he had thought it necessary. Marlow seems to me to enjoy Conrad's complete confidence— a feeling reinforced by the close similarities between their careers.

Marlow comes through to us not only as a witness of truth, but one holding those advanced and humane views appropriate to the English liberal tradition which required all Englishmen of decency to be deeply shocked by atrocities in Bulgaria or the Congo of King Leopold of the Belgians or wherever. Thus Marlow is able to toss out such bleeding-heart sentiments as these:

> They were all dying slowly—it was very clear. They were not enemies, they were not criminals, they were nothing earthly now—nothing but black shadows of disease and starvation, lying confusedly in the greenish gloom. Brought from all the recesses of the coast in all the legality of time contracts, lost in uncongenial surroundings, fed on unfamiliar food, they sickened, became inefficient, and were then allowed to crawl away and rest.

The kind of liberalism espoused here by Marlow/Conrad touched all the best minds of the age in England, Europe, and America. It took different forms in the minds of different people but almost always managed to sidestep the ultimate question of equality between white people and black people. That extraordinary missionary, Albert Schweitzer, who sacrificed brilliant careers in music and theology in Europe for a life of service to Africans in much the same area as Conrad writes about, epitomizes the ambivalence. In a comment which I have often quoted but must quote one last time Schweitzer says: "The African is indeed my brother but my junior brother." And so he proceeded to build a hospital appropriate to the needs of junior brothers with standards of hygiene reminiscent of medical practice in the days before the germ theory of disease came into being. Naturally, he became a sensation in Europe and America. Pilgrims flocked, and I believe still flock even after he has passed on, to witness the prodigious miracle in Lamberene, on the edge of the primeval forest.

Conrad's liberalism would not take him quite as far as Schweitzer's, though. He would not use the word "brother" however qualified; the farthest he would go was "kinship." When Marlow's African helmsman falls down with a spear in his heart he gives his white master one final disquieting look.

> And the intimate profundity of that look he gave me when he received his hurt remains to this day in my memory—like a claim of distant kinship affirmed in a supreme moment.

It is important to note that Conrad, careful as ever with his words, is not talking so much about *distant kinship* as about someone *laying a claim* on it. The black man lays a claim on the white man which is well-nigh intolerable. It is the laying of this claim which frightens and at the same time fascinates Conrad, ". . . the thought of their humanity—like yours . . . Ugly."

The point of my observations should be quite clear by now, namely, that Conrad was a bloody racist. That this simple truth is glossed over in criticism of his work is due to the fact that white racism against Africa is such a normal way of thinking that its manifestations go completely undetected. Students of *Heart of Darkness* will often tell you that Conrad is concerned not so much with Africa as with the deterioration of one European mind caused by solitude and sickness. They will point out to you that Conrad is, if anything, less charitable to the Europeans in the story than he is to the natives. A Conrad student told me in Scotland last year that Africa is merely a setting for the disintegration of the mind of Mr. Kurtz.

Which is partly the point: Africa as setting and backdrop which eliminates the African as human factor. Africa as a metaphysical battlefield devoid of all recognizable humanity, into which the wandering European enters at his peril. Of course, there is a preposterous and perverse kind of arrogance in thus reducing Africa to the role of props for the breakup of one petty European mind. But that is not even the point. The real question is the dehumanization of Africa and

Africans which this age-long attitude has fostered and continues to foster in the world. And the question is whether a novel which celebrates this dehumanization, which depersonalizes a portion of the human race, can be called a great work of art. My answer is: No, it cannot. I would not call the man an artist, for example, who composes an eloquent instigation to one people to fall upon another and destroy them. No matter how striking his imagery or how beautiful his cadences fall such a man is no more a great artist than another may be called a priest who reads the mass backwards or a physician who poisons his patients. All those men in Nazi Germany who lent their talent to the service of virulent racism whether in science, philosophy or the arts have generally and rightly been condemned for their perversions. The time is long overdue for taking a hard look at the work of creative artists who apply their talents, alas often considerable as in the case of Conrad, to set people against people. This, I take it, is what Yevtushenko is after when he tells us that a poet cannot be a slave trader at the same time, and gives the striking example of Arthur Rimbaud who was fortunately honest enough to give up any pretenses to poetry when he opted for slave trading. For poetry surely can only be on the side of man's deliverance and not his enslavement; for the brotherhood and unity of all mankind and against the doctrines of Hitler's master races or Conrad's "rudimentary souls."

Last year was the 50th anniversary of Conrad's death. He was born in 1857, the very year in which the first Anglican missionaries were arriving among my own people in Nigeria. It was certainly not his fault that he lived his life at a time when the reputation of the black man was at a particularly low level. But even after due allowances have been made for all the influences of contemporary prejudice on his sensibility, there remains still in Conrad's attitude a residue of antipathy to black people which his peculiar psychology alone can explain. His own account of his first encounter with a black man is very revealing:

> A certain enormous buck nigger encountered in Haiti fixed my conception of
> blind, furious, unreasoning rage, as manifested in the human animal to the end
> of my days. Of the nigger I used to dream for years afterwards.

Certainly, Conrad had a problem with niggers. His inordinate love of that word itself should be of interest to psychoanalysts. Sometimes his fixation on blackness is equally interesting as when he gives us this brief description:

> A black figure stood up, strode on long black legs, waving long black arms.[2]

as though we might expect a black figure striding along on black legs to have *white* arms! But so unrelenting is Conrad's obsession.

As a matter of interest Conrad gives us in *A Personal Record* what amounts to a companion piece to the buck nigger of Haiti. At the age of sixteen Conrad encountered his first Englishman in Europe. He calls him "my unforgettable Englishman" and describes him in the following manner:

[his] calves exposed to the public gaze . . . dazzled the beholder by the
splendor of their marble-like condition and their rich tone of young ivory . . .
The light of a headlong, exalted satisfaction with the world of men . . .
illumined his face . . . and triumphant eyes. In passing he cast a glance of
kindly curiosity and a friendly gleam of big, sound, shiny teeth . . . his white
calves twinkled sturdily.[3]

Irrational love and irrational hate jostling together in the heart of that tormented
man. But whereas irrational love may at worst engender foolish acts of
indiscretion, irrational hate can endanger the life of the community. Naturally,
Conrad is a dream for psychoanalytic critics. Perhaps the most detailed study of
him in this direction is by Bernard C. Meyer, M.D. In this lengthy book, Dr.
Meyer follows every conceivable lead (and sometimes inconceivable ones) to
explain Conrad. As an example, he gives us long disquisitions on the significance
of hair and hair-cutting in Conrad. And yet not even one word is spared for his
attitude to black people. Not even the discussion of Conrad's antisemitism was
enough to spark off in Dr. Meyer's mind those other dark and explosive thoughts.
Which only leads one to surmise that Western psychoanalysts must regard the
kind of racism displayed by Conrad as absolutely normal despite the profoundly
important work done by Frantz Fanon in the psychiatric hospitals of French
Algeria.

Whatever Conrad's problems were, you might say he is now safely dead.
Quite true. Unfortunately, his heart of darkness plagues us still. Which is why an
offensive and totally deplorable book can be described by a serious scholar as
"among the half dozen greatest short novels in the English language," and why it
is today perhaps the most commonly prescribed novel in the twentieth-century
literature courses in our own English Department here. Indeed the time is long
overdue for a hard look at things.

There are two probable grounds on which what I have said so far may be
contested. The first is that it is no concern of fiction to please people about whom it
is written. I will go along with that. But I am not talking about pleasing people. I am
talking about a book which parades in the most vulgar fashion prejudices and
insults from which a section of mankind has suffered untold agonies and atrocities
in the past and continues to do so in many ways and many places today. I am
talking about a story in which the very humanity of black people is called in
question. It seems to me totally inconceivable that great art or even good art could
possibly reside in such unwholesome surroundings.

Secondly, I may be challenged on the grounds of actuality. Conrad, after all,
sailed down the Congo in 1890 when my own father was still a babe in arms, and
recorded what he saw. How could I stand up in 1975, fifty years after his death
and purport to contradict him? My answer is that as a sensible man I will not
accept just any traveller's tales solely on the grounds that I have not made the
journey myself. I will not trust the evidence even of a man's very eyes when I
suspect them to be as jaundiced as Conrad's. And we also happen to know that

Conrad was, in the words of his biographer, Bernard C. Meyer, "notoriously inaccurate in the rendering of his own history."[4]

But more important by far is the abundant testimony about Conrad's savages which we could gather if we were so inclined from other sources and which might lead us to think that these people must have had other occupations besides merging into the evil forest or materializing out of it simply to plague Marlow and his dispirited band. For as it happened, soon after Conrad had written his book an event of far greater consequence was taking place in the art world of Europe. This is how Frank Willett, a British art historian, describes it:

> Gaugin had gone to Tahiti, the most extravagant individual act of turning to a non-European culture in the decades immediately before and after 1900, when European artists were avid for new artistic experiences, but it was only about 1904-05 that African art began to make its distinctive impact. One piece is still identifiable; it is a mask that had been given to Maurice Vlaminck in 1905. He records that Derain was "speechless" and "stunned" when he saw it, bought it from Vlaminck and in turn showed it to Picasso and Matisse, who were also greatly affected by it. Ambroise Vollard then borrowed it and had it cast in bronze. . . The revolution of twentieth century art was under way![5]

The mask in question was made by other savages living just north of Conrad's River Congo. They have a name, the Fang people, and are without a doubt among the world's greatest masters of the sculptured form. As you might have guessed, the event to which Frank Willett refers marked the beginning of cubism and the infusion of new life into European art that had run completely out of strength.

The point of all this is to suggest that Conrad's picture of the people of the Congo seems grossly inadequate even at the height of their subjection to the ravages of King Leopold's International Association for the Civilization of Central Africa. Travellers with closed minds can tell us little except about themselves. But even those not blinkered, like Conrad, with xenophobia, can be astonishingly blind.

Let me digress a little here. One of the greatest and most intrepid travellers of all time, Marco Polo, journeyed to the Far East from the Mediterranean in the thirteenth century and spent twenty years in the court of Kublai Khan in China. On his return to Venice he set down in his book entitled *Description of the World* his impressions of the peoples and places and customs he had seen. There are at least two extraordinary omissions in his account. He says nothing about the art of printing unknown as yet in Europe but in full flower in China. He either did not notice it at all or if he did, failed to see what use Europe could possibly have for it. Whatever reason, Europe had to wait another hundred years for Gutenberg. But even more spectacular was Marco Polo's omission of any reference to the Great Wall of China nearly 4000 miles long and already more than 1000 years old at the time of his visit. Again, he may not have seen it; but the Great Wall of China is the only structure built by man which is visible from the moon![6] Indeed, travellers can be blind.

As I said earlier, Conrad did not originate the image of Africa which we find in his book. It was and is the dominant image of Africa in the Western imagination and Conrad merely brought the peculiar gifts of his own mind to bear on it. For reasons which can certainly use close psychological inquiry, the West seems to suffer deep anxieties about the precariousness of its civilization and to have a need for constant reassurance by comparing it with Africa. If Europe, advancing in civilization, could cast a backward glance periodically at Africa trapped in primordial barbarity, it could say with faith and feeling: There go I but for the grace of God. Africa is to Europe as the picture is to Dorian Gray—a carrier onto whom the master unloads his physical and moral deformities so that he may go forward, erect and immaculate. Consequently, Africa is something to be avoided just as the picture has to be hidden away to safeguard the man's jeopardous integrity. Keep away from Africa, or else! Mr. Kurtz of *Heart of Darkness* should have heeded that warning and the prowling horror in his heart would have kept its place, chained to its lair. But he foolishly exposed himself to the wild irresistible allure of the jungle and lo! the darkness found him out.

In my original conception of this talk I had thought to conclude it nicely on an appropriately positive note in which I would suggest from my privileged position in African and Western culture some advantages the West might derive from Africa once it rid its mind of old prejudices and began to look at Africa not through a haze of distortions and cheap mystification but quite simply as a continent of people—not angels, but not rudimentary souls either—just people, often highly gifted people and often strikingly successful in their enterprise with life and society. But as I thought more about the stereotype image, about its grip and pervasiveness, about the willful tenacity with which the West holds it to its heart; when I thought of your television and the cinema and newspapers, about books read in schools and out of school, of churches preaching to empty pews about the need to send help to the heathen in Africa, I realized that no easy optimism was possible. And there is something totally wrong in offering bribes to the West in return for its good opinion of Africa. Ultimately, the abandonment of unwholesome thoughts must be its own and only reward. Although I have used the word *willful* a few times in this talk to characterize the West's view of Africa it may well be that what is happening at this stage is more akin to reflex action than calculated malice. Which does not make the situation more, but less, hopeful. Let me give you one last and really minor example of what I mean.

Last November the *Christian Science Monitor* carried an interesting article written by its Education Editor on the serious psychological and learning problems faced by little children who speak one language at home and then go to school where something else is spoken. It was a wide-ranging article taking in Spanish-speaking children in this country, the children of migrant Italian workers in Germany, the quadrilingual phenomenon in Malaysia and so on. And all this while the article speaks unequivocally about *language*. But then out of the blue sky comes this:

In London there is an enormous immigration of children who speak Indian or Nigerian dialects, or some other native language.[7]

I believe that the introduction of *dialects,* which is technically erroneous in the context, is almost a reflex action caused by an instinctive desire of the writer to downgrade the discussion to the level of Africa and India. And this is quite comparable to Conrad's withholding of language from his rudimentary souls. Language is too grand for these chaps; let's give them dialects. In all this business a lot of violence is inevitably done to words and their meaning. Look at the phrase "native language" in the above excerpt. Surely the only native language possible in London is Cockney English. But our writer obviously means something else—something Indians and Africans speak.

Perhaps a change will come. Perhaps this is the time when it can begin, when the high optimism engendered by the breathtaking achievements of Western science and industry is giving way to doubt and even confusion. There is just the possibility that Western man may begin to look seriously at the achievements of other people. I read in the papers the other day a suggestion that what America needs at this time is somehow to bring back the extended family. And I saw in my mind's eye future African Peace Corps Volunteers coming to help you set up the system.

Seriously, although the work which needs to be done may appear too daunting, I believe that it is not one day too soon to begin. And where better than at a University?

NOTES:

1   Albert J. Guerard, Introduction to *Heart of Darkness* (New York: New American Library, 1950), p. 9.

2   Jonah Raskin, *The Mythology of Imperialism* (New York: Random House, 1971), p. 143.

3   Bernard C. Meyer, M.D., *Joseph Conrad: A Psychoanalytic Biography* (Princeton, N.J.: Princeton University Press, 1967), p. 30.

4   *Ibid.,* p. 30.

5   Frank Willett, *African Art* (New York: Praeger, 1971), pp. 35-36.

6   About the omission of the Great Wall of China I am indebted to *The Journey of Marco Polo* as recreated by artist Michael Foreman, published by *Pegasus* Magazine, 1974.

7   *Christian Science Monitor,* Nov. 25, 1974, p. 11.

CONRAD'S NIGGER

Michael Echeruo

André Gide tells us that on his third visit to the Congo Rapids, he was able to cross one of the branches of the River Djou and come 'right up to the banks of the big river', where

> the height of the waves and the impetuosity of the current can be seen particularly well. The sky set its serene and radiant seal upon a spectacle that was more majestic than romantic. From time to time an eddy churns up the water; a jet of foam leaps up. There is no rhythm; and I cannot understand these irregularities in the current.[1]

When one of the guests remarked that it was incredible that 'a spectacle like this is still without its painter', Gide's reaction is an unspoken entry in his diary.

> This is an invitation to which I shall not respond. The quality of temperance is an essential one in art, and enormity is repugnant to it. A description is none the more moving because ten is put instead of one ... it is a common mistake to suppose that the sublimity of a picture depends on the enormity of its subject.[2]

Since Gide dedicated his *Travels* to Conrad, it is hardly surprising that this spectacle should remind him of his fellow-traveller of the Congo. But in this particular instance, Gide was thinking, not of Conrad's *Heart of Darkness*, but of *Typhoon,* a novel in which, according to him, Conrad seems to 'have done admirably in cutting short his story just on the threshold of the horrible and in giving the reader's imagination full play, after having led him to a degree of dreadfulness that seemed impossible.'[3] The compliment is important, because the restraint which Gide commends is one which a writer is hardly ever able to achieve when his subject is exo-cultural; when, that is, the audience has a strong culturally-derived attitude to the fictional subject. Hence in spite of himself, Gide loses that 'quality of restraint' in dealing with the 'mysterious' and 'exotic' world of Africa which he had commended in the Conrad of *Typhoon.* He writes:

> I have plunged into this journey like Curtius into the gulf; [a journey] imposed upon me by a sort of ineluctable fatality ... what joy to find oneself among Negroes!. . . On the wharf a swarm of Negroes hurry about like black ants, pushing trucks before them ... naked Negroes run about, shouting, laughing,

131

> quarreling, and showing their cannibal teeth . . . they will be brought back
> again on the return voyage. Admirable men for the most part but we shall only
> see them again with their clothes on.

And: "The natives' *indiscretion* can no doubt be explained by their *want of reserve:* one offers them a cigarette — they take the whole packet; a cake on a dish and they take the whole dish."[4]

In the same breath, Gide speaks of the 'rapture' with which he reread La Fontaine's fables. 'I can hardly think of a single quality he does not possess . . . his touch is often so slight and so delicate. He is a miracle of culture.'[5] Such delicacy would have been inappropriate to a subject as alien as the Congo. Hence Gide finds himself in the absurdly ironic situation in which to lack restraint and to be indelicate is to be cultured.

A similar lack of restraint is evident in Conrad's *The Nigger of the 'Narcissus'*, a novel that deals with an exo-cultural character. In the novels that preceded *The Nigger of the 'Narcissus'*, Conrad counted too much on the evocative language of his fiction to establish both the facts of his story and the emotional attitude he expected his audience to attach to these situations. In *Almayer's Folly,* for instance, Conrad's adjectives, as Newhouse says, 'insist too protestingly and the highly artificial rhythm strains too much'.[6] H. G. Wells drew attention to the same problem in his review of *An Outcast:* 'Mr. Conrad is wordy. He has still to learn the great half of his art, the art of leaving things unwritten.'[7] The triumph of the *Typhoon* from this point of view is, as Gide has mentioned, in Conrad's reticence; his realisation that a description is not the more impressive because 'ten is put instead of one'. Moreover, Conrad depended on the exotic setting of his novels and the unique experiences of his characters for the success of his fiction. In situations, therefore, where exaggeration and novelty are only partially appropriate, Conrad's prose gives the definite impression of straining hard at producing an effect; the emotions intended by the language of his work do not in any way correspond to those proposed by the author. In other situations, such as that of *The Nigger of the 'Narcissus'*, though the prose is the same, the strain is thought not to exist because the subject is exo-cultural.

In his review of recent approaches to the interpretation of Conrad's *The Nigger of the 'Narcissus'*, Ian Watt has condemned the tendency to read symbolic meanings into the character of James Wait, the Negro character of this novel. He does admit that Wait is a special kind of character whose 'portentous first appearance, and the way he later becomes the chief protagonist round whom the actions and the attitudes of the crew revolve . . . certainly justify our impulse to look for some hidden significance in him'.[8] What he objects to is the kind of symbol-hunting represented, for example, by the writings of Vernon Young and of James E. Miller who, in particular, claims that James Wait and the sea are 'symbols of death and life.'[9] Ian Watt says of this argument that it is a 'confessedly simplified paradigm'.

> Surely no one would have seized upon the particular pattern if he had not, in
> the first place, felt sure that there must be some such neat symbolic plot
> waiting to be discovered, and in the second, felt justified in giving decisive
> interpretative priority to a few selected details of character and incident which
> could be made to support it (p. 267).

Ian Watt similarly rejects Young's account, which, he says, 'reveals a very
Galahad of the symbol' (p. 268). Conrad's story, Watt contends, cannot be
schematised as if it were some allegorical drama.

Watt's argument is a theoretical one. It holds that the weakness in symbol-
hunting lies in the fact that the hunters are seeking what he terms *heterophoric*
rather than *homeophoric* symbols:

> The basic problem is to determine the kind of relationship between the literary
> symbol and its referent, between the narrative vehicle and its imputed larger
> tenor; most important, perhaps, are the distances between them and the basis
> on which the mutual rapport is ascribed. In the kind of interpretation I have
> been considering, the distance between the literary object and the symbolic
> meaning ascribed to it is rather great: and so I would describe making Wait a
> symbol of evil or Satan, an example of *heterophoric* interpretation, that
> is, it carries us to another meaning, it takes us beyond any demonstrable
> connection between the literary object and the symbolic meaning given to it
> (p. 272).

In so far, at least, as it concerns *The Nigger of the 'Narcissus'*, this distinction
is a very important but also a possibly misleading one. It warns us, rightly enough,
against too fanciful a reading of the novel. But it also seems to imply that Wait's
symbolic equivalent can be determined in the same way that, for example, we can
arrive at the symbolic function ᵒ ᶜShakespeare's Angelo, which is, in fact, not true.
The problem, for this novel and others like it, ought really to be stated in other
terms. For the difficulty is how to describe the reader's reaction to the presence of
the black hero without appearing to be imposing categories on the novel. In the
criticism of a Miracle or a Morality play, it is appropriate to speak of the symbols
of Vice and Grace, of Death and Salvation, of Devils and Angels. In those cases,
the form of the drama which operates outside the realm of character and
personality and concentrates on that of signification and idea, *requires* such an
approach. It is in this sense, after all, that these figures come to be thought of as
abstractions, and the modification of their form in characters like Shakespeare's
Angelo to be seen as symbolic. That is to say, we can talk of a character in a
morality play (or in plays that quite evidently exist under its inspiration) as being
symbolic, in both the *hetero-* and the *homeophoric* senses, without violence or
injustice to the true meaning of the work.

In *The Nigger of the 'Narcissus'*, however, the immediate physical reality
of Wait is so prominent that the search for a symbolic equivalent for his role leads
to two possibilities: Wait is either symbol enough in himself or we must find some
extravagant categories for aspects of an existing reality. Thus, when Harold E.

Davis says that Wait is 'equated with the devil, a "black idol", the prince of darkness, the tortured and dark areas of experience through which all men must pass to arrive at certainty',[10] we are not sure whether he means this as a symbolic analysis of the novel or is merely writing a metaphorical description of the literal experience of the story.

Watt calls a procedure such as Davis's a 'reductio ad symbolum' (p. 267). The rejection of this method should not, however, be combined with a refusal to deal with the fact that Conrad's treatment of Wait is, to say the least, unique. Ian Watt concedes that much, though he cites Conrad's antipathy to Melville, and Conrad's 1914 note 'To My Readers in America' to explain away the importance of this black hero. 'Conrad does not, in Melville's sense, believe in any absolute or transcendental "evil" and his Negro has not done any' (p. 270). Conrad's 1914 note categorically denies Wait: 'In the book (Wait) is nothing; he is merely the ship's collective psychology and the pivot of the action . . . .' The conclusion to draw from both of these comments — and Watt does not try to do so — is that Wait may well be a symbol in a more obvious and immediate sense than he or the symbol-hunters have imagined. This chapter seeks to explore this possibility, and thereby to redefine both the character of the black hero and the implications of the characterization not only for Conrad's readers but for his novel, too.

The problem can perhaps be seen from a better angle if, for a moment, we reflect on the function of Queequeg in Melville's *Moby Dick*. Whatever else he may be, Queequeg is offered as a very sharp contrast — in his person and his background — to the 'European'[11] and Christian part of the *Pequod* crew. He has a function essential to the theme and symbolic meaning of the novel. This function, however, is not arbitrary. It was not left absolutely to Melville to determine what it was to be; nor could it have been performed adequately by any of the regular American members of the crew. Moreover, Queequeg performs this function not in an individual capacity, as a person with experiences and attitudes all his own, but as a representative figure, a firm pagan counterpart to the Christian culture of the world of Melville and of the novel. We may, as readers, feel that we know Queequeg as well as we would ever want to. In fact, however, the individual, the inner man in Queequeg is not there; he is beyond us. What appears in Melville's novel is mainly an instrument of Melville's criticism. His racial features, the expectations of the reader, and the thwarting of those expectations — these are the character of his savage. In performing this role, then, Queequeg depends on his exo-cultural personality and background. In fact, much of the meaning of the novel depends on our appreciating that Ishmael ultimately finds more companionship and even brotherhood in that frightful-looking savage than in the world of civilised men which he rejected at the opening of the novel. Ishmael's first meeting with Queequeg is intended to established an initial *physical* revulsion on Ishmael's part from the man who later was to be his friend and saviour. Ishmael records this initial shock: "Good heavens! what a sight! Such a face! It was of a dark, purplish, yellow color, here and there stuck over with large, blackish looking squares."[12] Part of Ishmael's problem is one of ignorance:

> Ignorance is the parent of fear, and being completely nonplussed and confounded about the stranger, I confess I was as much afraid of him as if it was the devil himself who had thus broken into my room at the dead of night. In fact, I was so afraid of him that I was not game enough just then to address him, and demand a satisfactory answer concerning what seems inexplicable in him (p. 38).

What Ishmael in this ignorance imagines to be a devil's mask is in fact a man's face, Queequeg's *usual face*. That face was repulsive, first to Ishmael and subsequently, by a natural and reasonable extension, to Melville's readers. Or more exactly, Melville's readers would be expected to accept Ishmael's feelings of revulsion as justified. A critic could easily extract the comparison of Queequeg with the devil and construct from it a scheme of allegorical meanings. That would be particularly unnecessary if we realise that the comparison is not some ingenious discovery on Melville's part but a manner of words as naturally appropriate in European circles to Queequeg's appearance as calling a black man 'monkey' or, as in Elizabethan times, 'devil'. Melville is simply placing what turns out to be Queequeg's inner 'goodness' beside the 'devilishness' with which, on the basis of traditional associations, Queequeg is ordinarily connected. Queequeg can function satisfactorily as an ironic symbol of primitive goodness because Melville makes him the reversal of the obviously symbolic expectations of the audience from such a savage. Melville lets him operate essentially in a context in which he will constitute a permanent criticism of the civilised and hypocritical society of New England. In this sense, then, Watt is right in contrasting Melville's and Conrad's use of 'blackness' as symbol.

James Wait is in a similar predicament, though Conrad does not use him for the same fulfilment of any transcendental purposes similar to Melville's. Conrad presents his main character not as a *sick sailor* but as a *repulsive blackman*. Conrad plays on Wait's negroid features and (as it were) celebrates them to the point where they become not merely descriptions of the man, but an epitome of his nature. The man ceases, or rather, is subsumed in the Negro identity which Conrad has created for him. Wait is, thus, symbolic not in the ordinary sense that Conrad set him up to represent an abstract idea, but in the special sense that Conrad asserts a correspondence (Melville subverts this correspondence) between the imaginative predispositions of his European audience to this black sailor and his realised role in the novel. And, quite as importantly, Conrad does it by appearing to write entirely on the realistic plane. Where Melville treats the man as if he were a myth, Conrad treats the myth and the man as one.

Another comparison may be made, this time with Burns of Conrad's *The Shadow Line* who, like Wait, has been described as one of Conrad's 'Jonahs'. According to Frederick J. Masback 'both men appear . . . as an interruption of the established order and tranquility of the ship, causing a distinct sense of discomfort and even shock by their sudden appearance, and their surly and evasive attitude.'[13] Harold E. Davis comments: 'The pilgrimage scene is the basic pattern in the novel and it is this theme which is largely carried by the complex symbolism.

Into the world of the *Narcissus* comes Wait, a black, diseased fear, unknowable and thus more powerful, sowing dissension and violence.'[14] The comparisons with Burns and the reference to the pilgrimage theme are a hindrance rather than an aid to the understanding of the different roles which Wait and Burns play in the two novels. In the first place, of course, *The Nigger of the 'Narcissus'* is not concerned principally with the fact of a pilgrimage, although, in some sense, every sea journey which involves a struggle with the elements is a kind of pilgrimage. For another, Conrad does not characterise Wait and Burns in the same way. In *The Shadow Line*, Burns is an embittered man. As Conrad tells us, he had hoped to attain the mastership of the boat, but had been unfortunately disappointed in that hope. 'He took the ship to a point where he expected to be confirmed in his temporary command from lack of a qualified master to put over his head.'[15] We are not told this till late in the story, but we are expected to make use of this information in re-evaluating our impressions of him from the early scenes where we were made to feel that his malice is an irrational objection to the new captain. The captain had then complained of Burns' 'long, red moustache [which] determined the character of his physiognomy'. This physiognomy, he tells us, 'struck me as pugnacious in (strange to say) a ghastly sort of way' (p. 77). The qualifying parenthesis is an important clue to what Conrad intended us to feel about the narrator himself. It asks us to withhold our conclusion, and to accept that this physical appearance, 'the long, red moustache', did not have an intrinsic connection with pugnacious personality. The comparison is therefore a momentary, almost whimsical one, and Conrad saw that he could not depend exclusively on Burns' physiognomy for the establishment of his character. With Wait, as we shall see, the emphasis is different: his features had an intrinsic association.

Burns has also been described as 'repulsive', and this can be misleading if we do not pay close attention to how Conrad describes the man. Burns is more a man with hard and severe features than one who is, himself, replusive. 'His face in the full light of day appeared pale, meagre, even haggard. Somehow I had a delicacy as to looking too often at him; his eyes, on the contrary, remained fairly glued to my face. They were greenish and had an expectant expression' (p. 78). Even as he is about to die from sickness, Burns, though emaciated, is not despicable. Conrad does not describe him with any hints of revulsion. Instead he returns to the *facts* of his condition and to a repetition of his earlier comments on his character. Conrad thus refers to 'the preternatural sharpness of the ridge of his nose, the deep cavities of his temples'. 'He was so reduced that he would probably die very soon' (p. 136). In a final summing up of the man, Conrad tells us that Burns 'feared neither God, nor devil, nor man, nor wind, nor his own conscience. And I believe he hated everybody and everything. But I think he was afraid to die' (p. 138).

Burns, then, is a human being. His influence on the ship and on the captain can be established in terms of character and spiritual decadence. He is a temptation to the captain, who almost yields to Burns' fear that the spirit of the former captain, now dead, hovers over the ship, and that this spirit is really responsible for the dead calm. As he stumbles over Burns on all fours, the captain thinks he has seen the alleged ghost, 'that thing!' This fall is a symbolic act: a wind arises and the ship is on its way again.

Two points are worth noting here. The first is that though both Wait and Burns seem to call forth the storm and the calm plaguing their ships, the relationship of Burns to his story differs from that of Wait to his. James Wait has no personal history such as Burns has to account for his influence on the voyage. Burns is a tempter to the young captain; he is a positive character. Wait is not: his impact on the crew comes from the qualities with which the crew themselves invest him.

The other point is that Burns' story is a personal, even humane, story in a way that Wait's is not. We do not approve of Burns' moral position, but we understand why a man with his background can be thus deranged. His malady and his satanism have a human explanation. In *The Nigger of the 'Narcissus'*, Wait comes on board with his illness and his physical appearance, and both forces — the first augmenting the second — work the magic of his charm on the crew. Wait, as Conrad said, is nothing. He has no background, no being, no projected self. He is an enigma, a powerful portent. That portentous power derives from the combination in him of his negroid features, as these are seen by Conrad (or his fictional narrator), and the terror which is assumed to accompany these features.

It is the argument of this chapter, then, that the symbolic power of Wait's blackness is not a metaphorical construct but a kind of brutal fact to which Conrad draws attention in the story. In the characterisation of Burns (as well, incidentally, as in Melville's characterisation of Jackson in *Redburn*), the satanism of character is shown in terms of deformation of the body or face. Burns is haggard and skinny just before his death. Melville's Jackson had nothing left of him 'but the foul lees and dregs of a man; he was thin as a shadow; nothing but skin and bones; and sometimes used to complain that it hurt him to sit on the hard chests.'[16] In *The Nigger of the 'Narcissus'*, Wait is also sick and emaciated but his repulsive appearance is not described in terms of this condition, but of his racial appearance which his illness only heightens. Conrad makes this clear at the opening of the novel, when it is not a sickly but a *black* man that arrests the attention of the crew: 'The boy, amazed like the rest, raised the light to the man's face. It was black. A surprised hum — a faint hum that sounded like the suppressed mutter of the word "Nigger"— ran along the deck and escaped out into the night.'[17] In other words, the fact that Wait is a nigger had, in itself, a magical effect on the ship even before the crew came to know of his illness. Against this background of suppressed consternation, Conrad formally introduces James Wait as 'calm, cool, towering, superb'.

He overtopped the tallest by a half a head . . . The deep-ruling tones of his voice filled the deck without effort. He was naturally, scornfully, unaffectedly condescending, as if from his height of six foot three he had surveyed all the

vastness of human folly and had made up his mind not to be too hard on it . . .
he stood still surrounded by all these white men (pp. 34-5).

Conrad's tone here is difficult to determine since it is not clear whether he is
speaking as detached — and therefore impartial — observer, or as one of the
already excited crew. In the latter case, his comment would be a projection of his
fear. Whether, however, Conrad is being frank or ironic, the effect of the
description is to introduce Wait as the mighty and somewhat incongruous
opposite to the rest of the crew. In sum, Wait's power over the crew, hinted at in
their suppressed shudder on seeing his face, is paralleled by his physical tyranny
over them.

Having established these points, Conrad turns more carefully to the details
of Wait's physique, to the source of his power. Held up in the glare of a lamp,
Wait's head is seen as being: 'vigorously modelled into deep shadows and
shining lights—a head powerful and misshapen with a tormented and flattened
face — a face pathetic and brutal: the tragic, the mysterious, the repulsive mask of
a nigger's soul' (p.35).[18] The sentence says many things. Stylistically, it is a
tortured effort — notice the clausal breaks — to realise a difficult fact. More, the
sentence draws a sharp and very important contrast between the nigger's
appearance and his soul, though it does not say that this soul is any more pleasant
than the mask. At any rate, it is the 'mask', the appearance, that is described as
'repulsive'. This is no compliment to Wait, of course. But it does establish that
Conrad felt the distinction important, that he found in the negro features of Wait
the heart of his mystery. It is Wait's blackness and this includes his negroid
features in their natural, not their distorted, form, that is his chief 'attraction'. In
his colour and his features he carried almost all his magic.

Wait is inscrutable: 'You couldn't see that there was anything wrong with
him: a nigger doesn't show' (p. 51). His very presence seemed to be the antithesis
of light. When at one point in the story he comes on deck, he

> seemed to hasten the retreat of a departing light by his very presence; the
> setting sun dipped sharply as though fleeing before our nigger; a black mist
> emanated from him; a subtle and dismal influence; a something cold and
> gloomy that floated out and settled on all the faces like a mourning veil. The
> circle broke up. The joy of laughter died on stiffened lips. There was not a
> smile left among the ship's company. Not a word was spoken (p. 45).

Conrad returns to this comparison several times in the novel. In one passage
written obviously for effect but otherwise not an isolated purple passage, Conrad
recreates what beyond doubt was the exotic but weird attraction he found in
Wait's colour:

> When the light was put out, and through the door thrown wide open, Jimmy,
> turning on his pillow, could see vanishing beyond the straight line of top-
> gallant rail, the quick repeated visions of a fabulous world made up of leaping

fire and sleeping water. The lightning gleamed in his black face, and then
he would lie blinded and invisible in the midst of an intense darkness (p.89).

Because they are so conspicuous, these references to Wait's *colour* have been
extracted and fitted into ready categories by critics who only see his colour as
the abstract signal of symbolic meaning. Wait's physical appearance has not been
similarly taken into account, even though the text makes it clear that Conrad saw
Wait's physiognomy as another aspect of his Negro personality. Conrad
continually refers to Wait's eyes, for example, as 'bulging', 'startlingly prominent',
'staring', and rolling 'wildly'. Conrad does this with an insistence that makes it
evident that he is not referring to these eyes as an idiosyncratic feature of Wait's
but as a natural phenomenon — quite clearly non-European — which he finds
distracting and even disgusting. Apart from these eyes, Conrad also comments on
Wait's lips: 'The lower lip hung down, enormous and heavy' (p. 68). 'His heavy
lips protrude in an everlasting black pout' (p. 94). As Negro Wait had these
physical features of nose, cheeks and lips. Conrad (that is, the novel's narrator)
also found these features repulsive in themselves.

Wait's person is seen in sub-human terms. He is compared either to an animal
or to a corpse: 'There was an aspect astounding and animal-like in the perfection
of his expectant immobility — the unthinking stillness of a scared brute' (p. 98).
Or again: "He was becoming immaterial like an apparition; his checkbones rose,
the forehead slanted more; the face was all hollows, patches of shade; and the
fleshless head resembled a disinherited black skull, filled with two restless globes
of silver in the sockets of eyes. He was demoralizing' (p. 111). The same feeling
emerges when the crew try to rescue Wait: 'with concealing absurd gestures, like
a lot of drunken men embarrassed with a stolen corpse' they felt themselves
tottering together 'on the very brink of eternity' (p. 68). Conrad (as narrator) and
Donkin, alone, speak out their minds and call Wait 'a black-faced swine' (p. 52),
and 'the black brute' (p. 68). The others, though they share these sentiments, do
not try to express them. In their world, Wait is an uncomfortable companion, and
they are both scornful and frightened of him. Wait's strength comes from this
embarrassment on the part of the crew:

> They clustered around that moribund carcass, the fit emblem of their
> aspirations, and encouraging one another, they swayed, they tramped on one
> spot, shouting that they would not be put upon [p. 100]. Jimmy condescended
> to laugh. It cheered up everybody wonderfully [p. 91]. Had we (by an
> incredible hypothesis) undergone similar toil and trouble for an empty cask,
> that cask would have become as precious to us as Jimmy was. More precious,
> in fact, because we would have had no reason to hate the cask. And we hated
> James Wait [p. 69].

These contradictions in feeling are caused by the mysteriousness of Wait's
person, and his presence in their midst. Wait is a symbol, if we like, not in an
esoteric or technical sense, but in the obvious sense that he is virtually a devil

among them, an outsider, an occult creature, wearing a black and repulsive mask which the crew is necessarily incapable of piercing. They indeed admit that 'the man's a man if he is black' (p. 100). They nevertheless know that they cannot treat Wait either kindly or rudely, like one of themselves, without evident self-consciousness. As Conrad put it, it was as though they 'had been overcivilized, and rotten, and without any knowledge of the meaning of life. [They] had the air of being initiated in some infamous mysteries' (pp. 111-12).

It is quite clear here that Conrad is depending for this presentation of Wait on a long-standing tradition of associating the black man with the brute, and of equating physical with moral blackness. This is deducible from the fact that there are virtually no distinctions made in Conrad's narrative between literal descriptions of Wait and symbolic applications of his repugnant and demoralising personality. Moreover, Conrad is not using his references to Wait's malignity to confirm or supplement any traits of character which he had shown the hero to possess. Wait's magic is the magic of mere presence. In the vigour with which he describes Wait's impact on the crew, in the association of Wait with darkness, Conrad means us to see the 'demoralising' consequence of this presence. The moral decadence which Burns and Jackson introduce into the worlds of their novels comes from their history and their character. It is not a projection of the fears of the crew. Burns and Jackson are physically distorted as a consequence of their moral degeneracy: there is a kind of sympathetic logic. With Wait, the facts are otherwise. His natural features, described as exotic and repulsive, assume the proportions of sinister omens.

If, however, our comparison is between this novel and Conrad's *The Black Mate,* instead of between it and either *The Heart of Darkness* or *Benito Cereno,* we realize how unimportant for our analysis of the novel are those categories of symbols which do not spring from a recognition of Wait's natural repulsiveness. Published posthumously in *Tales of Hearsay*[19] but written about 1884, *The Black Mate* is essentially a typical Conrad story depending on mystery and ritual. It is in many ways a trite story, but that Conrad chose to write it, and to write it the way he did around a single embarrassment, is very revealing of some of his dispositions. The centre of the short novel is Bunter, the ship's mate. Bunter was apparently an exceptional sailor:

> [He] was noticeable to them in the street from a great distance; and when in the morning he strode down the jetty to his ship, the lumpers and the dock labourers rolling their bales and trundling the cases of cargo on their hand-trucks would remark to each other: Here's the black mate coming along (p. 85).

Bunter was not a black man, unfortunately. He only had black hair; 'absolutely black, black as a raven's wing' (p. 86). Conrad (or his narrator) objects very seriously to his appellation:

> That was the name [black mate] they gave him, being a gross lot who could
> have no appreciation of the man's dignified bearing. And to call him black was
> the superficial impression of the ignorant.
>   Of course, Mr. Bunter, the mate of the *Sapphire,* was not black. He
> was no more black than you or I, and not certainly as white as any chief mate
> of a ship in the whole of the port of London. . . . A man may have black hair
> without being a Dago (p. 86).

Conrad makes a distinction here between a casual blackness and an
intrinsic one, and suggests further that being a Dago (and having black hair as
well) was of the latter, intrinsic kind. A Dago, that is, might be called 'black'
without unfairness. This, in the logic of the story, would be particularly important,
since being called black had several associations. For example, to call Bunter
black would be to fail to appreciate 'the man's dignified bearing'.
     However that may be, Bunter found that he was looked upon, even in his
boat, with suspicion. Indeed Bunter's own captain did not feel differently from the
'gross lot': 'If anyone were to tell Captain Johns that he — Bunter — had a tail,
Johns would manage to get himself to believe the story in some mysterious
manner' (p. 92). Bunter had to dye his hair white. Conrad comments: 'Those eyes
that looked at you so steely, so fierce, and so fascinating out of the bush of a
buccaneer's black hair, now had an innocent, almost boyish expression in their
good-humoured brightness under those white eye-brows' (p. 116). As long as
Bunter had his black hair, he was a kind of 'diabolic' figure on board. Conrad
himself speaks of Bunter's 'usual stately deliberation, made sinister by the form of
his jet-black eyebrows' (p. 92). The Captain, even in his retirement, 'tries to tell
the story of a black mate he once had, "a murderous, gentlemanly ruffian", with
ravenblack hair which turned all white all at once in consequence of a
manifestation from beyond the grave. An avenging apparition' (p. 120).
     If we think Bunter's story is a *comic* parallel of the Wait story, we have to
explain our reaction. It seems clear, though, that the comedy lies in the
preposterous nature of the allegation being made, in the ludicrous nature of the
whole issue. In other words, the images of death and ferociousness, the references
to spirits and apparitions could not in themselves arouse any genuine feeling that
Bunter is capable of being any image or symbol. For this reason, we transfer the
absurdity of the comparisons from their object — Bunter — to the crew and the
captain. Because Bunter is not black in any true sense of the word, we discount
the possibility that he can be charged with being the agent of demons. Conrad is
with us in this feeling. Wait, on the other hand, has no such salvation. He is black
in a real sense and the equation of this blackness to devilishness is not as easily
written off as the aberration of the crew or of the narrator. In Bunter's story, we
are made to understand what is the truth and what is rumour in the narrative. The
narrator allows us a glimpse into his own prejudices and thus enables us to judge
his attitude to the story he is telling. In *The Nigger of the 'Narcissus',* the narrator
is outside the story, impersonal, though involved in the action. The degree of his
involvement is not made clear, however. As a result, we do not even consider the

possibility that we are perhaps dealing with an over-sensitive narrator. We are forced, accordingly, to assume that Conrad is speaking, as novelists do speak, through the narrator. That is, we do not qualify the exotic account of Wait's person by assuming that the whole story is the appraisal of the situation by just one of Conrad's characters, and not the most valid and general assessment of it. The result of all this is that Wait becomes an entirely mysterious person and we are in no position to verify stories about him, however strange they may be. Because of a limitation in point of view, there is an even greater limitation in our view of the hero.

Two implications seem inevitable in the light of the preceding discussion. The first is that we have to see Wait as an exo-cultural stereotype, a character who does not really belong to the ship and its world. Wait has a certain weird attractiveness about him, and it is this rather than the question of his individual character as a seaman, that concerns Conrad in the novel. Another way of phrasing this would be that Conrad found in Wait the antithesis of everything he expected of a sailor in his cultural context. To write a different story about Wait, Conrad would have had to adopt a totally different attitude to Wait's colour and his physiognomy. The symbol of evil and death which Wait is said to represent is merely the consequence of Conrad's supposedly factual description of an appearance which, to him, was literally brutal, tragic and sinister. If we must call Wait a devil, we must mean the name to be a measure of Conrad's revulsion from these aspects of Wait's physiognomy.

The second implication is related to the first. If we cannot accept a story about Bunter's devilishness because Conrad could not have meant us to take him seriously, we are really admitting that the real determinant of the symbolic relevance of a character is the imagination of the audience rather than the mere presence of those literary features usually associated with symbolism. Bunter cannot serve as a serious representation of anything because the man and his qualities, however we celebrate them, cannot sustain the serious meaning we intend them thereby to. Wait, it seems to me, serves such a symbolic function as is attributed to him because there is some disposition to accept the appropriateness of the equivalence which Conrad makes, because we have an appropriately con-ditioned imagination. This means, therefore, that when such spontaneous revulsion from the reality of Negro features does cease to appear correct, when, that is, any such *literary* expression of natural and correct revulsion should appear to us exaggerated, the reading and evaluation of the symbolic importance of Wait will suffer. The difference, very often, between tragedy and melodrama lies in the supporting system of belief, a concurring sensibility. No reading of *The Nigger of the 'Narcissus'* which does not begin with such a concurring attitude to Conrad's mystique of the black personality can escape being melodramatic. What sustains this novel, then, is not the assumed symbolic patterns to be found in it — whether they are *heterophoric* or *homeophoric* — but our concurrence with Conrad that his rites of colour and sin are also true, in the literal sense; our initial acceptance that Conrad's statement about Wait's face being the 'tragic, the mysterious, the repulsive mask of a nigger's soul' is not sheer nonsense. Because the conditioned imagination of Europe accepts Conrad's claim, the symbols are inevitable. Conrad's strength, in short, derives almost entirely from that of his exo-cultural hero.

NOTES:

1 *Travels in the Congo,* tr. Dorothy Bussy (Los Angeles, 1962) p. 13.

2 Ibid., p. 14.

3 Ibid., p. 14.

4 Ibid., pp. 4, 5, 7; 266.

5 Ibid., p. 4.

6 Neville H. Newhouse, *Joseph Conrad* (London, 1966), p. 39.

7 Quoted in Newhouse, p. 39.

8 Ian Watt, 'Conrad Criticism and *The Nigger of the "Narcissus"', Nineteenth Century Fiction,* XII (1958) 257-83. Subsequent references to this article are given in parentheses.

9 J. E. Miller Jr, *'The Nigger of the "Narcissus":* A Re-examination,' *PMLA,* LCVI (1951) 911-18; Vernon Young, 'Trial by Water: Joseph Conrad's *The Nigger of the "Narcissus"', Accent,* XII (1952) 67-81. See also W. R. Martin, "The Captain of the *"Narcissus"', English Studies in Africa,* VI (1963) 191-7.

10 'Symbolism in *The Nigger of the "Narcissus"', TCL,* II (1956) 29.

11 A term that also includes the other term 'white'.

12 Herman Melville, *Moby Dick,* ed. Alfred Kazin (Boston, 1956) p. 37.

13 F. J. Masback, 'Conrad's Jonahs', *College English,* XXII (1961) 332.

14 H. E. Davis, 'Symbolism in *The Nigger of the "Narcissus"',* p. 26.

15 *The Shadow Line: A Confession* (New York, 1917) p. 91.

16   Melville, *Redburn, His First Voyage* (New York, 1957) p. 55.

17   *The Nigger of the 'Narcissus'* (London, 1955). All subsequent references are to this
      edition and will be given in parentheses after quotations.

18   Cf. Melville, *Moby Dick,* p. 58:
      Savage though Queequeg was, and hideously marred about the face – at least
      to my taste — his countenance yet had a something in it which was by no
      means disagreeable. You cannot hide the soul. Through all his unearthly
      tattooings, I thought I saw traces of a simple honest heart . . . Queequeg was
      George Washington cannibalistically developed.

19   *Tales of Hearsay* (New York, 1925).

RACISM AND THE CLASSICS:
TEACHING *HEART OF DARKNESS*

Susan L. Blake

I would like to begin from the position that Joseph Conrad's *Heart of Darkness* is a racist novel. Although this position seems to run counter to the prevailing opinion that the novel attacks European imperialism,[1] it is not new. Jonah Raskin remarked briefly on Conrad's association of blackness with badness in *The Mythology of Imperialism* (1971); Chinua Achebe anatomized the racist assumptions in the novel's characterization of Africa and Africans in an article in *Research in African Literatures* in 1978.[2]

Achebe's argument that Conrad is "a bloody racist" (*RAL*, p. 9) rests on three main points. First, Conrad's portrayal of Africa and Africans is unreal. The landscape is a sort of solidified mixture of stillness and, quoting from Conrad, "black and incomprehensible frenzy" (*RAL*, p. 3). The people are, quoting again from Conrad, "a burst of yells, a whirl of black limbs, a mass of hands clapping, of feet stamping, of bodies swaying, of eyes rolling" (*RAL*, p. 4). They howl and grunt, but except for two statements in pidgin English, they do not speak, even among themselves. Second, his Africa and Africans represent something civilized people want to repress, something ugly but recognizable, and that, says Marlow, the narrator, "was the worst of it–this suspicion of their not being inhuman. It would come slowly to one. They howled and leaped, and spun, and made horrid faces; but what thrilled you was just the thought of their humanity–like yours–the thought of your remote kinship with this wild and passionate uproar. Ugly"(*RAL*, p. 4). Third, Conrad uses the confrontation of Europe and Africa to illustrate that all things have, and belong in, their place; the "black fellows" paddling a canoe "had bone, muscle, a wild vitality, an intense energy of movement, that was as natural and true as the surf along their coast." The African fireman on the steamboat, however, is compared to "a dog in a parody of breeches and a feather hat, walking on his hind legs" (*RAL*, pp. 5-6). Kurtz, who had fine ideals in Europe but has deteriorated in Africa, represents the other side of the same principle. The place for "wild vitality" is Africa; the place for civilization is Europe.

To these points, I would add a fourth. Although Marlow criticizes–indeed mocks–the colonial venture he has participated in as inefficient, inhumane, and hypocritical, he ultimately endorses it. The famous lie that he tells Kurtz's Intended keeps Europe from learning the horror of its own hypocrisy. (Kurtz has died pronouncing what Marlow calls "a judgement upon the adventures of his soul on this earth"; "The horror! The horror!"[3] But when the Intended, who believes in the nobility of his ideals, asks for "his last word–to live with," Marlow replies, "The last word he pronounced was–your name" [*HD*, p. 157].) And the comparison between the Congo and the Thames with which Marlow introduces the story of his adventures justifies hypocrisy. For "this also," says Marlow to his companions on a cruising yawl on the tranquil Thames, "has been one of the dark places of the earth" (*HD*, p.67). It was conquered by the Romans as the Congo was conquered by the Belgians. "The conquest of the earth," Marlow continues, "which mostly means the taking it away from those who have a different complexion or slightly flatter noses than ourselves, is not a pretty thing when you look into it too much. What redeems it is the idea only" (*HD*, p. 69). Conquest is not pretty, but it is redeemed. If we value order and enlightenment, we must accept the horror inevitable in their establishment.

One might argue that *Heart of Darkness* is about neither Africa nor colonialism, but the deterioration of one European mind or the chaos buried in any European mind. "Which," counters Achebe, "is partly the point. Africa as setting and backdrop which eliminates the African as human factor. Africa as a metaphysical battlefield devoid of all recognizable humanity" (*RAL*, p. 9). One might also argue, Achebe acknowledges, "that the attitude to the African in *Heart of Darkness* is not Conrad's but that of his fictional narrator, Marlow, and that far from endorsing it Conrad might indeed be holding it up to irony and criticism." But Conrad "neglects to hint however subtly or tentatively at an alternative frame of reference by which we may judge the actions and opinions of his characters . . . . Marlow seems . . . . to enjoy Conrad's complete confidence" (*RAL*, p. 7). Indeed, Achebe adds, Conrad in his own journals uses the same terminology and expresses the same perceptions as Marlow does in the story (*RAL*, p. 10).[4]

Achebe directs his discussion of *Heart of Darkness* toward the question of whether this novel, or any novel, "which depersonalizes a portion of the human race, can be called a great work of art" (RAL, p. 9). His answer, as you may suppose, is no. I would like to pose a more practical question: whether such a novel should be taught. By "such a novel" I mean one that has been considered great by many readers and depersonalizing by at least some. This category would include, for example, besides *Heart of Darkness, The Sound and the Fury,* in which the summary word on Dilsey is "They endured," and *Huckleberry Finn,* in which as Ellison puts it, Jim's "dignity and human capacity" emerge from behind a minstrel mask that also makes Jim appear forever a child.[5] It is not important to determine whether works such as these are racist or not, only to recognize that they have been considered so. The question of whether we teach them is important precisely because they are so highly regarded by the culture in general. Albert Guerard, in his introduction to the Signet edition, calls *Heart of Darkness* one of "the half-dozen greatest short novels in the English language" (*HD*, p. 8). Achebe surmises that it was "perhaps the most commonly prescribed novel in twentieth-century literature courses" at the University of Massachusetts, where he was teaching when he delivered the lecture later published in *RAL*. In my own department, it is on a required reading list for approximately twenty-five percent of the freshman class each year.

Partly because a novel such as *Heart of Darkness* is so highly acclaimed and widely taught by others, I think the answer to my question is yes, we should teach it. By "we" I mean those of us who acknowledge that it may be considered racist and decline to support racism in the name of art. I suggest we teach it, not out of deference to certified classics, but out of self-defense. Whether we teach such a work or not, our students will encounter it, perhaps without the critical frame of reference we would provide. Even if they never do encounter any particular classic, they live in the culture that has produced and applauded it. They had better be equipped to recognize and deal with the way this culture expresses itself in art.

Although it is important to provide a framework that will allow students to make negative judgements, it is not productive to teach literature only to denounce it. The further question, then, is *how* can we teach a novel that we don't wholly endorse? The method I have been using for the last several years is comparison–teaching with the questionable work another work about a comparable subject written from an opposing point of view.[6] This method has several advantages. First, of course, it throws the limitations of the work in question into relief without requiring the teacher to make a case against it; it allows the students to discover the results of different points of view themselves. You don't have to argue that Dilsey is seen from a white, though sympathetic, point of view if you have one of Ernest Gaines's enduring aunts available for comparison. Second, it illuminates the real basis of what emerges as racism in literature: that is, point of view itself. It helps us distinguish effect from intention in a work such as *Huckleberry Finn,* where the character of Jim is certainly meant to represent dignity and humanity but fails to escape the outlines of stereotype. All it takes is a glance at Frederick Douglass, whose narrative is a real-life freedom quest, as *Huck Finn* is a fictional one, to dramatize the difference between symbolic and actual dignity.

Depending on our particular teaching situations, these advantages may seem obvious or irrelevant. There is a third advantage, though, that applies to any teaching situation and may be less obvious. Comparing novels written from different social assumptions shows students how the technical elements of fiction function to produce meaning, how the implications of point of view govern the entire work, as art as well as social construct, and how literary values are tied to social values.

To demonstrate this point, let me share with you my experience in teaching *Heart of Darkness* with Ousmane Sembene's *God's Bits of Wood* in an introductory novel course. Although the two novels are set roughly sixty years apart in different parts of Africa, they have enough similarities of subject and structure to be comparable. Both concern the impact of colonialism–*Heart of Darkness* primarily on Europeans but also on Africans; *God's Bits of Wood* primarily on Africans but also on Europeans. Both are set along the length of a transportation route—*Heart of Darkness*, the Congo River; *God's Bits of Wood*, the Dakar-Niger railroad. In both, the vehicle–the steamboat, the train–represents the machine, the incursion of European technology and its consequences into African culture. Both focus on a shadowy hero–Kurtz, Bakayoko–who is known by his words but not seen until far into the story and who turns out to be someone less godlike than originally imagined. Both heroes experience a last-minute flash of self-perception; both novels trace the development of awareness of the meaning of colonialism in the other characters.

The difference in the images of Africa that the two novels present is, of course, dramatic. Conrad's Africa is dark and enclosed; Sembene's is light and open. In *God's Bits of Wood,* the people Conrad represented as disembodied limbs and rolling eyes become individual characters, with histories, values, problems, indeed entire stories of their own. They do not stamp and howl; they practice a quiet religion that calls for self-discipline and self-reflection. They do not grunt; they each speak several languages–a point emphasized in the characterization of ten-year-old Ad'jibid'ji, who ponders the philosophical basis of differences in Wolof, Banbara, and French vocabularies. Marlow calls the Africans savages; Ad'jibid'ji's grandmother applies that word to the Europeans.

But more interesting than the differences in their images of Africans are the differences in the ways Conrad and Sembene use the technical elements of fiction, for these differences show how point of view pervades a work. All the technical elements of *Heart of Darkness* contribute to the novel's inner-directedness; all the technical elements of *God's Bits of Wood* contribute to its outer-directedness. Inner-directedness underlines the pessimism of *Heart of Darkness,* as outer-directedness underlines the optimism of *God's Bits of Wood.*

The principal technical difference between the two novels is in the narrative point of view–first person in *Heart of Darkness,* third-person in *God's Bits of Wood.* As first person narrator, Conrad's Marlow objectifies everyone outside himself. The omniscient narrator of *God's Bits of Wood,* however, enters into the consciousness of a multitude of individual characters. Thus *Heart of Darkness* has only one developed character; *God's Bits of Wood* has many.

The implications of the difference in narrative point of view extend to the apparently similar elements of setting, symbolism, and characterization in the two works.

The linear setting of both novels suggests a quest and a path to its fulfillment. Marlow travels straight up the Congo, then straight back down. As he travels upriver he shuts himself further and further into himself until he finds Kurtz, who, he recognizes, is a manifestation of himself; his journey upriver is a journey into self. His return may be seen as a retreat from the insight he has achieved through Kurtz's vision of "the horror." The retreat climaxes in the lie to the Intended, which acknowledges Marlow's inability to act on what he has learned. The narrative consciousness of *God's Bits of Wood,* however, like the almost mythical Bakayoko, ranges up and down the railroad from Bamako to Dakar, not shutting other consciousnesses out, but drawing them in as it develops the stories of individual characters. When the novel returns at the end of each of the three primary locations, it is to show development in the people there, not to retreat to the original situation. As Marlow gains understanding of himself, he feels increasingly cut off from other people; as the characters in *God's Bits of Wood* gain understanding of themselves, they become more aware of their kinship with others. Conrad and Sembene view the line and the progress it represents differently. Conrad sees the line as direction to and from one point; Sembene sees it as the connector of an infinite number of points. For Conrad, progress is possible only in the individual consciousness; for Sembene, it is possible in the individual consciousness *because* it is possible in the aggregate of consciousnesses and *vice versa.*

The archetypal symbol of the machine, in both novels, brings the Africans and Europeans together; it transports Europeans into the interior of Africa and brings the Africans who work on it into a European setting. For Conrad, taking the point of view of the steamboat, that relationship is comic. The clumsy steamboat, patched like the Russian harlequin in Kurtz's camp, lumbering up the snag-filled river, is in continuous imminent danger of being sunk. And the African fireman trying to placate the spirit in the boiler looks like a parody of a dog in breeches. For Sembene, taking the point of view of a developing society, the relationship is complex. The striking railroad workers realize that the railroad represents both their strength and their dependence. It has been the means of their exploitation, but it has also given them both consciousness of the exploitation and the tools to combat it. For though the machine was built by the white man, it does not belong to him; it is inanimate power, at the service of whoever takes it; it represents a new way of life limited by "neither a language nor a race,"[7] but with the potential to transgress all kinds of barriers between peoples. In *Heart of Darkness,* the machine comes to represent not simply technology or modernity, but ethnocentricity; in *God's Bits of Wood* it represents the possibility of welding the best elements of conflicting cultures into a society designed for the good of all.

Finally, the characterizations of Kurtz and Bakayoko reveal the opposition between Conrad's and Sembene's concepts of the hero. Both heroes are shadowy because they are, in a sense, representations of the imaginations of others. By the end of *Heart of Darkness,* Marlow has taken over Kurtz's reputation; by the end of *God's Bits of Wood,* all the other characters, working together, have accomplished the revolution Bakayoko envisioned. But Kurtz represents both the evil that men are capable of when left to themselves and the honesty that allows them to acknowledge it, while Bakayoko represents the good that human beings can accomplish when they work together. Both Kurtz and Bakayoko are introduced as god-like characters; that is, though they are unseen, their influence, achieved through their words, is everywhere. As we get to know them, they fall in status–Kurtz to a devil; Bakayoko to a man, limited especially in his personal relations with other people, but capable of learning. Kurtz, devil though he is, becomes a hero to Marlow because he acknowledges his deviltry; heroism becomes a matter of the individual consciousness, unrelated to its effect on other people. Heroism in *God's Bits of Wood,* on the other hand, spreads out to include the whole community of men and women who succeed individually and collectively in changing their lives for the better. Bakayoko remains a hero as a part of that community, not as an individual superior to it. Heroism for Sembene is the interaction of human beings in the world.

As it reveals consistent opposition between the outward and optimistic reach of the African novel and the inward and pessimistic retreat of the European, a comparison of *Heart of Darkness* and *God's Bits of Wood* shows how thoroughly the technical elements of fiction depend upon and reflect social values. It shows, too, the general differences in values between European culture, focused on the individual, and African culture, focused on the community, and dramatizes the principle that social values are not universal but based on culture. Most importantly, a comparison of these two novels provides a basis for understanding the relationship between social and literary values and thus for questioning received values and determining one's own.

The inner-directedness that all of the literary elements of *Heart of Darkness* help to create is precisely what critics admire in the novel and what teachers lead their classes to see. "The book is not really about a journey up the Congo at all," students triumphantly discover, "but about a journey into the human heart." But inner-directedness is the foundation of the book's pessimism—or cynicism, depending on your point of view. It is at least in part because Marlow feels cut off from other people, feels alone in his understanding of Kurtz, that he fails to act on the implications of that understanding. His isolation enables him, perhaps forces him, to say that colonialism is justified by the very ideal he knows is hypocrisy. Neither Marlow nor Conrad, however, could retreat from the social reality of his story into an ideal if he thought of the Africans as people like himself (rather than simply "not inhuman"). In fact, in his willingness to sacrifice Africa to the ideal of order, Marlow himself—and Conrad through him—is analogous to the accountant who can "hate those savages. . . to the death" in the pursuit of correct entries (*HD*, pp. 84-85). So, too, are we if we are willing to ignore the social implications of Conrad's position in our reverence for our own ideal of inward vision. Our literary values reflect our social point of view; Africans do not dismiss Africa.

Thus teaching pairs of works written from specifically conflicting social points of view is not simply a way of getting around the offensive implications of a work one may feel constrained—for whatever reason—to teach. It is a positive way of helping students to see that "literary" techniques and values have social causes and implications. This insight is behind the rejection of works on the basis of their social values, but it might be more valuable to give students the insight as a basis for judging literature themselves than to use it to shield them from corruption or offense.

Lafayette College
Easton, Pennsylvania

NOTES:

1   Expressed in, for example, Eloise Knapp Hay, *The Political Novels of Joseph Conrad* (Chicago: University of Chicago Press, 1963); Jonah Raskin, "Imperialism: Conrad's *Heart of Darkness,*" *The Journal of Contemporary History,* 2, No. 2 (1967), 113-31; Avrom Fleishman, *Conrad's Politics: Community and Anarchy in the Fiction of Joseph Conrad* (Baltimore: The Johns Hopkins University Press, 1967).

2   Jonah Raskin, *The Mythology of Imperialism* (New York: Random House, 1971), pp. 160-61; Chinua Achebe, "An Image of Africa," *Research in African Literatures,* 9 (Spring 1978), 1-15. Quotations from Achebe will be cited within the text, identified by the initials *RAL.*

3   Joseph Conrad, *Heart of Darkness and the Secret Sharer* (New York: New American Library, 1950), pp. 147-48. All further quotations will be cited within the text, identified by the initials *HD.*

4   Molly Mahood, whose chapter on *Heart of Darkness* in *The Colonial Encounter* (London: Rex Collings, 1977) examines the relationship between Conrad and his narrator, corroborates Achebe's reading of the journals. She concludes: "There is nothing destructive or belittling in the irony that separates [Conrad] from his *alter ego.* Rather Marlow is the kind of Englishman that Conrad believed he might have been if he had been born in England"–and, she adds, sometimes was (p.23).

5   Ralph Ellison, *Shadow and Act* (New York: New American Library, 1965), pp. 65-66.

6   Mahood suggests this method in *The Colonial Encounter* by pairing novels by writers from each side of the colonial experience. So far as her method is comparative, however, her intention is "to put some of these novels from the new literatures alongside some of the best English novels of the twentieth century and by close and appreciative readings to establish their parity' (p. 2). She pairs *Heart of Darkness* with Achebe's *Arrow of God.*

7   Ousmane Sembene, *God's Bits of Wood* (Garden City, New York: Doubleday, 1970), p. 132.

UNDER AFRICAN EYES[1]

Ponnuthurai Sarvan

If any language may be described, in terms of extensive international usage and influence, as a world language then perhaps English has the best claim to the title. Conrad, as a major literary figure of a major language, is on the curricula of many schools and colleges throughout the world and his influence is wide. There are other reasons too why this influence, transcending Europe, should be felt in Asia and Africa. Apart from intrinsic literary merit, the setting of some of his work in the Far East and Africa stimulates an interest in readers from these regions. In the field of black African fiction, 1960 is often seen as a dividing line: novels preceding this date tend to deal with traditional society and the impact of Western imperialism and Christianity on it.[2] Conrad's *Heart of Darkness,* with its condemnation of the brutality of imperialism, is a useful external reference when dealing with this earlier group of novels. Novels published immediately after 1960 reflect the deep disillusionment which followed independence: Nigeria 1960; Uganda 1962; Kenya 1963. Conrad's opinion that revolutions are often betrayed by success, and that power and materialism erode ideals and principles is, sad to say, well understood in the so-called developing world. For various reasons, most black African novelists have chosen not to write in their own languages but have opted instead for English (Chinua Achebe, James Ngugi, Wole Soyinka) and French (Aime Cesaire, Leopold Senghor, Camara Laye, Ferdinand Oyono, Mongo Beti). Conrad is an inspiration to the African writer who ventures to express himself through a foreign linguistic medium, for was not English Conrad's third language? Thus, for a variety of reasons, Conrad has a large readership outside England, Europe and America.

In the following article I attempt to illustrate Conrad's influence by comparing James Ngugi's *A Grain of Wheat* with *Under Western Eyes.*[3] Such an examination will also exemplify how material drawn substantially from one source, when seen by another mind and translated into the terms of another culture, results in a completely different work–even when the similarity in plot and theme is evident. Ime Ikiddeh notices in passing the similarity between these two novels,[4] and Eustace Palmer in his *An Introduction to the African Novel* (London, 1972) briefly compares *A Grain of Wheat* with *Lord Jim:* "Its complexity of form recalls the involutions of Conrad's *Lord Jim,* on which it seems consciously to have been modelled" (pp. 24-25). It was left to Ebele

153

Obumselu to "read *A Grain of Wheat* against the background of its most immediate literary predecessor, *Under Western Eyes.*"5

Conrad's work, set in Russia under the Czars, is the story of a student, Razumov, "sought out in his obscure solitude, and menaced by the complicity forced upon him" (p. 366). Razumov, irrationally trusted by Victor Haldin, assassin (or, if one prefers, executioner) of Mr. de P–, President of the notorious Repressive Commission, betrays him to the police and becomes their instrument. He is sent to spy on the Russian expatriate group of revolutionaries in Switzerland, falls in love with Nathalie, sister of the late Victor Haldin, confesses his betrayal, is punished and ends his days deaf and crippled, attended by the "Samaritan" Tekla.

Ngugi's story is set in Kenya and covers the period of the successful culmination of the armed struggle against British colonial rule.6 As the work opens, we are but four days away from independence. Mugo, in Ngugi's novel, is like Razumov in that he is without family and fame, but has what Conrad says of his protagonist, "sane" and legitimate ambitions. Razumov, illegitimate son of Prince K–, lives alone and Mugo, an orphan, was brought up by an aunt, now dead. Razumov's immediate ambition is to win the silver prize at the essay contest organized by the Ministry of Education: a sure step to a later administrative appointment. Mugo is determined that "he would labour, sweat, and through success and wealth, force society to recognize him" (p. 11). Thus, neither of them has known love, nor the obligations which grow out of love. They neither owe nor are they owed to. "I was afraid of your mother. I never knew mine. I've never known any kind of love" (*Under Western Eyes,* p. 360).

Into the ordered world of Mugo, a world of work, plans and hopes, irrupts Kihika, dreaded leader of a band of men fighting the British. Kihika seeks shelter in Mugo's hut, trusting him as Haldin had trusted Razumov. What is worse, he wants Mugo's help in organizing the underground movement in the village. Fearing to refuse, yet fearing to cooperate; fearing for his life as for his future plans, tempted by thoughts of reward, Mugo betrays Kihika. A false reputation gathers round Mugo and he becomes a hero in the eyes of the community, even as Razumov had an honoured place in revolutionary circles. Kihika's sister, the beautiful Mumbi, confides in him. Attracted to her, unable to endure his false position, Mugo, like Razumov, confesses and is punished. Both Razumov and Mugo first confess in private to the sisters of the men they betrayed and then, since this does not jeopardize their lives and reputation, feel impelled to make a public confession, the former to the revolutionaries, the latter to the village community. The public confession is the atonement which at last sets them "free."

Razumov and Mugo had wished only to be left alone so that they might pursue their ambitions. Amidst oppression and upheaval, they attempted to follow their separate courses, but public issues intrude into private life and involvement cannot be avoided.

Thus Ngugi's story, like that of Conrad's, is set amidst a political struggle waged against oppression and is concerned with betrayal and confession. Haldin believed that he was compelled by circumstances to act violently: "You suppose that I am a terrorist, now–a destructor of what is. But consider that the true destroyers are they who destroy the spirit of progress and truth, not the avengers who merely kill the bodies of persecutors of human dignity" (p. 19). So too, Kihika:

> We don't kill just anybody. . . we are not murderers . . . Do you think we like scuffling for food like hyenas and monkeys in the forest? I, too, have known the comfort of a warm fire and a woman's love by the fireside. See? We must kill. Put to sleep the enemies of black man's freedom . . . . I spit on the weakness of our fathers. Their memory gives me no pride (pp. 216-17).

In *A Grain of Wheat* there is not a tragic figure of the betrayed's mother, but we have the old woman, mother of Gitogo. Gitogo was a strong man and a dutiful and affectionate son. During a raid for Mau Mau suspects, he runs to be with his aged mother, is challenged by British soldiers, but being deaf tragically runs on, and is shot. The old woman survives, withdrawn, half-demented. And here one feels that Ngugi has fused Mrs. Haldin and the pathetic Tekla who gives herself up not to "Causes" but to ministering to the suffering individual, to form the figure of Gitogo's mother. Tekla, rejected, has suffered much and is without illusions. Her suffering and loneliness have given her an acute perception and there is something of the sibyl in her. The old woman in *A Grain of Wheat*, though deeply shaken and silent, seems to have an intuitive knowledge, and whenever Mugo sees her, he is "agitated as if the woman recognized him" (p. 8). One day, Mugo attempts to speak to her, but she turns her head away. Mrs. Haldin, we remember, was suspicious of Razumov, virtual slayer of her son and, as she towards the end was deluded and held that her son was not dead and would one day return to her, so too Gitogo's mother believes in her son's return.

Because of their loneliness and focus on inner aspirations, Razumov and Mugo are reticent, and this quality inspires trust, making them the recipients of unsolicitated confidences. "Amongst a lot of exuberant talkers, in the habit of exhausting themselves daily by ardent discussion, a comparatively taciturn personality is naturally credited with reserve power" (*Under Western Eyes,* p. 6). And Mumbi tells Mugo, "I have never talked these things to anybody. . . You make me feel able to talk . . . Do you know my brother . . . said that if he had something really secret and important, he would only confide in somebody like you" (p. 157). The only person mentioned by Haldin in his letters to his sister is Razumov, described as one of those men leading "Unstained, lofty, and solitary existences" (p. 135).

After their respective acts of betrayal, Razumov and Mugo pass from reticence to taciturnity. As the gap between public belief and their own knowledge widens, they become schizophrenic, absent minded, slow moving, and incoherent in speech as they oscillate unhappily and unsteadily between inner self and public pose. "Razumov envied the materialism of the thief and the passion of the incorrigible lover. The consequences of their actions were always clear and their lives remained their own" (p. 78).

One may hunt for other similarities, but it should be clear by now that *A Grain of Wheat* is heavily indebted to *Under Western Eyes*. Indeed, in an interview reproduced in *African Writers Talking*, Ngugi states: "With Conrad, I'm impressed by the way he questions things, requestions things like action, the morality of action, for instance."[7] Ngugi also tells us (p. 126) that he began learning English when he was about thirteen: on these grounds, he feels an affinity with Conrad.

But of greater interest than similarities is the difference between the two works. It is a difference immediately felt but nonetheless difficult to state. There is, of course, the difference arising from the fact that Ngugi's work is set in rural Kenya, whereas much of Conrad's novel is set in Switzerland. The latter is neutral and almost any European capital would have sufficed. In *A Grain of Wheat*, the setting is drawn in detail, consciously.

Apart from this "visual" difference, what else is there that makes Ngugi's work worthy of independent assessment?—for the latter does have a right to be considered an original work, even as Anouilh's *Antigone* can be treated independently of Sophocles.

The main difference is one of belief and resulting attitude. As vivid as scenes in *Hard Times* and *Crime and Punishment* is the squalor the reader faces with Razumov as the latter walks the streets and comes to the eating-house: the old woman in the deep Russian winter, wrapped in "ragged shawls" and clutching a loaf of bread "with an air of guarding a priceless booty" (pp. 26-27); the "wet and bedraggled creature, a sort of sexless and shivering scarecrow" washing glasses in "an enormous slum, a hive of human vermin, a monumental abode of misery towering on the verge of starvation and despair" (p. 28). But Conrad lacked faith in progress and amelioration. As Jessie Conrad tells us in her biographical writings, Conrad's earliest experience had created in him a sense of tragedy, and he was not an optimistic man. Irving Howe notes that "beneath the controlled stiffness of Conrad's stoicism. . . there flows a bleak and terrible disbelief, a radical skepticism that corrodes the underside of everything he values."[8] With his view of human nature, Conrad believed that a good percentage of revolutionaries are impostors or sadists, inhabiting a world of falsehood and cruelty. "Hopes grotesquely betrayed, ideals caricatured—that is the definition of revolutionary success" (p. 135). Therefore, though Conrad has a contempt for the oppressors and some sympathy for the Haldins and Antonovnas of this world, he nevertheless feels that all their actions are doomed to failure. There is the perception of acute misery on the one hand, and a disbelief in collective action and progress on the other.

A Grain of Wheat accepts that imperialism, ruling over people by force and fear, can be removed through force and fear. Again, as Irving Howe observes, "Where freedom is absent, politics is fate" (p. 87). Ngugi writes with the historical vindication of the violent struggle launched by the people of Kenya, for, at the end of it, were independence and the restitution of the people's freedom and dignity. Therefore, there is not Conrad's sense of futility, a futility made terrible by his knowledge of the extreme suffering of the Russian people. In Ngugi, we see that it is the absence of freedom and the struggle for it which create abnormal conditions, and the novel ends with Gikonyo deciding to carve a woman's figure, "a woman big—big with child." As Shaw writes in his Preface to *John Bull's Other Island,* the independence struggle is an effort to restore normal life, normal preoccupations and pastimes. During the struggle, some will fall, victims of disjointed times, victims of a historical moment. Ngugi conveys the richness of society living out its normal, traditional life.

In Conrad, there is a strong element of prejudice against Russians, a prejudice which, though one can understand it in the light of Polish history and the suffering of Conrad's family, nevertheless mars the work. The tiger, says Conrad in his "Author's Note," cannot change its stripes, nor the leopard its spots: the Russians are incorrigible. Nikita is so grotesque that dogs bark at the sight of him (p. 267) and Sophia Antonovna must look "un-Russian" (p. 264) in order to be portrayed as noble. Ngugi, spared compulsory exile and writing after national independence, is able to achieve a greater degree of objectivity.

Conrad, like Hardy, is uncomfortable in handling sexual relationships and unsuccessful in his attempts to draw female characters. The teacher of English, explaining his feelings for Miss Haldin, is clumsy and succeeds only in being unintentionally amusing. Razumov confesses because he falls in love with Miss Haldin:

> You were appointed to undo the evil by making me betray myself back into truth. . . . (p. 358)
> And your pure forehead! It is low like the forehead of statues—calm, unstained. It was as if your pure brow bore a light which fell on me, searched my heart and saved me. (p. 361)

Razumov's love is given in the religious terms of a sinner suddenly seeing salvation. In contrast, the relationship between Mumbi and her husband, between her and Karanja, is conceived with understanding and compassion and set forth naturally. (The same cannot be said of the relationship between Mrs. Thompson and Dr. Dyke which is more in the vein of the cheap novelette.)

Ime Ikiddeh, in the article already cited, makes a brief comparison of these two works:

> As a story of betrayal, remorse and confession, I can only think of *Under Western Eyes* to parallel this. But then Conrad's novel slips out of the psychology of guilt into a spy story that runs across continents. Ngugi's story keeps up Mugo's nightmare to the end. (p. 9)

This is not a fair comment. In order to praise Ngugi, Conrad's novel should not be equated with a spy thriller. It is not necessary to damn the one in order to praise the other: as I hope this paper shows, *A Grain of Wheat* has its own merits.

Structurally, the two works are different. It might be said that if *A Grain of Wheat* is influenced in theme and plot by *Under Western Eyes,* in structure the influence is that of *Lord Jim. Under Western Eyes* opens with introductory comments by the teacher of English and then follows a straight narrative line. True, there is a major shift in scene and perspective as we leave Razumov facing the Councillor's "Where to?" and come to Switzerland and to new characters. But this is merely to prepare the ground for Razumov's arrival. Once he comes on the scene, the narrative resumes its briefly interrupted course. *A Grain of Wheat* has a deliberately disjointed plot structure. I do not wish to paraphrase but for purpose of illustration will summarize the first few events in the novel. It opens with Mugo waking up from troubled dreams and going to work on his piece of land. In a flashback, we are told of his childhood. The narrative shifts again and we see Mugo walking back to his hut to be met by members of the Party. This in turn leads to a brief resumé of the independence struggle, ending with Kihika and his betrayal. Thence we are introduced to Gikonyo and his strained relations with his wife, Mumbi. Thereafter, we meet the Thompsons via Karanja.

This technique enables us to see characters in greater depth, for we understand present predicament in the light of past events. The reader also gains a greater sense of familiarity with the characters, knowing their earlier years and background. But one feels that the technique is used to such a degree that it tends to become an end in itself: the over-disjointed narrative sequence ceases to have a significant function and becomes obtrusive. One cannot admire technique for its own sake and complexity is justified only if thereby effects are achieved which would not have been possible with simpler means.

Conrad makes no attempt to conceal the identity of Haldin's betrayer, and we are able to appreciate the irony of Razumov's position. Ngugi's novel commences with Mugo waking up from guilt-laden dreams, walking to work without zest, suspiciously examining even casual statements and greetings. Thereafter, particularly for one who has read the earlier *Under Western Eyes,* the key to Mugo's behavior is obvious. Yet the novelist tries to show torment, give clues and, at the same time, avoid open identification.

Ngugi does not have that mastery of the language which, together with other qualities, makes Conrad one of the greatest of novelists. Though Conrad's syntax is not simple, his sentences have such balance, polish and ease that they are admirable structures in themselves. Meaning is never obscured. Space does not permit illustration but the reader could, for example, compare Conrad's description of Mr. de P– (pp.7-8) with Ngugi's counterpart description of Thomas Robson, alias Tom the Terror (pp. 211-12). Or one could contrast Razumov's reaction to Haldin's confession with that of Mugo's reaction to Kihika's.

In *A Grain of Wheat* there is a diffusion of focus and we are in the minds of many and learn, for example, of the thoughts and feelings of Mr. and Mrs. Thompson, of the later's adulterous relationship with Dr. Dyke, and the rape of Dr. (Miss) Lynd. Conrad keeps the focus on Razumov and, therefore, involves us more deeply: of the other characters, we are told the necessary minimum. We well understand Razumov, the inner turmoil and suffering on which a mind of more than ordinary intelligence strives in vain to impose clarity. Mugo, on the other hand, is no intellectual and has neither the thoughts nor the language of Razumov: "I am a man of deep convictions. Crude opinions are in the air. They are not always worth combating. But even the silent contempt of a serious mind may be misinterpreted by headlong utopists" (p. 48).

In *A Grain of Wheat* there is an over-emphasis on the betrayal theme: Mrs. Thompson betrays her husband; Karanja, his oath; Mumbi, her husband; Mugo betrays Kihika and Gikonyo is "betrayed" by his member of parliament. But what Ngugi loses in concentration, he gains in the breadth of his canvas and we have a clear picture of a whole community.

Neither Conrad nor Ngugi judges or censures his protagonist. Explicit in Conrad and implicit in Ngugi is the belief that finally we decide, act, and suffer not as revolutionaries nor as conservatives but alone as individuals. "I am independent— and therefore perdition is my lot" (*Under Western Eyes*, p. 362).

University of Zambia

NOTES:

1   I gratefully acknowledge the valuable help given by my wife, Liebetraut, in writing this paper.

2   Cf. the present writer's "The Pessimism of Chinua Achebe," *Critique: Studies in Modern Fiction*, 15:3 (1974), 95-108.

3   James Ngugi, now known as Ngugi Thiong'O, a major black African writer, was born in Kenya in 1938. He studied there, in Uganda, and at Leeds University. His reputation rests largely on three novels (*Weep Not, Child*, 1964; *The River Between*, 1965; *A Grain of Wheat*, 1967), a play (*The Black Hermit*, 1968) and a collection of essays (*Homecoming*, 1972). The edition of Conrad's work which I have used is the one published by J. M. Dent & Sons Ltd., London, 1963; the edition of Ngugi's work is the one included in the African Writers Series (London: Heinemann, 1968).

4   *African Literature Today*, No. 2 (London: Heinemann Educational Books, 1969), pp. 3-10. I worked with Mr. Ikiddeh for two years in Nigeria and wish to record my thanks for the free use he gave me of his private library and the many discussions we had.

5   *The Benin Review*, 1 (1974), 80-91. Brilliant though this essay is, it has not sought to make a detailed comparison of the two novels. In doing so now, and in evaluating

them first comparatively and then separately, the present writer hopes his essay will complement Obumselu's and be of interest to *Conradiana* readers.

6   Due to the growth of the Mau Mau struggle, a State of Emergency was declared in 1952. In 1953 Jomo Kenyatta was arrested as the leader of this movement and imprisoned. He was released in 1959 and, in 1963, became the first Prime Minister of independent Kenya.

7   Edited by Dennis Duerden and Cosmo Pieterse (London: Heinemann, 1972), p. 124.

8   *Politics and the Novel* (New York: Horizon Press, 1957), pp. 80-81.

THE FRONTIER ON WHICH
HEART OF DARKNESS STANDS

Wilson Harris

I read Chinua Achebe's article on Joseph Conrad[1] with much interest and some sympathy. My sympathy rests on an appreciation of his uneasiness in the face of biases that continue to reinforce themselves in post-imperial western establishments. Perhaps the West does have the bad conscience Achebe attributes to it and is seeking, therefore, some assuagement of its guilt.

There are certainly writers, novelists, reporters, as he indicates, who seem predisposed to see nothing but bankruptcy in the Third World and one wonders in what unconscious degree perhaps the West may desire such bankruptcy—cultural and political–to become a fact of history, whereby it may justify its imperial past by implying that imperial order, across centuries of colonialism, was the only real support the modern world possessed, the only real governance the Third World respected.

Achebe's essay on "the dehumanisation of Africa and Africans" by "bloody racists"[2] is, therefore, in the light of western malaise and postimperial hangover, a persuasive argument, but I am convinced his judgement or dismissal of *Heart of Darkness*—and of Conrad's strange genius—is a profoundly mistaken one. He sees the distortions of imagery and, therefore, of character in the novel as witnessing to horrendous prejudice on Conrad's part in his vision of Africa and Africans.

As I weighed this charge in my own mind, I began to sense a certain incomprehension in Achebe's analysis of the pressures of form that engaged Conrad's imagination to transform biases grounded in homogeneous premises. By form I mean the novel form as a medium of consciousness that has its deepest roots in an intuitive and much, much older self than the historical ego or the historical conditions of ego dignity that bind us to a particular decade or generation or century.

The capacity of the intuitive self to breach the historical ego is the life-giving and terrifying objectivity of imaginative art that makes a painting or a poem or a piece of sculpture or a fiction endure long beyond the artist's short lifetime and gives it the strangest beauty or coherence in depth.

This interaction between sovereign ego and intuitive self is the tormenting reality of changing form, the ecstasy as well of visionary capacity to cleave the prison house of natural bias within a heterogeneous asymmetric context[3] in which the unknowable God–though ceaselessly beyond human patterns—infuses art with unfathomable eternity and grace.

I believe that this complex matter may arouse incomprehension in Africa where, by and large, tradition tends towards homogeneous imperatives. In South America where I was born this is not the case. The crucial hurdle in the path of community, if community is to create a living future, lies in a radical aesthetic in which distortions of sovereign ego may lead into confessions of partiality within sovereign institutions that, therefore, may begin to penetrate and unravel their biases, in some degree, in order to bring into play a complex wholeness inhabited by other confessing parts that may have once masqueraded themselves as monolithic absolutes or monolithic codes of behavior in the old worlds from which they emigrated by choice or by force.

It is in this respect that I find it possible to view *Heart of Darkness* as a frontier novel. By that I mean that it stands upon a threshold of capacity to which Conrad pointed though he never attained that capacity himself. Nevertheless, it was a stroke of genius on his part to visualize an original necessity for distortions in the stases of appearance that seem sacred and that cultures take for granted as models of timeless dignity.

There is a dignity in liberal pretensions until liberalism, whether black or white, unmasks itself to reveal inordinate ambitions for power where one least suspects it to exist.

The novel form Conrad inherited is the novel form in which most writers, black and white, write today. For comedy of manners is the basis of protest fiction, fiction of good guys and bad guys, racist guys and liberal guys. Comedy of manners is the basis of realism that mirrors society to identify refinements of behavior that are social or antisocial, heroic or antiheroic. All this is an oversimplification perhaps, but it may help to complement what is less obvious in this analysis.

The novel form Conrad inherited—if I may restate my theme in a more complex way—was conditioned by a homogeneous cultural logic to promote a governing principle that would sustain all parties, all characterizations, in endeavoring to identify natural justice, natural conscience behind the activity of a culture.

It was with such works of disturbing imagination as Edgar Allan Poe's *Arthur Gordon Pym* and James Hogg's *Confessions of a Justified Sinner,* both published in the 1830s, Melville's *Benito Cereno,* in the middle of the nineteenth century, and Conrad's *Heart of Darkness*, at the beginning of the twentieth century, that the logic of human-made symmetry or absolute control of diversity, the logic of benign or liberal order, disclosed hideous biases within a context of heterogeneous bodies and pigmentations. For the truth was that the liberal homogeneity of a culture becomes the ready-made cornerstone upon which to construct an order of conquest, and by degrees "the horror, the horror"[4] was intuitively manifest. Conquest is the greatest evil of soul humanity inflicts upon itself and on nature.

Such an admission—such a discovery that sacred human stasis may come to shelter the greatest evil—is a catastrophe for the liberal ego-fixated mind. In it, nevertheless, lies a profound creation myth that may begin to nourish a capacity for meaningful distortion of images through which to offset or transform the hubris of apparently sacred order and to create, by painful and yet ecstatic degrees, a profound, complex, and searching dialogue between confessing and confessional heterogeneous cultures that are no longer the monolithic or absolute civilizations they once were in Africa, China, Europe, India, or the Americas in the fourteenth century and fifteenth century before the circumnavigation of the globe and the fall of ancient America. Creation myth is a paradox. It is a vision of catastrophe and of coherence in depth *nevertheless* within or beneath the fragmented surfaces of given world orders. It is a vision of mysterious regeneration that apprises us of our limits and in so doing awakens a capacity to dream beyond those limits, a capacity for infinite conception of life and of humility, a capacity for complex risk, creativity, and dialogue with others through and beyond institutions inhibited by, or based on, the brute conquest of nature from which creation has recoiled again and again over long ages to leave us and our antecedents bereft and yet intensely aware of the priceless gift of being that begins all over again in the depths of animate perception.

The most significant distortion of imagery in *Heart of Darkness* bears upon Kurtz's liberal manifesto of imperial good and moral light. In that manifesto or consolidation of virtues the "extermination of all the [alien] brutes"[5] becomes inevitable. Thus Conrad parodies the notion of moral light that devours all in its path—a parody that cuts to the heart of paternalism with strings attached to each filial puppet. (The invasion of Afghanistan in the year of Machiavellian politics 1980 is a late twentieth century version of paternal Kurtz in which the virtues of the Soviet monolith make no bones about the symmetry of Communist power to encircle the globe.)

At no point in his essay does Achebe touch upon the crucial parody of the proprieties of established order that mask corruption in all societies, black and white, though this is essential, it seems to me, to a perception of catastrophe behind the dignified personae monoliths wear. (And, in this context, one is not speaking only of conquistadorial monoliths but of mankind the hunter whose folklore is death; mankind the ritualist who sacrifices female children to maintain the symmetry of males, or mankind the priest who once plucked the heart from the breast of a living victim to feed the sun.)

These distortions of the human mask (hunter, priest, ritualist) set their teeth upon African characters like an initiation ceremony at the heart of the Bush to bite deep as well into the European conquistador/butcher/businessman Kurtz.

Kurtz's manifesto, liberal manifesto, affected Marlow as follows:

All Europe contributed to the making of Kurtz; and by and by I learned that, most appropriately, the International Society for the Suppression of Savage Customs had intrusted him with the making of a report, for its future guidance.

And he had written it, too. I've seen it, I've read it. . . . Seventeen pages of
close writing he had found time for!. . . He began with the argument that we
whites, from the point of development we had arrived at, "must necessarily
appear to them (savages) in the nature of supernatural beings—we approach
them with the might of a deity," and so on and on. "By the simple exercise
of our will we can exert a power for good practically unbounded,' etc., etc.
From that point he soared and took me with him. . . . It gave me the notion of an
exotic Immensity ruled by an august Benevolence. It made me tingle with
enthusiasm. . . It was very simple, and at the end of that moving appeal to
every altruistic sentiment it blazed at you, luminous and terrifying, like a flash
of lightning in a serene sky: "Exterminate all the brutes!" The curious part was
that he had apparently forgotten all about that valuable postscriptum,
because, later on, when he in a sense came to himself, he repeatedly entreated
me to take good care of "my pamphlet."[6]

In this context of parody it is possible, I think, to register a foreboding
about the ultimate essence of *Heart of Darkness* and to sense an exhaustion of
spirit that froze Conrad's genius and made it impossible for him to cross the
frontier upon which his intuitive imagination had arrived. Achebe does not appear
to have given any thought to this matter in his essay. My view is that parody tends
to border upon nihilism, a fact all too clear in modern fiction and drama. Parody is
the flag of the death of god, the death of faith, and without faith imaginative art
tends to freeze and cultivate a loss of soul. Perhaps god has been so conditioned by
homogeneous or tribal idols that freedom of spirit seems a chimera. When I speak
of the necessity for faith I am not referring therefore to cults of idolatry but to a
conviction written into the stars as into one's blood that creation is a priceless gift
beyond human formula or calculation of Faustian will.

Conrad's despair is so marked that one is conscious of infinite desolation
within the very signals he intuitively erects that bear upon a radical dialectic of
form. His parody—like Beckett's parody—remains formidable because it cuts to
the bone and heart of liberal complacency. The transition beyond parody that
humanity needs neither Beckett nor Conrad fulfills.

I am convinced myself that there is a movement of transition in some
complex areas of twentieth century literature beyond parody but such an
exploration would require another essay. I shall give, however, two examples that
may suggest a groping transition. First of all, Wole Soyinka's masterpiece *The
Road* is influenced, I am sure, by Conrad in that the unscrupulous professor is
psychically related to Kurtz with the profound distinction that the professor's faith
in "the chrysalis of the Word"[7] prepares him for a descent into the fertility of the
African mask, so that he sustains in himself the wound that kills those who exist in
the depths of place and time. He is, as it were, the involuntary metaphysic that
illumines outcast humanity within the dissolution of the mask or persona
conferred by the savage god, Ogun, in contradistinction to Kurtz's totalitarian loss
of soul within the rigidity of the mask conferred by the hubris of material bias.

My second example of possible transition through and beyond post-
Conradian legacies is a remarkable asymmetric American fiction by the black

writer Jean Toomer in his book *Cane*, published in 1923, which comprises a series of half-fictions, half-plays shot through by stream of consciousness and lyrical moments as well as by short interludes or poems.

The characters appear implicitly clothed in property and landscapes they wear like bizarre roots and masks to suggest an unfreedom of personality locked in polarizations. This perception is psychic rather than behavioristic and, therefore, it may begin to undermine the polarizations since it is capable of seeing them not for what they appear to be—forms of strength—but for what they essentially are—fragmentations of a community dangerously divided within itself against itself. Paradoxically this psychic apprehension begins to grope for coherence in depth that needs to be grasped ceaselessly by imagery that points through itself, beyond itself, into a visionary comedy of wholeness that can never be structured absolutely. Indeed, where adamant property binds flesh and blood *Cane* is a revelation of bitterness and conflict since it evokes memories of the auction block on which persons were bought and sold, metaphorically nailed to the cross, as it were, as pieces of property.

I must confess, in bringing this article to a close, that I was rather surprised when Achebe quoted F. R. Leavis in support of his thesis. Leavis of all people! Leavis, as far as I am aware, possessed no sympathy whatever for imaginative literature that fell outside of the closed world of his "great tradition."

I would question Leavis's indictment of Conrad for an addiction to the adjective. The fact of the matter is that the intuitive archetypes of sensation and nonsensation by which Conrad was tormented are not *nouns*. They are qualitative and infinite variations of substance clothed in nouns. Nouns may reveal paradoxically, when qualified, that their emphasis on reality and their inner meaning can change as they are inhabited by variable psychic projections born of the mystery of creation. There is a *woodenness* to *wood*, there is also a *gaiety* to *wood* when it is stroked by shadow or light that turns *wood* into a mask worn by variable metaphysical bodies that alter the content within the mask. The livingness of wood is the magic of carven shapes that act in turn upon the perceiving eye and sculpt it into a window of spirit.

Marlow's bewilderment at the heart of the original forest he uneasily penetrated reveals unfinished senses within him and without him, unfinished perceptions that hang upon veils within veils.

> The *living* trees, lashed together by the creepers and every *living* bush of the undergrowth, might have been changed into *stone*, even to the *slenderest* twig, to the *lightest* leaf. It was not sleep—it seemed unnatural, like a state of trance. Not the *faintest* sound of any kind could be heard. You looked on amazed and began to suspect yourself of being *deaf*—then the night came suddenly, and struck you *blind* as well. About three in the morning some large fish leaped, and the *loud* splash made me jump as though a gun had been fired. When the sun rose there was a *white* fog, very warm and clammy, and more *blinding* than the night. . . . A cry, a very loud cry, as of infinite

desolation, soared slowly in the *opaque* air. It ceased. A complaining clamor, modulated in savage discord, filled our ears.[8]

At this stage I would like to add to the considerations I have already expressed by touching on the issue of "music" in imaginative literature.

The loud cry and clamor as of an orchestra at the heart of the Bush that come as a climax in the quotation from *Heart of Darkness* are of interest in the context of the human voice breaking through instruments of stone and wood and other trance formations to which the human animal is subject. Indeed it is as if the stone and wood *sing*, so that in mirroring hard-hearted dread and rigid desolation they suffer at the same time a disruption or transformation of fixed bias within themselves.

I am not suggesting that Conrad extends this notion into a profound discovery of new form or radical aesthetic but it is marginally yet significantly visible in the passage I have quoted.

Caribbean writers and poets have been interested in the ground of music in fiction and poetry. Edward Brathwaite, Derek Walcott, and others have complex approaches to music. I have intuitively explored in novels organic metaphors of music. In a recent article[9] I confessed to some of these intuitive archetypes and in particular to the pre-Columbian bone flute as a trigger of organic capacity to release a diversity of sombre or rock-hard images in alliance or attunement with phenomenal forests, walking trees, butterfly motifs within singing bodies of evolutionary hope in the midst of legacies of conquest and catastrophe.

I am reminded now, as I write this, of Beethoven's late quartets in which he wrestled with "the intolerable muteness" (as Anton Ehrenzweig puts it) "of a purely instrumental music; he tries to make the instruments sing in a human way . . . . In the end the human voice itself must break in as a symbol of extreme disruption in order to obey a more profound logic."[10]

NOTES:

1   Chinua Achebe, "An Image of Africa," *Research in African Literatures,* 9, 1 (1978), 9.

2   *Ibid.*

3   *Asymmetric context* implies that the unknowable God mediates between all structures. Thus if one were to say "the sun is a rose" one would visualize—in asymmetric context—an inimitable or unstructured mediation existing between *sun* and *rose*. Both

sun and *rose*, therefore, are partial signatures of—partial witnesses to—a universal principle of mediation, a universal principle of light beyond capture or structure. That principle of mediation at the heart of all metaphor may only be perceived as an *untameable* force mediating between *sun* and *rose*.

Symmetric context on the other hand would imply a binding locality or materiality or physicality in which *sun* and *rose* are *tameable* extensions or symmetric inversions of each other.

4   Joseph Conrad, *Heart of Darkness and The Secret Sharer* (New York: Bantam, 1978), p. 118.

5   *Ibid.,* p. 84.

6   *Ibid.,* pp. 84-85.

7   Wole Soyinka, *The Road* (London: Oxford University Press, 1965), p. 45.

8   Conrad, pp. 65-66. Italics in this quotation are mine.

9   Wilson Harris, "The Enigma of Values," *New Letters,* 40, 1 (1973), 141-49.

10   Anton Ehrenzweig, *The Hidden Order of Art* (London: Paladin, 1970), p. 219.

IV. Post-Colonial Legacy: In Conrad's Wake

CONRAD: THE PRESENTATION OF NARRATIVE

Edward W. Said

There are no words for the sort of things I wanted to say.—Lord Jim

In this essay I hope to be able to show that both in his fiction and in his autobiographical writing Conrad was trying to do something that his experience as a *writer* everywhere revealed to be impossible. This makes him interesting as the case of a writer whose working reality, his practical and even theoretical competence as a writer, was far in advance of *what* he was saying. Occurring at the time at which he lived and wrote, this irony of Conrad's writing therefore has a critical place in the history of the duplicity of language, which since Nietzsche, Marx and Freud has made the study of the orders of language so focal for the contemporary understanding. Conrad's fate was to have written fiction great for its presentation, and not only for what it was representing. He was misled by language even as he led language into a dramatization no other author really approached. For what Conrad discovered was that the chasm between words saying and words meaning was *widened*, not lessened, by his talent for words written. To have chosen to write then is to have chosen in a particular way neither to say directly nor to mean exactly in the way he had hoped to say or to mean. No wonder that Conrad returned to this problematic concern repeatedly, a problematic concern that his writing dramatized continuously and imaginatively.

I

Conrad's narratives pay unusual attention to the *motivation* of the stories being told; this is evidence of a self-consciousness that felt it necessary to justify in some way the telling of a story. Such attention to the motive for telling a story exactly conflicts with his account in *A Personal Record* of Conrad's beginning as a writer. Instead of a reasoned process by which a sailor became a writer, Conrad says that "the conception of a planned book was entirely outside my mental range when I sat down to write." One morning he called in his landlady's daughter:

> "Will you please clear away all this at once?" I addressed her in convulsive accents, being at the same time engaged in getting my pipe to draw. This, I admit, was an unusual request . . . I remember that I was perfectly calm. As

171

a matter of fact I was not at all certain that I wanted to write, or that I meant to write, or that I had anything to write about. No, I was not impatient.[1]

"This" is breakfast. Once cleared away, *Almayer's Folly* was begun: so much for an event of "general mysteriousness." Conrad's narratives deal simultaneously with actions without obvious rational motivation like this event in *A Personal Record*, and such actions as the telling of a story motivated by ascertainable causes. A clear example of what I am trying to describe is found in *Heart of Darkness*. Marlow's desire to visit the dark places is longstanding but really unexplained and yet his account of the journey to a group of listeners is related exactly to an occasion that motivates it. Marlow's "hankering after" blank spaces doesn't have a sequential history and it doesn't develop. It is fairly constant; even in *A Personal Record*, as he describes his "birth" as a writer, Conrad tells the same story as this one of Marlow's:

> Now when I was a little chap I had a passion for maps. I would look for hours at South America, or Africa, or Australia, and lose myself in all the glories of exploration. At that time there were many blank spaces on the earth, and when I saw one that looked particularly inviting on a map (but they all look that) I would put my finger on it and say, When I grow up I will go there. (VI, 52)

Years later one blank space

> had become a place of darkness. But there was in it one river especially, a mighty big river, that you could see on the map, resembling an immense snake uncoiled, with its head in the sea, its body at rest curving afar over a vast country, and its tail lost in the depths of the land. As I looked at the map of it in a shop window, it fascinated me as a snake would a bird—a silly little bird. (VI, 42)

If we compare this story of stupefied fascination with the occasion that gives rise to Marlow's telling of his African adventure we notice how, from even the tale's first paragraph, a rationale and a motive for the narration are described. The *Nellie* is forced to "wait for the turn of the tide" (XVI, 45), the five men have a common history of sea-faring, the lower reaches of the Thames suggest, not a snake fascinating a dumb bird, but a thread leading back to "the great spirit of the past . . . the dreams of men, the seed of commonwealths, the germs of empires" (XVI, 47) and then there is Marlow, with his well-known "propensity to spin yarns." Before the narration begins (and how unlike Conrad's inability to conceive of a planned book before he became an author) "we knew we were fated, before the ebb began to run, to hear about one of Marlow's inconclusive experiences." (XVI, 51)

As Conrad surveyed his novels for the Author's Notes he wrote at a late point in his career he was often impressed with the way his narratives resembled a species of gratuitous emanations. Frequently then he provided his reader with originating reasons for the story he had written. More often than not these reasons were an appealing anecdote, a bit of personal experience, a newspaper story and so on. Norman Sherry's prodigious labors have unearthed far more of that evidence than Conrad revealed, not only because Conrad was forgetful and evasive, but also because he was concerned mainly with *justifying* what he did as being reasonable. Conrad, I think, judged that to be more important than supplying clues to his methods of work. Hence, I think we ought to take seriously Conrad's protest in the Note to *Lord Jim* that Marlow's narration *could* have been spoken during an evening of swapping yarns. It is a very surprising line to take, but Conrad was addressing what was to him always an important point, the dramatized telling of the story, how and when it was told, for which the evidence was an integral part of the novel as a whole.

> Men have been known, both in the tropics and the temperate zone, to sit up half the night "swapping yarns." This, however, is but one yarn, yet with interruption affording some measure of relief; and in regard to the listeners' endurance, the postulate must be accepted that the story *was* interesting . . . That part of the book which is Marlow's narrative can be read through aloud, I should say, in less than three hours. Besides . . . we may presume that there must have been refreshments on that night, a glass of mineral water of some sort to help the narrator on. (XXI, vii)

Quite literally, therefore, Conrad was able to see his narratives as the place in which the motivated, the occasional, the methodical and the rational are brought together with the aleatory, the unpredictable, the inexplicable. On the one hand, there are conditions presented by which a story's telling becomes necessary; on the other hand, the essential story itself seems opposite to the conditions of its telling. The interplay of one with the other—and Conrad's attention to the persuasively realistic setting of the tale's presentation enforces our attention to it—makes the narrative the unique thing it is.

Such an interplay of antitheses moreover ought to be characterized as doing for Conrad what no other activity, whether verbal, plastic, or gestural, could have done for him. I attach a great importance to this observation. Too often Conrad's text is searched for supervening sub-texts or privileged meanings of the sort that seem more important than the book itself. Whereas not enough care is given the near-truism that the text such as it is, was for Conrad a produced thing, *the* produced thing—something he returned to as author, critic, defender, spectator or victim. The text was the never-ending product of a continuing process. For him, as many letters testify, the *necessity* of writing, once he had become an author, was pre-eminently the problem; for all the "general mysteriousness" of the "Rubicon" crossed into authorhood, he viewed his career as writer as a physical process and as a particularly onerous task that was his fate. "La solitude me gagne: elle m'absorbe. Je ne vois rien, je ne lis rien. C'est comme une éspèce de tombe, qui serait en même temps un enfer, où il faut écrire, écrire, écrire."[2] Loneliness, darkness, the necessity of writing, imprisonment: these are the pressures upon the writer as he writes, and there is scarcely any writer I have read who seems so profligate in his complaining. How different in tone this is from the aesthetic credo delivered by Conrad in his 1896 Preface to the *Nigger of the 'Narcissus'*. He speaks there of the artist's capacity for communal speech, and for the clarity of sight he affords the reader; those are achievements presumably won after much struggle with the writing itself.

> To snatch in a moment of courage, from the remorseless rush of time, a passing phase of life, is only the beginning of the task. The task approached in tenderness and faith is to hold up unquestioningly, without choice and without fear, the rescued fragment before all eyes in the light of a sincere mood. It is to show its vibration, its colour, its form; and through its movement, its form, and its colour reveal the substance of its truth—disclose its inspiring secret: the stress and passion within the core of each convincing movement. (XXIII, xiv)

Yet this is no set of euphemisms. To rescue a fragment and give it shape and form, to make the reader *see*, to do this by overcoming rational choice at the outset and fear during the performance: as imperatives they are much more formidable when we insist, as Conrad does a little earlier, that the medium is words. To produce or to read words is something quite different, obviously, than the more *visual* (and more well-known) goals Conrad formulates for his work. Indeed the perceptual transformation that occurs when writing or reading result in *sight* is very drastic, even antithetical. So antithetical in fact that one tends to forget the whole sentence in which Conrad formulates his primary ambition. "My task which I am trying to achieve is, by the power of the written word to make you hear, to make you feel—it is before all, to make you *see*" (xiv). Conrad's narratives thus embody (provide a locale for) the transformation in the act of taking place. Conrad's own efforts, he says, are to employ the power of *written* words, with their origin in the painstaking craft of writing, in order to make his reader experience the vitality and the dynamism of *seen* things. Most often, however, this happens through the mediation of spoken words.

For the dramatic protocol of much of Conrad's fiction is the swapped yarn, the historical report, the commonly exchanged legend, the musing recollection. This protocol implies (although often they are implicitly there) a speaker of course and a hearer and, as I said earlier, a sometimes very specific enabling occasion. If we go through Conrad's major work we will find, with the notable exception of *Under Western Eyes*, that the narrative is presented as transmitted orally. Thus hearing and telling are the ground of the story as it were, the tale's most stable sensory activity, the measure of its duration, whereas *seeing*, in marked contrast, is always a precarious achievement and a much less stable business. Consider, for a couple of examples, Kurtz and Jim. Both are heard about and spoken about more than they are seen directly in the narrative setting. When they are seen—and Jim is a particularly striking instance: "for me that white figure in the stillness of coast and sea seemed to stand at the heart of a vast enigma"—they are less clear than enigmatic, and in some curious way, grossly distorted. "Kurtz looked at least seven feet long . . . I saw him open his mouth wide—it gave him a weirdly voracious aspect, as though he had wanted to swallow all the air, all the earth, all the men before him" (XVI, 134). As Marlow speaks, furthermore, his voice remains steady as his listeners' sight of him fades. So frequent is that sort of disappearance that Conrad's stated goal in the 1896 Preface was for him an especially challenging one, since the course of narrative words seems frequently not only to run counter to vision, but to protract the silence of "an impenetrable darkness," despite the insistence of words either on the page or between speaker and hearer.

Perhaps it is useful to schematize some of what I have been saying. Narratives originate in the hearing and telling presence of people to each other. In Conrad's case this is usually true whether or not the narratives are told in the first person. Their subject is illusory, or shadowy, or dark: that is, whatever by nature is not easy to see. So much at least is ascertainable by the sheer telling of the tale, for what the tale usually reveals is the exact contours of this obscurity. Much of the time obscurity, regardless of even extravagant outward splendour (as is the case with Nostromo or Jim or the Black Mate), is a function of secret shame. Paradoxically, however, the secret is all too easily prone to the wrong kind of exposure, which Conrad's notoriously circumspect methods of narrative attempt to forestall. The reflective narrator is always a narrator preventing the wrong sort of interpretation. His narrative invariably assumes the currency of a rival version. For example, the whole of *Nostromo* is built out of competing histories of Costaguana, each claiming to be a more perspicacious record of momentous events, each implicitly critical of other versions. The same is true of *Under Western Eyes*, *Lord Jim*, and so on.

One can conceive of Conrad's narratives abstractly as the alternation in language of presence and absence. The presence of spoken words in time mitigates, if it does not make entirely absent, their written version; a speaker takes over the narrative with his voice, and his voice overrides the fact that he is absent (or unseen) to his listeners as he speaks; Conrad's goal is to make us see, or otherwise to transcend the *absence* of everything but words, so that we may pass into a realm of vision beyond the words. What is that realm? It is a world of such uncomplicated coincidence between intention, word and deed that the ghost of a fact, as *Lord Jim* has it, can be put to rest. There, rifts in the community of man, or in the damaged ego, are healed, and the space separating ambition from activity is narrowed. Retrospective time and events are corrected for divergences. Or, still more radically, the writer's intention of wishing to say something very clearly is squared completely with the reader's seeing—words bound to the page are, by the labors of a solitary writer, become the common unmediated property of the reader, who penetrates past the words to their author's visual intention, which is the same as his written presentation.

For Conrad the meaning produced by writing was a kind of *visual* outline to which written language can approach only from the outside and asymptotically. We can perhaps ascribe this hobbling limitation upon words to Conrad's concurrent faith in the supremacy of the visible and his radical doubt of the mimetic power available to written language. His use of such devices as the inquiry (*Lord Jim*), historical reporting (*Nostromo*), methodical quest (*Heart of Darkness*), the translation (*Under Western Eyes*), the ironic investigation (*The Secret Agent*) incarnates the process of drawing near in retrospective language to a sight (pun intended with "site") for which language might no longer be necessary. In all his narratives Conrad assumes that there is a central *place*, a heart of darkness which may be somewhere in central Africa, in Central America, or central London, that is better located, more centrally, for understanding action whose tendency is to proliferate from that place. To think of Conrad's fiction in those terms is to be hit by how compulsively the whole complex of ideas associated with "the center" (approach to the center, radiations away from the center) keeps appearing, especially since *writing* a narrative is the translation of a told narrative, which itself is a means for reaching that center. Thus in *Heart of Darkness* Marlow's trek inwards makes Kurtz the goal. Why? Because Kurtz is at the Inner Station and he is much spoken about; Marlow hopes by reaching him to put a stop to all the rumors, and finally to *see* (silently) for himself what exactly it is that Kurtz is and has done. Most of the time, however, the reader like Marlow must finally be satisfied with *fewer* words rather than no words once the center has been reached. Hence the haunting power in Conrad of minimal phrases such as "the horror" or "material interests": these work as the still verbal center glossed by the narrative and around which our attention turns and returns. *See* the thing they announce, and you have done with words. *Find* their visual equivalent, and you have a total presence for which the duplicitous order of language has made absent in the narrative. Nor for nothing is Conrad's first extended narrative, *Almayer's Folly*, about a structure called folly, designed to house the acquisition of gold brought out from the interior, gold never seen, never brought out, only spoken about.

So irrational must the coincidence between the effacement of words and the unmediated visual presence of meaning have become by the time of *The Secret Agent* (1907—twelve years after *Almayer*) that Conrad's use of a deranged boy's habitual activity to represent the coincidence is, I think, strongly self-commenting:

> ... innocent Stevie, seated very good and quiet at a deal table, drawing circles, circles; innumerable circles, concentric, eccentric, a coruscating whirl of circles that by their tangled multitude of repeated curves, uniformity of form, and confusion of intersecting lines suggested a rendering of cosmic chaos, the symbolism of a mad art attempting the inconceivable. The artist never turned his head; and in all his soul's application to the task his back quivered, his thin neck, sunk into a deep hollow at the base of the skull, seemed ready to snap. (XIII, 45-6)

Mr. Verloc merely "discloses the innocent Stevie" when he opens the kitchen door, for Stevie's autistic art intends no hearer, and it is unspoken. It is just a ceaseless, intense application to a repeated action whose meaning is unchanging. Conrad's choice of the word *task* here was probably an unintended quotation from the 1896 Preface whose moral seriousness he drew upon frequently. The solitary, repetitive, uniform, and confusing nature of Stevie's art parallels Conrad's description of writing ("un enfer où il faut écrire, écrire, écrire), just as the concentric, eccentric circles suggest the interplay of antithesis and the alternation in language of presence and absence to which I referred above. What is most remarkable is the *silence* of the whole scene and its "general mysteriousness." Can we say that Stevie is being overlooked, or overheard? For indeed it is hard to know whether Mr. Verloc's "grunt of disapproving surprise" means anything more than the merest awareness. Circles do not speak, they tell only of the inconceivable and that by a very attenuated symbolism, and they enclose blankness even as they seem partly to be excluding it. Moreover, Stevie's circles are pagebound; they tie him to a blank white space, and they exist no place else. I think it entirely likely that Conrad imagined Stevie as a kind of writer viewed *in extremis* who in being taken for a sort of pointless idiot is limited terribly to two poles: inscribing a page endlessly, or blown to bits and without human identity. (There are rough, but affecting antecedents for Stevie and the Verlocs in "The Idiots," a short story completed by Conrad in 1896. The story opens in very much the same way as "Amy Foster" (1901), which also deals with an alienated figure who appears to be insane, with the narrator *seeing* the vestiges of an old story as he visits a locale new to him. The story— "at last [it stood] before me, a tale formidable and simple"—is of a peasant couple who unaccountably produce four idiot children. The wife's hurt perplexity and rage drives her to kill her husband. She then kills herself by jumping off a cliff into the sea; a witness to the suicide hears "one shrill cry for help that seemed to dart upwards . . . and soar past, straight into the high and impassive heaven" (VIII, 84).

Still later, the language teacher in *Under Western Eyes* (1911) will comment further upon the attempt to transcend language by vision. Now, however, that folly has a political meaning as well, despite its formulation by him in verbal terms. "That propensity" he says "of lifting every problem from the plane of the understandable by means of some sort of mystic expression, is very Russian" (XXII, 104). Elsewhere he remarks on what it is like to listen to Russians speaking: "The most precise of her [Natalia Haldin's] sayings seemed always to me to have enigmatical prolongations vanishing somewhere beyond my reach" (XXII, 118). The verbs of physical action and perception to describe language put to extraverbal use are thoroughly consistent with Conrad's usual practice. *Lifting* of course suggests the *holding up* of the 1896 Preface, but it is associated here with the derogatory *mystic expression*, an unreliable instrument at best. The net effect of this kind of communication, no matter how precisely formulated, is to extend meaning so far away from the words that it disappears completely. What the old teacher constantly reiterates is that the tendency in Russian to mystic expression is a kind of ontological flaw present to a much lesser degree in the Western languages. Razumov feels the flaw hysterically when Haldin throws himself upon the poor student's mercy. Order is associated with the careful study and use of language (and after all it is not fortuitous that both the teacher and Razumov are students of the word), whereas disorder, transcendence and a kind of political aestheticism are linked to Haldin's revolutionary wish directly to see, to change, to embrace.

By the time *Chance* (1913) gave him an unexpected popularity Conrad had

determined that he was after all an English writer, not as some critics had
alleged a French one *manqué*, nor a crypto-Slav. In the second, much later
preface (1919) to *A Personal Record* he wrote this astonishingly "Russian"
account of his use of English. I quote it at length for its passion and its
determination not to press rationality too far:

> The truth of the matter is that my faculty to write in English is as natural
> as any other aptitude with which I might have been born. I have a strange
> and overpowering feeling that it had always been an inherent part of myself.
> English was for me neither a matter of choice nor adoption. The merest idea
> of choice had never entered my head. And as to adoption—well, yes, there
> was adoption; but it was I who was adopted by the genius of the language,
> which directly I came out of the stammering stage made me its own so
> completely that its very idioms I truly believe had a direct action on my
> temperament and fashioned my still plastic character.
>
> It was a very intimate action and for that very reason it is too mysterious
> to explain. The task would be as impossible as trying to explain love at first
> sight. There was something in this conjunction of exulting, almost physical
> recognition, the same sort of emotional surrender and the same pride of
> possession, all united in the wonder of a great discovery; but there was on it
> none of the shadow of dreadful doubt that falls on the very flame of our
> perishable passions. One knew very well that this was for ever.
>
> A matter of discovery and not of inheritance, that very inferiority of the
> title makes the faculty still more precious, lays the possessor under a life
> long obligation to remain worthy of his great fortune.... All I can claim
> after all those years of devoted practice, with the accumulated anguish of its
> doubts, imperfections and falterings in my heart, is the right to be believed
> when I say that if I had not written in English I would not have written at all.
> (VI, vii-viii)

Even if this is not the most lucid treatment of the problem at least one gets from
this passage an inkling of how complex, and how close to "Impossible" (the
capital is Conrad's), the problems were for Conrad as he considered the
dissemination, reception, and perception of language.

His letters portray Conrad perpetually struggling with language. His
narratives always dramatize how a story happens to someone else: he is either
told it or, if he is the protagonist, he experiences it like Jim with its rationale
herded under the heading Romance. "Romance had singled out Jim for its own—
and that was the true part of the story, which otherwise was all wrong." Written
language was essentially a *passive*, retrospective transcription of action. As
author therefore Conrad presented his writing as methodically overshadowed by
the speaking voice, the past, vision, and restful clarity. How revealing is this
moan in a letter of January 4, 1900 to Cunninghame Graham: "But difficulties
are as it were closing round me; an irresistible march of blackbeetles I figure it
to myself. What a fate to be so ingloriously devoured."[3]

Conrad *seemed* to have *overestimated* language, or at any rate its power
over him. I do not intend this as a judgment against him since from this
overestimation derives the extraordinary care Conrad took with the way his

narratives are delivered. *Heart of Darkness*, for instance, is a complex structure with half a dozen "languages" in it, each with its own sphere of experience, its time, its center of consciousness. To say that Conrad wrote in English therefore is to say really that Conrad makes highly imaginative distinctions within English, distinctions no other writer before him would have thought necessary, distinctions that were "physical recognition" of verbal sources for a story that always lay just beyond and outside him. These distinctions were Conrad's defence against the assault of language: by redisposing and redispersing, then reassembling language into voices, he could stage his work as a writer. The plurality of narrative components is then imagined as encircling a subject in many different ways. The net effect, as Mallarmé says in *Crise de vers*, is finally to concede "l'initiative aux mots, par le heurt de leur inegalités mobilisés."[4] What gets left out of the words is that intransigent remnant of the writer's identity that is not amenable to language. By a curious irony, which doubtless appeals to a writer who wishes to make you see, the excluded remnant is the actual inscribing *persona* himself, the author, and yet Conrad pretended that the author was secondary. Once again we note how voices leading to vision efface what Conrad called "the worker in prose," whose disappearance, according to Mallarmé, ought to yield *l'oeuvre pure*. Unlike both Mallarmé and Flaubert, however, this does not happen in Conrad's case. Let us now try to see why not.

II

Walter Benjamin's reflections of Leskov's storytelling take it that the success of narrative art has traditionally depended upon a sense of community between speaker and listener, and on the desire to communicate something useful. Those two conditions are interdependent. Information is useful only because it can be put to use by others with the same set of values, and a set of values is perpetuated only by the adherence to it of more than one individual. That this is no longer true in modern times, according to Benjamin,

> is a concomitant symptom of the secular productive forces of history, a concomitant that has quite gradually removed narrative from the realm of living speech and at the same time is making it possible to see a new beauty in what is vanishing . . . The storyteller takes what he tells from experience—his own or that reported by others. And he in turn makes it the experience of those who are listening to his tale. The novelist has isolated himself. The birthplace of the novel is the solitary individual, who is no longer able to express himself by giving examples of his most important concerns, is himself uncounseled, and cannot counsel others. To write a novel means to carry the incommensurable to extremes in the representation of human life.[5]

Conrad's personal history made him acutely sensitive to the different status of *information* in the sea life, on the one hand, and in the writing life on the other. In the former, community and usefulness are essential to the enterprise; in the latter the opposite is true. Thus Conrad had the dubious privilege of witnessing within his own double life the change from storytelling as useful, communal art to novel-writing as essentialized, solitary art.

What does the change specifically entail? First of all, since the status of information has become problematical, the medium of its delivery is given greater prominence. Second, the speaker has to vary his words and his tone enough to compensate for his doubts of the usefulness of what he is saying. James and Wilde, Conrad's contemporaries, repeatedly referred to this sort of variation as the creation of interest; interest in such an instance depends closely upon an uncertainty towards (or even an ignorance of) the usefully practical. Conrad's virtuosic skill in narrative management, which reached its apex in *Chance*, is always as important as—and usually more interesting and important than—any information the tale conveys. One can say this without in any way belittling either the sea lore in Conrad's fiction or its devotees among his readers. Third, the narrative no longer merely assumes a listener. It dramatizes him as well, so that frequently the author himself appears to be participating in the tale as an audience, or more precisely in Conrad's case, as the dramatized *recipient* of impressions. Fourth, narrative is conceived, in what Frye calls its radical of presentation, as *utterance* rather than as useful information. In Conrad's case the refinement of information into narrative utterance, as well as the fact that his language is usually in the mode of reported speech, are signs that the content of what is said need not by definition be as clear as who says it, why, and how.

I think that this last change has to be considered as an aspect of the general loss of faith in the mimetic powers of language to which I referred earlier. I said then that it was possible for the writer to lose such a faith and still to retain a belief in the supremacy of the visible. Writing therefore cannot represent the visible, but it can desire and, in a manner of speaking, can move towards the visible, without actually achieving the unambiguous directness of the visible. Michel Foucault has studied this apparent contradiction in his *Les mots et les choses* by treating it as a specific historical phase embodied in the work of de Sade, Mallarmé and Nietzsche: Conrad's narratives, I believe, offer particularly rich illustrations of it. Only within a general perspective of the sort Foucault draws can we understand the deep necessity of Conrad's decision to ground narrative epistemologically in utterance—that is, speech reported or spoken during periods dramatized as *enforced calm*—and not in action, community, or information.

The springs of Conrad's narrative utterances are what I shall call a) wanting-to-speak and b) the need to link a given utterance with other utterances. What makes a Conradian character the special creature he is comes from something he possesses that is in need of telling about. Often he possesses a guilty secret; at other times he is a man or woman of whom other people talk obsessively. At still other times he is a taciturn man, like James Wait, or Charles Gould, or MacWhirr, or Axel Heyst whose entire life *speaks* in an exemplary way to other men. Thus Conrad's tales are about such personages as all these but they are presented as *taken note of.* The internal continuity of each tale, however, derives from the utterance's sense of its own difference which, as I said above, is an awareness of conflicting or complementary utterances. In a sense therefore every narrative utterance in Conrad stands against another one: and Marlow's lie to Kurtz's Intended is only the most notable instance of a common enough habit. Nostromo's great ride out of Sulaco is the subject of Mitchell's admiring reports, but these must be judged to be but a few of the reports that generally treat the *capataz de cargadores* as Sulaco's savior. Then too Decoud's notes personify the cynic's attitude, in deliberate contrast to Gould's sentimentalism. Avellanos, Emilia, Giorgio Viola, Sotillo—each perceives and reports events in a manner turned either explicitly or implicitly towards other perceptions. In no place more than in *Chance* can the reader see Conrad make tension and conflict, and thereby a dynamic narrative texture, out of utterance at odds with and yet ineluctably linked to other utterance.

Lord Jim is one of the first of Conrad's extended narratives to make knowledge, intelligibility, and vision into functions of utterance. The novel "takes off" in "the act of intelligent volition" that directs Marlow's eyes to Jim's during the Inquiry. After a period of "endless converse with himself" and at a time when "speech was no use to him any longer" Jim at last meets a man whose presence loosens the tongues "of men with soft spots, with hard spots, with hidden plague spots." Marlow not only listened, but is "willing to remember Jim at length, in detail and audibly." True, Jim has "influential confidences" to confess, yet Marlow's propensity to tell and remember is at least as important to the book. ". . . With the very first word [of his narrative] Marlow's body, extended at rest in the seat, would become very still, as though his spirit had winged its way back into the lapse of time and were speaking through his lips from the past" (XXI, 33). Marlow's generosity towards Jim is rooted in precisely that same tendency to romantic projection because of which Jim so embarrassingly prefers courageous voyages in time to voyages in actuality. Neither man, whether hearer or storyteller, truly inhabits the world of facts. First Jim, then Marlow, wanders off "to comprehend the Inconceivable," an activity so urgent and rarefied at the same time as to involve "a subtle and momentous quarrel as to the true essence of life." Ultimately Conrad points out that Jim does not speak to Marlow, but rather *before* him, just as Marlow cannot (by definition) speak to the reader but before him.

What first seems like a meeting of minds turns into a set of parallel lines. Moreover Marlow explicitly says later that Jim exists for him, as if to say that Jim's confession before Marlow mattered more than what Jim confessed (both Marlow and Jim seem just about equally confused anyway). Only because of that performance—not just because of Jim's exploits in and of themselves— does Jim exist for his listener. I have already commented on Conrad's practice, which is evident in what Marlow says of Jim's enigmatic appearance and his need to talk, of alternating the visual and the oral modes: the way the narrative shows how "Romance had singled out Jim for its own" follows directly from this practice. Jim's appetite for disastrous adventure, like Marlow's narrative, like our attention to the tale, corresponds not to any communicable pattern of linear progress from, say, ambition to accomplishment, but rather to a more abstract impulse. The impulse can find no expression in action, and no image, other than the vague rubric of Romance, conveys the aim of Jim's troubled quest. The impulse resolves itself into the duration of reported speech or utterance whose exigencies are such relatively ethereal things as pattern, rhythm, phrase, sequence. What is the pressure upon Jim that makes him favor death over life, and which urges Marlow and Conrad towards "inconclusive experiences" that reveal less to the reader than he is entitled normally to expect? In all cases there exists a fatalistic desire to behold the self passively as an object told about, mused on, puzzled over, marveled at fully, in utterance. That is, Jim, Marlow and Conrad having everywhere conceded that one can neither completely realize one's own nor fully grasp someone else's life experience, are left with a desire to fashion verbally and approximately their individual experience in the terms unique to each one. Since invariably this experience is either long gone or by definition almost impossible, no image can capture this, just as finally no sentence can either.

Nevertheless the utterance is spoken, if not only to, then before another. Words convey the presence to each other of speaker and hearer but not a mutual comprehension. Each sentence drives a sharper wedge between intention (wanting-to-speak) and communication. Finally want-to-speak, a specifically verbal intention, is forced to confront the insufficiency, and indeed the absence, of words for that intention. It is not too extreme, I think, to say that in a very complex way Conrad is dramatizing the disparity between verbal intention apprehendable and possible, grammatically and formally, and verbality itself, as a way of being in the world of language with other men. In no place more than in "Amy Foster," that most poignant of all his stories, is the disparity spelled out in particular human detail. Washed ashore in England, Yanko Goorall lives amongst people who cannot make him out and to whose language he is always a foreigner:

> These were the people to whom he owed allegiance, and an overwhelming loneliness seemed to fall from the leaden sky of that winter without sunshine. All the faces were sad. He could talk to no one, and had no hope of ever understanding anybody. It was as if these had been the faces of people from the other world—dead people he used to tell me years afterwards. Upon my word, I wonder he did not go mad. He didn't know where he was. Somewhere very far from his mountains—somewhere over the water. Was this America, he wondered?
> . . . The very grass was different, and the trees. All the trees but the three old Norway pines on the bit of lawn before Swaffer's house, and these reminded him of his country. He had been detected once, after dusk, with his forehead against the trunk of one of them, sobbing, and talking to himself. They had been like brothers to him at that time, he affirmed. Everything else was strange . . .
> Many times have I heard his high-pitched voice from behind the ridge of some sloping sheepwalk, a voice light and soaring, like a lark's but with a

> melancholy human note, over our fields that hear only the song of birds. And I would be startled myself. Ah! He was different; innocent of heart, and full of good will, which nobody wanted, this castaway, that, like a man transplanted into another planet, was separated by an immense space from his past and by an immense ignorance of the future. His quick, fervent utterance, positively shocked everybody. (XX, 128, 129, 132)

Conrad's excruciatingly detailed understanding of this predicament makes utterance something far more urgent than a comfortable aesthetic choice. It is clear he believed that only a fully imagined scene between a speaker and a *watching* hearer could present—continuously, directly, and, since it occurs in story after story, repeatedly—the fundamental divorce he stood for as a writer: the rift between a fully developed but, with regard to other people, an intentional or virtual capacity, and an inescapable human community. "There are no words for the sort of things I wanted to say." Hence, for example, Conrad's penchant for repeating phrases like "he was one of us" together with reminders of how unique each individual and his experiences were. Moreover the text Conrad worked at ceased simply to be a written document and became instead a distribution of utterances around both sides of the rift. They are held together by the reader's attention to both sides. In its duration for the length of the book such overarching attention binds together Jim's verbal intention with Marlow's forbearance as a witness. In the domain of intention and fantasy to which Conrad's heroes have what appears to be a fatal attraction, and only there, can there be completion for schemes of the kind Jim devises for himself; but such a place is apprehendable only during the constantly progressing narrative of his doom and failure. When Marlow sees Jim for the last time, there is the following passage:

> Jim, at the water's edge, raised his voice. "Tell them . . ." he began. I signed to the men to cease rowing, and waited in wonder. Tell who? The half-submerged sun faced him. I could see its red gleam in his eyes that looked dumbly at me . . . "No—nothing," he said, and with a slight wave of his hand motioned the boat away. I did not look again at the shore till I had clambered on board the schooner.
> . . . He was white from head to foot, and remained persistently visible with the stronghold of the night at his back, the sea at his feet, the opportunity by his side—still veiled? I don't know. For me that white figure in the stillness of coast and sea seemed to stand at the heart of a vast enigma. The twilight was ebbing fast from the sky above his head, the strip of sand had sunk already under his feet, he himself appeared no bigger than a child—then only a speck, a tiny white speck, that seemed to catch all the light left in a darkened world . . . And suddenly, I lost him . . . " (XXI, 336)

Much is brought together here. Jim's terminal silence indicates that once again "a silent opportunity" takes over his life. He seems for a moment to have become the point of visual, as well as intellectual, reference for which words are both inadequate and never relinquished. Then he disappears. His life is covered over with the minimal traces—a letter, an incomplete narrative, a patchy oral report—that Marlow can garner much later. But at least Jim holds the privacy of his intentionality intact, something Axel Heyst, for example, cannot hold to himself for very long. Heyst is the last of those substantial Conradian figures to attempt a life of almost pure virtuality and, almost, by definition, the last of men whose passivity is an invitation to the assaults of Romance. Yet in *Victory* (1915) Heyst's insular seclusion is of itself no guarantee. No man, in short, can become invisible so long as he retains even the slenderest contact with the actual. The subject of Schombert's malicious gossip, or Ricardo's venality, of the Archipelago's gossip, Heyst cannot use his father's philosophy of detachment to much purpose. Besides, Heyst's attraction to Lena is too strong for him, just as earlier his sympathy for Morrison's plight crushes his reserve.

Of course there is an important sexual theme in *Victory*, yet Conrad's deliberate juxtaposition of Morrison's boat with Lena as objects of Heyst's romantic intervention into the world belongs, I think, to another, more strictly verbal enterprise of his, one easily found in many other places in the fiction. I have said that Conrad's primary mode, although he is a writer, is presented as the oral, and his ambition is to move towards the visual. These are the situations that employ yarns, tales, and utterances for their depiction, and which in the end present us with the disparity between intention and actuality, or in sensuous terms between hearing on the one hand, and seeing and comprehending on the other. In my discussion of *Lord Jim* I had been indicating also the *play* of all this in the text, as well as the intense attraction to each other, despite the gulf between them, of intention (not silence) and actuality. But, it needs hardly to be said, Conrad is a novelist, not a philosopher, and not a psychologist. This brings me to my final point, which I'd like now to sketch briefly. I imagine that during the writing of his fiction Conrad had certain substantial quantities or qualities in mind, for both his memory and his senses, though transmuted into words as he wrote, were focussed on material objects. Despite what I have said about utterance and presentation one remembers *objects* in Conrad's fiction, not merely words. In his fiction an essential place is filled by substances around which a great deal of the action in the utterance is organized: Lingard's gold, Kurtz's ivory, the ships of sailors, Gould's silver, the women that draw men to change and romance, and so forth. A large proportion of the tension in Conrad's fiction gets generated as the author, or the narrator, or the hero tries to make us *see* the object that draws out the writing, the thought, the speech on and on. I said earlier that with telling or reporting as their basis, these activities approach substantiality. But why? And why, after all, did Conrad ground all these activities, given verbal form, in utterance or reported speech, and not for example in the impersonal purity adopted by Mallarmé or Joyce?

The main interest of this question is, I think, that it purports to distinguish, however minimally and schematically, between Conrad's psychology (which is really the exclusive subject of psychoanalytic studies like *Joseph Conrad: A Psychoanalytic Biography*, by Bernard C. Meyer) and the psychology of Conrad's writing. As a source of evidence of the man's psychohistory, fiction is "finished" by literary process in a way that everyday behaviour, itself conditioned by culture and history, is not. Moreover, as I have tried to show elsewhere,[6] there is a particular psychological dynamic to a literary career and a literary text that is very doubtfully construed as either direct or indirect evidence of a *man's* psychology considered *tout court*. But does a literary career or text, and consequently an *author*, mean confirmation or denial of psycho-pathology? Is there any relatively useful and non-trivial way of separating "the man who suffers and the mind which creates?" To be more specific, is there an exact analogy between an author's personal writing and artistic writing on the one hand, and, on the other hand, the same man's discourse and his dreams?

Writing, whether personal or artistic, and dreams are subject to different sorts of control than the ones governing a man's spoken discourse. Yet it is difficult to conceive of writing-work done under conditions that resemble those of the dream-work. Wakefulness, a pen or a typewriter, paper, one's past writing, a plan for what is being written, a set of physical gestures, what one has consciously learned about writing: these, I think, count importantly in differentiating writing and dreaming, at least if one is to insist that the two activities are valid as psychoanalytic evidence. The differences become more interesting, however, when writing is denied its importance in the writer's work itself, especially by the writer like Conrad for whom it was sheer agony.

If we say, as I think we must, that Conrad in his writing is generally unhappy with the idea of writing, so much so that when he is not complaining about it he is always turning it into substitute speech, then we can go as far as saying that Conrad's writing tries in fact overtly to negate itself *as writing*. Of negation Freud has said that it is a way of affirming what is repressed. But what does it mean for a writer to affirm writing that is repressed? Again Freud is helpful. "By the help of the symbol of negation the thinking-process frees itself from the limitations of repression and enriches itself with the subject-matter without which it could not work efficiently."[7] Writing, and its negation in the ways I have discussed, was for Conrad a way of *permitting himself* a number of things otherwise impossible. Amongst these things are the use of English, the use of experiences from out of his past that are reconstructed and, most of the time, deformed into "fictional" novels and stories, the use of events about which no explanation can (or need) be satisfactory.

Let us continue a step further with Freud's argument. Negation is the result of an intellectual judgment made on two grounds. First there is a judgment as to whether a thing has, or has not, a particular property. Second, a judgment is made as to whether or not an image exists in reality. In both cases criteria of internality (respectively: I want this inside me, or, that image is inside me) and criteria of externality (respectively: I reject this, or, that image also has an existence in reality outside me) are used, both of them making reference to the judging ego. Freud had been led to these discoveries because, he says, "in the course of analytic work we often bring about a further very important and somewhat bewildering modification of the same situation. We succeed in defeating the negation too and in establishing a complete intellectual acceptance of what is repressed—but the repression itself is still not removed (182)." Therefore when a *negative* reality-judgment about an image is made the ego may still be affirming the image's existence by repression; for an *image* is a rediscovery of what has already been lost. Thus only when "the symbol of negation has endowed thought with a first degree of independence from the results of repression and at the same time from the sway of the pleasure principle (195)" is there a proper judgment.

Writing for Conrad was an activity that constituted negation—of itself, of what it dealt with—and was also repetitive. That is, writing negated, reconstituted, negated again, and so forth indefinitely; hence the extraordinarily patterned quality of Conrad's writing. The utterance is the *form* of the negation. As such therefore its function is to postpone judgment indefinitely, on itself and its subject matter: it too is repetitive, for we see Conrad imagining narrative *being uttered* from one tale to the next while the reality of what Marlow calls "life-sensation" remains private, developed, uncommunicable except by negatives (e.g. "we live, as we dream—alone . . ."). But Conrad's characters, at some stage in their lives, are powerfully affected by material objects: women, treasure, ships, land, etc. Most of the time, however, these objects are at the outset passively endowed with force. Charles Gould inherits his father's mine. Only after that does he build the imperial power of the San Tomé Mine. At the point in Conrad's fiction that that process of mythical building becomes apparent, an important cleavage appears between the character reported about and the report. The fact of utterance from being a form of negation becomes then the instrument of Conrad's judgment. Writing transforms the writer from failed speaker, the character or the "narrating pen" who had direct, visual and even material goals passively accepted because of heritage or convention, into the reflective writer, the *author* who *takes on* the form of utterance habitually from novel to novel and forces it through a maximum of different and interesting developments. In each tale therefore Conrad's autobiographical presence plays numerous roles: first as man to whom events happened, as speaker, as listener, then finally as author who at one moment *presents* narrative, negates it by pretending it is speech, then negates that (in his letters) by denouncing its difficulties, then negates even that (late in his career) by sounding like Everyman's Favorite Old Novelist. My argument, put very bluntly, is that Conrad's writing was a way of repeatedly *confirming* his authorship amidst a variety of narrative and quasi-narrative contingencies, and not simply a way of representing his neuroses.

Conrad in short tried to use prose for the transcendence of writing and the *embodiment* both of direct utterance and vision. Every experience begins for him in the presence of speaker to hearer and vice versa; consequently each speaker tells of action whose goal is clarity, or realized intention. Yet in almost every case, what enables the latter fulfillment is an inert substance like silver given power over life. Such a substance is felt mistakenly to be capable of embodying the visible, the timeless, the unmediated sensory possession of all reality. But also in each case, this substance turns out to embody the ego's nearly limitless capacity for extension. Surely this insight is what makes *Nostromo* the impressively pessimistic edifice that it is, for the novel reposes upon the impregnation of silver with an imaginative conception of its power. The totality of this conception encompasses both life and death, and thus the Goulds for all their pretention to humanity are no different from the Professor in *The Secret Agent* or Kurtz in *Heart of Darkness*. ". . . By her imaginative estimate of its power she [Emilia Gould] endowed that lump of metal with a justificative conception, as though it were not a mere fact, but something far-reaching and impalpable, like the true expression of an emotion or the emergency of a principle . . . . For the San Tomé Mine was to become an institution, a rallying point for everything in the provinces that needed order and stability to live. Security seemed to flow upon this land from the mountain range" (IX, 107, 110).

Matter is transmuted into value as, in an ideal world, emotion can be converted into "true expression." Matter for Conrad's heroes becomes a system of exchange underlying language. The self, which is the source of utterance, attempts the reconciliation of intention with actuality; words are really being bypassed as a direct embodiment in material sought by the imagination, at the same time that the ego reports its adventures and its disappointments. If language fails ultimately to represent intention and analogously, if the mimetic function of language is sorely inadequate to make us see—then by using substance *instead of words* the Conradian hero, like Conrad himself, aims to vindicate and articulate his imagination. Every reader of Conrad knows how this aim too is bound to fail. In the end the hero, like the dying Kurtz, becomes a talking insubstantiality. For every brief success like Gould or Verloc there is a Nostromo or a Stevie whose destroyed body tells on. And for every Kurtz and Jim there is a Marlow by whose memory a body can be recaptured in all its splendour and youth. That this takes place only in "the lapse of time" and because the speaker's words are being written does not diminish its achievement except as words diminish, without actually delivering, a man entire. Conrad is the writer whose work exactly is this fertile irony.

1   All references to Conrad are to the *Complete Works*, 26 vols. (Garden City, New York: Doubleday, Page and Company, 1925) VI, 70. Volume and page numbers are noted parenthetically.

2   *Lettres françaises* (Paris: Gallimard, 1930), p. 50.

3   *Joseph Conrad: Letters to Cunninghame Graham,* ed. C.T. Watts (Cambridge: Cambridge University Press, 1969), p. 129.

4   *Oeuvres Complètes* (Paris: Gallimard, 1945), p. 366.

5   *Illuminations,* ed. Hannah Arendt, trans. H. Zohn (New York: Harcourt, Brace, 1968), p. 87.

6   "Notes on the Characterization of a Literary Text," *MLN,* 85, No. 6 (1970), 765-790.

7   *Collected Papers,* Vol. 5, trans. Joan Rivière (New York: Basic Books, 1959), p. 182.

CONRAD'S DARKNESS

V. S. Naipaul

It has taken me a long time to come round to Conrad. And if I begin with an account of his difficulty, it is because I have to be true to my experience of him. I would find it hard to be detached about Conrad. He was, I suppose, the first modern writer I was introduced to. It was through my father. My father was a self-taught man, picking his way through a cultural confusion of which he was perhaps hardly aware and which I have only recently begun to understand; and he wished himself to be a writer. He read less for pleasure than for clues, hints, and encouragement; and he introduced me to those writers he had come upon in his own search. Conrad was one of the earliest of these: Conrad the stylist, but more than that, Conrad the late starter, holding out hope to those who didn't seem to be starting at all.

I believe I was ten when Conrad was first read to me. It sounds alarming; but the story was "The Lagoon"; and the reading was a success. "The Lagoon" is perhaps the only story of Conrad's that can be read to a child. It is very short, about fifteen pages. A forest-lined tropical river at dusk. The white man in the boat says, "We'll spend the night in Arsat's clearing." The boat swings into a creek; the creek opens out into a lagoon. A lonely house on the shore; inside, a woman is dying. And during the night Arsat, the young man who is her lover, will tell how they both came there. It is a story of illicit love in another place, an abduction, a chase, the death of a brother, abandoned to the pursuers. What Arsat has to say should take no more than fifteen minutes; but romance is romance, and when Arsat's story ends the dawn comes up; the early morning breeze blows away the mist; the woman is dead. Arsat's happiness, if it existed, has been flawed and brief; and now he will leave the lagoon and go back to his own place, to meet his fate. The white man too has to go. And the last picture is of Arsat, alone in his lagoon, looking "beyond the great light of a cloudless day into the darkness of a world of illusions."

In time the story of "The Lagoon" became blurred. But the sense of night and solitude and doom stayed with me, grafted, in my fantasy, to the South Sea or tropical island setting of the Sabu and Jon Hall films. I have, unwillingly, looked at "The Lagoon" again. There is a lot of Conrad in it–passion and the abyss, solitude and futility and the world of illusions–and I am not sure now that it isn't the purest piece of fiction Conrad wrote. The brisk narrative, the precise pictorial writing, the setting of river and hidden lagoon, the nameless white visitor, the story during the night of love and loss, the death at daybreak: everything comes beautifully together. And if I say it is a pure piece of fiction, it is because the story speaks for itself; the writer does not come between his story and the reader.

"The Lagoon" was parodied by Max Beerbohm in *A Christmas Garland*. Writers' myths can depend on accidents like that. "The Lagoon," as it happens, was the first short story Conrad wrote; and though later, when I read the parody, I was able to feel that I was in the know about Conrad, from my own point of view "The Lagoon" had been a cheat. Because I was never to find anything so strong and direct in Conrad again.

There is a story, "Karain," written not long after "The Lagoon." It has the same Malayan setting and, as Conrad acknowledged, a similar motif. Karain, inspired by sudden sexual jealousy, kills the friend whose love-quest he had promised to serve; and thereafter Karain is haunted by the ghost of the man he has killed. One day he meets a wise old man, to whom he confesses. The old man exorcises the ghost; and Karain, with the old man as his counselor, becomes a warrior and a conqueror, a ruler. The old man dies; the ghost of the murdered friend returns to haunt Karain. He is immediately lost; his power and splendor are nothing; he swims out to the white men's ship and asks them, unbelievers from another world, for help. They give him a charm; a Jubilee sixpence. The charm works; Karain becomes a man again.

The story is, on the surface, a yarn about native superstition. But to Conrad it is much more; it is profounder, and more wonderful, than "The Lagoon"; and he is determined that its whole meaning should be grasped. All the suggestions that were implicit in "The Lagoon" are now spelled out. The white men have names; they talk, and act as a kind of chorus. So we are asked to contemplate the juxtaposition of two cultures, one open and without belief, one closed and ruled by old magic; one, "on the edge of outer darkness," exploring the world, one imprisoned in a small part of it. But illusions are illusions, mirage is mirage. Isn't London itself, the life of its streets, a mirage? "I see it. It is there; it pants, it runs, it rolls; it is strong and alive; it would smash you if you didn't look out; but I'll be hanged if it is yet as real to me as the other thing." So, romantically and somewhat puzzlingly, the story ends.

The simple yarn is made to carry a lot. It requires a more complex response than the plainer fiction of "The Lagoon." Sensations–night and solitude and doom–are not enough; the writer wishes to involve us in more than his fantasy; we are required–the chorus or commentary requires us–to stand outside the facts of the story and contemplate the matter. The story has become a kind of parable. Nothing has been rigged, though, because nothing is being proved; only wonder is being awakened.

In a preface to a later collection of stories Conrad wrote: "The romantic feeling of reality was in me an inborn faculty." He hadn't deliberately sought out romantic subjects; they had offered themselves to him.

> I have a natural right to [my subjects] because my past is very much my own.
> If their course lie out of the beaten path of organized social life, it is, perhaps,

because I myself did in a sort break away from it early in obedience to an impulse which must have been very genuine since it has sustained me through all the dangers of disillusion. But that origin of my literary work was very far from giving a larger scope to my imagination. On the contrary, the mere fact of dealing with matters outside the general run of everyday experience laid me under the obligation of a more scrupulous fidelity to the truth of my own sensations. The problem was to make unfamiliar things credible. To do that I had to create for them, to reproduce for them, to envelop them in their proper atmosphere of actuality. This was the hardest task of all and the most important, in view of that conscientious rendering of truth in thought and fact which has been always my aim.

But the truths of that story, "Karain," are difficult ones. The world of illusions, men as prisoners of their cultures, belief and unbelief: these are truths one has to be ready for, and perhaps half possess already, because the story does not carry them convincingly within itself. The suggestion that the life of London is as much a mirage as the timeless life of the Malayan archipelago is puzzling, because the two-page description of the London streets with which the story ends is too literal: blank faces, hansom cabs, omnibuses, girls "talking vivaciously," "dirty men. . . discussing filthily," a policeman. There isn't anything in that catalogue that can persuade us that the life described is a mirage. Reality hasn't fused with the writer's fantasy. The concept of the mirage has to be applied: it is a matter of words, a disturbing caption to a fairly straight picture.

I have considered this simple story at some length because it illustrates, in little, the difficulties I was to have with the major works. I felt with Conrad I wasn't getting the point. Stories, simple in themselves, always seemed at some stage to elude me. And there were the words, the words that issued out of the writer's need to be faithful to the truth of his own sensations. The words got in the way; they obscured. *The Nigger of the "Narcissus"* and *Typhoon*, famous books, were impenetrable.

In 1896 the young H. G. Wells, in an otherwise kind review of *An Outcast of the Islands,* the book before *The Nigger,* wrote: "Mr. Conrad is wordy; his story is not so much told as seen intermittently through a haze of sentences. He has still to learn the great half of his art, the art of leaving things unwritten." Conrad wrote a friendly letter to Wells; but on the same day–the story is in Jocelyn Baines's biography–he wrote to Edward Garnett: "Something brings the impression off—makes its effect. What? It can be nothing but the expression–the arrangement of words, the style." It is, for a novelist, an astonishing definition of style. Because style in the novel, and perhaps in all prose, is more than an "arrangement of words": it is an arrangement, even an orchestration, of perceptions; it is a matter of knowing where to put what. But Conrad aimed at fidelity. Fidelity required him to be explicit.

It is this explicitness, this unwillingness to let the story speak for itself, this anxiety to draw all the mystery out of a straightforward situation, that leads to the mystification of *Lord Jim.* It isn't always easy to know what is being explained. The story is usually held to be about honor. I feel myself that it is about the theme–much more delicate in 1900 than today–of the racial straggler. And, such is Conrad's explicitness, both points of view can be supported by quotation. *Lord Jim,* however, is an imperialist book, and it may be that the two points of view are really one.

Whatever the mystery of *Lord Jim,* it wasn't of the sort that could hold me. Fantasy, imagination, story if you like, had been refined away by explicitness. There was something unbalanced, even unfinished, about Conrad. He didn't seem able to go beyond his first simple conception of a story; his invention seemed to fail so quickly. And even in his variety there was something tentative and uncertain.

There was *The Secret Agent,* a police thriller that seemed to end almost as soon as it began, with a touch of Arnold Bennett and *Riceyman Steps* in that Soho interior, and a Wellsian jokeyness about London street names and cabbies and broken-down horses – as though, when dealing with the known, the written-about, the gift of wonder left the writer and he had to depend on other writers' visions. There was *Under Western Eyes,* which, with its cast of Russian revolutionaries and its theme of betrayal, promised to be Dostoevskyan but then dissolved away into analysis. There was the too set-up fiction of *Victory:* the pure, aloof man rescues a girl from a musical company touring the East and takes her to a remote island, where disaster, in the form of gangsters, will come to them. And there was *Nostromo,* about South America, a confusion of characters and themes, which I couldn't get through at all.

A multiplicity of Conrads, and they all seemed to me to be flawed. The hero of *Victory,* holding himself aloof from the world, had "refined away everything except disgust"; and it seemed to me that in his fictions Conrad had refined away, as commonplace, those qualities of imagination and fantasy and invention that I went to novels for. The Conrad novel was like a simple film with an elaborate commentary. A film: the characters and settings could be seen very clearly. But realism often required trivial incidental dialogue, the following of trivial actions; the melodramatic flurry at the end emphasized the slowness and bad proportions of what had gone before; and the commentary emphasized the fact that the characters were actors.

But we read at different times for different things. We take to novels our own ideas of what the novel should be; and those ideas are made by our needs, our education, our backgrounds or perhaps our ideas of our background. Because we read, really, to find out what we already know, we can take a writer's virtues for granted. And his originality, the news he is offering us, can go over our heads.

It came to me that the great novelists wrote about highly organized societies. I had no such society; I couldn't share the assumptions of the writers; I didn't see my world reflected in theirs. My colonial world was more mixed and second-hand, and more restricted. The time came when I began to ponder the mystery– Conradian word–of my own background: that island in the mouth of a great South American river, the Orinoco, one of the Conradian dark places of the earth, where my father had conceived literary ambitions of himself and then for me, but from which, in my mind, I had stripped all romance and perhaps even reality: preferring to set "The Lagoon," when it was read to me, not on the island I knew, with its muddy rivers, mangrove and swamps, but somewhere far away.

It seemed to me that those of us who were born there were curiously naked, that we lived purely physically. It wasn't an easy thing to explain, even to oneself. But in Conrad, in that very story of "Karain," I was later to find my feelings about the land exactly caught.

> And really, looking at that place, landlocked from the sea and shut off from the land by the precipitous slopes of mountains, it was difficult to believe in the existence of any neighborhood. It was still, complete, unknown, and full of a life that went on stealthily with a troubling effect of solitude; of a life that seemed unaccountably empty of anything that would stir the thought, touch the heart, give a hint of the ominous sequence of days. It appeared to us a land without memories, regrets, and hopes; a land where nothing could survive the coming of the night, and where each sunrise, like a dazzling act of special creation, was disconnected from the eve and the morrow.

It is a passage that, earlier, I would have hurried through: the purple passage, the reflective caption. Now I see a precision in its romanticism, and a great effort of thought and sympathy. And the effort doesn't stop with the aspect of the land. It extends to all men in these dark or remote places who, for whatever reason, are denied a clear vision of the world: Karain himself, in his world of phantoms; Wang, the self-exiled Chinese of *Victory,* self-contained within the "instinctive existence" of the Chinese peasant; the two Belgian empire-builders of "An Outpost of Progress," helpless away from their fellows, living in the middle of Africa "like blind men in a large room, aware only of what came in contact with them, but unable to see the general aspect of things."

"An Outpost of Progress" is now to me the finest thing Conrad wrote. It is the story of two commonplace Belgians, new to the new Belgian Congo, who find that they have unwittingly, through their Negro assistant, traded Africans for ivory, are then abandoned by the surrounding tribesmen, and go mad. But my first judgment of it had been only literary. It had seemed familiar; I had read other stories of lonely white men going mad in hot countries. And my rediscovery, or discovery, of Conrad really began with one small scene in *Heart of Darkness.*

The African background–"the demoralized land" of plunder and licensed cruelty–I took for granted. That is how we can be imprisoned by our assumptions. The background now seems to me to be the most effective part of the book; but then it was no more than what I expected. The story of Kurtz, the up-river ivory agent, who is led to primitivism and lunacy by his unlimited power over primitive men, was lost on me. But there was a page which spoke directly to me, and not only of Africa.

The steamer is going up river to meet Kurtz; it is "like travelling back to the earliest beginnings of the world." A hut is sighted on the bank. It is empty, but it contains one book, sixty years old. *An Inquiry into Some Points of Seamanship,* tattered, without covers, but "lovingly stitched afresh with white cotton thread." And in the midst of nightmare, this old book, "dreary . . . with illustrative diagrams and repulsive tables of figures," its "honest concern for the right way of going to work," seems to the narrator to be "luminous with another than a professional light."

This scene, perhaps because I have carried it for so long, or perhaps because I am more receptive to the rest of the story, now makes less of an impression. But I suppose that at the time it answered something of the political panic I was beginning to feel.

To be a colonial was to know a kind of security; it was to inhabit a fixed world. And I suppose that in my fantasy I had seen myself coming to England as to some purely literary region, where, untrammelled by the accidents of history or background, I could make a romantic career for myself as a writer. But in the new world I felt the ground move below me. The new politics, the curious reliance of men on institutions they were yet working to undermine, the simplicity of beliefs and the hideous simplicity of actions, the corruption of causes, half-made societies that seemed doomed to remain half-made: these were the things that began to preoccupy me. They were not things from which I could detach myself. And I found that Conrad–sixty years before, in the time of a great peace—had been everywhere before me. Not as a man with a cause, but a man offering, as in *Nostromo,* a vision of the world's half-made societies as places which continuously made and unmade themselves, where there was no goal, and where always "something inherent in the necessities of successful action . . . carried with it the moral degradation of the idea." Dismal, but deeply felt; a kind of truth and half a consolation.

To understand Conrad, then, it was necessary to begin to match his experience. It was also necessary to lose one's preconceptions of what the novel should do and, above all, to rid oneself of the subtle corruptions of the novel or comedy of manners. When art copies life, and life in its turn mimics art, a writer's originality can often be obscured. *The Secret Agent* seemed to be a thriller. But Inspector Heat, correct but oddly disturbing, was like no policeman before in fiction–though there have been many like him since. And, in spite of appearances, this grand lady, patroness of a celebrated anarchist, was not Lady Bracknell:

> His views had nothing in them to shock or startle her, since she judged them from the standpoint of her lofty position. Indeed, her sympathies were easily accessible to a man of that sort. She was not an exploiting capitalist herself; she was, as it were, above the play of economic conditions. And she had a great pity for the more obvious forms of common human miseries, precisely because she was such a complete stranger to them that she had to translate her conception into terms of mental suffering before she could grasp the notion of their cruelty. . . . She had come to believe almost his theory of the future, since it was not repugnant to her prejudices. She disliked the new element of plutocracy in the social compound, and industrialism as a method of human development appeared to her singularly repulsive in its mechanical and

unfeeling character. The humanitarian hopes of the mild Michaelis tended not towards utter destruction, but merely towards the economic ruin of the system. And she did not really see where was the moral harm of it. It would do away with all the multitude of the parvenus, whom she disliked and mistrusted, not because they had arrived anywhere (she denied that), but because of their profound unintelligence of the world, which was the primary cause of the crudity of their perceptions and the aridity of their hearts.

Not Lady Bracknell. Someone much more real, and still recognizable in more than one country. Younger today perhaps; but humanitarian concern still disguises a similar arrogance and simplicity, the conviction that wealth, a particular fortune, position or a particular name are the only possible causes of human self-esteem. And in how many countries today can we find the likeness of this man?

> The all but moribund veteran of dynamite wars had been a great actor in his time. . . . The famous terrorist had never in his life raised personally so much as his little finger against the social edifice. He was no man of action . . . . With a more subtle intention, he took the part of an insolent and venomous evoker of sinister impulses which lurk in the blind envy and exasperated vanity of ignorance, in the suffering and misery of poverty, in all the hopeful and noble illusions of righteous anger, pity, and revolt. The shadow of his evil gift clung to him yet like the smell of a deadly drug in an old vial of poison, emptied now, useless, ready to be thrown away upon the rubbish-heap of things that had served their time.

The phrase that had struck me there was "sinister impulses which lurk . . . in . . . noble illusions." But now another phrase stands out: the "exasperated vanity of ignorance." It is so with the best of Conrad. Words, which at one time we disregard, at another moment glitter.

But the character in *The Secret Agent* who is the subject of that paragraph hardly exists outside that paragraph. His name is Karl Yundt; he is not one of the figures we remember. Physically, he is a grotesque, a caricature, as are so many of the others, for all Conrad's penetration–anarchists, policemen, government ministers. There is nothing in Karl Yundt's dramatic appearance in the novel, so to speak, that matches the profundity of that paragraph or hints at the quality of reflection out of which he was created.

My reservations about Conrad as a novelist remain. There is something flawed and unexercised about his creative imagination. He does not–except in *Nostromo* and some of the stories–involve me in his fantasy; and *Lord Jim* is still to me more acceptable as a narrative poem than as a novel. Conrad's value to me is that he is someone who sixty to seventy years ago meditated on my world, a world I recognize today. I feel this about no other writer of the century. His achievement derives from the honesty which is part of his difficulty, that "scrupulous fidelity to the truth of my own sensations."

Nothing is rigged in Conrad. He doesn't remake countries. He chose, as we now know, incidents from real life; and he meditated on them. "Meditate" is his own, exact word. And what he says about his heroine in *Nostromo* can be applied to himself. "The wisdom of the heart having no concern with the erection or demolition of theories any more than with the defense of prejudices, has no random words at its command. The words it pronounces have the value of acts of integrity, tolerance, and compassion."

Every great writer is produced by a series of special circumstances. With Conrad these circumstances are well known: his Polish youth, his twenty years of wandering, his settling down to write in his late thirties, experience more or less closed, in England, a foreign country. These circumstances have to be considered together; one cannot be stressed above any other. The fact of the late start cannot be separated from the background and the scattered experience. But the late start is important.

Most imaginative writers discover themselves, and their world, through their work. Conrad, when he settled down to write, was, as he wrote to the publisher William Blackwood, a man whose character had been formed. He knew his world, and had reflected on his experience. Solitariness, passion, the abyss: the themes are constant in Conrad. There is a unity in a writer's work; but the Conrad who wrote *Victory,* though easier and more direct in style, was no more experienced and wise than the Conrad who, twenty years before, had written *Almayer's Folly.* His uncertainties in the early days seem to have been mainly literary, a trying out of subjects and moods. In 1896, the year after the publication of *Almayer's Folly,* he could break off from the romantic turgidities of *The Rescue* and write not only "The Lagoon" but also "An Outpost of Progress." These stories, which stand at the opposite ends, as it were, of my comprehension of Conrad, one story so romantic, one so brisk and tough, were written almost at the same time.

And there are the aphorisms. They run right through Conrad's work, and their tone never varies. It is the same wise man who seems to be speaking. "The fear of finality which lurks in every human breast and prevents so many heroisms and so many crimes": that is from *Almayer's Folly,* 1895. And this is from *Nostromo,* 1904: "a man to whom love comes late, not as the most splendid of illusions, but like an enlightening and priceless misfortune"–which is almost too startling in the context. From *The Secret Agent,* 1907, where it seems almost wasted: "Curiosity being one of the forms of self-revelation, a systematically incurious person remains always partly mysterious." And, lastly, from *Victory,* 1915: "the fatal imperfection of all gifts of life, which makes of them a delusion and a snare"–which might have been fitted into any of the earlier books.

To take an interest in a writer's work is, for me, to take an interest in his life; one interest follows automatically on the other. And to me there is something peculiarly depressing about Conrad's writing life. With a writer like Ibsen one can be as unsettled by the life as by the plays themselves. One wonders about the surrender of the life of the senses; one wonders about the short-lived satisfactions of the creative instinct, as unappeasable as the senses. But with Ibsen there is always the excitement of the work, developing, changing, enriched by these very doubts and conflicts. All Conrad's subjects, and all his conclusions, seem to have existed in his head when he settled down to write. *Nostromo* could be suggested by a few lines in a book, *The Secret Agent* by a scrap of conversation and a book. But, really, experience, was in the past; and the labor of the writing life lay in dredging up this experience, in "casting round"–Conradian words–for suitable subjects of meditation.

Conrad's ideas about fiction seem to have shaped early during his writing career. And, whatever the uncertainties of his early practice, these ideas never changed. In 1895, when his first book was published, he wrote to a friend, who was also beginning to write:

> All the charm, all the truth of [your story] are thrown away by the construction–by the mechanism (so to speak) of the story which makes it appear false.... You have much imagination: much more than I ever will have if I live to be a hundred years old. Well, that imagination (I wish I had it) should be used to create human souls: to disclose human hearts–and not to create events that are properly speaking *accidents* only. To accomplish it you must cultivate your poetic faculty . . . you must squeeze out of yourself every sensation, every thought, every image.

When he met Wells, Conrad said (the story is Wells's): "My dear Wells, what is this *Love and Mr. Lewisham about?* What is all this about Jane Austen? What is it all *about?*" And later–all these quotations are from Jocelyn Baines's biography—Conrad was to write: "The national English novelist seldom regards his work–the exercise of his Art–as an achievement of active life by which he will produce certain definite effects upon the emotions of his readers, but simply as an instinctive, often unreasoned, outpouring of his own emotions."

Were these ideas of Conrad's French and European? Conrad, after all, liked Balzac, most breathless of writers; and Balzac, through instinct and unreason, a man bewitched by his own society, had arrived at something very like that "romantic feeling of reality" which Conrad said was his own inborn faculty. It seems at least possible that, in his irritated rejection of the English novel of manners and the novel of "accidents," Conrad was rationalizing what was at once his own imaginative deficiency as well as his philosophical need to stick as close as possible to the facts of every situation. In fiction he did not seek to discover; he sought only to explain; the discovery of every tale, as the narrator of *Under Western Eyes* says, is a moral one.

In the experience of most writers the imaginative realizing of a story constantly modifies the writer's original concept of it. Out of experience, fantasy, and all kinds of impulses, a story suggests itself. But the story has to be tested by, and its various parts survive, the writer's dramatic imagination. Things work or they don't work; what is true feels true; what is false is false. And the writer, trying to make his fiction work, making accommodations with his imagination, can say more than he knows. With Conrad the story seems to be fixed; it is something given, like the prose "argument" stated at the beginning of a section of an old poem. Conrad knows exactly what he has to say. And sometimes, as in *Lord Jim* and *Heart of Darkness,* he says less than he intends.

Heart of Darkness breaks into two. There is the reportage about the Congo, totally accurate, as we now know: Conrad scholarship has been able to identify almost everyone in that story. And there is the fiction, which in the context is like fiction, about Kurtz, the ivory agent who allows himself to become a kind of savage African god. The idea of Kurtz, when it is stated, seems good: he will show "what particular region of the first ages a man's untrammelled feet may take him into by way of solitude." Beguiling words, but they are abstract; and the idea, deliberately worked out, remains an applied idea. Conrad's attitude to fiction–not as something of itself, but as a varnish on fact–is revealed by his comment on the story. "It is experience pushed a little (and only very little) beyond the actual facts of the case for the perfectly legitimate, I believe, purpose of bringing it home to the minds and bosoms of the reader."

Mystery–it is the Conradian word. But there is no mystery in the work itself, the things imagined: mystery remains a concept of the writer's. The theme of passion and the abyss recurs in Conrad, but there is nothing in his work like the evening scene in *Ghosts:* the lamp being lit, the champagne being called for, light and champagne only underlining the blight of that house, a blight that at first seems external and arbitrary and is then seen to come from within. There is no scene like that, that takes us beyond what we witness and becomes a symbol for aspects of our own experience. There is nothing–still on the theme of blight–like "The Withered Arm," Hardy's story of rejection and revenge and the dereliction of the innocent, which goes beyond the country tale of magic on which it was based. Conrad is too particular and concrete a writer for that; he sticks too close to the facts; if he had meditated on those stories he might have turned them into case histories.

With writers like Ibsen and Hardy, fantasy answers impulses and needs they might not have been able to state. The truth of that fantasy we have to work out, or translate, for ourselves. With Conrad the process is reversed. We almost begin with the truths–portable truths, as it were, that can sometimes be rendered as aphorisms–and work through to their demonstration. The method was forced on him by the special circumstances that made him a writer. To understand the difficulties of this method, the extraordinary qualities of intelligence and sympathy it required, and the exercise of what he described as the "poetic faculty," we should try to look at the problem from Conrad's point of view. There is an early story which enables us to do just that.

The story is "The Return," which was written at the same time as "Karain." It is set in London and, interestingly, its two characters are English. Alvan Hervey is a City man. He is "tall, well set-up, good-looking and healthy; and his clear pale face had under its commonplace refinement that slight tinge of overbearing brutality which is given by the possession of only partly difficult accomplishments;

by excelling in games, or in the art of making money; by the easy mastery over animals and over needy men." And it is already clear that this is less a portrait than an aphorism and idea about the middle class.

We follow Hervey home one evening. We go up to his dressing room, gaslit, with a butterfly-shaped flame coming out of the mouth of a bronze dragon. The room is full of mirrors and it is suddenly satisfactorily full of middle-class Alvan Herveys. But there is a letter on his wife's dressing table: she has left him. We follow Hervey then through every detail of his middle-class reaction: shock, nausea, humiliation, anger, sadness: paragraph after ordered paragraph, page after page. And, wonderfully, by his sheer analytical intelligence, Conrad holds us.

Someone is then heard to enter the house. It is Hervey's wife: she has not, after all, had the courage to leave. What follows now is even more impressive. We move step by step with Hervey, from the feeling of relief and triumph and the wish to punish, to the conviction that the woman, a stranger after five years of marriage, "had in her hands an indispensable gift which nothing else on earth could give." So Hervey arrives at the "irresistible belief in an enigma . . . the conviction that within his reach and passing away from him was the very secret of existence–its certitude, immaterial and precious." He wants then to "compel the surrender of the gift." He tells his wife he loves her; but the shoddy words only awaken her indignation, her contempt for the "materialism" of men, and her anger at her own self-deception. Up to this point the story works. Now it fades away. Hervey remembers that his wife has not had the courage to leave; he feels that she doesn't have the "gift" which he now needs. And it is he who leaves and doesn't return.

Mysterious words are repeated in this story—"enigma," "its certitude, immaterial and precious." But there is no real narrative and no real mystery. Another writer might have charted a course of events. For Conrad, though, the drama and the truth lay not in events but in the analysis: identifying the stages of consciousness through which a passionless man might move to the recognition of the importance of passion. It was the most difficult way of handling the subject; and Conrad suffered during the writing of this eighty-page story. He wrote to Edward Garnett: "It has embittered five months of my life." Such a labor; and yet, in spite of the intelligence and real perceptions, in spite of the cinematic details– the mirrors, the bronze dragon breathing fire–"The Return" remains less a story than an imaginative essay. A truth, as Conrad sees it, has been analyzed. But the people remain abstractions.

And that gives another clue. The vision of middle-class people as being all alike, all consciously passionless, delightful and materialist, so that even marriage is like a conspiracy, that is the satirical vision of the outsider. The year before, when he was suffering with *The Rescue,* Conrad had written to Garnett: "Other writers have some starting point. Something to catch hold of . . . . They lean on dialect–or on tradition–or on history–or on the prejudice or fad of the hour; they trade upon some tie or conviction of their time–or upon the absence of these things

–which they can abuse or praise. But at any rate they know something to begin with—while I don't. I have had some impressions, some sensations—in my time . . . . And it's all faded."

It is the complaint of a writer who is missing a society, and is beginning to understand that fantasy or imagination can move more freely within a closed and ordered world. Conrad's experience was too scattered; he knew many societies by their externals, but he knew none in depth. His human comprehension was complete. But when he set *The Return* in London he was immediately circumscribed. He couldn't risk much; he couldn't exceed his knowledge. A writer's disadvantages, when the work is done, can appear as advantages. *The Return* takes us behind the scenes early on, as it were, and gives us some idea of the necessary oddity of the work, and the prodigious labor that lay behind the novels which still stand as a meditation on our world.

It is interesting to reflect on writers' myths. With Conrad there is the imperialist myth of the man of honor, the stylist of the sea. It misses the best of Conrad, but it at least reflects the work. The myths of great writers usually have to do with their work rather than their lives. More and more today, writers' myths are about the writers themselves; the work has become less obtrusive. The great societies that produced the great novels of the past have cracked. Writing has become more private and more privately glamorous. The novel as a form no longer carries conviction. Experimentation, not aimed at the real difficulties, has corrupted response; and there is a great confusion in the minds of readers and writers about the purpose of the novel. The novelist, like the painter, no longer recognizes his interpretative function; he seeks to go beyond it; and his audience diminishes. And so the world we inhabit, which is always new, goes by unexamined, made ordinary by the camera, unmeditated on; and there is no one to awaken the sense of true wonder. That is perhaps a fair definition of the novelist's purpose, in all ages.

Conrad died fifty years ago. In those fifty years his work has penetrated to many corners of the world which he saw as dark. It is a subject for Conradian meditation; it tells us something about our new world. Perhaps it doesn't matter what we say about Conrad; it is enough that he is discussed. You will remember that for Marlow in *Heart of Darkness* "the meaning of an episode was not inside like a kernel but outside, enveloping the tale which brought it out only as a glow brings out a haze, in the likeness of one of those misty halos that sometimes are made visible by the spectral illuminations of moonshine."

THE LIMITS OF THE LIBERAL IMAGINATION:
ONE HUNDRED YEARS OF SOLITUDE AND *NOSTROMO*

Jean Franco

When Joseph Conrad's novel *Nostromo* appeared in 1904, British imperialism was at its self-confident height, for the Boer War had, if anything, increased nationalist fervour. Like all imperial powers, Britain had legitimised direct aggression and informal colonisation by claiming a civilising mission on the Roman model whose visible symbols were the statues of Victoria, orb in hand, presiding like Minerva over the neo-classical facades of banks and exchanges. Wars might rage in far-flung outposts; but within the island, at least, there was relatively little interest in questioning the legitimacy of the *pax britannica.* Even those novelists who apparently dissented from the materialist goals of Victorian society usually turned a blind eye to empire. The colonies, when mentioned at all in fiction, were represented by Thackeray's nabobs, Dickens' Miss Fuzzy Wuzzy; or they were those mysterious 'foreign parts' into which characters conveniently disappeared or out of which they returned with large, unexplained fortunes. Not until 1902 when J. A. Hobson published *Imperialism: A Study* was there any detailed, theoretical critique of the economics of empire building; not until the appearance of Conrad's novels was there real awareness of the complexity of the effects of empire on the aggressors as well as on the victims of neo-colonialism, nor any novel which charted the national differences between European imperialist ideologies.

Nostromo is a penetrating study of European manipulation of the politics of a dependent country. Precisely because the drama focuses on Europeans whose activities transform the society of Sulaco, the novel presents us with the reverse side of Macondo in Gabriel García Márquez's *One Hundred Years of Solitude,* a place whose inhabitants never project their desires into durable institutions. The tragedy of Sulaco is conceived in terms of the Europeans who are corrupted because their ambitions are acted out upon the stage of a dependent nation. The tragedy of Macondo is that of a dependent population whose very imagination is no longer inviolate.

The two novels are not, of course, analogous projects. The constraint under which Conrad worked was that of verisimilitude, and contemporary critics tended to judge his work according to his ability to create plausible characters and situations. In *Nostromo,* however, he was up against a difficulty: no amount of verisimilitude would shake the British conviction that Latin America was a comic opera world. Even the sympathetic *Manchester Guardian* critic was intolerably patronising on this score:

> Most of us have from time to time read idly of some crisis or revolution in a South American republic and perhaps dismissed idly the 'farcical' episodes in the life of a community which seems to change its government with the weather. It is to one of these episodes in the separation of the 'Occidental Republic' from 'Costaguana' that Mr. Conrad has addressed himself. It need hardly be said that he does not lack the humourous perception of the events that he records, and in a corner of the world that is hardly worthy of our perfunctory and impatient regard that he finds a richness and variety of life that cannot be matched in our careful civilisation.[1]

The apparently objective and universal standard of verisimilitude breaks down when the novel extends its scope to include people 'hardly worthy' of the 'perfunctory and impatient regard' of the European reader. By the time that García Márquez comes to write, the critical *desideratum* has changed; and it is the writer's ability to create 'another reality' or a 'total fiction' which is to be praised. The danger now is that implausibility instead of having a liberating effect may well reflect the separation of reality from the imagination which is ideologically given.

It is easy to see why Conrad, after writing of Africa and the Far East, should have wished to set a novel in 'Latin America,' where the complexity of forces could not be reduced to some simplistic novelised formula. The Hispanic ways of life (so contrary to the British ethic) and the developed superstructures of state organisation and legal institutions called for a densely populated novel if verisimilitude was to be achieved. The single figure of the lone trader as outcast of capitalism and bearer of its ideology no longer sufficed as protagonist. Nor, as Conrad discovered as he began to write, was his brief experience of Latin America enough . . . "pour bâtir un roman dessus."[2] He therefore drew heavily on some of the dozens of travel books, many written by Britishers who felt themselves in-spired by the patriotic urge to extend their country's hegemony over these once forbidden realms. The brothers Robertson in Paraguay, Francis Bond Head and Woodbine Parish in the Argentine, Basil Hall in Chile among others were not simply travel writers, but emissaries of a civilisation which considered local traditions obstacles to progress, and the Catholic religion backward. Yet more than the well-attested influence of Masterman's *Seven Eventful Years in Paraguay* or Eastwick's *Venezuela* and other travel books, it is the sublime metropolitan self-confidence which is important to *Nostromo*.[3] Not that the travellers were entirely uncritical of their own civilisation. Francis Bond Head, who rode across the Argentine pampa in the hope of taking over silver mines abandoned by the Spaniards, found his vision of the undiluted benefits of industrial civilisation somewhat shaken as he compared the wizened appearance of Chilean miners to the healthy freedom of the gaucho.[4] What is merely a passing mood in Head's travels turns into fierce questioning in the work of W. H. Hudson and R. B. Cunninghame Graham, who were two of Conrad's closest friends.

Hudson had been brought up in the Plate Region, though his adult life was lived, for the most part, in Victorian London. In 1885, he published an autobiographical novel, *The Purple Land,* whose full title (later shortened) was *The Purple Land That England Lost.* Its protagonist, Richard Lamb, leaves Montevideo to seek his fortune in the interior of the Banda Oriental (as Uruguay was then called) and becomes, in the course of his wanderings, a true gaucho. His experiences make him lose faith in the undisputed superiority of the British way of life; and at the end of his journey he meditates on the "wild delightful flavour" that would certainly disappear with the material prosperity "resulting from Anglo-Saxon energy." Were this to happen, he writes:

> I must breathe the wish that this land may never know such prosperity.... We do not live by bread alone, and British occupation does not give to the heart all the things for which it craves. Blessings may even be curses when the gigantic power that bestows them on us scares from our midst the shy spirits of Beauty and Poesy.[5]

It is very much the attitude of Conrad's Mrs. Gould who preserves the original beauty of the San Tomé ravine in her water-color sketches but who, at the end of *Nostromo,* sees the silver mine as the spirit of evil, "feared, hated, wealthy, more soulless than any tyrant, more pitiless and autocratic than the worst government, ready to crush innumerable lives in the expansion of its greatness."[6] As for Conrad's other close friend, Cunninghame Graham, whose romantic rebelliousness was not altogether to Conrad's taste, something of his quixotic disdain for the material apparatus of "perfected civilisation" with its obliteration of "the individuality of old town under the stereotyped conveniences of modern life" found its way into the novel.[7]

In his study, Hobson had suggested that imperialism encouraged perverted forms of nationalism, whether it be self-defensive nationalism or "the nationalism which glows with the animus of greed and self-aggrandisement at the expense of others."[8] Conrad, on the other hand, appears more concerned with the way that certain national ideals promote the neo-colonialist venture whilst masking its true nature from the participants. His main interest is, therefore, in ideology. The fact that his Englishmen are entrepreneurs, his Americans financiers, his Italians railway-workers, foremen and innkeepers, and that his Frenchman is an intellectual underscores the historic role of these countries in Latin America. It is precisely the accuracy of his reconstruction of nineteenth-century Latin American politics during the period of transition from the colonial era to the era of financial and industrial dependency that gives weight to the criticism of the materialist goals implicit in the 'fable.'[9] To achieve this accuracy required both insight and recourse to historical data. To take one example: the dictator Guzmán Bento, who tyrannizes over Costaguana shortly after its independence from Spain, is closely modelled on two Paraguayan dictators, President López and Dr. Francia. Indeed, so close is the resemblance that, like Dr. Francia, Guzmán Bento's body is spirited from the tomb soon after burial. But this 'bricolage' of historical fact suggests, more than self indulgence, the existence of a problematic. For Conrad has to show the changes that come to Costaguana through the portrayal of specific individuals caught up in a political situation with which few of his readers were familiar. As it happened, however, painstaking and accurate detail was not enough to make Costaguana more than a comic opera setting in the eyes of the British readers; and Conrad himself was not able to transcend the ideological limitations of a liberal critique which, whatever its reservations about the materialism of the age, was not prepared to see the European domination of the underdeveloped world as anything other than inevitable.

The symbolic agents in the transformation of Sulaco are two: the railway and the Ocean Navigation Company, which opens up the port and hence allows silver to be exported. Conrad gives the company steamships classical names—Minerva, Juno and Cerberus–as if these deities were intended to legitimise, in the name of civilisation, a British imperial expansion based on trade rather than armed conquest. As raw material, the silver is useless without the British-owned railway and steamship line. Together they form the triad on which financial-industrial dependency is to be based. To protect them, Charles Gould and the other foreigners must become directly involved in the politics of Costaguana. It is they who support the benevolent civilian dictator, Ribiera, a figure closely modelled on those Latin American liberals who encouraged foreign investment in the name of a civilisation which differentiated them from their more barbarous countrymen. The downfall of Ribiera after a coup that exploits anti-foreign elements precipitates the civil war out of which the mining interests emerge strengthened by the declaration of Sulaco's independence from Costaguana. This final stroke (which opens up Sulaco to "development") was almost certainly suggested by Panama's declaration of independence, which was in the air precisely when Conrad was writing his novel.

There is, nevertheless, one curious limitation even in Conrad's impressive reconstruction of the course of nineteenth-century Latin American politics: in the depiction of character, Conrad loads the dice in favor of those natives who are most amenable to European manipulation, and hence he reproduces the very liberal ideology which helped promote dependency. It was the cultivated and enlightened liberals of Argentina and Mexico, for example, who most eagerly welcomed railways and foreign investment as signs of progress while ignoring or glossing over the structure of dependency which these implied. In sympathy with the Europeans are the more "civilised" inhabitants of Sulaco: the historian, Don José Avellanos, and his daughter, Antonia; the old independence fighter, Don Pepe; and, of course, the president of Costaguana, Don Vincente Ribiera, whom Conrad describes as a man of "delicate and melancholy mind." The weighting of forces in favour of civilisation becomes even more blatant when even the noble "barbarians" are recruited to the European cause. Thus, the loyalist General Barrios is modelled on those "men on horseback" who terrorised post-Independence politics; yet, as Conrad depicts him, he is the perfect bourgeois whose one desire is to "convert our swords into ploughshares and grow rich. Even I, myself," he confides to Mrs. Gould, "as soon as this little business is settled, shall open a *fundación* on some land I have on the Llanos and try to make a little money in peace and quietness." More surprisingly and even less probable from the point of view of historical verisimilitude, the Europeans recruit the primitive rebel, Hernández, who becomes the Minister of War in independent Sulaco, and Father Corbelán, once an ascetic missionary among remote Indian tribes and hence the epitome of the Hispanic disdain for material progress that the British found so inexplicable.

In contrast, the reader is given no opportunity to take the rebel side seriously. After all, Conrad was not really concerned with the conflict between civilisation and barbarism as played out in Latin America but rather with what was going on in the European mind. His rebel general is dismissed as a sinister "vaquero." He has, it is hinted, negro blood in his veins. The son of a lackey who had served a well-known European traveller and hence has received a smattering of education, General Montero is not civilised enough to play the European game. His brother, Pedro, is an even more interesting example of loaded characterisation. Represented as an ambitious politician who has lived in Paris and conceived an admiration for the Duc de Mornay, his rise to power can only be ascribed to the backwardness of a people who, like the primitive peoples of the past, admire successful duplicity and "who went straighter to their aim and were more artless in their recognition of success as the only standard of morality." Pedro and all the other members of the rebel forces are distinguished by their need of immediate gratification and a corresponding inability to work for long-term or supra-national goals. Comandante Sotillo, the rebel admiral, is, for instance, not only a drunkard but also a man obsessed with the desire to recover the silver. His obsession prevents him from joining up with Montero's forces, thus ruining the rebel cause. Pedro Montero's actions are also "usually determined by motives so improbable in themselves as to escape the penetration of a *rational* person" (my italics). And the Monterist revolution itself is "rooted in the political immaturity of the people, in the indolence of the upper classes and the mental darkness of the lower." Conrad's novel is thus based on the assumption that dependency is inevitable given the "immaturity" of Latin Americans.

The critical insights in *Nostromo* belong to the mature wisdom of the Artist and the Healer. Dr. Monygham is a survivor from the days of Guzmán Bento, under whose regime he suffered torture and solitary confinement which had bound him "indissolubly" to Costaguana "like an awful procedure of naturalisation." It was this experience that involved him deeply in national life "far deeper than any amount of success and honour could have done." Mrs. Gould with her water-colors and her Hudson-like love of nature, is Monygham's natural ally. "Even here," she remarks at one point, "there are simple and picturesque things that one would like to preserve." But this conversation is with the railway magnate, who would certainly not allow those simple and picturesque things to stand in the way of progress. A woman of "endurance and compassion," her critique is contained by the limits which a paternalistic society puts on females. Thus, she is caught in the conflict between regretting change and supporting her husband who is its instrument. In a telling phrase, moreover, Conrad reveals that even her charity is based on a sense of distance from the native people whose "flat, joyless faces. . . looked all alike" to her. Thus the mature critique of the Artist and the Healer alters not at all the "inevitable" process of development. It is a critique which, like the novel itself, at no point endangers the rules of "civilised" communication.[10]

Within these limitations, Conrad's novel is a devastating and perceptive account of the internalisation of those nationalist drives which, as Hobson had shown, had been exacerbated in imperialism. Behind them all, shaping them all, is the "future" power of the United States. "We shall run the world's business whether the world likes it or not," promises Holroyd, whose company finances the mine. "The world can't help it—and neither can we, I guess." Once again, Conrad has underlined the inevitability of the process, hinting that this future will also see "more subtle, outwardly unmarked" changes that will affect "the minds and hearts of the workers." But of central importance in the novel are not these forces of the future so much as those of the present. In his Europeans, Conrad explores the hypostatisation of certain values—honesty, honour, intellectual detachment and romantic passion—which are, in reality, ideological masks hiding the drive for power. It is precisely because individuals act in the name of honesty or courage that they are effective in furthering the ends of neo-colonialism. And it is Conrad's particular genius to have shown the interconnection between moral values and ideology.

The British offer a particularly interesting example of the internalisation of socially useful values, for their reliance on the apparently disinterested virtues of "good faith, order, honesty, peace" (to use the language of the railway magnate) is the element cementing the structures of the empire. These virtues formed the basis for carrying on trade, but because they were defined by the metropolis they were also double-edged. The benevolent dictator, Vincente Ribiera, is a man whose honesty is, in the British view, above reproach; yet his countrymen know he has sold them out to the foreigners. It is no accident then that the pivotal point of the action is Nostromo's theft of the silver that he was supposed to prevent from falling into the enemy's hands during the civil war. His theft, however, is trivial compared with the long term exploitation of the natives in the mine and the "innumerable lives" that are sacrificed to it. Individuals might try to live according to "good faith" and with "honesty" yet as the novel reveals, practiced within the dependency context such virtues merely further a development whose main beneficiary was the metropolis. Bourgeois society divides the private from the public domain and encourages the belief that there can be an unviolated personal life. Nostromo shows the two to be inseparable. Neither the impeccable Charles Gould nor the incorruptible Nostromo escape the tainting influence of the silver, which contaminates precisely because of its role within the total system. Gould's conviction that he is working for the public good is thus a delusion. He believes that "once material interests get a firm footing. . . . they are bound to impose the conditions on which alone they can continue to exist. . . A better justice will come afterwards." In this he shares the optimism of a Macauley for whom the spread of railways would bring about "universal brotherhood and peace" or of a Spencer who declared that "as surely as there is . . . any meaning in such terms as habit, custom, practice, so surely must evil and immorality disappear; so surely must man become perfect."[11] Yet Gould's final solitude is also the indication of how far Conrad himself was removed from this undiluted optimism.

The way in which Decoud's intellectual (and secretly romantic) passion, and the peculiarly Italian combination of abstract idealism (Viola) and manly virtues (Nostromo) also represent European ideologies is less obvious. The French, whose revolutionary tradition made that country a model for Latin America, were not above using intellectual prestige in the furtherance of economic interests, and from early on exercised a spiritual hegemony through publishing houses and magazines while also pursuing maximilianesque-like adventures. Decoud's intellectual *hubris*—the fact that he is the self-appointed architect of Sulaco's independence, the founder of the newspaper *El Porvenir* and the passionate admirer of Antonia for whom he is prepared to risk his life—not only constitutes a nice foil for British pragmatism but provides a specific example of French ideology at work. It is particularly interesting that this man who communicates through *writing* and has a certain intellectual detachment should be considered Conrad's mouthpiece by several critics.[12] They are, of course, betraying their own ideological preferences for the intellectual. Yet Conrad's irony should guard against such a reading, for Decoud's fate parallels that of Gould and Nostromo. His intellectual detachment is just as much an ideological mask as Gould's practical involvement and Nostromo's incorruptibility.

The Italians do not reflect imperialist ideology (though Italy had just embarked on African ventures) as much as they reveal the attitudes of the immigrant who formed a major proportion of new settlers in the nineteenth-century Americas. They brought with them revolutionary ideals and were founders of anarchist and socialist movements; and they also engaged in mafia-like activies. That is why, at the end of *Nostromo*, Conrad has the Sulaco Democratic party depending "on these socialistic Italians. . . with their secret societies, camorras and such like." The very nickname Nostromo (so reminiscent of today's *cosa nostra*) suggests the reciprocal bond of personal loyalty to a fearless leader which characterises Nostromo's relationship with the harbour workers and which, in another context, produced the Mafia. Unlike the British emphasis on honesty for its own sake, the Mediterranean concept of honour depended very much on public recognition of manliness and generosity. That is why Nostromo hides out when he has no money to spend and why his incorruptibility depends on its public recognition as such. His friend, Viola, on the other hand, is the pure revolutionary, one whose abstract ideal is undiluted by practice. And—as was actually the case with many Italian immigrants to the Argentine—this idealism was not incompatible with racist distrust of the natives.

In *Nostromo*, the novelist can show what the historian can only conjecture: how the goals of capitalist society are internalised by individuals and how this in turn conceals the fact that relationships are mediated by money and based on exploitation. It is this contradiction between the sense of individual worth and the real forces of society which drives each one of the main characters to that solitary end just before which his values are seen to be illusory. Gould, reified by the mine, becomes remote from his wife and remains without an heir who might have made his work more meaningful. Decoud, stranded on an island and thwarted in his heroic gesture, "entertains doubts as to his own individuality." His suicide by drowning is the supremely ironic negation of his life. Nostromo's theft turns him into two people, as if the public and private aspects of his personality could no longer be made to fit together. To the public, he is the respectable trader, Captain Fidanza; in his own eyes, he is the furtive thief, Nostromo. His violent death when he is mistakenly killed by his old friend Viola could not have happened but for this split in his personality, which is of the utmost symbolic significance in the overall meaning of the novel. For it is as if, in a system which rests on exploitation and injustice the virtues of courage, honesty and intelligence can only be maintained at the cost of schizophrenia.

Conrad perhaps did not see it quite in this way and possibly the novel tells us more than he himself consciously knew. Because he could not envisage a viable Third World ideology, mature realisation is reserved to the Europeans whom he nevertheless perceives as "helpless" pawns in the "whole scheme of things." By reducing the natives to a chorus, and by separating the Europeans into blind activists and helpless observers, Conrad reproduced the division of labour within the metropolis and the dependency relationships underpinning the whole capitalist structure.

In *Nostromo,* the characters are, in a sense, allegorical or, at least, representative in the Lukacsian sense. In *One Hundred Years of Solitude,* on the other hand, the Buendías represent nothing but themselves; for there is no identifiable signified for which they are the signifiers. Consider, for instance, the José Arcadio who has circumnavigated the globe seven times and on his return to Macondo Indian-wrestles five men at a time in the local bar. The bar-keeper, Catarino, "bet him twelve pesos that he could not move the counter. José Arcadio pulled it out of the place, lifted it over his head and put it in the street. It took eleven men to put it back".[13] What singles out this activity is its gratuitousness, the fact that it has no other purpose than pleasure. This refusal to put their talents—whether strength, inventiveness, sexuality—to any practical end makes the Buendías quite unlike the Samsons, Casanovas or the Napoleons they might have been. Their activities are confined, apparently by choice, to a play world which has the non-instrumentality of fiction itself. Thus the founder, José Arcadio, who uses his scientific instruments to conceive "a notion of space that allowed him to navigate across unknown seas, to visit uninhabited territories and to establish relations with splendid beings without having to leave his study" is quite different from the Renaissance scientists whose discoveries were closely connected with maritime expansion. Moreover, José Arcadio clearly prefers his imaginary world. It is therefore fitting that the Buendía line should come to an end with the narcissistic

José Arcadio who drowns in a lily-pond, and the incestuous Aureliano who deciphers his own past.

By flouting exogamy, the founder of Macondo has, in reality, rejected the primal taboo on which society has been built; for social man communicates through exchange and differentiation, a transaction in which exogamy has an important role. Without the incest taboo, society and culture become impossible.[14] But in the realm of fiction, the Utopian is still available. Hence, Macondo's economic system does not demand exploitation or master-slave relationships. There is a money economy which includes *reales* and *pesos;* but except for vegetables and fruit, Ursula's toffee animals, and José Arcadio's golden fish, nothing is *produced.* Instead of serving to differentiate status the fish are used to *identify* the Colonel's followers during the civil war. Once the war is over, the Colonel can only manufacture new fish by melting down the old in a circular production system. Thus Macondo neither recognises the incest taboo nor engages in the processes of exchange and capital accumulation on which the economy of the Western world was built. Surplus production—when it occurs— simply results in increased consumption. After the devastating rainstorms which ruin Macondo, domestic animals are raffled according to a system which reduces the possibility of anyone's accumulating wealth, for the winners consume their prizes on the spot:

> . . .at dusk food and drink stands would be set up in the courtyard and many of those who were favored would slaughter the animals they had won right there on the condition that someone else supply the liquor and music, so that without having wanted to, Aureliano Segundo suddenly found himself playing the accordion again and participating in modest tourneys of voracity.

This is the reverse of a work ethic. Indeed, apart from the banana plantation and domestic labour which is, by definition, unproductive, work is overshadowed in Macondo by festivity and play. The production of the toffee animals and the golden fish is a kind of game. Thus Macondo posits in Marcusian terms the free play of human faculties "*outside* the realm of alienated labor" and the negation of the "performance principle."[15] Ursula's toffee animals, Aureliano's golden fish, Aureliano Segundo's lottery belong to the realm of freedom and fulfillment, not to work. Similarly, the invention of a boat to navigate Macondo's swiftly-running river, the discovery of a route to the sea and knowledge that the world is round do not have any practical application whereas, historically, they were all linked to the expansion of the West. And this separation of play from work and function corresponds to the line between the real and the imaginary.

Because they have chosen this Utopia of play, the Buendías cannot, however, aspire to the apotheosis of history. For this reason, their lives and deaths, though pathetic, never have the exemplary force of historical events. They frequently die obscurely like the José Arcadio whose execution is a casual event, witnessed fortuitously by Rebecca who "had scarcely time to wave him goodbye." The Colonel, once supreme commander of the revolutionary forces "with jurisdiction and command from one border to another "dies without glory; and people soon forget the person behind the street name that was intended to commemorate him. His feats of arms fail to achieve the status of history, being merely unconfirmed rumours that he had been "victorious in Villanueva, defeated in Guacamayal, eaten by Motilone Indians, had died in one of the swamp villages and had risen again in Urumita." To his family, he appears as a "mythic warrior" who had "placed a distance of three metres between himself and the rest of the world"; and this mythic space which distances the Colonel from other human beings is, in reality, around all the Buendías.

To have history at all, we suppose a design in which events have more than individual or family significance and hence become part of a public and civic discourse. But in Macondo, events which should be included in such discourse are actively forgotten rather than commemorated, so that the hundreds of victims of a massacre are wiped from the memory of men even before their bodies are thrown into the sea. Gerineldo Márquez's funeral procession becomes not an apotheosis of great deeds but their negation. In pouring rain, the procession carries a coffin draped with a shameful flag "that had been rejected by more honourable veterans":

> On the coffin they had also placed the sabre with tassels of silver and copper, the same one that Colonel Gerineldo Márquez used to hang on the coat rack in order to go into Amaranta's sewing room unarmed. Behind the cart, some barefoot and all of them with their pants rolled up, splashing in the mud were the last survivors of the surrender of Neerlandia, carrying a drover's staff in one hand and in the other a wreath of paper flowers that had become discoloured in the rain. They appeared like an unreal vision along the street which still bore the name of Colonel Aureliano Buendía.

We are reminded of the fact that the epigraph of one of García Márquez's earlier novels had been taken from Creon's speech in Sophocles' *Antigone* in which he had condemned Polynices to the worst of fates—that of remaining unburied and a prey to the scavenging birds.[16] Not to honour the dead is to condemn them to oblivion; yet, for the dead to be consecrated, there must be society and history or, at least, a tribal memory. None of these are possible in Macondo so that those objects which in other cultures serve as historical and social symbols—the victor's sabre, the flag, the flowers that symbolise regeneration—here become the symbols of defeat, fragility or simply of private life. Thus the Buendías are not only without a society in a real sense, but in consequence are without social symbols and myths which serve to keep the past alive and hence to give a sense of continuity.[17]

The gulf between history and fiction is therefore complete. The Buendías' flight from the pirates, their incest and their defiance of physical laws put them outside any possible social organisation and even absolved them, in some instances, from the law of gravity. Like the Spanish galleon which José Arcadio finds in the jungle, they occupy a privileged space which should protect them from the ravages of time. But the tragedy of Macondo is precisely this; that the immortality and universality traditionally promised to those who dedicate themselves to art are denied them. The privileged space of Macondo is constantly invaded by alien forces and is susceptible to destruction by natural catastrophe. The carnival princesses are killed by real gunfire. The platitudinous declaration read by the army officers to the plantation strikers is backed up by real arms. Imagination is no match for this reality:

> The captain gave the order to fire and fourteen machine-guns answered at once. But it all seemed like a farce. It was as if the machine-guns had been loaded with caps because their panting rattle could be heard and their incandescent spitting could be seen, but not the slightest reaction was perceived, not a cry, not even a sigh among the compact crowd that seemed petrified by an instantaneous invulnerability.

Because it takes place in Macondo, the massacre seems like carnival or theatre. What does it destroy anyway but figments of the imagination? Among the dead, there are even intruders from novels by Carpentier, Cortázar and Carlos Fuentes. What is swept away is only "the whorish world where Ursula Iguarán had sold so many little candy animals." Yet in bringing about this confrontation, García Márquez reveals the limitations of his imaginary universe.[18]

For Macondo is the space available to the liberal imagination in Latin America. By this I mean that if we take as the liberal ideal respect for individual freedom, the possibility of self-development with as little authoritarian or arbitrary interference as possible, and 'civilised' discourse and relationships, then plainly these conditions can only exist in an imaginary Latin American state; any novelist who pretends to be mimetic or adopts 'truth to life' as a strategy will also find it difficult to reproduce characters like those 'autonomous' beings of, say, the nineteenth- and twentieth-century English novel.[19] By freeing themselves from the mimetic and by cutting the ropes which tied the 'balloon of fiction' to the ground, many Latin American novelists writing in the 1960's constructed a space in which freedom and dialogue became possible. One has only to think of Lezama Lima's *Paradiso,* for example, or Cortázar's *Rayuela* or, of course, *One Hundred Years of Solitude.* Significantly, recent novels by Roa Bastos, Alejo Carpentier and García Márquez[20] himself have centred on the extreme power and freedom of dictators in Latin America. And equally significantly, all these novels are in the form of monologues. In contrast, *One Hundred Years of Solitude* presents a set of characters who (except for the Colonel) are untainted by the original sin of power, and Macondo represents an ideal space in which to set in motion the *individual* virtues of heroism and intellectual daring. Since the 'bourgeois' novel cannot provide a model, García Márquez adopts the tone of the archaic storyteller who captures his listeners' attention by promising them untold marvels.

The storyteller is, of course, not constrained by verisimilitude. For centuries, oral tradition in Latin America transmitted the tales of knightly deeds and the exploits of obscure saints; and such traditions have even represented a

focus of resistance to the homogenisation and submission to print culture that
came with 'modernisation' in a dependency context. However, though García
Márquez can reproduce the storyteller's enjoyment of the marvellous, he cannot
reproduce the living relationship to a community which oral tradition implies and
he is doomed to the solitude of print. In order to rescue pleasure and the libido
from the crushing effects of systematisation and homogeneity, he constructs a
Utopia whose inhabitants defy what Marcuse calls "the performance principle"
which is based on the deferment of gratification.[21] Furthermore, within the text
of the novel there is a distinction between the 'instrumental' writing of decrees
and proclamations and the 'gratuitous' nature of the Buendías' activities. And this
distinction, in turn, reflects a separation common among avant-garde writers
from Flaubert onwards between the 'instrumentality' of ordinary language and
the 'non-instrumentality' of poetic language.[22] In *One Hundred Years of
Solitude, written* labels have to be devised to remind people of the *function* of
things only when the entire population lose their memories during a plague of in-
somnia. These 'instrumental' labels are rendered useless when the gypsy
Melquiades restores sleep and memory with a magic potion. It is the alchemist,
Melquiades, however, who also introduces non-instrumental writing when he
begins to encode the family history in a language which they cannot read. He does
this in a room which is like the space of literature itself, for in it privileged people
feel "protected by the supernatural light . . . by the sensation of being invisible."
Yet Melquiades himself is only too mortal, having "a human weight, an earthly
condition that kept him involved in the small problems of daily life." The alchemy
of literature thus salvages what society cannot use, but it is available only to a
minority of those who, like Aureliano Babilonia, are prepared to run the risk of
deciphering its meaning.

    It is significant that the last of the Buendías should bear the name of a
civilisation (Babylon) which had a god of writing and which came to an end when
writing appeared on the wall, for Aureliano devotes himself to the deciphering of
Melquiades' words. Yet the limitation of this solitary voyage of discovery, which is
always retrospective, never totally present, becomes clear at the end of the novel.
Aureliano skips whole passages in order to "ascertain the date and circumstances
of his death'; yet literature can never rejoin the reality of the present "for it was
foreseen that the city of mirrors (or mirages) would be wiped out by the wind and
exiled from the memory of men at the precise moment when Aureliano Babilonia
would finish deciphering the parchments, and that everything written on them was
unrepeatable since time immemorial and forever more, because races condemned
to one hundred years of solitude did not have a second opportunity on earth."

    The storyteller is silent. Scheherezade will survive for another night but
must tell a different story tomorrow. This 'unrepeatability' is the very mark of the
creative presence in bourgeois society, distinguishing artistic creation qualitatively
from the automatised, the repetitious and the historical. Art, it was supposed,
formed a zone of unalienated work within the generally alienated labour
conditions of capitalism. To salvage this unalienated space, the writer severed

literature from "instrumental" language and the contamination of reality, creating "another reality" whose very positing constituted a transgression of the system. We are reminded, moreover, that this "other reality" had its brief apotheosis in 1968, only one year after the publication of *One Hundred Years of Solitude* when Paris students proclaimed "l'imagination au pouvoir." The fact that García Márquez's novel also reveals the vulnerability of the imagination has tended to be obscured by a critical reception which reflects the system's encouragement of harmless fantasy. The condition on which imagination is allowed to survive is that it should not represent any real interference (in the communications sense) with the ideology of the technical-industrial stage of dependency and hence scramble the message of the consumer society beyond all recognition. Without diminishing the real achievement of *One Hundred Years of Solitude,* it is legitimate to question the separation of reality from imagination, of play from work when society furthers this very division, and turns imagination into a safety valve for all that is not socially useful. Conrad's verisimilitude could not prevent an ideological reading of *Nostromo* which confined Latin America to the realm of the absurd; *One Hundred Years of Solitude* defiantly accepts this, but in a manner which is too disarming. The danger is that, with the real world in the hands of the multinational corporations and the mass media, literature can safely be left to the Tolkiens and the Richard Adams.[23]

NOTES:

1   Norman Sherry (ed.), *Conrad: The Critical Heritage* (London and Boston, 1973). This unsigned review was first published on 2nd November, 1904.

2   Ibid., p. 159.

3   Critics have long acknowledged that Conrad drew on Edward Eastwick, *Venezuela: or Sketches of Life in a South American Republic* (London, 1868) and G. F. Masterman, *Seven Eventful Years in Paraguay* (London, 1868). Norman Sherry, *Conrad's Western World* (C.U.P., 1971) discusses the influence of Captain Basil Hall's *Extracts From a Journey Written on the Coasts of Chile, Peru and Mexico in the Years 1820, 1821, 1822,* (Edinburgh, 1824), and has noted that Conrad used Alexandre Dumas (ed.), *Garibaldi, An Autobiography* tr. William Robson (London, 1860) for Viola. In 'The Original Nostromo: Conrad's Source,' R. E. S., new ser. x, no. 37 (1959), pp. 45-52, John Halverston and Ian Watt have noted the source of the silver theft anecdote as Frederick Benton Williams, *On Many Seas, The Life and Exploits of a Yankee Sailor* (1897).

4   Francis Bond Head, *Journeys Across the Pampas and Among the Andes* (London, 1826), first published as *Rough Notes Taken During Some Rapid Journeys Across the Pampas and Among the Andes* (London, 1826).

5   W.H. Hudson, *The Purple Land* (London, 1949), p. 296. This is a reset of the 2nd edition (London, 1904).

6   I have used the Modern Library edition of *Nostromo* (New York, 1951) with an introduction by Robert Penn Warren.

7   The words are Conrad's, *Nostromo*, p. 107. Joseph Conrad's *Letters to R.B. Cunninghame Graham* (Cambridge U. P., 1969) shed some interesting light on their relationship, especially on Cunninghame Graham's criticism of North American capitalism and his belief that in Kipling's work 'the Imperial Mission' was a euphemism for 'the Stock Exchange Militant'. The note on *Nostromo* in C. T. Watts' introduction to the letters, pp. 37-52, offers an interesting comment on the influence of Graham's views. Graham, who had been involved in the civil war between *Blancos* and *Colorados* in the Banda Oriental (Uruguay) was, of course, a critic whose opinion of the novel Conrad valued highly and in his letters he shows himself sensitive to Graham's comments on certain incorrect uses of Spanish: *Letters*, pp. 157-8.

8   J.A. Hobson, *Imperialism: A Study*, 3rd ed. (London, 1938), p. 9.

9   I am here using the periodisation which has been elaborated by 'new dependency' theorists. For a brief survey, see Ronald H. Chilcote, 'A Critical Synthesis of the Dependency Literature', *Latin American Perspectives I* (Spring, 1974).

10   There is a vast critical literature on *Nostromo* of which the most 'political' interpretation to date seems to be that of Irving Howe, *Politics and the Novel* (Freeport N.Y., 1957), pp. 100-13. See also Avron Fleishman, 'Class Struggle as Tragedy' in *Conrad's Politics* (Johns Hopkins Press, 1967), pp. 161-84.

11   These quotations from the *History of England* (1848-55) by Macauley and from *Social Statics* (1852) by Herbert Spencer are given by E. Houghton in the chapter 'Optimism', *The Victorian Frame of Mind* (Yale, 1957), pp. 27-53.

12   This was the opinion of the anonymous *Manchester Guardian* critic to whom I have already referred. See Sherry (ed.), *Conrad, The Critical Heritage*, p. 173. Robert Penn Warren has some discussion of the issue in his introduction to the Modern Library edition of *Nostromo*, pp. xxvi-xxvii.

13   The quotations are from Gregory Rabassa's translation, *One Hundred Years of Solitude* (New York, 1970).

14   This is forcibly expressed by Bronislaw Malinowski, *Sex and Repression in Savage Society* (New York: 1968), p. 216.

15   Herbert Marcuse, *Eros and Civilisation* (New York, 1955), especially 'The Aesthetic
      Dimension', pp. 157-179.

16   Pedro Lastra, 'La tragedia como fundamento estructural en *La Hojarasca*' in Helmy
      F. Giacoman, *Homenaje a G. Garcia Márquez* (New York, 1972), pp. 43056 [sic.]

17   Carlos Blanco Aguinaga, 'Sobre la lluvia y la historia en las ficciones de García
      Márquez' in *De Mitologias Y Novelistas* (Madrid, 1975) argues along similar lines.
      He shows convincingly that the novel does not belong to the circular time of myth
      but is 'linear and chronological' and that the 'circularity' and 'lo fantástico' represent
      an evasion on the author's part. At the time of writing, the collection of essays had
      not been published but the article appeared in *Narradores Hispanoamericanos De
      Hoy* (North Carolina, 1973).

18   I have dealt with this in more detail in an article on 'Literary History and the
      Dependency Context' in the *Minnesota Review* (September, 1975).

19   F. R. Leavis, *The Great Tradition* (London, 1955). This is the *Locus Classicus* of
      normative criticism. Admittedly, Leavis speaks only of English tradition but
      according to his criterion ('a vital capacity for experience, a kind of reverent
      openness before life, and a marked moral intensity') even Flaubert is ruled out of the
      great tradition and plainly no Latin American novelist would qualify for this
      particular paradise.

20   I refer to Augusto Roa Bastos, *Yo El Supremo* (Mexico, 1975); Alejo Carpentier,
      El Recurso Del Método (Mexico, 1974); and Gabriel García Márquez, *El Otoño
      Del Patriarca* (Barcelona, 1975).

21   H. Marcuse, op. cit., pp. 40-41.

22   This distinction has come under attack by linguists and notably by Mary Pratt in an
      unpublished dissertation, *Towards A Theory of Literary Discourse* (Stanford,
      1975).

23   The topics of the novel as 'another reality,' of critical constraints on writers,
      'normative' evaluations elaborated in Europe and North America which are then
      applied on non-European literatures etc. are all to be discussed in a book I am
      preparing on *The Crisis of the Liberal Imagination*.

OUT OF DARKNESS:
CONRAD AND OTHER THIRD WORLD WRITERS

Peter Nazareth

My chapter on Conrad's *Nostromo* in my first critical book was based on a dissertation I wrote at Leeds University in the mid-sixties.[1] I had not always liked Conrad. V. S. Naipaul's initial response to *Nostromo* was mine. "I felt with Conrad I wasn't getting the point," he says. "Stories, simple in themselves, always seemed at some stage to elude me. And there were the words, the words that issued out of the writer's need to be faithful to the truth of his own sensations. The words got in the way; they obscured. *The Nigger of the 'Narcissus'* and *Typhoon,* famous books, were impenetrable."[2] Conradian word, impenetrable: we find a lot of Conradian words in Naipaul.

What drew me to Conrad was Ngugi wa Thiong'o. Ngugi had decided as a student at Makerere University College not to take my advice to study D. H. Lawrence as his special subject but to focus on Conrad. "I'm impressed with the way he questions things, requestions things like action, the morality of action, for instance," he was to say later.[3] But for me at the time, in the words of Naipaul, "And there was *Nostromo,* about South America, a confusion of characters and themes, which I couldn't get through at all."[4] Yet if Ngugi found Conrad valuable, there had to be something there, something which eluded me, and so I felt it was worth pursuing him: which I did at Leeds.

There, at Leeds, I went through a series of unhappy, I would say racist, experiences. Naipaul speaks for me again when he says, "To be a colonial was to know a kind of security; it was to inhabit a fixed world."[5] I had come to England precisely at the point at which this fixed world was breaking up. Uganda had become independent less than a year earlier. Independence had shaken the ground under most Goans (and Asians) in Uganda. It was, not coincidentally, the time of the Civil Rights movement, political assassinations of radical Third World intellectuals like Malcolm X and Pio Gama Pinto. At Leeds, I experienced a "breakdown," that is, a psychic dissolution of the fixed world I had known and taken for granted. At this point, Conrad (and Fanon) began to make sense, for I had to break apart my old perception of the world and to re-educate myself almost from scratch.

Writing about *In a Brown Mantle,* G. S. Amur says that an Indian reader's immediate reaction to novels like mine, Ngugi's, and Achebe's is to wonder why there are so few novels like them in his own literature.[6] "Is it merely a question of literary influences?" Amur wonders. He notes, "Conrad who has been such a formative influence on the African writers has never had much of an appeal to the Indian writer." The point is that Conrad does not make sense to persons belonging to monolithic societies, communities whose world-view is so secure that nothing is permitted to penetrate, question and change it. Such would be Naipaul's Hindu community in Trinidad and my Goan community in East Africa. Wilson Harris elaborates: the adjectives in Conrad are not irrelevant but, by qualifying nouns, reveal "qualitative and infinite variations of substance," showing that perceptions of *reality* can change.[7]

The supreme monolithic world-view comes from colonialism. As Grant Kamenju says, quoting Marx and Engels, the European bourgeoisie "compels all nations, on pain of extinction, to adopt the bourgeois mode of production; it compels them to introduce what it calls civilization into their midst, i.e. to become bourgeois themselves. In one word, it creates a world after its own image."[8] Colonialism and its latter-day version, neocolonialism, are primarily economic and political exploitation, but they have their cultural/psychic counterpart, which is both cause and consequence. *Colonialism, in this counterpart sense, means the imposition of one world-view on peoples of another.* Colonialism was justified at home as a process of civilizing the savages. A perpetual colonial machine could be created as most of the people running it believed they were doing good to the savages. This is perhaps what Harris means when he says, "the liberal homogeneity of a culture becomes the ready-made cornerstone upon which to construct an order of conquest."[9] The Judaeo-Christian consciousness looks at the world in an either/or, black/white way, the evil being out there, the good inside: the good guys versus the bad guys, the good with the white hats, the bad with black, instead of the hats being white and black. Thus Achebe notes the constant need of the Western world to win grace for itself by putting down Africa.[10]

At Leeds University, when I was beginning to experience the "breakdown" I have mentioned, I said to my (white) professor that I felt I had lived all my life in a glass cage. I was trying to explain why the academic study of English literature had suddenly become irrelevant. I shall never forget his sarcastic laughter: some professors do not believe in instinctual metaphors even though they feed off literature. But that metaphor was true, innocent, unmanufactured: colonialism puts one into an invisible cage, it imposes a glass dome over our world. How can one break through? This may be the meaning of Wilson Harris's drawings in which an arrow is shown piercing through a dome. The monolithic worldview must be broken up; the language too, which was imposed and carries that monolithic worldview, must be made less inevitable, more tentative, the personality encased in the words thus freed, the glass cage broken up.

Ngugi saw that this was what Conrad was doing: saw this very early while East Africa was still under colonial rule. Ngugi saw the concept of the good guy *in* instead of *versus* the bad guy, contained in the very title "The Secret Sharer," as central to Conrad. In an early essay on *Lord Jim,* Ngugi says that Brown represents what Jim's thwarted will is potentially capable of becoming and concludes:

> When he allows Brown to go, Jim becomes the agent of his own destruction. It is as if he realizes that Brown is part of him. But Jim has now come to know himself better. He can face himself and not be terrified as in the earlier parts. His acceptance of himself is an acceptance of his total humanity; the criminal element in him and the saint in him; the side perpetually turned to the light of day, and that side of us which exists stealthily in perpetual darkness.[11]

Analyzing the significance of "The Secret Sharer," Ngugi says of the relationship of the untried Captain to Legatt, "The doubleness of personalities which makes one man see himself in the other is symbolical of the doubleness in the soul of the individual. That is, the soul of the individual is a complexity with many sides; the side turned to the light and the side turned to the darkness; the 'criminal' self which also can be the basis of great actions, and the other more conscious self, the more ordinary day-to-day self which we turn to other people." The imposition of the Judaeo-Christian either/or world-view on Africa meant that Europeans could project their "dark self" onto the "dark people." At the end of Paule Marshall's *Brown Girl, Brownstones,* Selina, a black American of Barbadian parents, is running away from her first experience of racism. "Her dark face must be confused in their minds with what they feared most," she thinks, "with the night, symbol of their ancient fears, which seethed with sin and harbored violence, which spawned the beast in its fen; with *the heart of darkness within them. . .*"[12]

Where is the heart of darkness? Marlow has begun his adventure in Africa believing, like all Europeans, that the darkness is *out there,* in the Africans, not in himself. Thus much that he first sees of colonial exploitation in the Congo (the ship firing into the bush, Africans in chains, an Eldorado expedition of white men) seems disconnected, illogical. Marlow was a liberal, like Kurtz, who, the story tells us, was created by all of Europe. Kurtz had also been writing liberal lies about the great civilizing mission of Europe in Africa; until, in a burst of honesty, he scribbled across his manifesto, "Exterminate the brutes!" And that is what Kurtz, *the great ivory agent,* has been doing, for the greater profit of Europe.

It is not just the "what happened" in the story that is important, however; it is in the way the story is told that meaning is to be found. Marlow is telling his story in the present about the past. He is both re-creating his experience as it was and evaluating it as he talks, implicating the listeners, including the unknown "I." Actually, it is the "I" who is recounting the story. Who is the "I"? Is he just part of Conrad's *cordon sanitaire,* as Achebe charges?[13] Or is he the "I" of Europe, in the sense of "eye" and the ego, counterpointed with the "yellow complexion" Marlow sitting "cross-legged" like Buddha, a figure from the non-white world? The other listeners are "the Lawyer," "the Accountant," and "the Director of Companies": manipulators of the whole colonial machine. Marlow lacked the courage to open the eyes of Kurtz's fiancée to what he was really doing in Africa and how he really died: he let her retain her romantic vision about the great civilizing mission. But *the story* has a different conclusion. We are told that the Thames was the great waterway on which Drake and Franklin, "the knights-errant of the sea," set out, *The Golden Hind* "returning with her round flanks full of treasure." They were "the adventurers and the settlers," "hunters for gold or pursuers of fame," "messengers of might": in other words, pirates.

It is after two-and-a-half pages of such precise description that Marlow begins his story, saying suddenly, "And this also has been one of the dark places of the earth." The "I" explains that the meaning of an episode to Marlow does not lie inside a kernel (the *what happened* of a story) but outside, a definition often quoted to explain Conrad as a writer. Marlow continues by imagining what the English were to the Romans who came in by the river Thames to exploit and did not know the people or the landscape. Note the reversal: the superior Englishmen of the time the story was published, ruling the non-white world supposedly because of their moral and cultural superiority, are presented as unknown barbarians. The invading Romans, Marlow says, must have thought of them as "savages"; noting that there was little to eat inland "for a civilized man," the Romans "were men enough to face the darkness," they would march inland to "feel the savagery, the utter savagery."[14] Marlow is moving towards a conclusion articulated nearly a century later by one of the colonials: Pirate Jack says in Ishmael Reed's *Flight to Canada* in reply to the accusation by Princess Quaw Quaw that he is a savage for killing her father and brother, "The difference between a savage and a civilized man is determined by who has the power."[15]

Marlow gets explicit. The exploitation of the non-white world, which was for profit, could only take place if one dehumanized the non-white people. As for the colonial agents: "They were conquerors, and for that you want only brute force–nothing to boast of, when you have it, since your strength is just an accident arising from the weakness of others. They grabbed what they could get for the sake of what was to be got. It was just robbery with violence, aggravated murder on a great scale, and men going at it blind–as is very proper for those who tackle a darkness. The conquest of the earth, which mostly means the taking it away from those who have a different complexion or slightly flatter noses than ourselves, is not a pretty thing when you look into it too much. What redeems it is the idea only."[16] Notice not only the explictness of the indictment but also the use of "blind" and "darkness." "What redeems it is the idea only," says Marlow. This is just a qualification: those with an unselfish belief in the idea are more admirable than those who are merely out to grab the loot, but even those with the idea end up no better than the naked robbers. Conrad's Kurtz is the forerunner of Ngugi's European characters in *Weep Not Child* and *A Grain of Wheat*, namely, Howlands and Thompson, the former a settler, the latter a colonial administrator, both obsessed by an idea and an ideal, both responding to the guerilla movement to end colonialism by becoming brutes and torturers.[17]

Achebe and Frances Singh are not entirely wrong to say that there is racism in Marlow. Marlow's aunt who helped him get to Africa talked of "weaning those ignorant millions from their horrid ways."[18] But there is an erosion of his inherited racist framework through the direct experience of Africa, through reflection on that experience, and through the telling of the story. The early Ngugi recognized this, saying, "Now, it is only those people who accept their total humanity that find their link with other men. . . In *Heart of Darkness,* Marlow finds his link with the Africans and even with Kurtz."[19] Marlow finds it hard to break out of his glass cage but he helps others (as does the "I") in *the use of language.* As Leonard Johnston, the black Canadian owner of *The Third World Books and Crafts* in Toronto, told me, the English language is inherently racist, an example being that when the lights go out, it is not called a "white-out" but a "blackout."[20] Conrad, Marlow and the "I" work against this by reversing images of whiteness and blackness. When he was a boy, Marlow says, he was fascinated by "a white patch" on the map, which was Africa, before "it had become a place of darkness;"[21] that is, before the European colonialists got in and he was taught to think of it as dark. When he first gets to the Congo and sees six black men in chains, guarded by another black man with a rifle, he notes that the guard hoists his weapon to his shoulder with alacrity, "white men being so much alike at a distance that he could not tell who I might be."[22] This reverses the stereotype in the European world that all black men look alike, reducing it to cultural blindness. He even, as Frances Singh points out, calls Brussels a "whited sepulchre,"[23] thus using the color *white,* not *black*, as a symbol of death as well as indicating that the development of the European capital is based on death, which we shall see as the story progresses.

There was censorship in the colonial world: no Marx or Lenin. But there was Conrad, sneaking through as a member of Leavis's Great Tradition, actually undermining that tradition. Jane Austen's characters in *Mansfield Park* could live a luxurious life while the patriarch left for the colonies; Conrad actually takes us to the colonies to show us what happened there when the patriarch or his agents arrived and how his wealth at home came from brutal colonial action. Conrad was therefore a mental liberator: not only for those blinded at home but also for those who were to come later, the colonized elite wearing the eyes of Europe.

"But we read at different times for different things," says Naipaul. "We take to novels our own ideas of what the novel should be; and those ideas are made by our needs, our education, our backgrounds or perhaps our ideas of our background. Because we read, really, to find out what we already know, we can take a writer's virtues for granted. And his originality, the news he is offering us, can go over our heads."[24] We must pay careful attention to this disturbing statement. Although he notes that one can miss the new vision a writer really has to offer because of one's preconceptions, thus showing an awareness that the writer may have a new vision, Naipaul pulls back from what I said earlier: that at the point at which those preconceptions begin to crack, the writer (specifically, Conrad) can widen the cracks and completely destroy them. Instead, Naipaul is denying the role of the imagination in, and the imaginative response to, literature. He says we read writers only for what we want to take from them. The statement is palatable if we limit Naipaul's observation to that of a writer cannibalizing other writers, for we know writers frequently do this. But it becomes an important clue to understanding a critical problem with Naipaul because we are talking here of *the writer as colonial remaining determinedly colonial.* Although he is frequently presented in the West as the one writer who really understands the Third World, the writer who is the Third World descendant of Conrad himself, in fact Naipaul travels the same physical territory as Conrad but sees it utterly differently for, as he admits, "we can be imprisoned by our own assumptions."[25]

Let us explore. Adil Jussawalla has complained that Naipaul's novel *A Bend in the River* has been unfairly compared to Conrad's *Heart of Darkness.*[26] But the comparison is not unfair: Naipaul's work stands in deliberate relationship to Conrad's work. Naipaul's protagonist comes from the other side, the East (from East Africa, and by ancestral origin, from India), finding his way to the heart of Africa on the Congo river. Compare the following passages:

> "In the darkness of river and forest you could be sure only of what you could see— and even on a moonlight night you couldn't see much. When you made a noise-dipped a paddle in the water you heard yourself as though you were another person. The river and the forest were presences, much more powerful than you. You felt unprotected, an intruder."

> "Not the faintest sound of any kind could be heard. You looked on amazed, and began to suspect yourself of being deaf–then the night came suddenly, and struck you blind as well. About three in the morning some large fish leaped, and the loud splash made me jump as though a gun had been fired."

It is difficult to tell from a casual reading which passage is by Naipaul and which by Conrad. Look again. The one reinforcing the solidity of personality, troubled by an incomprehensible world out there, is by Naipaul; the one in which the world out there begins to erode the solid walls of personality is by Conrad. The references to deafness and blindness tell us that the second one is by Conrad.[27] Unlike Ngugi, Naipaul has permitted himself to understand Conrad only superficially, letting his own prejudices remain unchanged. The "political panic" he was beginning to feel at the end of colonial rule, because "to be a colonial was to know a kind of security," never ended.[28] So Naipaul shares geography with Conrad but misses the heartland. "And I found that Conrad–sixty years before, in the time of great peace–had been everywhere before me," he says. "Not as a man with a cause, but a man offering, as in *Nostromo,* a vision of the world's half-made societies as places which continuously made and unmade themselves, where there was no goal, and where always 'something inherent in the necessities of successful action . . . carried with it the moral degradation of the idea.' " Dismal, but deeply felt: "a kind of truth and half a consolation."[29] This is a perverse misreading of Conrad for Naipaul does not attribute the quote to a specific character, does not see it in the context of a whole speech and the structure of the novel. The words are from Mrs. Gould and she is blinding herself to excuse the moral failure of her capitalist husband. Charles Gould believed that developing capitalist interests (financed by a North American) in a Latin

American country would automatically bring about law, order and justice for all the people; but at a time of "revolution" (is this what Naipaul means by "a time of great peace"?), the ideal is shown to have been hollow. Gould has become linked, through a host of images, with the earlier, cruder colonialists of Europe and even with pirates willing to blow up the ship rather than surrender it. His obsession with his silver mine had driven him away from his wife. And she cannot face the reality and see that her husband's ideal was doomed to failure: it is not his ideal, that of capitalism, that was at fault, she says; the failure was inherent in human existence, in the necessities of successful action. But we must not read this as *Conrad's* judgment, not only because Dr. Monygham later makes an explicit comment on capitalism's moral failure, but also because the thoughts of Mrs. Gould before the line quoted by Naipaul begin, "Poor boy!. . . He was perfect— perfect. What more could she have expected? It was a colossal and lasting success; and love was only a short moment of forgetfulness, a short intoxication."[30] Poor boy. . . perfect, perfect. . . colossal: the language warns us. But Naipaul is intentionally blind. He refuses to see that Mobutu in his essay about the Congo prior to the novel[31] and the President of his novel are not in opposition to the Western world when colonialism has ended but a result of continuing Western interests. Just a little research in American newspapers and a few books about (not by) the C.I.A. after Watergate would reveal this. Naipaul will not see, even after the event is blatant: Conrad saw to such a degree that even a right-wing one-time secret agent like Edward Luttwak could say, *"Nostromo* is a brilliant prophetic analysis of the causes and consequences of 'neocolonialism.' "[32]

We are talking of blindness not only to Conrad's political vision but also to language. Wilson Harris quotes a passage from *Heart of Darkness,* from when Marlow sees the heart of the forest he has penetrated, adding italics:

> The *living* trees, lashed together by the creepers and every *living* bush of the undergrowth, might have been changed into *stone,* even to the *slenderest* twig, to the *lightest* leaf. It was not sleep—it seemed unnatural, like a state of trance. Not the *faintest sound of any kind could be heard. You looked on amazed and began to suspect yourself of being deaf*—then the night came suddenly, and struck you *blind* as well. About three in the morning some large fish leaped, and the *loud* splash made me jump as though a gun had been fired. When the sun rose there was a *white* fog, very warm and clammy, and more *blinding* than the night. . . . A cry, a very loud cry, as of infinite desolation, soared slowly in the *opaque* air. It ceased. A complaining clamor, modulated in savage discord, filled our ears.[33]

The words of the above passage, which include three sentences I quoted earlier, show that the forest is *living,* challenging Marlow's fixed mode of perception and therefore his fixed personality. True, Marlow has not seen how the Africans live, but he is being prepared to understand his lack of understanding. But in Naipaul, there is no sense of things being alive and differentiated in the forest, of the problem of perception being in the observer. Instead, there is hysteria about the encroaching "bush" when the European colonizers leave. "This, for all their talk of authenticity and the way of the ancestors, was their fear: to be returned from the sweet corruptions of Kinshasa to the older corruption of the bush, to be returned to Africa," says Naipaul in his Congo essay. He continues, "And the bush is close. It begins just outside the city and goes on forever."[34] Six pages later, he says, "If the steamers do not fail, if there are no more wars, it is the Congo hyacinth that may yet imprison the river people in the *immemorial* ways of the bush." And two pages further, "The bush is a way of life; and where the bush is so overwhelming, organized agriculture is an illogicality." Naipaul's terror against the bush which comes in when the white man leaves is such that he distorts *Heart of Darkness,* which he took as his guide for the trip, the essay and the novel. He includes the novella in "one kind of imperialist writing."[35] He quotes Marlow's comment that imperialism is only redeemed by an idea *in order to justify imperialism,* overlooking the fact that Marlow has explicitly condemned imperialism as exploitation a few lines before. For Marlow, the "primitiveness" of the Africans he saw was undermined by his recognition of their kinship with him, and that they had no excuse, unlike the white man, for being there; but Naipaul talks of "the rage of primitive men coming to themselves and finding that they have been fooled and affronted."[36] Naipaul even goes so far as to misinterpret Kurtz's degeneration, blaming it, like a latter-day colonial apologist, on the Africans: "It was there, in Conrad's story, that Kurtz reigned, the ivory agent degraded from idealism to savagery, taken back to the earliest ages of man, by wilderness, solitude and power, his house surrounded by impaled human heads."[37] So Kurtz, according to Naipaul, is not brought to brutality by his own unrecognized darkness: it is the environment and the Africans to blame. Lest we miss the point, Naipaul says that it is Mobutu who is the successor to Kurtz. No, Naipaul is not saying that it is now Mobutu who is looking after Western interests as Kurtz had done earlier: Mobutu, says Naipaul, is a man "maddened not by contact with wilderness and primitiveness, but with the civilization established by those pioneers who now lie on Mont Ngaliema, above Kinshasa rapids."[38] The bush drives Naipaul mad. He cannot stand the idea of African students aspiring to intellectualism for where have they come from? "They have come from the bush, but already they talk of Stendhal and Fanon. . . "[39]

Naipaul's brother Shiva does not do much better–or does just as well, depending on one's perspective. Making a trip to East Africa around the same time as his brother, also to write a book, he, too, draws the same superficially Conradian ("impenetrable," "inscrutable," "frenzied") but actually anti-Conradian, racist conclusions. "As for Western civilization, that had been aborted almost from the beginning," this Naipaul says. "Civilized man, it seems, can no more cope with prolonged exposure to the primitive than the primitive can cope with prolonged exposure to him."[40] His reference to "the new imperialism" is just to state, like his brother, that the local bosses are worse imperialists than the white rulers they have displaced, messing things up completely: not that the local bosses represent continuing imperial interests. The two Naipauls must have shared notes or instructions on their African trip. V. S. Naipaul's protagonist in *A Bend in the River* is horrified not at the way the West has exploited the colonies but at how the Arabs with their oil are going to bring down the West.

"The bush runs itself," says Salim near the end of a *A Bend in the River*, a statement that means more than he or his creator realize, as we shall see.[41] Both Naipauls went to the colonies and, like Marlow talking to Kurtz's fiancée, refuse to show what the West was really doing out there. Conrad tells the truth through his novella, although he did not have the opportunity to read Achebe's *Things Fall Apart,* Ngugi's *The River Between,* or other African novels that show that the "bush" was not just "bush"; there were people living there with their own cultural matrix and their own relationship to the environment before the white man came and tore them apart. V. S. Naipaul had that opportunity and made nothing of it. His brother did worse: he read with approval precisely those writers Ngugi exposed as colonialist and only one African novel, Meja Mwangi's fourth (and poorest), in order to extract "evidence" that the colonialist writers were right. He says that Mwangi's protagonist can trace his ancestry to Elspeth Huxley's mission boy, a young man who "behaves like a performing circus animal, an animal that had been snatched from its proper existence and trained to ride a bicycle, drink tea, jump through a hoop and dance a jig," which leads him (Naipaul) to conclude, "when one is talking to Africans who seem thoroughly modern, something is said that. . . brings one up short and makes one realize that not all is what it seems to be."[42] I had written to Shiva Naipaul after reading his account of his East African journey in one of the English journals, urging him to read more East African writing, including mine, but I did not receive a reply. In my fiction, I consider the reader's perceptions (including those of the Goan community) to be part of the problem: my fiction challenges the blindness of those perceptions.[43] The Naipauls cannot see what Conrad is saying because of their preconceptions: even more, it is more convenient for them deliberately to refuse to see.

However, even Achebe interprets Conrad's *Heart of Darkness* the same way V. S. Naipaul does, doing this to disapprove. "Conrad is a bloody racist," concludes Achebe.[44] One could explain this by saying that Achebe is a bad critic because, like Naipaul, he does not pay enough attention to words.[45] More than that, the explanation is that once Conrad helped colonials break out, some of them looked back and found him unnecessary. "The night was impenetrably dark" could have come from Conrad but in fact is the beginning of Chapter 11, Part I of Achebe's *Things Fall Apart.*[46] Even Ngugi is revisionist. In his *Writers in Politics,* published in 1981, Ngugi says, "For Joseph Conrad, the African characters in *Heart of Darkness* are part of the primitive savagery that lay below the skin of every civilized being. He was telling his fellow Europeans: You go to Africa to civilize, to enlighten a heathen people; scratch the thin veneer of civilization and you will find the savagery of Africa in you too."[47] This is Naipaul's conclusion about Conrad, but this is not what Conrad is saying. Ngugi, enjoining battle against neocolonialism, has no patience with subtleties anymore.

Yet he cannot really dismiss Conrad as a racist for halfway through the book, he praises *Nostromo* for being anti-imperialist, for rooting morality, religion and ethics in class. He concludes "The African writer and Joseph Conrad share the same world and that is why Conrad's world is so familiar. Both have lived in the world dominated by imperialism."[48]

Edward Said said of Conrad, "He was a self-conscious foreigner writing of obscure experiences in an alien language and he was only too aware of this. . . Conrad's prose is not the unearned prolixity of a careless writer, but rather the concrete and particular result of his immense struggle with himself. If at times he is too adjectival, it is because he failed to find a better way of making his experience clear."[49] True, except that I would put it more positively: it was the best way Conrad had of bringing unpleasant truths home, of shattering the benign worldview of colonialism projected at home and, by extension, on the educated elite of the Third World. I do not agree with Harris that Conrad experienced an exhaustion of spirit after Marlow stood on the threshold of new perceptions. Harris is thinking of what would have happened in one of his own novels. The passage from *Heart of Darkness* he quoted (see note 33) could have been written by Harris himself. Compare it to the scene in Harris's *Palace of the Peacock* when the protagonist goes into the forest for the first time:

> The *whispering* trees spun their leaves to a *sudden fall* wherein the ground seemed to *grow lighter* in my mind and *to move* to meet them in the air. The carpet on which I stood had *an uncertain place* within splintered and timeless roots whose fibre was *stone* in the *tremulous* ground. I lowered my head a little, *blind* almost, and begin forcing a *new path* into the trees away from *the river's opening* and side.[50]

The personality of the protagonist becomes more fluid, ready to change into a higher state. The "I" is both the "eye" that sees and the dreamer, watching and identifying with the other self, Donne, the doer, the exploiter, the last landlord. The journey into the interior is one of destroying the ego; not only does Donne move to a higher state of being but also the "I" disappears in the storytelling until the end. But Conrad's Marlow, being "real," being European, wanting to return to the European world, could not know *from the inside* what African life was; he could only become aware that there was more in the African world than was dreamt of in his European philosophy.

The job of exorcising the ghosts that have possessed the educated elite of the Third World, trained in the image of the Western bourgeois to serve as their agents, is continued by other Third World writers who return to the "bush." In Okot p'Bitek's *Song of Lawino*, a woman from the "bush" smashes up the colonial dome element by element. Spelling out the totality of her world, she attacks her alienated husband:

> He abuses all things Acoli,
> He says

The ways of black people
Are black
Because his eyeballs have exploded,
And he wears dark glasses,
My husband's house
Is a dark forest of books.
Some stand there
Tall and huge
Like the *tido* tree
Some are old
Their barks peeling off
And they smell strongly.
Some are thin and soft. . .
Some have pictures on their backs,
Dead faces of wild-looking men and women,
Unshaven, bold, fat-stomached
Bony-cheeked, angry revengeful-looking people,
Pictures of men and women
Who died long ago.[51]

Lawino warns about being thus possessed:

If you stay
In my husband's house long
The ghosts of the dead men
That people this dark forest,
The ghosts of the many white men
And white women
That scream whenever you touch any book,
The deadly vengeance ghosts
Of the writers
Will capture your head
And like my husband
You will become
A walking corpse.[52]

With her "bush" cunning and wisdom, Lawino names an abstract thing, calling it a ghost, and then she can exorcise it. Note that the collection of white men's books is "a dark forest," because her husband cannot see he wears "dark" glasses, and he is possessed by ghosts, which are *white*. Lawino is continuing the task of smashing up the dome to let light through, a task begun in literature by Conrad.

While Idi Amin was still in power, having been put there by certain Western powers to protect their interests but having gotten out of hand, a novel was published entitled *Target Amin* by James Konrad.[53] James Konrad? We recall that Joseph Conrad's last name was originally spelled with a "K". This is a clue to the nature of the novel, clearly written by a Ugandan who knew the inside story.

The pseudonym is indeed a clue, for the action of the story is the crisis caused by the intended visit to England of Idi Amin with the blood of Archbishop Luwum and thousands of other Ugandans on his hands. The English cannot stand the idea that this bloody monster should come to their place. It is the duty of the chief of intelligence to ensure that Amin is not murdered on their doorstep. What we see is the consternation caused by a latter-day Kurtz coming back home. Nearly a hundred years later, Conrad is still helping refocus the Third World under Western Eyes.

University of Iowa

NOTES:

1   Peter Nazareth, "The Significance of Nostromo and the Silver in the Moral Pattern of *Nostromo,*" *Literature and Society in Modern Africa* (Nairobi/Kampala/Dar es Salaam: East African Literature Bureau, 1972); also published as *An African View of Literature* (Evanston, Illinois: Northwestern University Press, 1974).

2   V.S. Naipaul, "Conrad's Darkness," published in Robert D. Hamner, ed., *Critical Perspectives on V.S. Naipaul* (Washington: Three Continents Press, 1977 and London: Heinemann, 1979), p. 56. The essay is also included in V.S. Naipaul, *The Return of Eva Perón* (New York: Vintage Books, 1980). All quotations from this essay will be from the book edited by Hamner.

3   *African Writers Talking,* ed. Dennis Duerden and Cosmo Pieterse (London: Heinemann, 1972), p. 124, quoted by Ponnuthurai Sarvan, "Under African Eyes," *Conradiana,* 9 (1976), 7.

4   Hamner, p. 57.

5   Hamner, p. 59.

6   G.S. Amur, *Images and Impressions* (Jaipur: Pancheel Prakashan, 1979), p. 22.

7   Wilson Harris, "The Frontier on Which *Heart of Darkness* Stands," *Research in African Literatures,* 12:1 (1981), 91.

8   Grant Kamenju, "Black Aesthetics and Pan-African Emancipation," in Pio Zirimu and Andrew Gurr, eds., *Black Aesthetics* (Nairobi/Kampala/Dar es Salaam, EALB, 1973), p. 175.

9   Harris, p. 88. An alternative interpretation of what Harris means is that it is easy for a homogeneous culture to be conquered by another homogeneous culture.

10   Chinua Achebe, "An Image of Africa," *RAL,* 9:1 (1978), 2.

11   James Ngugi, unpublished essay written in 1963 at Makerere University College on the question of whether *Lord Jim* is broken-backed. The next quotation is from "The Significance of *The Secret Sharer"*, unpublished essay written by Ngugi in 1963. (Ngugi later changed his name to Ngugi wa Thiong'o.)

12   Paule Marshall, *Brown Girl, Brownstones* (Old Westbury, New York: The Feminist Press, 1981), p. 291. The novel was first published in 1959.

13   Achebe, p. 7.

14   Joseph Conrad, *Heart of Darkness,* from *Joseph Conrad's Heart of Darkness,* ed. Leonard F. Dean (Englewood Cliffs, New Jersey: Prentice-Hall, 1960), p.4; hereafter abbreviated *HD.*

15   Ismael Reed, *Flight to Canada* (New York: Random House, 1976), p. 149.

16   *HD,* pp. 4-5.

17   James Ngugi, *Weep Not Child* (London: Heinemann, 1964) and *A Grain of Wheat* (London: Heinemann, 1967).

18   Achebe, p. 9; also see Frances B. Singh, "The Colonialistic Bias of *Heart of Darkness,"* *Conradiana,* 10 (1978), 44, and *HD,* 9.

19   Ngugi, "The Significance of *The Secret Sharer."*

20   Interview with Leonard and Gwen Johnston by Peter Nazareth, to be published in a collection of interviews with Third World Writers.

21   *HD,* p. 5.

22   *HD,* p. 12.

23   Frances B. Singh, p. 42, *HD,* 7.

24   Hamner, pp. 57-58.

25   Hamner, p. 58. See *Newsweek* and *The New York Times* from 1978 onwards.

26   Adil Jussawalla, "V.S. Naipaul: The Civilized Malcontent." The article was published in an Indian journal in 1979. Unfortunately, although Jussawalla sent me the article, he did so by ripping out the pages from the journal. I therefore do not have details of the journal.

27   V.S. Naipaul, *A Bend in the River* (New York: Vintage Books, 1980), p. 8: *HD,* p. 32.

28   Hamner, p. 59.

29   Hamner, p. 59.

30   See Nazareth, p. 121. My chapter draws to some extent on an unpublished essay
      Ngugi wrote in 1964 entitled, "Why *Nostromo?*" Also see Joseph Conrad,
      Nostromo (London: Penguin, 1963), p. 427.

31   See "A New King for the Congo: Mobutu and the Nihilism of Africa" in *The Return
      of Eva Perón.*

32   Edward Luttwak, *Coup d'Etat (A Practical Hand Book)* (New York: Fawcett,
      1969), p. 37, n. 2.

33   Harris, p. 9; *HD*, p. 32.

34   *The Return of Eva Perón,* p. 191.

35   *Ibid.*, p. 206. Naipaul also says, "*Lord Jim*, however, is an imperialist book . . ."
      in Hamner, p. 57.

36   *The Return of Eva Perón,* p. 208.

37   *Ibid.,* p. 209.

38   *Ibid.,* pp. 209-10.

39   *Ibid.,* p. 219.

40   Shiva Naipaul, *North of South: An African Journey* (New York: Simon and
      Schuster, 1979), p. 347.

41   *A Bend in the River,* p. 272.

42   Shiva Naipaul, pp. 54-55. See Ngugi's attack on Elspeth Huxley and Karen Blixen
      (Isak Dinesen) as racist apologists for imperialism in *Homecoming* (London:
      Heinemann, 1972), pp. 9, 43, and *Writers in Politics* (London: Heinemann, 1981),
      pp. 17-19, 33. It is no surprise that Elspeth Huxley praises Naipaul's book: it had her
      laughing and crying, the cover of the book says. See also the article entitled, "On
      Isak Dinesen's Land, Old Kenyan Reminisces," *New York Times,* 13 September
      1981, p. 14. The diseased herd boy Isak Dinesen had rescued and turned into a
      servant as described in her *Out of Africa* had a collection of stories in 1975 edited by
      Peter Beard, now the husband of Cheryl Tiegs, with an Afterword by Jacqueline
      Onassis, published by Harcourt Brace Jovanovich at $19.95. The author claims
      that he has not received a cent from the book. Angered by the title of the book, he
      says, "What darkness? What does it mean? When was I ever in darkness?" This
      book is entitled *Longing for Darkness: Kamante's Tales from Out of Africa.*

43   See my interview in Bernth Lindfors, *MAZUNGUMZO* (Athens, Ohio: Ohio State University Press, 1980). See also my "Practical Problems and Technical Solutions in Writing My Two Novels," *Afriscope,* ed. Uche Chukwumerije (Yaba, Lagos, Nigeria), Vol. 10, No. 9, September, 1980.

44   Achebe, p. 9.

45   For example, see Towhé Esubiyi, "FLYING: A Maverick Reading of Achebe's Festac Poem," *African Writing Today,* special double issue of *Pacific Quarterly Moana,* ed. Peter Nazareth. Hamilton, New Zealand, Vol. 6, Nos. 3-4.

46   Chinua Achebe, *Things Fall Apart* (New York: Fawcett, 1959), p. 90.

47   Ngugi wa Thiong'o, *Writers in Politics,* p. 19.

48   *Ibid.,* pp. 76-77.

49   Edward Said, *Joseph Conrad and the Fiction of Autobiography* (Cambridge: Harvard University Press, 1966), p. 4. Said's purpose is to prove that one can understand the camouflage in Conrad's fiction by reading his explicit letters to close friends and colleagues.

50   Wilson Harris, *Palace of the Peacock* (London: Faber and Faber, 1977), p. 27.

51   Okot p'Bitek, *"Song of Lawino"* and *"Song of Ocol"* (Nairobi: East African Publishing House, 1974), pp. 184-85.

52   *Ibid.,* p. 187.

53   James Konrad, *Target Amin* (London: Sphere Books, 1977).

NOTES ON CONTRIBUTORS

Achebe, Chinua.
> Nigerian novelist and short story writer. *Things Fall Apart* (1958), *No Longer at Ease* (1960), *Arrow of God* (1964), *A Man of the People* (1966), *Morning Yet on Creation Day* (1975).

Blake, Susan L.
> U.S. citizen. Associate Professor of English at Lafayette College, Pennsylvania. Fulbright Senior Lectureship, Université du Benin, Togo, 1983-84.

Clemens, Florence.
> U. S. citizen. Ph. D. on Conrad at Ohio State University (1937). Taught three years in Penang, Malaysia.

Clifford, Sir Hugh C. (1866-1941)
> British diplomat in foreign service: Colonial Secretary for Trinidad and Tobago, for Ceylon; Governor of Gold Coast and Nigeria; High Commissioner for Malay States and British Agent in Borneo. Author of *Studies in Brown Humanity* (1898).

Echeruo, Michael.
> Nigerian poet, Professor of English at the University of Ibadan. National Editor for *Conradiana*. Poems *Morality* (1968); criticism includes *Joyce Cary & the Novel of Africa* (1973), and *The Conditioned Imagination from Shakespeare to Conrad* (1978).

Fernando, Lloyd.
> Malaysian novelist, Professor of English at the University of Malaya. Author of *Scorpion Orchid* (1976), *"New Women" in the Late Victorian Novel* (1977).

Franco, Jean.
> Born in England, Professor of Spanish and Comparative Literature at Stanford University. *Modern Culture of Latin America* (1967), *Cesar Vallejo: The Dialects of Poetry and Silence* (1976).

Goonetilleke, D. C. R. A.
> Sri Lanka, Senior Lecturer in English at the University of Sri Lanka. Ph.D. from the University of Lancaster as Commonwealth Scholarship recipient.

233

Harris, Wilson.
> Guyanese novelist and critical theorist, now residing in London. Novels too numerous to list, poetry, and essays: *Tradition and the West Indian Novel* (1965), *Tradition, the Writer and Society* (1967), *The Womb of Space: The Cross-Cultural Imagination* (1983).

Hilson, J. C. [Ian],
> England, Lecturer in English literature at Leicester University until his death in 1980.

McLauchlan, Juliet.
> England, Chairman of the Joseph Conrad Society (U.K.); retired, but currently teaching extension courses at Oxford and Cambridge.

Marle, Hans van.
> Netherlands, Dutch National Editor for *Conradiana.*

Nazareth, Peter.
> Ugandan novelist, playwright. Teaching in the International Writing Program at the University of Iowa. Novel: *In a Brown Mantle* (1972), and more recently, *The General Is Up* and *The Footnote Man.* Literary criticism: *An African View of Literature* (1974), *The Third World Writer* (1975).

Naipaul, V. S.
> Trinidadian writer, now resides in England. Novels and short stories too numerous to list set in the West Indies, England and Africa. Travel books on the Caribbean, India, the Near and Far East.

Said, Edward W.
> Born in Palestine, now Parr Professor of English and Comparative Literature at Columbia University. Author of *Joseph Conrad and the Fiction of Autobiography* (1966), *Orientalism* (1978), *Covering Islam* (1981), *The World, the Text, & the Critic* (1983).

Sarvan, C. Poonuthurai.
> Zambia, Lecturer in English at the University of Zambia.

Timms, David.
> England, Lecturer in American Literature at Manchester University.

Bibliographical Distribution
by Area and by Decade

Separate placement has been observed for the metropolitan and Third World nations. Because of similar development, Australia and Canada are counted together; due to geographic proximity to each other, South America and the Caribbean, India and Sri Lanka, and Southeast Asia and the Pacific islands are placed into three appropriate groups.

With the exception of horizontal columns for counting writers, numbers from the decades add up correctly both horizontally for each country category, and vertically for sums in all columns. The discrepancy in the horizontal columns for writers is accounted for by the fact that some writers published several articles or books in succeeding decades. Each writer is counted within each decade in which he published; however, writers are counted only once for the horizontal total given beside their respective countries. The overall totals of these accounts for countries are, therefore, correct in all the vertical columns in every category.

Table
Bibliographical Distribution By Area & By Decade

Third World Country/Area	1890s	1900s	1910s	1920s	1930s	1940s	1950s	1960s	1970s	1980s	Totals
AFRICA											
Writers								3	15	9	22
Articles								3	16	7	26
Books										1	1
CARIBBEAN/SOUTH AMERICA											
Writers						1	1	3	1	2	7
Articles						1	1	3	1	2	8
Books											0
INDIA/SRI LANKA											
Writers								9	14	5	26
Articles								9	17	5	31
Books									2	1	3
SOUTHEAST ASIA/PACIFIC											
Writers	2						1	3	6	6	15
Articles	2						1	9	8	6	26
Books								1	1		2
Metropolitan Commonwealth Countries											
AUSTRALIA											
Writers								3	3	1	7
Articles								3	3	3	9
Books											0
CANADA											
Writers	1							4	5	5	10
Articles	1							7	8	5	21
Books										1	1
SUBTOTALS (Third World & Metro. Commonwealth)											
Writers	3					1	2	25	44	27	87
Articles	3					1	2	34	53	28	121
Books								1	3	3	7

Bibliographical Distribution by Area & By Decade

Industrialized West	Decades										Totals
	1890s	1900s	1910s	1920s	1930s	1940s	1950s	1960s	1970s	1980s	
ENGLAND											
Writers	13	5		3	1	1	2	10	8	4	41
Articles	13	7		4	1	1	2	12	8	3	51
Books								1	2	1	4
EUROPE											
Writers				3	1	2		2	11	4	20
Articles				3	1	3		3	12	4	23
Books				1							1
UNITED STATES											
Writers	3			1	1	2	8	19	35	17	76
Articles	3			1	1	3	8	16	38	22	92
Books								4	3	2	9
SUBTOTALS (Industrialized West)											
Writers	16	5		7	3	3	10	31	55	25	137
Articles	16	7		8	3	4	10	31	58	29	166
Books				1				5	5	3	14
OVERALL TOTALS (ALL AREAS)											
Writers	19	5		7	3	4	12	56	99	52	224
Articles	19	7		8	3	5	12	65	111	57	287
Books				1				6	8	6	21

A JOSEPH CONRAD BIBLIOGRAPHY: THIRD WORLD PERSPECTIVES

The primary works Conrad set in the outposts of empire make an impressive list. They are his best, the repository of his right to remain a major figure in English literature. That they continue to be the object of lively criticism is not surprising. The following list of works is but a fraction of the work devoted to analysis of his writing, but it represents the fascination he holds for new writers and critics from the Third World, and for readers in cosmopolitan countries who are interested in the legacy of imperialism.

From the beginning, there are frustrating problems involved in determining what the qualifying standards should be for secondary sources. Obviously, natives of any of the former colonies and countries of the Third World should be included. Knowing who they are, however, is not always easy. Not only do people move around with increasing frequency in the second half of the twentieth century, but the reliability of ethnic and regional surnames is less than certain. Adding to this basic problem is the fact that in spite of modern communications technology, the writing in many developing countries is not widely known. Numerous short-lived journals and newspapers appear and disappear without being indexed in major publications. Once the existence of an item becomes known, then comes the procedure of trying to locate a copy.

Materials of the second type that seemed to be appropriate for this bibliography, are those articles and books concerned with the colonial/imperial aspects of Conrad's work, no matter what the writer's geographic origin. Once again, surnames are suspect and datelines of publications provide only tenuous clues. In some cases, critics and authors have left clear evidence of their national origin, only to establish residence elsewhere. Geography and nationality aside, the complexity of the basic subject matter leaves many borderline articles subject to interpretation. Conrad leads readers into politically sensitive areas that are not always distinctively or directly related to colonialism as such. Perhaps no choice can be made without its political implications.

Articles deal with Conrad's autobiographical realism, with his treatment (or stereotypical avoidance) of colored races, his choice of language (being a Pole, coming to England and English as a foreigner), his revealing Freudian or Jungian symbolism, his antirevolutionary fervor and his ambivalence toward Victorian ideals. Each of these themes could be pertinent to the central question of Conrad's treatment of alien cultures forcibly confronting each other under imperial colonialism. Yet in many instances, the principal thrust of a given essay takes it away from Conrad's function as a "colonial" author. If such a distinction can be made, it must be with humility and great trepidation.

Such are the tactical problems involved in the process of selection. Nevertheless, the basic list has grown over the years to total 308 items. Beyond the fact that the number of publications on Conrad's colonialism seems to have risen and fallen along with his being generally in and out of favor with successive generations of readers, there is an obvious, steady increase of such articles since the 1950s. At the turn of the century, there was a flurry of interest in this new writer of exotic tales of faraway adventures, then scant attention between the 1920s and the colonial independence movements beginning after World War II.

Metropolitan scholars realized Conrad's relevance to these emerging nations in the 1950s, but the significant new element in the field is the contribution by Third World critics who were virtually unknown before 1960. Of the six books and fifty-seven essays published in this field since 1979, half have been produced by critics from Commonwealth countries. The combined totals so far in the 1980s for all the nations involved in this survey, already exceed half the 111 articles and eight books I have located from the 1970s. At the present rate, these numbers could well be surpassed by 1990. The following is, at best, a bibliography in the process of becoming.

SELECTED BIBLIOGRAPHY

I. Primary sources relating to Conrad's Colonial/Imperial Writing

A. Eastern Works (Indo-Malaysian)
- 1895 *Almayer's Folly*
- 1896 *An Outcast of the Islands*
- 1897 "Karain," "The Lagoon,"
- 1898 "Youth," "An Observer in Malaya," plus a review of *Studies in Brown Humanity* (by Sir Hugh Clifford) in *Academy*, 23 April.
- 1900 *Lord Jim*
- 1902 *Typhoon*, "The End of the Tether"
- 1903 "Falk"
- 1908 "The Black Mate"
- 1910 "The Secret Sharer"
- 1911 "A Smile of Fortune"
- 1912 "Freya of the Seven Isles"
- 1914 "Because of the Dollars," "The Planter of Malata"
- 1915 *Victory*
- 1917 *The Shadow Line*
- 1920 *The Rescue* (*The Rescuer* in 1896)
- 1924 "Geography and Some Explorers," in *Last Essays*

B. Africa
- 1897 "An Outpost of Progress"
- 1899 *Heart of Darkness*
- 1925 "The Congo Diary" in *Last Essays*

C. *Caribbean/Latin America*
- 1903 *Romance*
- 1904 *Nostromo*
- 1906 "An Anarchist" (in Cayenne, partly), "Gaspar Ruiz"

D. Others
- 1897 *The Nigger of the 'Narcissus,'* title character a West Indian Negro aboard a ship bound from Bombay around Africa to England
- 1906 *The Mirror of the Sea*, references to voyages, the scattered ports of Conrad's sea experience

II. Secondary Sources

Achebe, Chinua. "An Image of Africa." *The Massachusetts Review,* 18:4 (Winter 1977), 782-94. Rpt. *Research in African Literatures,* 9:1 (1978), 1-15. Conrad a "bloody racist" in *Heart of Darkness.*[1]

_____. "Viewpoint." *Times Literary Supplement,* 1 Feb. 1980, p. 113. *Heart of Darkness* confirms European prejudices.

Aithal, S. Krishnamoorthy. "Conrad's *Lord Jim.*" *Explicator,* 38:1 (Fall 1979), 3-4. Jim a "trapped, cornered, imprisoned" figure.

_____. "Imagery in Conrad's *Lord Jim.*" *Neophilologus,* 63 (n.d.), 309-19. Associative qualities reveal characters, events, themes.

_____. "A Postscript to Criticism on Conrad's *Lord Jim.*" *English Studies,* 57:5 (Oct. 1976), 425-31. Jim victim of inevitable fate. Integrity in Conrad's withholding verdict on Jim.

Altick, Richard Daniel. "The Search for Sambir." In *The Scholar Adventurers,* New York: Macmillan, 1950. Rpt. New York: The Free Press, 1966, pp. 289-97. John Gordon's discovery that Sambir in *Almayer's Folly* is Berouw in Borneo and that Almayer is based on Carel Olmeijer.

Amur, G. S. " 'Heart of Darkness' and 'The Fall of the House of Usher': The Tale as Discovery." *The Literary Criterion* (Mysore), 9:4 (Summer 1971), 59-70. Parallels in structure, narrative approach, plot and theme.

Anderson, James A. "Conrad and Baroja: Two Spiritual Exiles." *Kwartalnik Neofilologiczny.* 20:4 (1973), 363-71. Compares Conrad, a "spiritual exile," Pio Baroja, a writer about exiles.

Anderson, Linda R. "Ideas of Identity and Freedom in V. S. Naipaul and Joseph Conrad." *English Studies.* 59:5 (Oct. 1978), 510-17. Alike in exile, alienation, cultural confrontation. Conrad's possibility for commitment.

Aynard, Joseph. "L'exotisme de Joseph Conrad à propos de *Lord Jim*" *Journal Des Debats,* 134 (18 Nov. 1922), 3. Exotic settings, but common human experience beneath surface is principal importance.

Bantock, G. H. "Conrad and Politics." *English Literary History,* 25-2 (June 1958), 122-36. Conrad admires individual's motives, not philosophical creed or social force.

Bass, Eben. "The Verbal Failure of Lord Jim." *College English,* 26(1965). 438-44. Jim's faulty idiom turned to asset; his stutter, auditory errors, reticence in keeping with his insecurity. Conrad's experiences in an alien language.

Beeton, Ridley. "Conrad and the African Experience." In *Generous Converse: English Essays in Memory of Edward Davis.* Ed. Brian Green. Cape Town: Oxford U. P., 1980, pp. 102-12. Range of Conrad's knowledge of Africa. Civilized man needs contact with civilization.

Benson, Donald R. " 'Heart of Darkness': The Grounds of Civilization in an Alien Universe." *Texas Studies in Literature and Language,* 7:4 (Winter 1966), 339-47. Novel searches origins of civilization in an alien, naturalistic universe, not just "inner journey."

Birje-Patil, J. "From *Heart of Darkness* to a *Free State.*" *Colonial Consciousness in Commonwealth Literature: Essays Presented to Professor C. D. Narasimhaiah.* Eds. G.S. Amur, S.K. Desai. Bombay: Somaiya Publications, 1984, pp. 110-18.

Bitterli, Urs. *Conrad, Malraux, Greene, Weiss: Schriftsteller und Kolonialismus.* Zurich: Benziger, 1973. Conrad as colonial writer, pp. 27-60.

Blake, Susan L. "Racism and the Classics: Teaching *Heart of Darkness.*" *CLA Journal,* 25:4 (June 1982), 395-404. *Heart of Darkness* should be treated as racist novel.[1]

Bogue, Ronald L. "The Heartless Darkness of *Apocalypse Now.*" *The Georgia Review,* 35:3 (Fall 1981), 611-26. Film adaptation of *Heart of Darkness.*

Bolton, W. F. "The Role of Language in *Lord Jim.*" *Conradiana,* 1:3 (Summer 1969), 51-59. Argues for the pervasive, purposeful use of language as spoken word and as textual artifact.

Bonney, William W. " 'Eastern Logic under My Western Eyes': Conrad, Schopenhauer, and the Orient." *Conradiana,* 10:3 (1978), 225-52. Rpt. in his *Thorns & Arabesques: Contexts for Conrad's Fiction.* Baltimore: Johns Hopkins U. P., 1980, pp. 3-30, 224-27. Conrad's inconsistencies and irregularities are outgrowth of his conception of life as "a sequence of unique perceptual coagulations" which may be related, but are not necessarily consistent.

Brashers, H. C. "Conrad, Marlow, and Gautama Buddha: On Structure and Theme in *Heart of Darkness.*" *Conradiana,* 1:3 (Summer 1969), 63-71. Parallels between plot of *Heart of Darkness* and Buddha's "Noble Eight-Fold Path."

Braun, Andrzej. "Indonezja Conradowska" (Conradian Indonesia). *Swiat* (World), Nos. 11-14 (17 Mar.-7 Apr. 1968), n.p.* Series of articles identifying real locations cited in Conrad's fiction.

_____. "The Myth-Like Kingdom of Conrad." *Conradiana,* 10:1 (1978), 3-16. Compares official Bugis kingdom of Wadjo to Conrad's fictional state in "Karain," *The Rescue, Lord Jim,* "The Lagoon."

_____. "Sladami Conrada." *Zycie Literackie* (Literary Life), No. 5 (2 Feb. 1969), 8-9. Trans. by Elias J. Schwartz. "In Conrad's Footsteps." *Conradiana,* 4:2 (1972), 33-46. Braun's first-hand impressions of scenes Conrad witnessed in Eastern settings.

_____. "Wizyta w Patusanie" (A Visit in Patusan). *Tworczosc* (Creation), 27:3 (Mar. 1972), 58-81. Location of Lord Jim's island.

"Brown Humanity." *Outlook* (London), 23:1 (Apr. 1898), 372. Conrad not limited to South Seas. Settings in *Tales of Unrest* in West Africa and London.

Cândido, Antonio. *Tese e Antitese: Ensaios.* São Paulo: Cia Editora National, [1964?], Conrad, pp. 59-93. Dramatizes humans, regardless of circumstances of place.

Carpenter, Richard C. "The Geography of Costaguana, or Where Is Sulaco?" *Journal of Modern Literature,* 5:2 (Apr. 1976), 321-26. Difficulties of fixing geographic setting for *Nostromo.*

Chatterjee, Kalyan. "Marlow's Tragic Vision in *Lord Jim.*" *The Bulletin* (Calcutta University, Department of English), N.S. 8:1 (1972-73), 9-14. Complexities of viewers and objective world major subject of novel.

Chatterjee, Sisir. "Joseph Conrad: The Power of the Written Word." In *Problems in Modern English Fiction.* Calcutta: Bookland Private, 1965, pp. 112-22. Examines experimental techniques and characterization in various works. Compares with Henry James.

Chiampi, Rubens. *"Heart of Darkness."* *ITA Humanidades* (Sao Jose dos Campos, Brazil), 5 (1969), 52-68. Style composite of Stevenson, Kipling, James, French naturalism, Slavic and Russian novel.

Christmas, Peter. "Conrad's *Nostromo:* A Tale of Europe." *Literature and History,* 6:1
        (1980), 59-81.* Possessiveness signified in title supplies principal meaning.
Cleary, Thomas R. and Terry Sherwood. "Women in Conrad's Ironical Epic: Virgil,
        Dante and *Heart of Darkness." Conradiana,* 16:3 (1984), 183-94. Borrowings
        from Virgil and Dante guide symbolic journey and shape ironic treatment of
        women.
Clemens, Florence. "Conrad's Favorite Bedside Book." *South Atlantic Quarterly,* 38:3
        (July 1939), 305-15. Utilization of Alfred Wallace's *The Malay Archipelago*
        (1869) for background, character and description.
_____. "Conrad's Malaysia." *College English,* 2 (Jan. 1941), 338-46. Authoritative
        recording of political, geographic, social scene. Concentrates on whites, not
        native individuals.[1]
_____. "Joseph Conrad as a Geographer." *Scientific Monthly,* 51 (Nov. 1940), 460-
        65. Substantiates places and names for Malaysian settings of novels and stories.
Clifford, Hugh. "The Art of Mr. Joseph Conrad." *The Spectator,* 29 Nov. 1902, pp. 827-
        28. Doubtful psychological insight into Oriental mind.
_____. "Concerning Conrad and His Work." *Empire Review,* 47 (May 1928), 287-
        94. Knowledge of Malayan people "superficial and inaccurate in an infuriating
        degree."
_____. "The Genius of Mr. Conrad." *North American Review,* 178 (June 1904),
        843-52. Asiatics of interest for their impression scored on sensitive, European
        observer.[1]
_____. "Joseph Conrad: Some Scattered Memories." *Bookman's Journal and Print
        Collector,* 2 (Oct. 1924), 3. Conrad admits shallow knowledge of Malayan mind.
        Clifford aids in serialization of *Chance.*
_____. "The Trail of the Book-Worm: Mr. Joseph Conrad at Home and Abroad."
        Singapore Free Press (Weekly Mail edition), 1 Sept. 1898, p. 142. Conrad's
        inaccuracy in presenting Malayan people.
Collins, Harold. R. "Kurtz, the Cannibals, and the Second-Rate Helmsman." *The
        Western Humanities Review* (Autumn 1954), pp. 299-310. Significance of the
        confrontation of cultures and personalities for individuals, and races. Demorali-
        zation of misplaced persons.
Conroy, Mark. "Lost in Azuera: The Fate of Sulaco and Conrad's *Nostromo. Glyph:
        Textual Studies,* 8 (1981), 148-69. European's deterministic view of mytho-
        logized South America constitutes further imperialism.
Coonan, Michael. "Conrad's Vocabulary." *American Notes and Queries,* 18 (1979),
        38-39. Misusages result of unfamiliar sound patterns in second language.
Crews, Frederick. "The Power of Darkness." *Partisan Review* (Fall 1967), pp. 508-25.
        No artificial contradictions, Conrad lived amid prejudices of his age, and
        personal angst.
Curle, Richard. "Conrad in the East." *Yale Review,* N.S. 12 (Apr. 1923), 497-508.
        Despite accurate details of Eastern settings and real-life characters in fiction,
        Conrad imaginatively colors his memories of East. Major concern with man, not
        nature.
Daiches, David. "Experience and the Imagination: The Background of 'Heart of
        Darkness.' " In *White Man in the Tropics: Two Moral Tales.* Ed. David
        Daiches. New York: Harcourt, Brace and World, 1962, pp. 3-16. Profound
        paradox of 'Heart of Darkness' is that society (which men need) corrupts
        inevitably and individual isolation (which is desirable) maddens or destroys.

Daniel, Nechama. "A Glimpse of Conrad's Patusan." *Joseph Conrad Today,* 9:3 (Fall 1984), 258-61. Photographs and comparison between Lord Jim's Patusan and personal recollections of Mountain Districts of Central Celebes.

Das, Ram Jiwan. *Joseph Conrad: A Study in Existential Vision.* New Delhi: Associated Publishing, 1980. Shows chaotic, godless, meaningless world where order is based on individual self.

Davidson, Arnold E. "The Abdication of Lord Jim." *Conradiana,* 13:1 (1981), 19-34. Despite various optimistic interpretations, Jim's ultimate failure.

_____. "Delimiting *Victory*: The Ending of Joseph Conrad's Last Major Novel." *Modern British Literature,* 3 (1978), 88-100.

_____. "Deluded Vision in Conrad's *Under Western Eyes.*" *International Fiction Review,* 4:1 (1977), 23-31.

_____. "The Open Ending of *The Secret Agent.*" *Ariel,* 7:1 (1976), 84-100.

_____. Rev. of three books on Conrad. *Modern Fiction Studies,* 19-4 (Winter 1973-74), 631-35. Rev. of Adams, *Joseph Conrad*; Coolidge, *The Three Lives of Joseph Conrad;* Saveson, *Joseph Conrad: The Making of a Moralist.*

_____. "The Sign of Conrad's Secret Agent." *College Literature,* 8:1 (Winter 1981), 33-41.

Dean, Leonard F. "Conrad and the Congo." In *Joseph Conrad's "Heart of Darkness": Backgrounds and Criticisms.* Ed. Leonard F. Dean. Englewood Cliffs, N.J.: Prentice-Hall, Spectrum Books, 1960, p. 143. Relationship of Conrad's Congo diary, Mrs. Jessie Conrad and Captain Otto Lutken.

Dorall, E. N. "Conrad and Coppola: Different Centres of Darkness." *Southeast Asian Review of English* (Kuala Lumpur), 1:1 (Dec. 1980), 19-26. *Heart of Darkness* filmed as *Apocalypse Now.*

Duncan, Sara Jeannette. Rev. of *An Outcast of the Islands. Indian Daily News* (Calcutta), 12 Oct. 1896, n.p. Rpt. in *Sara Jeannette Duncan: Selected Journalism.* Ed. Thomas E. Tausky. Ottawa: Tecumseh Press, 1978, pp. 119-20. Astonishing book to rise out of "Samarany Roads;" account is real and truthful, could well be about India.

Eagleton, Terry. "Joseph Conrad and *Under Western Eyes.*" In his *Exiles and Emigrés.* New York: Schocken Books, 1972, pp. 21-32. Pseudoneutrality of narrative, ambiguities, irony "sustain a precariously fine tension between 'English' and 'foreign' experiences."

Echeruo, Michael J. C. "Conrad's Nigger." In *The Conditioned Imagination from Shakespeare to Conrad.* New York: Holmes and Meier, 1978, pp. 93-112. James Wait stereotypical, conditioned for European Negrophobia.[1]

Elayouty, Amin. "Romantic Realism in Conrad's *Lord Jim" Journal of English,* 6: pp. 54-78.*

Emmett, Victor J. Jr. "The Esthetics of Anti-Imperialism: Ironic Distortions of the Vergilian Epic Mode in Conrad's *Nostromo.*" *Studies in the Novel,* 4:3 (Fall 1972), 459-72. *Heart of Darkness* not imperialistic. Inevitability is central theme of *Nostromo.*

Envall, Markku. "Politiikka ja filsosofia Joseph Conradin *Heart of Darkness*-toeksessa." *Kirjallisuudentutkijain Seuran Vuosikirja* (Helsinki), 27 (1973), 5-19.*

Faulkner, Peter. "Vision and Normality: Conrad's 'Heart of Darkness.' " *Ibadan Studies in English,* 1 (1969) 36-47. Perception of observer explored, Conrad and characters.

Fernando, Lloyd. "Conrad's Eastern Expatriates: New Version of His Outcasts." *Publications of the Modern Language Association*, 9:1 (Jan. 1976), 78-90. Covers lack of primary knowledge with sensitive understanding. Colonialism deflects expatriate and native alike from familiar patterns.[1]

_____. "Other Worlds, Other Seas: The Imperial Theme in British Fiction." *Victorian Studies,* 20:3 (Spring 1977), 299-309. Covers Stevenson, Kipling, Conrad.

Fleishman, Avrom. "Colonists and Conquerors." In *Conrad's Politics: Community and Anarchy in the Fiction of Joseph Conrad.* Baltimore: Johns Hopkins Press, 1967, pp. 79-125. Among contemporary anti-imperialists, Conrad concerned with social disruption for natives and moral disorientation for Europeans. Selectivity in settings reflects judgmental view.

Ford, Ford Madox. "On Conrad's Vocabulary." *Bookman* (New York), 67 (June 1928), 405-408. On Ford's collaboration toward new novel form, conversational tone. Secret of Conrad's style is "mosaic of little crepitations of surprise."

Foulke, Robert. "Postures of Belief in *The Nigger of the 'Narcissus.' " Modern Fiction Studies,* 17 (1971), 249-62. Technique requires fine analysis, multiple narrative voices.

Franco, Jean. "The Limits of the Liberal Imagination: *One Hundred Years of Solitude* and *Nostromo." Punto de Contacto/Point of Contact,* 1:1 (Dec. 1975), 4-16. Comparative study. Conrad reserves maturity to Europeans. Imperialist intervention in nationalist drives.[1]

Frederic, Harold. Rev. of "The Nigger of the 'Narcissus.' " *Saturday Review,* 12 Feb. 1898, p. 211.

Fwasatadi, Wabeno. *"Heart of Darkness:* Le Voyage de Marlow vers l'interieur." *Cahiers de Littérature et de Linguistique Appliquée,* 7-8 (1975), 85-92. Journey as classical artistic device.

[Garnett, Edward]. "Mr. Conrad's Art." *Speaker,* 12 Nov. 1904, pp. 138-39. Captivating racial genius of gracious, semibarbarous South America penetrates European consciousness. Importance of environment.

_____. Rev. of *Youth, A Narrative; and Two Other Stories. Academy and Literature,* 6 Dec. 1902, p. 606. Rates "Youth" above *Heart of Darkness* and "The End of the Tether." Barbarism of Africa, deterioration of white man's morale in the tropics.

Geddes, Gary. "Clearing the Jungle: The Importance of Work in Conrad." *Queen's Quarterly,* 73:4 (Winter 1966) 559-72. Interruption of work pattern threatens survival.

_____. "Conrad and the Darkness Before Creation." *The Antigonish Review,* 7 (Autumn 1971), 93-104. Anguish underlies Conrad's creative act.

_____. "Conrad and the Fine Art of Understanding." *The Dalhousie Review,* 47:4 (1967), 492-503. Requires sympathetic imagination to enter fiction of unrestricted interplay between reality and consciousness.

_____. *Conrad's Later Novels.* Montreal: McGill-Queen's U. P., 1980. Later, more stylized and self-conscious novels are variation on romance form—the "ironic romance."

_____. *"The Rescue:* Conrad and the Rhetoric of Diplomacy." *Mosaic,* 7:3 (Spring 1974), 107-25. *The Rescue* about hearing and listening, the difference between statement and fuller meaning.

_____. "The Structure of Sympathy: Conrad and the Chance That Wasn't." *English Literature in Transition,* 12:4 (1969), 175-88. Ambivalent critics underestimate Conrad's power. Dialectic or ironic counterpoint in by-play between Marlow and narrator.

_____. "That Extra Longitude: Conrad and the Art of Fiction." *University of Windsor Review,* 3:2 (Spring 1968), 65-81. Philosophical, analytical novelist exploring illusory quality of life.

Gillon, Adam. "Cosmopolitanism in Conrad's Work." *Proceedings of the International Comparative Literature Association.* Ed. François Jost. The Hague: Mouton, 1966, vol. 1, pp. 94-99. Reasons for cosmopolitan attitudes among characters in international settings: divided men, no national roots, needing brotherhood transcending economic, political, racial, cultural differences.

Glassman, Peter J. *Language and Being: Joseph Conrad and the Literature of Personality.* New York: Columbia U. P., 1976 Accounts for Conrad's "unindividuated" life, wherein fiction replaces the "personality structures of family, nation, sexuality, love."

Goonetilleke, D. C. R. A. "Conrad's African Tales: Ironies of Progress." *Ceylon Journal of the Humanities,* 2:1 (Jan. 1971), 64-97. Rpt. in his *Developing Countries,* q.v.

_____. "Conrad's *Victory* Reconsidered." *Sri Lanka Journal of the Humanities,* 1:1 (1975), 1-7. Flawed, mixed values in novel depend on understanding Heyst's drama, not an evocation of European man in Sourabaya.

_____. *Developing Countries in British Fiction.* Totowa: Rowman and Littlefield, 1977. Conrad, Kipling, Forster, Lawrence, Carey. Four Chapters on Conrad: his most important themes personal, not political, does not reach deepest parts of cultures or issues.

_____. "On Conrad's Portrayal of Malayans." *ACLALS Bulletin* (1974), pp. 6-9. His Malayans tribalists, not transplanted Polish nationalists.

Gordon, J. D. "The Four Sources." In his *Joseph Conrad, the Making of a Novelist.* New York: Russel & Russel, 1963, pp. 28-74. Traces characters and events in novels and stories to actual persons.

_____. "The Rajah Brooke and Joseph Conrad." *Studies in Philology,* 35 (1938), 619-25. Inspiration for Lingard.

Green, Martin. "Conrad." in his *Dreams of Adventure, Deeds of Empire.* New York: Basic Books, 1979, pp. 297-319. Chronological overview of Conrad's career. Conrad rich in "political and psychological insight into the sins and follies of imperialism," but equivocates and is too ambivalent to be "master of these insights...."

Greiff, Louis K., and Shirley A. Grieff. "Sulaco and Panama: A Geographical Source in Conrad's *Nostromo." Journal of Modern Literature,* 3:1 (Feb. 1973), 102-4. *Nostromo* set in Panama.

Gupta, N. Das. "Conrad." In his *Literature of the Twentieth Century.* Gwalior: Kitab Ghar, 1967, pp. 163-70. Impressionistic method reveals inner self. Avoids didacticism, showing problems not solutions.

Gutierrez, Donald. "Uroboros, the Serpent, and Conrad's *Heart of Darkness." Nantucket Review,* 5 (Dec. 1975), 40-45. Psychology of serpent tradition in literature.

Halverston, John, and Ian Watt. "The Original Nostromo: Conrad's Source." *Review of English Studies,* N.S. 10:37 (Feb. 1959), 45-52. Parallels between *Nostromo* and details from book by "Frederick Benton Williams" (pseudonym of Herbert Elliott Hamblen), *On Many Seas: The Life and Exploits of a Yankee Sailor,* New York:

Macmillan, 1897.

Hamner, Robert D. "Colony, Nationhood and Beyond: Third World Critics Contend with Joseph Conrad." *World Literature Written in English,* 23:1 (Winter 1984), 108-16. Influences of Conrad on writers, critical reactions.

_____. "Conrad and Third World Critics: Reflections on a Bibliography." *Joseph Conrad Today,* 8:1-2 (Jan.-Mar. 1983), 212-15. Range of interest in Conrad's colonial/imperial works.

_____. "Joseph Conrad and the Colonial World: A Selected Bibliography." *Conradiana,* 14:3 (1982), 217-29.

Harris, Wilson. "The Frontier on Which *Heart of Darkness* Stands." *Research in African Literatures,* 12:1 (Spring 1981), 86-93. Conrad parodies liberal complacency, stands on frontier of complex wholeness which transcends parody. Confronts Achebe's charges of "racism."[1]

Haugh, Robert F. "Joseph Conrad and Revolution." *College English,* 10:5 (Feb. 1949), 273-77. Revolutionary forces in *Under Western Eyes* like sea in *Lord Jim.*

Hawkins, Hunt. "Conrad and Congolese Exploitation." *Conradiana,* 13:2 (1981), 94-100. Possibility of personal exposure to atrocities. Contemporary accounts of Congo.

_____. "Conrad's Critique of Imperialism in *Heart of Darkness.*" *Publications of the Modern Language Association,* 94:2 (1979), 286-99. Four main critics on Conrad's imperialism differ widely. Finds no positive "colonists" in any of the works, but "paternalists," condemned for their "dominative intervention."

_____. "The Issue of Racism in *Heart of Darkness.*" *Conradiana,* 14:3 (1982), 163-71. Complex attitude, but remarkably fair-minded for period.

_____. "Joseph Conrad, Roger Casement, and the Congo Reform Movement." *Journal of Modern Literature,* 9:1 (1981-82), 65-80. Distrusts materialistic movements, little faith in reforms.

Hay, Eloise. *The Political Novels of Joseph Conrad: A Critical Study.* Chicago: Chicago U. P., 1963. Complex "contemporaneity" of Conrad's political orientation. His strict discipline denied "recourse to any institution, whether of school, party or church."

Hidalgo, Pilar. "Los Raices Literarias de 'Apocalypse Now.' " *Arbor,* 412 (1980), 41-48. *Heart of Darkness* on theme central to present literature.

Higdon, David Leon, and Floyd Eugene Eddleman. "A Glossary of Malay Words in Conrad's *Almayer's Folly.*" *Conradiana,* 10:1 (1978), 73-79. Balance of familiar and exotic to communicate. Conrad views basic parallels between London and Borneo.

Hilson, J. C., and D. Timms. "Conrad's 'An Outpost of Progress' or, the Evil Spirit of Civilization." *Cahiers Victoriens et Edouardiens* (Montpellier), 2 (1975), 113-28. Attacks European masquerade of philanthropy.[1]

Hosillos, Lucila. "A Reliable Narrator: Conrad's Distance and Effects Through Marlow." *Diliman Review,* 18:2 (Apr. 1970), 154-72. Growing consciousness of uses of Marlow-narrator in successive stories. Creates set of facts enveloped by subjective mood.

Howarth, Herbert. "Conrad and Imperialism: *The Rescue.*" *Ohio Review,* 13:1 (Fall 1971), 62-72. Lingard the adventurer debilitated by contact with British elite, condemns himself.

Howe, Irving. "I. Order and Anarchy: The Political Novels." *Kenyon Review,* 15:4

(Autumn 1953), pp. 505-21. Part II. In *Kenyon Review* 16:1 (Winter 1954), 1-19. Despite distaste for political causes, Conrad pursued certain political themes. Reflects attempt "by symbolic indirection, to justify or expiate his 'desertion' from a national [Polish] cause."

Inniss, Kenneth. "Conrad's Native Girl: Some Social Questions." *Pacific Coast Philology,* 5 (1970), 39-45. Anglo-American xenophobia, complicated by Puritanism and attitudes toward inferior races, involved in Conrad's presentation of native women.

Jabbi, Bu-Buakei. "Conrad's Influence on Betrayal in *A Grain of Wheat.*" *Research in African Literatures,* 11 (1980), 50-83. Ngugi ingests and translates Conrad's work into his own masterpiece.

Jacobs, Diane. "Coppola Films Conrad in Vietnam." In *The English Novel and the Movies.* Eds. Michael Klein and Gillian Parker. New York: Ungar, 1981, pp. 211-17.

Jacobson, Dan. "Commonwealth Literature: Out of Empire." *New Statesman,* 69 (29 Jan. 1965), 153-54. On Novels of British imperialism. Typical British attitudes toward colonialism explored especially in *Heart of Darkness* and *Nostromo.*

Jean-Aubry, G[eorges]. *Joseph Conrad in the Congo.* Boston: Little, Brown & Co., 1926. Rpt. New York: Haskell House Publishers, 1973. Geographical spread of novels, merger of experience and fiction.

_____. *Joseph Conrad in the Congo.* London: "The Bookman's Journal Office," 1926. Rpt. Folcroft, Pa.: Folcroft Press, 1969. Traces Conrad's experience leading to and during his employment on the Congo. Parallels with *Heart of Darkness.*

_____. "Joseph Conrad et l'Amérique Latine." *Revue de l'Amérique Latine,* 2 (Apr. 1923), 290-99. Rpt. as "Joseph Conrad and Latin America." *Living Age,* 307 (12 May 1923), 350-55. Study of three works set in South America. Realism enhanced by ability to draw atmosphere from knowledge of books.

Jenkins, Gareth. "Conrad's *Nostromo* and History." *Literature and History: A New Journal for the Humanities,* 6 (1977), 173-78. Literary-fictional criteria favored over historical-critical explanation in Conrad's style.

Kapur, Ranjit K. *Joseph Conrad: Theme and Treatment of Evil.* New York: Asia Publishing House, 1978. Dialectics of evil through thematic structure, imagery, rhetoric and symbol.

Kemoli, Arthur and David K. Mulwa. "The European Image of Africa and the African." *Busara,* 2:2 (1969), 51-53. Carey and Conrad caricature, idealize and falsify.

Killam, G. Douglas. "Kurtz's Country." *Lock Haven Review,* No. 7 (1965), 31-42. Rpt. in his *Africa in English Fiction 1874-1939.* Ibadan: Ibadan U. P., 1968. Writers since Conrad still exotic romancers. Frequently endow Africa with capacity to test characters.

Kitonga, Ellen M. "Conrad's Image of African and Coloniser in *Heart of Darkness.*" *Busara,* 3:1 (1970), 33-35. Juxtaposition of civilized and savage ironic. Marlow parody of racist reader's view.

Klooss, Wolfgang. "Die Metaphorik des Kolonialismus: Joseph Conrad's *Heart of Darkness* als Problem literarischer Wirklichkeitsauffassung un die Jahrhundertwende." *Germanisch-Romanische Monatsschrift,* 31:1 (1981), 74-92. *Heart of Darkness* key to understanding treatment of colonialism in Conrad.

Knipp, T. R. "Black African Literature and the New African State." *Books Abroad,* 44

(1970), 373-79. General overview. Two literary traditions: Rider Haggard's heroic white, noble savage; Conrad's dark symbol of human spirit.

Kocówna, Barbara. "The Problem of Language." In *Joseph Conrad: A Commemoration.* Ed. Norman Sherry. London: Macmillan, 1976, pp. 194-98. Adopting second culture involves problems of loyalty, guilt, alienation.

Krenn, Heliena. "The Perfidy of Fidelity in Joseph Conrad's Fiction." *Fu Jen Studies: Literature and Linguistics* (Taipei), 13 (1980), 27-40.*

_____. "Vae Soli: Joseph Conrad's Predilection for Isolated Characters." *Fu Jen Studies: Literature and Linguistics* (Taipei), 3 (1970), 63-85.*

Kuesgen, Reinhardt. "Conrad and Achebe: Aspects of the Novel." *World Literature Written in English*, 24:1 (Summer 1984), 27-33. Novel form, a white invention, now available to general culture and capable of satisfying "both white and world-wide needs."

Kulkarni, H. B. "Buddhistic Structure and Significance in Joseph Conrad's *Heart of Darkness.*" *South Asian Review*, 3 (1979), 67-75. Parallels life journeys in *Mahāyāna* and *Hinayāna.*

La Bossière, Camille Rene. "The Eastern Logic of Conrad's *Ars Poetica.*" *Conradiana,* 11:3 (1979), 267-80. Imaginative eye fuses objective reality and subjective perception.

_____. " 'A Matter of Feeling' : A Note on Conrad's Comedy of Errors in *Under Western Eyes.*" *Thalia: Studies in Literary Humor,* 2:i-ii (1979), 35-38.

Langland, Elizabeth. "Society as Formal Protagonist: The Examples of *Nostromo* and *Barchester Towers.*" *Critical Inquiry,* 9:2 (Dec. 1982), 359-78. Society as protagonist alters narrative choices and perception of unity.

Larsen, Golden L. "The Contemporaneity of Joyce Cary: A Comparison with Joseph Conrad." In his *The Dark Descent: Social Change and Moral Responsibility in the Novels of Joyce Cary.* New York: Roy Publishers, 1966, pp. 1-21. Seeks perspective into Cary through comparing Conrad's treatment of Africa.

Laskowsky, Henry J. *"Heart of Darkness:* A Primer for the Holocaust." *Virginia Quarterly Review,* 58:1 (Winter 1982), 93-110. Traces influences on Coppola's *Apocalypse Now. Heart of Darkness* as prophetic "Holocaust" literature.

Lee, Robert F. *Conrad's Colonialism,* Hague: Mouton, 1969. Approves Britain's assumption of "white man's burden." Colonial power great for good and evil.

Lee, Sang-ok. "Experience into Fiction: An Aspect of Joseph Conrad's Idea of the Novel." *English Language and Literature,* No. 49 (Spring 1974), 63-84. Paradigmatic case of writing from experience. Not fact, but process of transforming into fiction is crucial concern.

Lester, John. "Conrad and Islam." *Conradiana,* 13:3 (1981), 163-79. Conrad's presentation of Islam may be surrogate criticism of superstition, hypocrisy, and bigotry in institutionalized belief of Victorians.

_____. "Conrad's Narrators in *The Nigger of the 'Narcissus.'* " *Conradiana,* 12:3 (1980), 163-72. Exploits advantages of each point of view to reveal maximum insights.

_____. "A Fictional Chronology of Conrad's Eastern World." *Conradiana,* 15:1 (1983), 65-71. Sequence of events in combined Eastern fiction.

Levin, Harry. "Literature and Exile." *The Listener,* 62 (15 Oct. 1959), 613-17. Overview of notable exiled writers from Ovid to Nabokov. Problems inherent in expatriation, yet experience can reinforce other gifts, encourage non-conformity.

Levinson, Andre. "Joseph Conrad est-il un escrivain français?" *Nouvelles Littéraires,* 4 Aug. 1928, p.8.*

Lewis, John S. "Conrad's Principal Sources for 'The Lagoon.'" *UNISA English Studies: Journal of the Department of English* (Pretoria), 9:2 (1971), 21-26. Sources: McNair's *Perak and the Malays,* Keppel's *The Expedition of HMS 'Dido' for the Suppression of Piracy.*

Little, Roger. "Saint-John Perse and Joseph Conrad: Some Notes and an Uncollected Letter." *Modern Language Review,* 72 (Oct. 1977), 811-14. No literary influences exchanged, but Conrad had strong personal impact on M. Leger.
_____. "Saint-John Perse, Poet Anglais." *Revue de Litterature Comparèe,* 46 (1972), 505-13.*

Lombard, Francois. "Conrad and Buddhism." *Cahiers Victoriens et Edouardiens* (Montpellier), 2 (1975), 103-12. Schopenhauer's Buddhistic ideas evident in several works.

Lovett, Robert Morss. "The Real of Conrad." *Asia,* 23 (May 1923), 325-27, 337-78. Hardyesque novelist of environment. Human contacts are occasional, the result of circumstances.

McClure, John A. *Kipling and Conrad: The Colonial Fiction.* Cambridge: Harvard U. P., 1981. Contrasting experiences account for Conrad and Kipling's different views. Conrad explores damaging drives of imperialists.

McCullough, Norman Verrle. *The Negro in English Literature: A Critical Introduction.* Ilfracombe, Devon: A. H. Stockwell, 1962, pp. 136-41. Discusses underlying human connections in *Heart of Darkness* and *The Nigger of the "Narcissus".* 41.

Mackaness, George. "Joseph Conrad and Australia." In his *Bibliomania: An Australian Book Collector's Essays.* Sydney: Angus and Robertson [1965], pp. 159-63. Cites scenes and impressions of Australia in Conrad's stories.

McLauchlan, Juliet. "Almayer and Willems—'How Not to Be.'" *Conradiana,* 11 (1979), 113-41. Life-death antithesis in dreams of Almayer and Nina. Willems in prison of self-absorption.[1]
_____. "The Politics of *Nostromo.*" *Essays in Criticism,* 18:4 (Oct. 1968), 475-77. Sharpens definition of "politics" and "symbolic" place names in *Nostromo.*

McMillan, Dougald. *"Nostromo:* The Theology of Revolution." In *The Classic British Novel.* Ed. H. M. Harper and C. E. Edge. Athens: University of Georgia Press, 1972, pp. 166-82. Underlying the intricacy and complexity is pattern of guilt and redemption from secularized Christian myth and theology.

Mahood, Molly Maureen. "Idols of the Tribe: Conrad's 'Heart of Darkenss.'" In her *The Colonial Encounter: A Reading of Six Novels.* London: Collings, 1977, pp. 4-36, 192-96. Two types of colonialism: Polish—Russian conquest and exploitation masked as philanthropy. English—workman-like faith in future beneficence.

Maini, Darsan Singh. "Conrad's Moral Drama." *Literary Criterion (Mysore),* [5] (Winter 1967), 79-84. Conrad daring, provocative, not Victorian. Starkness of undeveloped countries adds bold relief to events that would appear shabby in sophisticated society.

Marle, A. van. "The Location of Lord Jim's Patusan." *Notes and Queries,* N.S. 15:8 (Aug. 1968), 289-91. Patusan could have been Tenom in Sumatra, as Clemens suggests earlier, q.v.

Marle, Hans van. "Jumble of Facts and Fiction: The First Singapore Reaction to *Almayer's Folly.*" *Conradiana,* 10:2 (1978), 161-66. Reproduces text of previously unnoted review from Singapore *Straits Times* and text of letter to *Straits Times* concerning *Almayer's Folly* (both dated 1896).[1]

Marsh, D. R. C. "Moral Judgments in *The Secret Agent." English Studies in Africa,* 3:1 (Mar. 1960), 57-70. Characters contaminated by self-interest, lack of loyalty, no long-range values. Despite complexity and anarchy, life remains valuable.

Martin, W. R. "Charting Conrad's Costaguana." *Conradiana,* 8:2 (1976), 163-68. Details, maps, discussion of problems.

_____. "Compassionate Realism in Conrad and *Under Western Eyes." English Studies in Africa,* 17 (1974), 89-100. Settings allow detachment of laboratory observation. Conrad critical, but compassionate.

Messenger, William E. "Conrad and His 'Sea Stuff.' " *Conradiana,* 6:1 (1974), 3-18. Conrad's ambivalence toward his reputation as writer of sea adventure.

_____. "Conrad and Melville Again." *Conradiana,* 2:2 (1969-70), 53-64. Influences of Melville in spite of Conrad's antipathy toward him.

Meyers, Jeffrey. "Conrad and Roger Casement." *Conradiana,* 5:3 (1973), 64-69. The several contacts between Conrad and Casement. Conrad's growing dislike of Casement.

_____. *Fiction and the Colonial Experience.* [Totowa, New Jersey]: Rowman and Littlefield, [1973]. Conrad compared with Kipling, Forster. *Nostromo* and *Heart of Darkness* suggest incompatibility of materialism and moral principles.

_____. "Savagery and Civilization in *The Tempest, Robinson Crusoe,* and *The Heart of Darkness." Conradiana,* 2 (1970), 171-79. *Heart of Darkness* first major fiction to deny benevolence of nature and civilization.

Mnthali, Felix. "Continuity and Change in Conrad and Ngugi." *Kunapipi,* 3:1 (1981), 91-109, Skepticism of revolutionary change leads to caricature in *Under Western Eyes.* Accepts racist shibboleths in *Heart of Darkness. Nostromo* politically amoral.

Moorthy, P. Rama. "Nigger of the 'Narcissus'." *Literary Criterion* (Mysore), [3] (Winter 1965), 49-58. Wait contradictory. Adamic element in crewmen's complicity in his seeking to deny his condition.

Morley, Patricia A. "Conrad's Vision of the Absurd." *Conradiana,* 2:1 (Fall 1969-70), 59-68. Pessimism underlying *The Secret Agent* traced to type of anguish typified by the Theatre of the Absurd.

Morrissey, L. J. "The Tellers in *Heart of Darkness:* Conrad's Chinese Boxes." *Conradiana,* 13:2 (1981), 141-48. Enclosing narrative structures.

Mphahlele, Ezekiel. "The White Man's Image of the Non-White in Fiction." In *The African Image.* London: Faber & Faber, 1962, pp. 101-65. Does not recognize boundaries in human characters. Nina, Aissa untethered by didactic purpose, no need for self-justification.

"Mr. Conrad's New Book." Rev. of *Youth: A Narrative and Two Other Tales. Manchester Guardian,* 10 Dec. 1902, p. 3. *Heart of Darkness* attacks colonial expansion. Reassurance in conclusion of "how far we have travelled."

Mroczkowski, Przemyslaw. "Joseph Conrad's International World of Men." *Kwartalnik Neofilologiczny,* 21 (1974), 171-91. Characters represent range of geographic locations, languages, races.

Mudrick, Marvin. "Conrad." In his *On Culture and Literature.* New York: Horizon

Press, 1970, pp. 93-107. Survey of critical perceptions of Conrad's varied career.

Mukerji, N. "The Problem of Point of View in *Under Western Eyes.*" *The Bulletin of the Department of English* (Calcutta University), N.S. 8:2 (1972-73), 73-80. Double focus of Russian and Western views, uses irony.

_____. "The Secret Agent: Anarchy and Anarchists." *Calcutta Review,* 172 (Aug. 1964), 139-48. Study of irony, and comic characterization in pseudo-revolutionaries. Self-professed prophets of people, their madness, criminal futility.

Na, Yong-Gyun. *Aesthetic Distance in Joseph Conrad.* Seoul: Ewha Women's U. P., 1975.*

_____. "The Sense of Absurdity in *The Secret Agent.*" In *Festschrift Presented to Professors B. Y. Hong and K. S. Kim on Their Sixtieth Birthdays.* Seoul: Ewha Women's U.P., 1974, pp. 122-43.

Naipaul, V. S. "Conrad's Darkness." *New York Review of Books,* 19 (19 Oct. 1974), 16-21. Rpt. in his *The Return of Eva Peron with the Killings in Trinidad.* New York: Knopf, 1980, pp. 205-28. Conrad preceded Naipaul in depicting world's "half-made" societies.[1]

_____. "A Note on a Borrowing by Conrad." *New York Review of Books,* 29:20 (16 Dec. 1982), 37-38. Passage in "The Return" similar to one in *Madame Bovary.* Conrad knew English middle class through his reading.

Nazareth, Peter. "Out of Darkness: Conrad and Other Third World Writers." *Conradiana,* 14:3 (1982), 173-87. Conrad a mental liberator for metropolitans and for colonized elite who wear the "eyes of Europe." Achebe and Naipaul blind to fuller meanings, q.v.[1]

_____. "The Significance of Nostromo and the Silver in the Moral Pattern of 'Nostromo.' " In his *Literature and Society in Modern Africa.* Nairobi: East Africa Literature Bureau, 1972, pp. 94-127. *Nostromo* not cynical or futile; has moral code. Sees through politics and economics to individuals.

Ngugi wa Thiong'o, (James). "Writers in Politics." *Busara,* 8:1 (1976), 5. Rpt. in his *Writers in Politics.* London: Heinemann, 1981, pp. 71-81. Conrad and African writer share same world of imperialism.

Obumselu, Ebele. "A Grain of Wheat: Ngugi's Debt to Conrad." *The Benin Review,* 1 (June 1974), 80-91. Ngugi parallels *Under Western Eyes;* uncertain in style and tone, but gives illusion of reality.

Ordonez, Elmer A. *The Early Joseph Conrad: Revisions and Style.* Quezon City: University of the Philippines Press, 1969. Evolution of narrative voices. Speakers achieve individualized idiolects.

_____. "The Literary Impressionist as Critic: Conrad and Ford." *Diliman Review,* 12:1 (Jan. 1964), 101-15. Impressionism of Crane, Conrad and Ford, in theory and practice.

_____. *"The Nigger of the 'Narcissus':* From Manuscript to Print." *Philippine Social Sciences and Humanities Review,* 30:1 (Mar. 1965), 34-39. Comparative study of revisions in several versions, to perfect a style regarded by Henry James as "unique and peculiarly worthy of recognition."

_____. Notes on the 'Falk' Manuscript." In *Twenty-seven to One.* Ed. Bradford B. Broughton. Ogdensburg, N.Y.: Ryan Press, 1970, pp. 45-51.

_____. "Notes on the Revisions in *An Outcast of the Islands.*" *Notes and Queries,* N.S. 15:8 (Aug. 1968), 287-89. On textual changes leading to final copy.

Orisabiyi, N. O. *"Heart of Darkness* as an Anatomy of Moral Failure." *Lares,* 1:1 (Jan. 1979), 94-103. Even ideal man reverts to devil when free of moral restraint.

"Our Awards for 1898—The 'Crowned' Books: Mr. Joseph Conrad and 'Tales of Unrest.' " *Academy.* 14 Jan. 1899, pp. 65-67. Transfers very heart of the East; is "one of the notable literary colonists."

Parrill, Anna Sue. "Joseph Conrad's Revolutionists." *Phi Kappa Phi Journal,* 57:3 (Summer 1977), 16-22. Novelist can give greater sense of reality than history books and newspapers. Analysis of motives and types of revolutionaries in *The Secret Agent* and *Under Western Eyes;* the opportunists, dreamers, fanatics.

Parry, Benita. *Conrad and Imperialism: Ideological Boundaries and Visionary Frontiers.* London: The Macmillan Press, Ltd., 1983.

Payn, James. Rev. of *Outcast of the Islands. Illustrated London News,* 4 Apr. 1896, p. 418. In spite of general preference for stories laid on British soil, this novel depicts other places and people well.

Perse, St.-John. [Letter concerning friendship with Conrad]. *Conradiana,* 2:3 (1970), 17.

Pinsker, Sanford. "The Conradian Hero and the Death of Language: A Note on *Nostromo." Conradiana,* 1:1 (Summer 1968), 49-50. Language unable to comprehend external experience. Layers of rhetoric in *Nostromo,* political, religious, historical, ironic.

_____. "Conrad's Curious 'Natives': Fatalistic Machiavellians/Cannibals with Restraint." *Conradiana,* 14:3 (1982), 199-204. Victorian protagonists among natives as dramatic foils. Conrad not racist or imperialist. Before Beckett and Ionesco, Conrad explored silence and failure of language.

_____. *The Languages of Joseph Conrad.* Amsterdam: Rodopi, 1978. Focuses on areas where Conrad's "doubts about the efficacy of verbal construct were most pronounced." Categories of language are of East, narration, sea, politics.

Pital, Sergio. "Conrad en Costaguano." *Cuadernos Hispanoamericanos,* No. 256 (Apr. 1971), 58-73. Polish political background. Holroyd equivalent of Belgians in Congo.

Pooviah, Nimmi. "Nostromo: The Silver Mine and the Widening Circles of Evil." *Commonwealth Quarterly,* 2:8 (1978), 82-93. Negative influence of treasure on each character.

Pritchett, V. S. "The Exile." *New Statesman,* 24 Aug. 1957, p. 229. Conrad learned exile as a child; its moral freedom and terror, anticipate the general modern experience.

_____. "The Moralist of Exile." *New Statesman,* 30 Jan. 1960, pp. 157-58. Rev. Baines' *Conrad a Critical Biography,* q.v.

_____. "A Pole in the Far East." In *The Living Novel,* New York: Reynal and Hitchcock [1947], pp. 143-48. London: Chatto and Windus, 1946, pp. 139-144.

Pulc, I. P. "Andrzej Braun's Visit to Atjeh." *Conradiana,* 5:2 (1973), 86-94. Report on Braun's travels in pursuit of Conrad's references to real places in East.

_____."Karain's Domain and the Rajah Potalolo." *Conradiana,* 6:1 (1974), 63-67. Rev. Andrzej Braun's "Byl panem skrawka ziemi" [He was. . .master of a... foothold on the earth]. *Miesiecznik Literacki* (June 1970), pp. 3-12. Braun's search for Conradiana in Dongala, several pages quoted in translation.

Rajiva, Stanley F. "The Singular Person: An Essay on Conrad's Use of Marlow as Narrator." *The Literary Criterion* (Mysore), [6] (Summer 1968), 35-45. Three

Marlows: detached in *Chance,* filtering in *Lord Jim,* introspective spirit in *Heart of Darkness.*

Raskin, Jonah. "Imperialism: Conrad's *Heart of Darkness.*" *The Journal of Contemporary History,* 2:2 (Apr. 1967), 113-31. Rapacity behind pious ideals of civilization. Not natives, but colonialism makes barbarians of civilized men.

————. *The Mythology of Imperialism: Rudyard Kipling, Joseph Conrad, E. M. Forster, D. H. Lawrence, and Joyce Cary.* New York: Random House, 1971. Two Conrads: One, Polish colonial, hating imperialism; and two, the patronizing Englishman. Conrad warped because he hates revolutionaries as much as autocrats.

Raval, R. K. "Lord Jim: An Existential Analysis." *Journal of the Maharaja Sayaji Rao University of Baroda,* 17:1 (Apr. 1968), 57-70. Jim's jumping from *Patna* is self-betrayal. Sisyphean process of living out personal sense of honor.

Raval, Suresh. "Conrad's *Victory:* Skepticism and Experience." *Nineteenth-Century Fiction,* 34:4 (1980), 414-33. Inner and outer sources of evil implicated in each other. Heyst's skepticism prevents normal emotions and action against intruders.

————. "Narrative and Authority in *Lord Jim:* Conrad's Art of Failure." *English Literary History,* 42:2 (Summer 1981), 387-410. Ambiguous view: emphasizes Jim's inscrutable nature and also says he's "one of us." Jim's ideal becomes surrogate for living—his trap.

Ray, M. S. "The Gift of Tongues: The Languages of Joseph Conrad." *Conradiana,* 15:2 (1983), 83-109. Conrad's defense of using English. Artistic consequence of choice is detachment from his medium and suspicion about nature of his language.

Reid, Stephen A. "The 'Unspeakable Rites' in *Heart of Darkness.*" In *Conrad: A Collection of Critical Essays.* Ed. Marvin Mudrick. Englewood Cliffs: Prentice-Hall, 1966, pp. 45-54. Kurtz's unnamed rites concern human sacrifice and cannibalism in keeping with G. James Frazer's analysis of primitive societies.

Reitz, Bernhard. "The Meaning of the Buddha-Comparisons in Joseph Conrad's *Heart of Darkness.*" *Fu Jen Studies: Literature and Linguistics,* 13 (1980), 41-53.*

Renner, Stanley. "The Garden of Civilization: Conrad, Huxley, and the Ethics of Civilization." *Conradiana,* 7:2 (1975), 109-20. Evolution as a force in Conrad's fiction. Civilization cultivates its garden, from primitive state to refined order. Dangers of ego in the gardener.

Resink, Gertrudes Johan. "Axel Heyst and the Second King of the Cocos Islands." *English Studies,* 44:6 (Dec. 1963), 443-47. The possible original for character of Heyst.

————. "De archipel voor Joseph Conrad." *Bijdragen tot de Tall-, Land- en Volkenkunde,* 115:1 (1959), 192-208.

————. "The Eastern Archipelago Under Joseph Conrad's Eyes." In his *Indonesia's History Between the Myths: Essays in Legal History and Historical Theory.* The Hague: W. van Hoeve, 1968, pp. 307-23. Economy and politics in Conrad's fiction compared with official Dutch documents.

————. "Het Juweel Van Landak, Kaatje Stoltes Dochter, en Emma van Heine." *De Gids,* 124:10 (Oct. 1961), 183-87. Discussion of *Lord Jim.*

————. "Jozef Korzeniowski voornaamste lectuur betreffende Indonesie." *Bijdragen tot de Tall-, Land- en Volkenkunde,* 117:2 (1961), 209-37. Examines sources underlying Conrad's Indonesian fiction.

_____. "Samburan Encantada." *English Studies,* 47:1 (Feb. 1966), 35-44. Tracing possible influences on Conrad of Melville's works.

Rev. of *Almayer's Folly. Bookman,* Sept. 1895, p. 176. Mysterious East casts spell on Conrad, seems to be "muttering" his tale.

Rev. of *Almayer's Folly. Daily News,* 29 Apr. 1895, p. 6. Author acquainted with Borneo; European among Arabs and Malays.

Rev. of *Almayer's Folly. Guardian,* 3 July 1895, p. 1001. Charming romance of strange Malay world.

Rev. of *Almayer's Folly. Literary News,* Sept. 1895, pp. 268-69. Strikes new vein in fiction, truths underlying land and people almost unknown to West.

Rev. of *Almayer's Folly. Nation* (USA), 17 Oct. 1895, p. 278. Borneo suitable to study monkeys, not man.

Rev. of *Almayer's Folly. Scotsman,* 29 Apr. 1895, p. 3. Depicts Malay life if not intimately, at least with imagination.

Rev. of *Almayer's Folly. Speaker,* 29 Jun. 1895, pp. 722-23. Character declines from life in semi-barbaric setting.

Rev. of *Lord Jim. Spectator,* 24 Nov. 1900, p. 753. More than others, Conrad identifies with standpoint of natives—their aspirations, motives, glamour of landscape. The narrator never loses touch with the *"ethos* of his race."

Rev. of *An Outcast of the Islands. Nation* (USA), 15 Apr. 1897, p. 287. Novel of poor judgment, peopled by "society, black and white, of a sort which no reputable person would meet at home."

Rice, Thomas Jackson. "Conrad's 'The Lagoon'": Malay and Pharisee." *Christianity and Literature,* 25:4 (1978), 25-33. Key to ambiguity, dual structure and controversial style of "The Lagoon" is traditional Christian symbolism.

Rivera, Ruben O. "The 'Silver of the Mine': Conrad's *Nostromo." Diliman Review,* 13:2 (Apr. 1965), 199-214. Silver unifies disrupted structure of two stories in novel.

Robertson, P. J. M. *"Things Fall Apart* and *Heart of Darkness:* A Creative Dialogue." *International Fiction Review,* 7:2 (Summer 1980), 106-11. Achebe's intemperate attack on Conrad undermines his credibility. *Heart of Darkness* promotes black-white dialogue Achebe seeks. Conradian irony closes *Things Fall Apart.*

Roderick, Colin. "Joseph Conrad's Affiliations with Australia." *L'Epoque Conradienne* (France), 3 (1977), 1-14.

Rogers, Philip. "No Longer at Ease: Chinua Achebe's 'Heart of Whiteness," *Research in African Literatures,* 14 (1983), 165-83. Suggests *No Longer at Ease* close to parody of *Heart of Darkness.*

"A Romance of the Far East." *Daily Chronicle,* 16 Mar. 1896, p. 3. *An Outcast of the Islands* favorably compared with Melville and Stevenson for scenic tropics. Civilized men deteriorate.

Rosenfield, Claire. *Paradise of Snakes: An Archetypal Analysis of Conrad's Political Novels. Chicago: Chicago U. P., 1976.* Archetypal approach to *Nostromo, Secret Agent, Under Western Eyes,* and other works.

Rossman, Charles. "A Note on Puns and the Spanish in *Nostromo." Modern British Literature,* 1:1 (Fall 1976), 88-90. Puns on proper and place names.

Rothfork, John. "The Buddha Center in Conrad's 'Youth.' " *Literature East and West* 21:1-4 (Jan.-Dec. 1977), 121-29. Sources in Buddhism for archetypal, cyclical life patterns. Theravada rather than Bodisattva Buddhism prevalent in southeast Asia.

Roy, Virendra Kumar. *The Romance of Illusions: A Study of Joseph Conrad with Special Reference to "Lord Jim" and "Heart of Darkness."* Delhi: Doaba House, 1971. Covers life and career as writer. Interpretations of *Lord Jim* and *Heart of Darkness* bring in most leading analyses by recognized critics.

Ryan, Patrick J. "Images of the White Liberal." *America,* 119:11 (12 Oct. 1968), 316-17, 320-321. White liberals despair that they might be rejected by Black Power leaders. Conrad's inconsistent anti-colonialism.

Said, Edward W. "Conrad: The Presentation of Narrative." *Novel: A Forum on Fiction,* 7:2 (Winter 1974), 116-32. Conrad in practice and theory advanced beyond what he said. Written words render dynamism of objects seen. Many faceted narrative reveals views, but never the author's persona.[1]

_____. *Joseph Conrad and the Fiction of Autobiography.* Cambridge: Harvard U. P., 1966. Interplay of real experience and creativity in Conrad's practice as a writer.

Sandison, Alan. "Joseph Conrad: Window onto Chaos." In his *The Wheel of Empire.* London: Macmillan, 1967, pp. 120-48. Imperial idea is correlative for exploring antithesis between fragile consciousness and hostile principle which threatens it. Man's personal estrangement underscores imperial urge.

Sarang, Vilas. "A Source for *The Hollow Men.*" *Notes and Queries,* 15:2 (Feb. 1968), 57-58. Line "Life is very long" could derive from *An Outcast of the Islands.*

Sarvan, Charles Ponnuthurai. "Racism and the *Heart of Darkness.*" *The International Fiction Review,* 7:1 (Winter 1980), 6-10. Conrad and African writer share world of capitalism, imperialism, colonialism. Conrad assails darkness in man, not Africa.

_____. "Under African Eyes." *Conradiana,* 8:3 (1976), 233-40. Rpt. as "Conrad's Influence on Ngugi." *Kucha,* 1:1 (Nov. 1977), 39-44. Informative contrast between *Under Western Eyes* and Ngugi's *A Grain of Wheat.* Ngugi's focus diffused, lacks Conrad's grasp of language.[1]

Saveson, John E. "Conrad's View of Primitive Peoples: *Lord Jim* and *Heart of Darkness.*" *Modern Fiction Studies,* 16:2 (Summer 1970), 163-83. Rpt. in his *Joseph Conrad: The Making of a Moralist.* Amsterdam: Rodopi, 1972, pp. 37-63. Relevance of several anthropological theories, traces of influence.

_____. "Sources of *Nostromo.*" *Notes and Queries,* 19:9 (Sept. 1972), 331-34. Suggests two less well known historical texts as background for novel.

Sherry, Norman. "Conrad and the Bangkok *Times.*" *Nineteenth-Century Fiction,* 20:3 (Dec. 1965), 255-66. Rpt. in his *Conrad's Eastern World,* q.v. Conrad's accuracy using certain actual events in fiction.

_____. "Conrad's Eastern Port: The Setting of the Inquiry in *Lord Jim.*" *Review of English Literature,* 6 (Oct. 1965), 52-61. Rpt. in his *Conrad's Eastern World,* q.v.

_____. Ed. *Conrad: The Critical Heritage.* London: Routledge and Keegan Paul, 1973. Examples of criticism from 1895-1933, trends summarized.

_____. *Conrad's Eastern World.* London: Cambridge U.P., 1966. Verifies attention to factual detail—names of ships, places, people, gossip of sea ports, weights, distances, atmosphere. Accuracy in Aristotelian sense of probable or necessary consequences.

_____. *Conrad's Western World.* Cambridge: Cambridge U.P., 1971. Close scrutiny of materials relating to incidents and characters in novels and stories with Western settings: primarily *Heart of Darkness, Nostromo* and *Secret Agent.* Conrad's creativity required imaginative use, not invention of "original" themes, plots and characters.

_____. " 'Rajah Laut'—A Quest for Conrad's Source." *Modern Philology,* 62 (Aug. 1964), 22-41. Argues William Lingard is original of adventurer figure in several of the Malayan novels.

Shukla, Narain Prasad. "The Light Imagery in *Lord Jim.*" *Osmania Journal of English Studies,* 15 (1979), 43-48. Flame imagery as thematic and structural device.

_____. "The Theme of Escape in Conrad's *Victory.*" *Journal of the Department of English* (Calcutta University), 17:1 (1981-82), 99-106.

Singh, Frances B. "The Colonialistic Bias of *Heart of Darkness.*" *Conradiana,* 10:1 (1978), 41-54. Shows Africans as victims of European sin, but equates primitive with evil and black with spiritual darkness. Too ambivalent to be truly anti-colonial.

Singh, Ramchander. *"Nostromo:* The Betrayed Self." *The Literary Criterion* (Mysore), 10:3 (Summer 1973), 61-66. Impact of social organization on the self. Nostromo betrays values for silver.

Spencer, G. W. "The Form of Part III of *Nostromo.*" *Conradiana,* 3:1 (1970-71), 81-86. Defends length of *Nostromo* for thematic relevance and sustained drama.

Srivastava, Avadhesh K. *Alien Voice: Perspectives on Commonwealth Literature.* Lucknow: Print House, 1981. Scattered comparisons and references to Conrad.

Stape, J. H. "Conrad's 'Certain Steamship': The Background of 'Tradition.' " *Conradiana,* 16:3 (1984), 236-39. Conrad's sources for essay on torpedoed ship.

_____. "Two Unpublished Letters and a Reply." *Conradiana,* 14:3 (1982), 230-32. Conrad letters to Hallam Murray on behalf of John Gallsworthy.

Stein, William Bysshe. "Conrad's East: Time, History, Action, and *Maya.*" *Texas Studies in Literature and Language,* 7:3 (Autumn 1965), 265-83. Eastern influence on Conrad's psychological environments. Individual encounters with nothingness and absurdity, seen in light of Indian scripture, especially *Karma-yoga.*

_____. "The Eastern Matrix of Conrad's Art." *Conradiana,* 1:2 (Fall 1968), 1-14. Exposure to an alien culture.

_____. *"The Heart of Darkness:* A Bodhisattva Scenario." *Conradiana,* 2:2 (1969-70), 39-52. Interprets in terms of Marlow's *karmic* motives in relating his journey up the Congo.

_____. "The Lotus Posture and 'The Heart of Darkness.' " *Modern Fiction Studies,* 2:4 (Winter 1956-57), 235-37. Offers understanding of the lotus posture as key to Marlow's descent into underworld.

Stewart, Garrett. "Coppola's Conrad: The Repetitions of Complicity." *Critical Inquiry,* 7:3 (Spring 1981), 455-74.

_____. "Lying as Dying in *Heart of Darkness.*" *Publications of the Modern Language Association,* 95:3 (May 1980), 319-31. Marlow's lie to protect the "Intended" destroys the integrity of Kurtz's dying pronouncement.

Stone, Wilfred. "Rev. of *Conrad's Colonialism,*" by Robert F. Lee. *Journal of Modern Literature,* 1 (1971), 753-54. Conrad used to display Lee's racial, political prejudices, q.v.

Stoneback, H. R. " 'The Only Real Poet of the Sea'?—Joseph Conrad and Saint-John Perse." *Joseph Conrad Today,* 9:2 (Summer 1984), 246-47. Evidence Saint-John Perse influenced by Conrad.

Street, Brian. "Joseph Conrad and the Imaginative Literature of Imperialism." In *Literature and Imperialism.* Ed. Bart Moore-Gilbert. A conference organized by the English Department of the Roehampton Institute in February 1983. London: Roehampton Institute of Higher Education, 1983. Anthropological ideology of period appears unevenly in Conrad. At times uses it for ironic commentary; other times defers to "authorities" whose testimony is more questionable than his own.

Subramani. "The Mythical Quest: Literary Responses to the South Seas." *Literary Half-Yearly,* 18:1 (1977), 165-86. Melville, Maugham, Conrad and others find South Seas material unsustaining, resort to Western conflicts and contradictions.

Subramanyam, N. S. "Henry James (1843-1916) and Joseph Conrad (1857-1924): The Point of Veiw on Reality and the Projection of Situations." In his *Movements in Modern English Novel.* Gwalior: Kitab Ghar, 1967, pp. 79-95. Expands novel horizontally to foreign lands and vertically through narrative techniques to explore mental and moral values.

Sullivan, Zohreh T. "Civilization and its Darkness: Conrad's *Heart of Darkness* and Ford's *The Good Soldier." Conradiana,* 8:2 (1976), 110-20. Comparison study centers on the *fin-de-siècle* fascination with doom in corrupt, overly civilized Europe.

_____. "Enclosure, Darkness, and the Body: Conrad's Landscape." *The Centenial Review,* 25:1 (Winter 1981), 59-79. Sea, river and jungle project nightmarish fear of black, bestial womb of devouring mother.

Teets, Bruce E. Rev. of *Fiction and the Colonial Experience,* by Jeffrey Meyers. *Conradiana,* 6 (1974), 221-24, q.v.

Thumbo, Edwin. "Some Plain Reading: Marlow's Lie in *Heart of Darkness." The Literary Criterion* (Mysore), 16:3 (1981), 12-22. Marlow preserves discrimination, learns cost of protecting another human being.

Tomlinson, T. B. "Conrad's Trust in Life: *Nostromo." The Critical Review* (Melbourne), 14 (1971), 62-81. Counters argument that despair and skepticism of characters overwhelm Conrad and his novel.

Trigona, Prospero. "Il Dramma del Colonialismo nei Primi Romanzi di Joseph Conrad." *Trimestre,* 6 (1972), 127-48. Role of colonialism in series of novels.

Truter, H. W. "Uit 'Donker' Africa." *Tydskrif Vir Geesteswtenskappe,* 11 (1971), 186-203. Treatment of Ibo life during colonial period in Conrad, Achebe and a Dutch novel.

Tucker, Martin. *Africa in Modern Literature.* New York: Frederick Ungar Pub. Co., 1967. Discusses the trends in writing about Africa set by Rider Haggard, Conrad. Surveys status of twentieth-century African literature.

Ureña, Max Henriquez. "La América de Joseph Conrad." *Noverim* (Havana), 2:9 (Nov. 1958), 7-21. Imagination and glimpses of real place combine. South Americans play secondary roles.

Verschoor, Edith E. "Joseph Conrad's World." *UNISA English Studies: Journal of the Department of English* (Pretoria), 8:2 (1970), 12-18.*

Vidon, Ivo. "St.-John Perse's Visit to Conrad: A Letter by Alexis Saint-Leger to G. Jean-Aubry." *Conradiana,* 2:3 (1970), 17-22. Perse appreciative of Jean-Aubry's *Vie de Conrad,* recalls visiting Conrad. Letter from 1947 rpt.

Viola, André. "La Symbolique du Mandala dans *Victory* de Joseph Conrad." *Cahiers*

Victoriens et Edouardiens (Montpellier), 16 (Oct. 1982), 105-24. Interprets circular motifs, references to Jung and Oriental symbolism.

Volkening, Ernesto. "Evocación de una Sombra." *Eco; Revista de la Cultura de Occidente* (Bogotá), 6:4 (Feb. 1963), 358-75. Comments on *Heart of Darkness*, theme, Kurtz.

Wagner, Geoffrey. "John Bull's Other Empire." *Modern Age*, 8 (Summer 1964), 284-90. Examines situation of colonizer in several works. Assails fantasized versions of imperialism easily accepted by casual observers.

_____. "The Novel of Empire." *Essays in Criticism,* 20:2 (Apr. 1970), 229-42. Image of imperialism in fiction of Forster, Conrad, Kipling, Haggard, Orwell.

Watt, Ian. "Conrad Criticism and *The Nigger of the 'Narcissus.'* " *Nineteenth-Century Fiction,* 12[1957], 257-83. Controversial interpretations of point of view expose critical value systems. Reexamines critical motivation.

Watts, Cedric [T.]. *Conrad's 'Heart of Darkness': A Critical and Contextual Discussion.* Milan: Mursia International, 1977. Subtle devices assure reader only to undermine complacency, question nature and ultimate results of imperialism.

_____. "A Minor Source for *Nostromo.*" *Review of English Studies,* 16 (May 1965), 182-84. Suggests Ramón Paez's *Wild Scenes in South America; or Life in the Llanos of Venezuela* (London 1863) as source for *Nostromo's* political and descriptive detail.

Waugh, Arthur. "London Letter." *Critic,* 11 May 1895, p. 349. Fears success of *Almayer's Folly* might release "torrent of Bornean fiction."

"White Man and Brown." *Daily Chronicle,* 11 May 1895, p. 3. *Almayer's Folly* shows effect of East on neurotic Westerner. Atmosphere realistic, not merely a backdrop.

Wilhelm, Cherry. "Joseph Conrad: Four Tales." *Crux: A Journal on the Teaching of English,* 10:2 (1976), 23-30. Antitheses in Conrad's character account for his uniqueness, not merely use of "foreign" tongue. Romantic using realism, pessimist with faith in code of service.

Willy, Todd G. "The Call to Imperialism in Conrad's 'Youth': An Historical Reconstruction." *Journal of Modern Literature,* 8 (1980), 39-50. British sentiment would have viewed "Youth" as "endorsement of bellicose Conservative imperialism." Stressing dangers and questioning results of imperialism, ploys to make it more attractive.

_____. "Measures of the Heart and of the Darkness: Conrad and the Suicides of 'New Imperialism.' " *Conradiana,* 14:3 (1982), 189-98. Durkheim would view suicides in Conrad fiction as pathology of degenerating society. Victorians found self-sacrifice noble, exciting.

Wohlfarth, Paul. "War Joseph Conrad ein Englishcher Dichter?" *Germano-Slavica,* 4 (1936), 143-51. Considering the Polish motifs, the anti-Russian elements, and other "Slavic" traits, Conrad is foreign enricher of his adopted English language.

Wright, Edward. "The Romance of the Outlands." *Quarterly Review,* 203 (July 1905), 55-61. Oddities of Conrad's life and letters. Concerned with character, not exciting action. Romantic trait preserves him from melancholy.

Yaseen, Mohammad. *Joseph Conrad's Theory of Fiction.* 2nd Ed. Bombay: Asia Publishing House, 1970. In "Slavo-Franco-English" tradition, blends uniquely. Traces four phases of development.

Young, Gloria L. "Quest and Discovery: Joseph Conrad's and Carl Jung's African

Journeys." *Modern Fiction Studies,* 28:4 (Winter 1982-83), 583-89. References to Jung's and Conrad's experiences in, and treatment of, Africa in their works. Similarities in play on the subconscious, types of symbols, primitives.

Young, W. J. "Conrad Against Himself." *Critical Review* (Melbourne), No. 11 (1968), 32-47. Psychoanalytical analyses of Conrad's neuroses serve curiosity, but his abnormalities do not invalidate his vision.

Zabel, Morton Dauwen, Introd. *The Nigger of the "Narcissus."* New York: Harper, Harper's Modern Classics, 1951, pp. vii-xxxi. Practical experience of ships and the East provided material for fiction. Role of *Nigger of the "Narcissus"* in Conrad's developing style and themes.

Zelnick, Stephen. "Conrad's *Lord Jim:* Meditations on the Other Hemisphere." *Minnesota Review,* 11 (Fall 1978), 73-89. Evaluates five theoretic approaches to Conrad. Marxist critics encouraged to use their integrative power and learn from other schools of thought.

Zimmerman, Peter. "Joseph Conrad's Südostasienwerke: Probleme Realistischer Gesellschaftsanalyse im Zeitalter des Frühimperialismus." *Zeitschrift für Anglistik und Amerikanistik,* 24 (1976), 37-56.

Zins, Henryk. *Joseph Conrad and Africa.* Nairobi: Kenya Literature Bureau, 1982. (Available through Third World Publications, Birmingham, England.) The influence of Conrad's Polish experience on treatment of Africa. Answers post-colonial criticism that Conrad dehumanizes Africans.

Zuckerman, Jerome S. "The Motif of Cannibalism in *The Secret Agent." Texas Studies in Literature and Language,* 10:2 (Summer 1968), 295-99. References and uses of cannibalism in various works. In *Secret Agent,* represents manner in which men exploit others.

[1]This article is collected in the present volume.
*I have not been able to obtain a copy of this item.

Addenda to Bibliography

Publication of this book was unavoidably delayed after the text had been typeset in 1985. In the interim, the number of essays and articles regarding Conrad's relationship to various aspects of the Third World has grown rapidly. Although I could not incorporate these most recent studies within the annotated bibliography and distribution chart, the following partial listing indicates the degree to which Conrad has become integral to Third World scholarship. Of these fifty-five additional entries, only fourteen predate 1985.

Anderson, Walter E. " 'Heart of Darkness': The Sublime Spectacle." *University of Toronto Quarterly,* 57: 3 (Spring 1988), 404-21.

Armstrong, Paul B. "Conrad's Contradictory Politics: The Ontology of Society in *Nostromo.*" *Twentieth Century Literature*, 31: 1 (Spring 1985), 1-21.

Bardolph, Jacqueline. "Ngugi wa Thiong'o's *A Grain of Wheat* and *Petals of Blood* as Readings of Conrad's *Under Western Eyes* and *Victory.*" *Conradian*, 12: 1 (May 1987), 32-49.

Bignami, Marialuisa. "Joseph Conrad, the Malay Archipelago, and the Decadent Hero." *Review of English Studies*, N.S. 38: 150 (May 1987), 199-210.

Brantlinger, Patrick. *"Heart of Darkness*: Anti-Imperialism, Racism, or Impressionism?" Criticism, 27: 4 (Fall 1985), 363-85.

Brydon, Diana. " 'The Thematic Ancestor': Joseph Conrad, Patrick White and Margaret Atwood." *World Literature Written in English*, 24: 2 (Autumn 1984), 386-97.

Burkman, Katherine H., and Reid J. Meloy. "The Black Mirror: Joseph Conrad's *The Nigger of the 'Narcissus'* and Flannery O'Connor's 'The Artificial Nigger.' " *Midwest Quarterly,* 28: 2 (Winter 1987), 230-47.

Caracciolo, Peter. "Buddhist Teaching Stories and Their Influence on Conrad, Wells, and Kipling: The Reception of the Jataka and Allied Genres in Victorian Culture." *Conradian*, 11: 1 (May 1986), 24-34.

During, Simon. "Postmodernism or Post-Colonialism Today." *Textual Practice*, 1.1 (Spring 1987), 32-47.

Gibert, Teresa. " 'An Outpost of Progress': La Ironia Imperial de Joseph Conrad." *Epos: Revista de Filologia*, 4 (1988), 469-82.

Golanka, Mary. "Mr. Kurtz, I Presume? Livingstone and Stanley as Prototypes of Kurtz and Marlow." *Studies in the Novel*, 17: 2 (Summer 1985), 194-202.

263

Goonetilleke, D.C.R.A. "Conrad as a Modernist Writer: *The Secret Agent.*" *Sri Lanka Journal of the Humanities*, 5 (1979), 37-53.

Hampson, Robert G. "Conrad, Guthrie, and 'The Arabian Nights.' " *Conradiana,* 18: 2 (1986), 141-43.

Hawkins, Hunt. "Conrad and the Psychology of Colonialism." In *Conrad Revisited: Essays for the Eighties.* Ed. Ross C. Murfin. University: University of Alabama Press, 1985, 71-87.

Hawthorne, Jeremy. "The Incoherences of *The Nigger of the 'Narcissus.' "* *Conradian*, 11:2 (Nov. 1986), 98-115.

Higdon, David Leon. "An Australian Quarrel with Conrad." *Conradiana,* 17: 2 (1985), 149-51.

Hoagland, Edward. "Africa Brought Home: *Heart of Darkness* and Its Journey Downriver." *Harper's* 270 (May 1985), 71-72.

Huggan, Graham. "Anxieties of Influence: Conrad in the Caribbean." *Commonwealth,* 11: 1 (Autumn 1988), 1-12.

Jordan, Elaine. "Conrad's Latin American Adventure: 'An Obscure and Questionable Spoil. ' " In *America in English Literature*. Ed. Neil Taylor. London: RoehamptonInstitute, 1980, pp. 78-101.

Kenny, Alan Heywood. "Almayer and the Upas Tree." *Conradian*, 8 (1983), 12-13.

Kharbutli, Mahmoud K. "The Treatment of Women in *Heart of Darkness.*" *Dutch Quarterly Review of Anglo-American Letters*, 17: 4 (1987), 237-48.

Kolupke, Joseph. "Elephants, Empires, and Blind Men: A Reading of the Figurative Language in Conrad's 'Typhoon.' " *Conradiana*, 20: 1 (Spring 1988), 71-85.

Krenn, Heliéna, "Joseph Conrad's Polish Heritage of Hopefulness in 'Youth.' " *Fu Jen Studies: Literature and Linguistics.* (Taipei), 15 (1982), 37-53.

_____. "The Shadow of a Successful Man: Conrad's Hollow Man in *An Outcast of the Islands. Fu Jen Studies: Literature and Linguistics* (Taipei), 16 (1983), 33-48.

Lessay, Franck. "Joseph Conrad et les Chemins de l'Empire." In *Migrations*. Paris: Centre d'Hist. des Idées dans les Iles Britanniques, Univ. Paris, 1986, pp. 122-39.

Lester, John S. "Conrad and the *Timaru Herald.*" *Conradiana*, 19: 3 (1987), 214.

Lindenbaum, Peter. "Hulks with One and Two Anchors: The Frame, Geographical Detail and Ritual Process in *Heart of Darkness.*" *Modern Fiction Studies*, 30: 4 (Winter 1984), 703-10.

Lippe, Hans. "*Lord Jim:* Some Geographic Observations." *Conradiana*, 10: 2 (Nov. 1985), 135-38.

Lord, George de Forest. "Imperial Horror: Conrad's *Heart of Darkness.*" *Trials of the Self: Heroic Ordeals in the Epic Tradition*. Hamden, Connecticut: Archon Books, 1983, pp. 192-216.

Marle, Hans van. "Conrad and Richard Burton on Islam." *Conradiana*, 17: 2 (1985), 137-42.

McClure, John. "Problematic Presence: The Colonial Other in Kipling and Conrad." In *The Black Presence in English Literature*. Ed. David Dabydeen. Manchester: Manchester U. P., 1985, pp. 154-67.

Meyers, Jeffrey. "The Ranee of Sarawak and Conrad's *Victory*." *Conradiana*, 18: 1 (1986), 41-44.

Milne, Fred L. "Marlow's Lie and the Intended: Civilization as the Lie in *Heart of Darkness*." *Arizona Quarterly*, 44: 1 (Spring 1988), 106-12.

Modrzewski, Stanislaw. "The Consciousness of Cultural Models in 'The Planter of Malata.'" *Conradian*, 13: 2, (Dec. 1988), 171-82.

Neilson, Renn G. "Conrad's 'Heart of Darkness.'" *Explicator*, 45: 3 (Spring 1987), 41-42.

Okafor, C.A. "Conrad, Joseph and Achebe, Chinua—2 Antipodal Portraits of Africa." *Journal of Black Studies*, 19: 1 (1988), 17-28.

Pittock, Murray. "Rider Haggard and *Heart of Darkness*." *Conradiana*, 19: 3 (Autumn 1987), 206-8.

Prescott, Lynda. "Past and Present Darkness: Sources for V.S. Naipaul's *A Bend in the River*." *Modern Fiction Studies*, 30: 3 (Autumn 1984), 547-59.

Raval, Suresh. "On Reading Conrad." *Studies in the Novel*. 13.4 (Winter 1981), 439-48.

Rawson, Claude. "Gulliver, Marlow and the Flat-Nosed People: Oppression and Race in Satire and Fiction." *Dutch Quarterly Review of Anglo-American Letters,* 13 (1983), 162-78, 282-99.

Robinson, Jeffrey. "The Aboriginal Enigma: *Heart of Darkness, Voss* and *Palace of the Peacock*." *Journal of Commonwealth Literature*, 20: 1 (1985), 148-55.

Said, Edward W. "Through Gringo Eyes; with Conrad in Latin America." *Harper's,* 276 (Apr. 1988), 70-72.

Schwartz, Nina. "The Ideologies of Romanticism in *Heart of Darkness. New Orleans Review*, 13: 1 (Spring 1986), 84-95.

Seidel, Michael. "Defoe in Conrad's Africa." *Conradiana,* 17: 2 (1985), 145-46.

————. "Isolation and Narrative Power: A Meditation on Conrad at the Boundaries." *Criticism*, 27: 1 (Winter 1985), 73-95.

Shaheen, Mohammed. "Tayeb Salih and Conrad." *Comparative Literature Studies*, 22: 1 (Spring 1985), 156-71.

Thorpe, Michael. "Echoes of Empire (IV); Conrad and Caliban." *Encounter*, 66 (Mar. 1986), 43-51.

Viola, André. "Conrad et les Autres: Les Ecueils du Langage dans *Coeur des Ténèbres*." Cycnos, 2 (Winter 1985-86), 91-101.

Watts, Cedric. " 'A Blood Racist': About Achebe's View of Conrad." *Yearbook of English Studies*, 13 (1983), 196-209.

Wilding, Michael. "Heart of Darkness." *Sydney Studies in English*, 10 (1984-85), 85-102.

Williams, Mark. "Containing Continents: The Moralized Landscapes of Conrad, Greene, White and Harris." *Kunappi,* 7: 1 (1985), 34-45.

Wilt, Judith. "The Imperial Mouth: Imperialism, the Gothic and Science Fiction."
    Journal of Popular Culture, 14 (1981), 618-28.

Yong, Margaret. "Explorations in the *Heart of Darkness:* Turning Landscape into Art in
    Slipstream and *The Year of Living Dangerously*." In *Discharging the Canon:
    Cross -Cultural Readings in Literature*. Ed. Peter Hyland. Singapore:
    Singapore U.P., 1986, pp. 10-37.

Zall, J. "The Modulations of Terror: The Oblique Elements in *The Secret Agent*."
    University of Cape Town Studies in English, 11 (1981), 29-43.

Zhang. Weiwen. "A Tentative Comment on Conrad's *Heart of Darkness*." *Foreign
    Literature Studies* (China), 27: 1 (Mar. 1985), 39-45.

Index